World Food Marketing Systems

About the editor

Erdener Kaynak is Visiting Professor of Marketing and International Business at the Faculty of Business Administration of the Chinese University of Hong Kong. He is a tenured Professor of Marketing, Department of Business Administration, Mount Saint Vincent University, Halifax, Nova Scotia, Canada. He holds an economics degree from the University of Istanbul, a Masters degree in Marketing from the University of Lancaster, and a doctorate in Marketing Management from the Cranfield Institute of Technology. He has taught at Hacettepe University in Ankara, Turkey and Acadia University in Wolfville, Nova Scotia, Canada. Furthermore he has conducted post-doctoral research studies at Michigan State University, USA, the Universities of Lund and Uppsala, Sweden and the University of Stirling, Scotland. Dr Kaynak has lectured widely in diverse areas of marketing and management and held executive training programmes in Europe, North America, the Middle East, the Far East and Latin America. He is the founder and president of a Halifax-based company, Cross-Cultural Marketing Services Incorporated.

Dr Kaynak has served as a business consultant to a number of Canadian and international organizations, been the recipient of a number of research scholarships and distinctions, has published many articles and books, and chaired many conferences in different countries. He is also the editor of various journals and, in addition, sits on the editorial boards of several journals.

World Food Marketing Systems

Edited by
Erdener Kaynak, BEcon, MA, PhD
Professor of Marketing and Chairman,
Department of Business Administration,
Mount Saint Vincent University,
Halifax, Nova Scotia, Canada

Butterworths
London Boston Durban Singapore Sydney Toronto Wellington

First published, 1986

© **Butterworth & Co. (Publishers) Ltd, 1986**

British Library Cataloguing in Publication Data

World food marketing systems.
    1. Food industry and trade   2. Marketing
    I. Kaynak, Erdener
    381'.456413   HD9000.5

    ISBN 0-407-00358-4

Library of Congress Cataloging in Publication Data
Main entry under title:

World food marketing systems.

    Bibliography: p.
    Includes index.
    1. Produce trade.   2. Food industry and trade.
3. Farm produce–Marketing–case studies.   4. Food–
Marketing–case studies.   I. Kaynak, Erdener.
HD9000.5.W587   1986   380.1'456413   85-28371
ISBN 0-407-00358-4

Photoset by Butterworths Litho Preparation Department
Printed and Bound in England by Butler & Tanner Ltd, Frome and London

Foreword

Few issues are more vital to the well being of the world than the food we eat. The concern for agricultural productivity often obscures the inescapable need for improved marketing effectiveness. As such, Dr Erdener Kaynak's enterprise in bringing together the several contributors that have written this book is to be greatly commended.

The work is comprehensive in every respect and will act as a major text for the increasing number of programmes for undergraduates and professional managers in the field of food marketing.

Its most significant contribution for me, however, is the manner in which it offers scope for comparison of the realities of marketing in more and less developed economies. The contributions discuss Africa and Sweden, the Gulf and Holland, the Mediterranean and Finland.

Comparative insight is a vitally important ingredient ensuring that the food marketing systems that are encouraged and developed by international agencies and governments fit the real needs and wants rather than all too often seeking to fulfil unreal aspirations.

I commend the book for the important contribution it makes to feeding the world more effectively by the application of marketing art and science.

Dr Gordon Wills
Principal and Professor of Customer Policy,
International Management Centre from Buckingham, UK

Acknowledgements

I am in great debt to some twenty-eight contributors to this volume who come from different countries of the world. In the midst of their busy schedules, they created the time needed for completion of their chapters and submitted them to me in plenty of time. Unlike its predecessors, this book has attracted quite a large number of people with practical experience which enhances the impact of the volume. I sincerely thank the respective organizations with which these authors are affiliated for allowing them to contribute chapters to this volume. This endeavour, of course, has created a balance between theory and practice.

Sincere thanks and appreciation go to those staff at Butterworths involved, for their help and assistance in bringing this book to fruition, and also for the foresight and enthusiasm of Butterworths for undertaking to publish a project of this magnitude. My family were once again a constant source of encouragement for which I am very grateful and thankful.

I am, of course, solely responsible for any errors or omissions in this volume.

Erdener Kaynak
Shatin NT,
Hong Kong

Preface

This is a pioneering study of the characteristics of food marketing systems around the world. The study is both descriptive and analytical in nature, the former because it points out the characteristics of food marketing systems in various parts of the world and the latter in the sense that it tries to compare these systems prevalent in different areas of the globe. The book, in general, relates any existing differences and similarities in the food marketing systems to the environment within which they are operating and contrasts the findings with previously established theories, conceptual frameworks (constructs) and techniques of marketing. To this end, this book enables us to understand the functions, processes, institutions, and environment of the food marketing system members, as well as the interaction between them.

This book is anthology of readings containing a wealth of information that covers a selection of papers coming from different parts of the world from people with varying backgrounds and perspectives. There are eleven sections in the book reflecting a broad spectrum of topics and subjects of food marketing systems at cross-national/cultural levels. The topics and subject areas selected cover most of the important problem areas in food marketing and offer solutions to them. Most notably, specific food marketing topics like food market structure analysis, analytical techniques and tools used in food marketing, methods for food market planning, control, societal responsibility of food marketing and actual experience and problems in a number of chosen food marketing fields examined. As well, marketing processes of various types of food products and of food-related services are delineated.

The book is a useful source of information for public policy makers, marketing practitioners, educators and researchers. To this end, this book will be of tremendous assistance to government policy makers as an easy reference guide for planning food marketing systems of a country, providing a means for them to learn from the experiences of others. Food marketing practitioners will be able to find certain prescriptions in this volume for making future strategies and designing food marketing facilities. This book is also a facilitatory tool for researchers, educators and trainers for providing comparative information on the food marketing problems and their solutions in countries around the world.

Food is one of the largest industries in most countries of the world and it is the largest item in a typical household budget. The food industry is a complex set of many integral parts with many different products and processes and, with large numbers of people working for food manufacturing, processing and distribution enterprises. In recent years, there have been changes in the kinds and qualities of food produced and marketed, the technologies utilized, numbers and size of enterprises, channels of distribution used, efficiency in production and distribution, food industry orientation and organizational structures, procurement and merchandising methods used in food industry and the nature of competition therein. These changes and developments are taking place at an accelerating rate, although this does vary from country to country. Because food expenditures constitute a large percentage of an average family's budget, developments in food marketing and distribution are an integral part of economic development of countries of the world.

In this book, the reader is acquainted with a multitude of facts about the environment and institutional structure of food marketing. To this end, the core of the study is the analysis of how the various activities of different actors of the food marketing process affect marketing productivity and efficiency. In some places, the study is prescriptive which offers solutions to food problems of different countries of the globe.

The primary objective of the book has been to develop information that would define the structure and trade practices within selected countries of the world or different food products. The volume also identifies potential problems or obstacles to successful food marketing operation, and provides recommendations as to organizational arrangements and sales methods which would be most suitable for the marketing of these products.

Erdener Kaynak
Shatin NT,
Hong Kong

Contributors

John C. Abbott
Consultant, Marketing and Credit Service, Food and Agriculture Organization of the UN, Rome, Italy

Lyn S. Amine
Associate Professor of Marketing, College of Business and Economics, University of Wisconsin–Whitewater, Wisconsin, USA

Stephen B. Ash
Chief of Staff, Ministry of Communications, Ottawa, Canada

Robert H. Bates
Henry R. Luce Professor, Department of Political Science, Duke University, Durham, North Carolina, USA

Louis P. Bucklin
Professor of Business Administration, School of Business Administration, University of California, Berkeley, California, USA

Giovanni Cannata
Professor of Agricultural Economics, Institute of Economic Studies, Free University of Social Studies of Rome, Rome, Italy

S. Tamer Cavusgil
Professor of Marketing and Director, Center for Business and Economic Research, Bradley University, Peoria, Illinois, USA

Bo Edvardsson
Assistant Professor in Business Administration, Karlstad University, Karlstad, Sweden

Abdel Aziz El-Sherbini
Director, Planning and Economic Analysis Division, International Fund for Agricultural Development, Rome, Italy

Gordon Foxall
Reader in Marketing, Cranfield Institute of Technology, and Director of the Consumer Behaviour Research Centre, Cranfield School of Management, Cranfield, Bedfordshire, England

Bogdan Gregor
Faculty Member, Institute of Marketing, University of Lodz, Lodz, Poland

Barbara Harriss
Research Fellow and Lecturer, Nutrition Policy Unit, Department of Human Nutrition, London School of Hygiene and Tropical Medicine, London, England

Ben Issa A. Hudanah
Associate Professor of Marketing, Department of Business Administration, Garyounis University, Benghazi, Libya

Erdener Kaynak
Professor of Marketing and Chairman, Department of Business Administration, Mount Saint Vincent University, Halifax, Nova Scotia, Canada

Bruce M. Koppel
Research Associate, East–West Center Resource Systems Institute, Honolulu, Hawaii, USA

Martin Kriesberg
President, Kriesberg Associates (economic consulting firm), Washington DC, USA

Eeva Helena Mäkinen
Acting Professor of International Marketing, Turku School of Economics and Business Administration, Turku, Finland

Frank Meissner
Staff Member, Inter-American Development Bank, Washington DC, USA

M. T. G. Meulenberg
Professor of Marketing, Department of Marketing and Marketing Research, Agricultural University, Wageningen, The Netherlands

Hans J. Mittendorf
Chief, Marketing and Credit Service, Agricultural Services Division, Food and Agriculture Organization of the UN, Rome, Italy

Klaus Moll
Director, Chile Office, International Labour Organization, Santiago, Chile

Narry Nyström
Professor of Marketing and Organization Theory, Agricultural University of Sweden, Uppsala, Sweden

John A. Quelch
Assistant Professor of Business Administration, Harvard Graduate Business School, Harvard University, Boston, Massachusetts, USA

Vincent Tickner
Director, Government and Agricultural Marketing Consultants (GAMCO), 24 Crown Gardens, Brighton, England

C. Peter Timmer
John D. Black Professor of Agriculture and Business, Harvard Graduate Business School, Harvard University, Boston, Massachusetts, USA
Faculty Fellow, Harvard Institute for International Development, Boston, Mass., USA

Secil Tuncalp
Associate Professor of Industrial Management, College of Industrial Management, University of Petroleum and Minerals, Dhahran, Saudi Arabia

Howard Wagstaff
Lecturer in Agricultural Economics, Edinburgh School of Agriculture, West Mains Road, Edinburgh, Scotland

Solveig R. Wickström
Professor of Marketing and Consumer Affairs, Department of Business Administration, University of Lund, Lund, Sweden

Attila Yaprak
Associate Professor of Marketing, School of Business Administration, Wayne State University, Detroit, Michigan, USA

Ugur Yavas
Associate Professor of Industrial Management, College of Industrial Management, University of Petroleum and Minerals, Dhahran, Saudi Arabia

Contents

Introduction

Over the last three decades, food marketing systems in the industrialized countries have undergone drastic changes. New technology in packaging, processing, transport, storage and information processing has permitted the development of supermarket chains that are closely integrated both horizontally and vertically. Concentration of wholesale purchasing through these food marketing chains has had important repercussions on the organization of food supply at the farm, assembly and processing levels. The demand for large quantities of well-packed and standardized food products has gone much further; organization to meet this demand has permitted mass merchandizing. The productivity of labour in food marketing has thus increased considerably, bringing down costs, and this in turn has opened up new and expanded markets for farmers' produce.

It has been tempting to take this pattern of development as a model for less developed countries. Many people involved in food and agricultural marketing in these countries have considered their traditional marketing systems to be outdated and, technology-wise, obsolete. Investment funds have gone into elaborate forms of storage and processing, conveyor line grading and packing and other visibly advanced marketing facilities, without sufficient attention to how these fit into the marketing system and to the economics of maintaining them. Development agencies went along with these proposals only to find out later that the new refrigerated stores or processing facilities were used far below capacity or not at all. It is now increasingly recognized that technologies for marketing must be chosen with reference to local conditions, in particular labour costs, marketing organization and the sociocutural environment.

The bias of financing agencies towards the provision of physical facilities for marketing has been a continuing constraint to a balanced development of marketing. A second major problem in many less developed countries has been the negative attitudes of government towards private enterprise, which has been considered inefficient, exploitative and lacking in innovation. Government policy has been to promote the growth of cooperative marketing organizations, assigning them monopolies for the handling of major products, and also to set up parastatals with monopolies in important areas of marketing. The general justification for such developments was the need to assist smaller farmers to market their produce or obtain inputs, together with the need to deliver food to low-income consumers at subsidized prices.

Whether parastatal organizations faced with a range of responsibilities can maintain efficient performance is not clear as evaluation and monitoring is difficult. Under the pressure of the high cost of governments of supporting some of their organizations, the trend in the middle of the eighties is to shift marketing strategies towards more competitive systems and to place more emphasis on the contribution local initiatives can make to marketing development.

Policy makers in less developed countries and their advisers still lack a conceptual framework for the formulation of development strategies adaptable to differing sets of conditions. This collection of papers, mostly written by authors with first-hand experience, should contribute to a better understanding of the development issues in food marketing under a range of requirements and conditions. It is hoped that it will promote an independent and critical analysis of marketing strategies in less developed countries as a basis for policies for the years to come.

H. J. Mittendorf
Food and Agriculture Organization
of the United Nations

Part I

Introduction

In this section the food marketing system is defined as a primary mechanism for coordinating the three inter-related total business system activities, namely: production, marketing/distribution and consumption. Marketing activity includes the exchange activities associated with the transfer of property rights to food products, the physical handling, storage and transportation of food products, the institutional and facilitatory arrangements necessary for performance of marketing activities and, finally, the consumption activities that complete the cycle.

There are two types of active participants in a food marketing system of a country: the micro (firm level) behaviour of participants in food production – distribution systems; the macro (country level) consequences that take place affecting the well-being of various participant groups in the food system.

In this book, the 'system orientation' emphasis, concerned with the coordination of different economic activities as a system of inter-related and interdependent activities, was used. To this end, production and distribution of farm inputs, farm production and food distribution are viewed as a system because they are interdependent, hence inter-related. Generally, small increases in productivity in one part of the food system may greatly improve the potential for the whole marketing system. In this chapter, food marketing systems are divided into two categories: private and institutional marketing systems. The nature and character of a country's food marketing system would, in most cases, be related not only to the prevailing political system but also to the country's socioeconomic and technological development level and, whichever food marketing system is used, examination of its operation is carried out at (*a*) primary (farm), (*b*) wholesale, and (*c*) retail levels.

Marketing activities can be divided into two halves: bulking/collecting, consisting of the accumulation and transmission of successively larger shipments of a food product until a limiting consignment size is reached, and distributing which is the reverse of bulking, i.e. the transmission of successively smaller parcels reaching minimum size at the last transaction between retailer and consumer. During both bulking/collecting and distributing, certain food marketing outlets, functions and services are carried out, but these outlets and their services vary in size, extent and magnitude from country to country.

In the developed countries of the West, marketing methods have been notably improved with the wide application of self-service in retailing and partly in wholesaling; the extensive introduction of computers and the wide standardization of containers, products and operational methods have all increased labour productivity. These have all led to a large increase in the scale of operations at all levels of the food marketing system.

In less developed countries, simple marketing systems still prevail. Individual traders with very little capital cannot afford to deal with such a long and expensive marketing process and, in most cases, each trader forms a link in a long chain of intermediaries, each making only a small profit. In early commercial development, marketing chains become gradually longer. At a later stage, increasing demand and bulk transport facilities lead to the shortening of the marketing chain as the small-scale, mainly rural, intermediaries are undercut and bypassed by large, urban wholesalers using a high input of capital; a long tradition of internal trading ensures harmony between supply and demand of food products.

Chapter 1

World food marketing systems: integrative statement

Erdener Kaynak

Introduction

Growing world food shortages and increased awareness of human nutrition problems in recent years have intensified renewed efforts to establish viable food marketing systems. To this end, many concerted efforts are needed to focus primarily upon links of the production–processing–marketing–consumption food chain. This chapter broadly reviews food supplies and needs in terms of interconnected links of a total food chain or system; development of all such links must be coordinated if the food chain itself is to function effectively[14].

Building viable and efficient food chains requires balanced agribusiness development of farm inputs, production, processing, marketing and distribution of the food commodities. It is no longer sufficient just to develop one vital component of the overall system, assuming that development of, say, the production side will trigger other needed developments. In most less developed countries (LDCs), public policy makers and economic development planners give undue emphasis to production by neglecting the most important link – marketing. The entire complex of key activities (system's inputs) should be integrated in a cohesive way (*Figure 1.1*).

Generally, interdependency considerations are critical in understanding and improving the performance of the food production–distribution system. For example, the development of low-cost food retailers in low-income neighbour-hoods is dependent on the development of effective wholesale institutions that can greatly reduce supply procurement problems as well as supply credit and technical/managerial skills. The development of such a wholesaler system is largely dependent on the assurance that a market will exist for the services. Thus, neither the lower cost retailer nor the wholesaler institution is likely to develop in isolation. Both must move together, although either may initiate the movement toward an organized wholesale–retail chain[8].

Food market structure

The food manufacturing industry is heterogeneous in its product ranges as well as in its structure, which includes companies of varying size and nature. Approximately

4

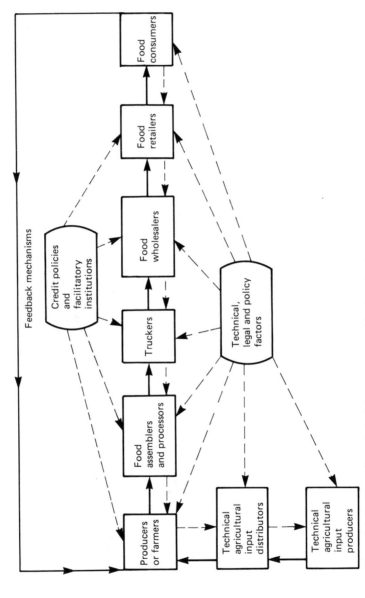

Figure 1.1. An illustration of principle components of food production–marketing systems in developed countries. (Adapted from E. Kaynak, 1982, *Marketing in the Third World*, P. 9, New York, Praeger Special Studies)

half of the world's largest 100 food and drink companies are based in the USA. Of those outside the USA, the UK has a dominant market share[2]. Between 1965 and 1976, these largest 100 food and drink companies increased their share of food manufacturing assets from 59% to 73% through vertical integration. Today, their share is likely to exceed 75%[12].

The world food manufacturing and marketing industries are asymmetrically structured, with relatively few huge conglomerate firms and thousands of smaller-sized companies. The largest firms have high market concentration and dominant market position, and confer market power conducive to supracompetitive profits. In most cases, food conglomerates can use their excessive profits to engage in competitive tactics not available to specialized firms. To increase their comparative advantage, the conglomerates use profits earned in one market to subsidize competitive adventures in other markets[13].

During the last two decades, there has been a continuous merger activity among large food corporations which concentrated their assets on relatively few huge conglomerate corporations. For instance, Foremost Dairy, which merged with McKesson in 1967, was transformed from a specialized dairy company to a large conglomerate. By 1980 and about 50 mergers later, total food sales accounted for only about 25% of Foremost–McKesson's sales, the remaining coming from non-food sales due to company diversification strategies. Beatrice Food followed another merger route. It has become the most conglomerated food corporation by acquiring about 200 companies in a variety of diverse fields. By 1980 Beatrice Foods had sales of US$8.3 billion, a 419% increase over 1970. National Dairy Products was the last large dairy processor to conglomerate. In the late 1970s, it changed its name to Kraft Corporation, which seemed to reflect a commitment to food manufacturing. In 1980, the company merged with Dart Industries, which had sales of US$2.4 billion, and it diversified in non-food lines. Dart and Kraft had sales in 1980 of US$9.4 billion, a 235% increase over the sales of National Dairy Products in 1979[12].

What is a food marketing system?

Food 'marketing system' is a primary mechanism for coordinating production, distribution and consumption activities in the food chain. In this context, marketing includes the exchange activities associated with the transfer of property rights to commodities, the physical handling of products and the institutional arrangements for facilitating these activities. There are two types of participants: the micro (firm level) behaviour of participants in food production distribution systems and the macro (country level) consequences that occur over time and affect the well-being of various participant groups, such as consumers, retailers, wholesalers, processors, assemblers and produce farmers. *Figure 1.2* shows the functional organization of US food agribusinesses whereas *Figure 1.3* shows the channels of food distribution in the United Kingdom. Channels of distribution comprise a system with different direct and indirect participants who facilitate the food distribution process.

The 'systems orientation' emphasizes interdependence of related activities and is concerned with the coordination of economic activities as a system. Thus, production and distribution of farm inputs, farm production and food distribution are viewed as a system because they are interdependent. Small increases in

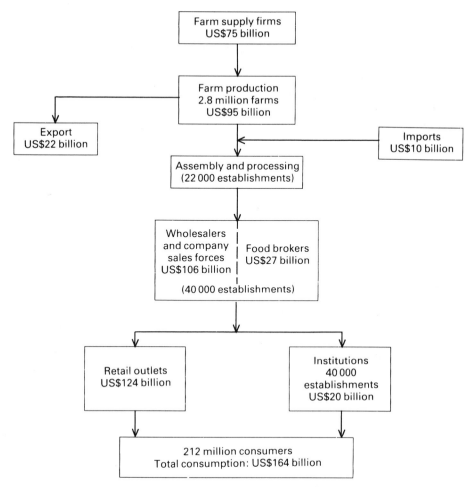

Figure 1.2. Functional organization of US food agribusinesses. (From R.A. Goldberg, unpublished paper, reprinted in G. L. Cramer and C. W. Jensen, 1979, *Agricultural Economics and Agribusiness*, p. 34, New York, Wiley)

productivity in one part of the system may greatly improve the potential for the whole system.

For analytical purposes, food marketing systems are usually divided into two categories: (*a*) private marketing system and (*b*) institutional marketing system. Most of the aspects are discussed under each level of the food marketing chain, namely, (i) primary (farm) level, (ii) wholesale level, and (iii) retail level[7].

Evolution of food marketing systems around the world

The issue of food is structurally linked to the political economy of the industrialized society. Increased food production becomes essential with population growth and with an increasing part of the population engaged in non-agricultural sectors. The subsistence production (production primarily for own use) is in conflict with the

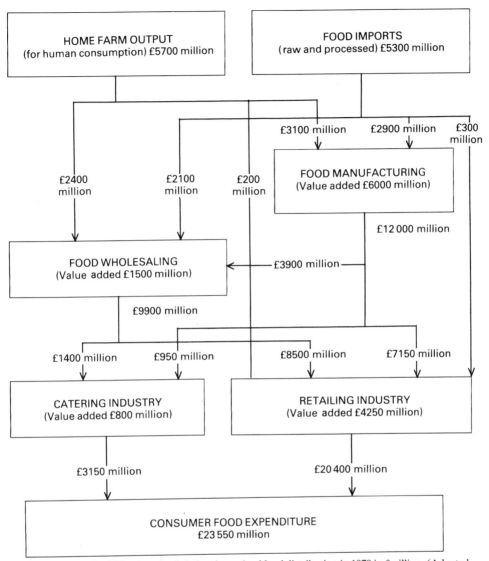

Figure 1.3. The United Kingdom food chain: channels of food distribution in 1979 in £million. (Adapted from J. Burns, J. McInerney and A. Swinbank (eds), 1983, *The Food Industry: Economics and Policies*, p. 2, London, Heinemann)

logic of the industrial economy. With the formation of the industrial economy, the need to link and subordinate food production to the development of the national economy becomes steadily more urgent[15].

The sequence of transactions and commodity movements between the producer and the ultimate consumer is called the 'marketing chain'. As internal market systems become more sophisticated, the importance of direct producer to consumer transactions usually decreases and the importance of trading intermediaries increases. This change may be attributed to increasing specialization by producers and to a general increase in the average distance between the producers and consumers in the more advanced food marketing system. In developed economies, a single intermediary possesses large sums of capital and can afford to buy directly from many different producers, transport his purchases to a convenient place of sale and finally sell directly to the consumers.

Generally, the marketing chain can be clearly divided into two halves. These are bulking or collecting and distributing[9]. Bulking consists of the accumulation and transmission of successively larger parcels of a commodity until a limiting consignment size is reached. Distribution is the reverse of bulking – the transmission of successively smaller parcels until finally they reach their minimum size at the last transaction, between retailer and consumer. During both bulking/collecting and distributing, certain food marketing outlets as well as marketing functions and services are performed. However, the extent, size and magnitude of these outlets and their services vary from country to country (see Figure 1.4). The wholesalers with most capital are likely to deal with the stages of marketing near to the limiting consignment. In these stages, large loads are frequently transported long distances and economies of scale can be achieved by a high input of capital. In contrast, the stages at either end of the chain are characterized by high inputs of labour and low inputs of capital, major scale economies not usually being possible[1].

Developed country practices

Considerable changes in organization, structure and methods of food marketing system participants have taken place in the last two decades in western Europe. The marketing system has become a corresponding dynamic force in economic development and has brought about corresponding changes in the following aspects of food marketing[3].

First of all, marketing methods have been improved, most notably the wide application of self-service in retailing and partly in wholesaling, e.g. Cash and Carry; the extensive introduction of computers and the wide standardization of containers, products and operational methods have all increased labour productivity. The wide application of newer marketing techniques has led to a large increase in the scale of operations at all levels of the food chain. The increase in the scale of operations has been accompanied by a rapid concentration in purchasing, sales promotion activities and by an increasing cooperation in organization and technical matters between independent food marketing enterprises. The formation of associated retail groups, voluntary chains, in western European countries has greatly contributed to a higher degree of productivity of independent food retailers[5]. Marketing costs and margins for selected foods in the USA is shown in Table 1.1 which reflects the improvements in marketing methods.

Less developed country practices

In less developed countries individual traders, in most cases, have very little capital and they cannot afford to deal with such a long and expensive marketing process on their own. As a result, each trader forms a link in a long chain of intermediaries, making only a small profit, but using relatively little capital in their transactions[1]. Marketing costs and margins as a percentage of consumer price for major food

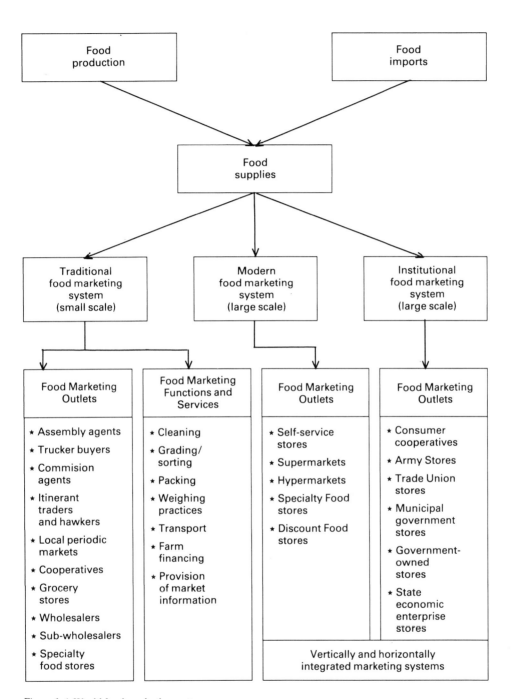

Figure 1.4. World food marketing systems.

TABLE 1.1. Marketing costs and margins for selected foods in the USA

Food item and year	Farm value (US cents)	Assembly and procurement (US cents)	Processing (US cents)	Intercity transportation (US cents)	Wholesaling (US cents)	Retailing (US cents)	Retail price (US cents)
Pork (pound)							
1978	74.5	2.1	28.9	2.2	6.3	29.6	143.6
1977	63.6	2.0	31.2	2.2	5.2	21.2	125.4
Broilers (pound)							
1978	37.2	1.0	8.7	1.4	3.8	14.4	66.5
1977	33.0	1.1	8.0	1.4	3.7	12.9	60.1
Butter (pound)							
1978	96.4	3.4	17.2	2.7	6.4	20.9	145.2
1977	85.8	3.2	15.4	2.6	6.1	20.0	133.1
Potatoes (fall) (10-pound bag)							
1978	41.4	n.a.	20.0	22.8	16.3	72.6	173.1
1977	44.3	n.a.	16.9	24.1	13.2	66.6	165.1
Oranges, Calif. (dozen)							
1978	50.2	2.3	26.9	16.7	13.2	79.1	188.4
1977	36.2	2.3	20.6	14.5	11.2	55.5	140.3
Lettuce, Calif. (head)							
1978	15.0	0.4	7.7	8.9	3.4	21.6	57.0
1977	5.1	0.4	7.3	9.4	3.7	20.1	46.0
Orange juice, frozen (6-ounce can)							
1978	19.1	0.6	8.8	1.8	4.3	8.1	42.7
1977	10.7	0.6	12.1	1.7	3.0	5.9	34.0
Tomatoes, Calif., whole (303 can)							
1978	4.8	0.7	17.4	3.6	2.6	8.5	37.6
1977	3.9	0.6	21.1	3.4	1.5	6.8	37.3
Tomato catsup, Calif. (14-ounce bottle)							
1978	7.1	1.1	18.9	4.4	7.5	9.9	48.9
1977	5.7	0.9	23.7	4.2	3.5	10.8	48.8

n.a. not available
Source: Food Margins Analysis: Aims, Methods and Uses (1981) Agricultural Products and Markets, Organisation for Economic Cooperation and Development, Paris 1981 p. 74.

TABLE 1.2. Marketing costs and margins for major food items in selected less developed countries

Major food items	Marketing costs and margins as percentage of consumer price	Cost items as percentage
Cereals		
Rice	30–60	9–18 (transport costs)
		9–18 (milling costs)
		12–24 (other costs such as assembly and retailing)
Wheat	60–80	The largest part of the gross margin was taken up by the baker's and retailer's margin
Maize	40	Major cost items were assembly and milling costs
Livestock and meat		
Livestock Meat	20–45	5–11 – retail costs (lower income countries)
	20–50	10–23 – retail costs (higher income countries)
	1–3	Assembly costs
		Slaughtering costs
Eggs		
Eggs	20–30	10–15 (retailing costs)
		10–15 (assembly and wholesaling costs)
Potatoes		
Potatoes	20–40	20–30 (retailing costs)
		60–70 (assembly and wholesale costs including transport)

items in selected less developed countries are shown in *Table 1.2.* Forman and Reigelhaup[6] suggested that, in early commercial development, marketing chains become gradually longer and small-scale intermediaries proliferate. At a later stage, increasing demand and bulk transport facilities lead to the shortening of the marketing chain as the small-scale, mainly rural, intermediaries are undercut and bypassed by large, urban wholesalers, using a high input of capital and having a high turnover but a relatively low profit margin. Intricate networks of food channel intermediaries facilitate food distribution over long distances, and the existence of storage facilities (although most are quite rudimentary but nevertheless effective) and a long tradition of internal trading ensures harmony between supply and demand of food products. Generally, spatial and temporal arbitrage take place, but traders and consumers nevertheless are quite responsive to price variations. Food intermediaries are quite specialized, and there are several different kinds of factors involved in the internal food trading process[10] (*see Figure 1.5*).

Vegetables and fruit

Being a very heterogeneous group of commodities, marketing costs and margins, expressed as a percentage of the consumer price, vary according to the perishability and market value of the commodity. There are also differences in marketing services involved which have a bearing on the share of marketing margins in relation to the consumer price[11]*.

* The countries involved in this study were: Bangladesh, India, Indonesia, Korea, Nepal, Pakistan, Papua New Guinea, Thailand, Bolivia, Colombia, Peru, Chile, Jordan, Turkey, Kenya, Zambia, Philippines, Jamaica, Mexico, Cyprus.

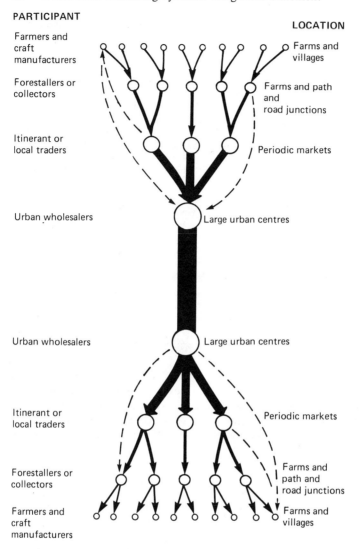

Figure 1.5. A graphic model of the internal trading process. (From J. McKay, 1973, *Development in Tropical Environments*, p. 16, Symposium of the 45th Congress, Perth, Australia, August)

What lessons may less developed countries learn from experiences of developed countries?

While drawing any lessons from developed country practices one has to be aware of the basic economic and technological differences between industrialized and non-industrialized countries. At the farm level one has to be aware of the wide differences in the food supply systems of developed and less developed countries. The small-scale food producers in less developed countries require much more technical marketing assistance before they can meet the requirements of a modern integrated food marketing system[10].

At the intermediary level, namely food wholesaling and retailing, careful economic analysis is needed. Low income of the consumer limits the assortment of the retail store and the customer's outreach. Small stores located near the consumer homes seem, therefore, essential for convenient daily food purchasing. Since labour costs are low, the application of labour-saving equipment should have low priority. Taking these basic differences, namely low labour costs and low consumer incomes, into consideration, the scope for marketing system development in less developed countries should be on the following focal points[4].

(a) How to improve and strengthen the services of food marketing system participants for the benefit of consumers, producers and other participants in the food chain to reach the major objective of a food marketing system becoming a major dynamic force for economic development.

(b) Reduction of costs through improving marketing logistics system.

(c) Form of marketing structure, namely what is the most suitable type of food marketing enterprise to be promoted and what should be the most suitable marketing structure for it.

(d) In view of the important role some cereal products play in the family budget, particular attention should be given to improving cereal distribution system, particularly under conditions of shortage.

(e) Given present food shopping behaviour of LDC consumers, how can we develop an efficient food marketing system which can not only satisfy the needs of low income consumers, but also offer reasonable return without being a burden on tax payers.

The total production, marketing, processing and distribution functions for different food products in a country can be viewed as a 'marketing system' (food chain) of linked steps through which the products flow to final consumers. It is of paramount importance to understand the interfaces between production and distribution for each group of food products as a component of a system. This necessitates systematic planning and development of all vital activities which are necessary to effectively produce, process, market, distribute and utilize a food product. Generally, food system effectiveness is measured in terms of how all components of the food chain function together. To this end, the total food system approach can serve as an important tool in planning, implementing and evaluating system-oriented food marketing development activities. In other words, there should be a food marketing system whereby changing consumer demands and retail and wholesale marketing structures and practices can be promptly reflected back to the farm production through the rural assembly markets.

So far, nearly all the activities in the way of food market system development have been physical facility or physical distribution oriented. Careful planning should be done on the human, institutional and operational aspects of the existing food marketing systems.

References

1. BROMLEY, R. J. (1971) Markets in the developing countries: a review. *Geography* **56**, 129–130
2. BURNS, J. A. (1983) The UK food chain with particular reference to the inter-relations between manufacturers and distributors. *Journal of Agricultural Economics* **34**, 366

3. FAO (1973) *Development of Food Marketing Systems for Large Urban Areas.* Buenos Aires, Argentina, FAO, pp. 13–21
4. FAO (1975) *Development of Food Marketing Systems for Large Urban Areas.* Kuala Lumpur, Malaysia, FAO, March–April, pp. 25–44
5. FAO (1975) *Food Marketing Systems in Asian Cities.* Food and Agricultural Organization of the UN, Bangkok, pp. 5–6
6. FORMAN, S. and RIEGELHAUPT, J. F. (1970) Market place and market system: towards a theory of peasant economic integration. *Comparative Studies in Society and History* **12,** 202
7. GUNUWARDENA, P. J. (1982) Some issues in marketing of vegetables in Sri Lanka. *Agricultural Administration* **11,** 24
8. HARRISON, K., HENLEY, D., RILEY, H. and SHAFFER, J. (1974) *Improving Food Marketing Systems in Developing Countries: Experiences from Latin America.* Research Report No. 6, Latin American Studies Center, Michigan State University, East Lansing. pp. 3–6
9. HILL, P. (1963) Markets in Africa. *Journal of Modern African Studies* **1,** 451
10. McKAY, J. and SMITH, R. H. T. (1973) The role of internal trade and marketing in development. In *Development in Tropical Environments Symposium,* p. 15. 45th Congress, Perth, Australia
11. MITTENDORF, J. J. and HERTAG, O. (1982) Marketing costs and margins for major food items in developing countries. *Food and Nutrition* **8,** 27–31
12. MUELLER, W. F. (1982) The food conglomerates. In *Food Policy and Farm Programs,* Vol. 34, No. 3. Ed. by D. F. Hadwiger and R. B. Talbot. Proceedings of the Academy of Political Science, New York
13. OKOSO-AMAA, K. (1975) *Rice Marketing in Ghana,* pp. 57–58. Scandinavian Institute of African Studies, Uppsala
14. PHILLIPS, R. and UNGER, S. G. (1978) *Building Viable Food Chains in the Developing Countries,* p. 1. Food and Feed Grain Institute, Manhattan, Kansas
15. SANO, H-O. (1983) *The Political Economy of Food in Nigeria 1960–1982.* Research Report No. 65, p. 77. Scandinavian Institute of African Studies, Uppsala
16. SMITH, R. H. T. and HAY, A. M. (1969) A theory of the spatial structure of internal trade in underdeveloped countries. *Geographical Analysis* **1,** 122–126

Part II
The framework of the food marketing process and analysis

In the first chapter of Part II, the necessity of modernizing distribution systems is addressed, particularly food distribution in less developed countries with large or growing urban centres. Modernization efforts devoted to this sector are considered to be as important as modernization or establishment of manufacturing industries. Economic and technical improvement possibilities are discussed separately. The role of systems integration is heavily emphasized and the advantages of voluntary chains highlighted since they can be implemented more easily while maintaining the entrepreneurial independence of all of their affiliates.

Alternative systems presently under study are not perceived as performing better in handling the bulk of the food requirements, but, in the light of the growing unemployment problem, the growth of the informal sector and the apparent restructuring of economic patterns, efforts should be pursued to develop new viable formulae; these should be rigorously tested and evaluated in comparison to all other alternatives. At the same time modernization in line with proven models should be actively implemented.

The trend of food supports for less developed countries and their interpretation are discussed in the second chapter in which an analysis is presented across countries of changes in the food supply balances and cereal imports from the early 1960s to the late 1970s. Changes in food energy supplies have not corresponded closely with changes in domestic food production per head, and the increase in imports tends to be greater in middle income than in low income countries. The balance of payments implications are examined, and the chapter concludes with a consideration of the reliability of international market supplies.

Chapter 2

Stimulation of industrial development through modern management of food distribution*

Klaus Moll

Introduction

Modernizing distribution, especially the distribution of food products, is a vital requirement particularly for the population in the rapidly growing urban centres†. It is furthermore an economic activity of substantial proportions, the volume of which is often underestimated because of the unspectacular appearance of food retailing outlets, food markets, brokers offices etc., particularly in less developed countries. In Paris, the sheer size of the antiquated system designed to provide food for the metropolis was once a tourist attraction. As the Halles disappeared the city became the forerunner of an entirely new, and controversial, system of distributing food: the network of hypermarkets where consumers buy food, and non-food articles, in sales areas of one hectar each. Wholesale markets in less developed countries are often very impressive as, for instance, the supersized market in the city of Buenos Aires. It tends, however, to be overlooked that in the same city 50 000 retail stores procure the population with its nutritional requirements, and that these retail stores represent a far bigger economic activity than the combined activities of sellers and buyers at the wholesale market.

It is, perhaps, of interest to observe that the distributive sector, even in highly industrialized countries, makes a contribution to the gross national product of about one-half to two-thirds of the contribution made by manufacturing industries. In many of the less developed countries, distribution contributes more to the gross national product than all manufacturing activities combined. As food distribution represents about half of the activities of the distributive sector, food wholesaling and retailing become one of the most important economic activities in any country. This is a natural consequence of industrialization and urban concentration. Food

---

* This chapter (an original version of which had appeared as a discussion paper for UNIDO), although much of its content is based on earlier work with ILO and later exchanges with FAO, does not necessarily reflect the views of any of these organizations. The author has updated the original to reflect his present understanding and views in relation to the subject discussed.

† For instance within the programme of action of the World Employment Conference in 1976, the need to strengthen distribution systems is mentioned repeatedly, in the beginning within the framework of macroeconomic policies (Point 7b) and later within the ambitus of overall employment policy (Point 11). There are numerous further references to this problem in international conferences organized by the FAO, the OECD and the UN itself.

processing, in turn, is the leading manufacturing activity, particularly in less developed countries where it reaches a share of up to 32% of total food manufacturing industry, e.g. in Indonesia. Its share of the gross national product as a percentage of all manufacturing activities is normally 20–25% in less developed countries.

In the process of economic development, the creation of new production capacity often receives limelight attention. Too often, it is overlooked that industry cannot exist or grow without equally modern distribution facilities. What implications are there in the modernization of food distribution systems? What does modernization mean in this respect? The answer to this question will focus on two aspects of distribution which are both inter-related:

- The creation of vertically and later horizontally integrated distribution systems.
- The appearance of technical innovations in food retailing and wholesaling.

The impact of economic changes in food distribution

Economic integration in the area of food distribution means that, in one country with, for instance, a population of 60 million, only 50 persons need to be convinced today of a given product to ensure its distribution in 90–95% of all retail stores, as

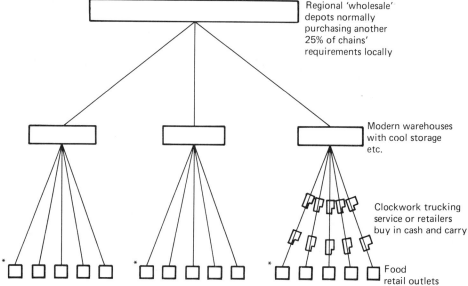

Regional 'wholesale' depots normally purchasing another 25% of chains' requirements locally

Modern warehouses with cool storage etc.

Clockwork trucking service or retailers buy in cash and carry

Food retail outlets

Figure 2.1. Model of an integrated food distribution system. Central Purchasing and Coordinating Office normally buys approximately 25% of the systems' requirements in large quantities from domestic and foreign manufacturers, food processors, agricultural cooperatives, importers and other food intermediaries. As was observed in all countries studied, integrated systems work with smaller margins than non-integrated systems, as long as they compete with each other. This is the case practically everywhere. Only horizontal integrations of trades with specific products have been observed to develop monopolistic patterns, particularly in less developed countries.
*Retail outlets: unless owned by the system, they buy up to 50% of their requirements from suppliers outside the system, items such as fresh fruit and vegetables, locally manufactured goods and products which are sold by door-to-door service of manufacturing companies, e.g. freshly roasted coffee

only that many decide on the products to be purchased. It also means regional and national purchasing of 40 000 independent retailers through two retailer cooperatives, plus a similar number of retailers organized in about a dozen wholesaler cooperatives, both systems coexisting with an important organization of consumer cooperatives and a certain number of retail chains. The integration follows the same pattern for each one of the different networks (*see Figure 2.1*).

Vertical integrations, in view of their economic power and difference in orientation, have been strong enough to break such monopolistic patterns by seeking direct access to the producer.

The advantages of such integration to the development of food processing industry are:

- The reduction of the selling cost of the industry, which can now organize its sales system in a more efficient way.
- The security of a reliable demand represented by periodic large quantity purchases, once a commodity is introduced.
- Finally, and perhaps somewhat more controversial, the imposition of high quality standards combined with low cost production which the food industry must accept from the modern purchasing offices of integrated distribution systems.

Selling cost by the industry, in the absence of integrated systems, is best illustrated by the experience in one less developed country with a total population of 10 million people, where the following conditions were observed. One manufacturer of milk and dairy products with a sales volume in the order of US$80 million per year maintained 300 salesmen to visit continuously the same 60 000 retail outlets of the country. Another manufacturer of sweets, candies and similar items with total sales in the order of US$30 million had 400 delivery cars visiting the same retail shops and maintained 9 large cool deposits for redistribution in different areas of the country. Retailers who were interviewed complained about the up to 30 sales representatives they received daily to promote different items of different manufacturers. Food manufacturers, who cannot maintain such an impressive sales force, are either reduced to small-scale, high margin production or have to look for strong partners, as happened to another company in the same country which maintained four independently operated sales systems in the capital city where it was selling an equal number of different product lines.

One might argue that the benefit of integrated, rather than industry operated, food distribution systems in these cases would not be to industrial development but exclusively to the consumer, who would pay less for the products as a consequence of the reduction of cost at the manufacturer's level. However, simplified distribution procedures would make it possible for other companies to enter the market and, through competition, increase their combined volume of production as has been observed in many similar cases.

The possibility of periodic large quantity purchases, once the products of a food manufacturing company are introduced in integrated systems, by the sheer size of demand they represent, is an additional advantage to food processors, in particular to those companies which would otherwise have had to rely on sporadic purchases by market wholesalers. It is not necessarily an advantage to those firms who already have a strong market position through their organized, but costly, sales force.

The controversial question, whether the power displayed by modern purchasing offices is of advantage to the food processing industry, might be answered as follows:

> Those companies, who learn to comply with higher quality standards, which tend to be imposed by these offices, and who are able to reduce their production costs through rationalization, will have a more than proportional growth as they will absorb the sales of less competitive firms in their areas. The capacity to produce according to standards and at low cost, is one of the prerequisites to industrial growth.

It may be of interest to observe other tendencies which sooner or later adversely affect the less efficient companies:

- The increasing capacity and interest of governments to control the quality of food items sold to the population.
- The increasing pressure for higher quality from the population itself. In some countries a pronounced interest in the keeping dates on packages is observed. These have to now be printed on the package. Thus, it is unthinkable nowadays that one can find food products in retail stores which have been on the same shelf for one or two years. This was still possible 25 years ago in smaller retail stores, for instance in West Germany.

It has been said that product policy is the key to industrial development and, in particular, to exports. Therefore, a country with modern integrated food distribution systems possesses a most valuable tool to raise the standards of its own industry, and agriculture, to the level required for competition in international markets.

The impact of technical changes in food distribution

The advantages of technical improvements in food distribution are of an even greater importance to food processing industries. The introduction of self-service, while reducing the cost of retailing, requires prepackaging of products which were previously sold in bulk. Not only the food industry, but particularly the packaging industry, which registered substantial annual growth rates, benefit from this development. Prepackaging of milk, sugar, dried vegetables, and also cheese, fruit, sausages, meat, plus other similar food products under generally better hygienic conditions than those existing in retail stores, is an industrial activity of mutual benefit to the consumer and the industry, the latter being greatly increased through this distribution method. The growth of the packaging industry is one of the indicators of overall development. Some areas of the packaging industry are labour intensive and do not require highly skilled workers, as in the case of wooden crates and packages.

The availability of refrigerated cabinets at the retail level, cooling facilities at the wholesale level and clockwork-type trucking services, make it possible to sell fresh products in retail stores, where previously large losses and deteriorations of quality were registered when the purchases from the market could not be sold the same morning. There again, food processing in the form of grading and occasionally of packaging is required.

The advent of efficient systems for the wholesaling and retailing of agricultural products makes food processing near the farm possible. The higher cost of grading and packaging is often more than offset by the elimination of waste. In this connection, a study of 11 agricultural products in a tropical country revealed losses between 18.6% (oranges) and 63.6% (avocados) from the producer to the consumer. In the case of avocados, these would have had to be sold to the consumer at a price at least three times that paid to the farmer – just to cover the cost of waste, transportation and handling. Such multiplications of price are indeed often observed in less developed countries, at least part of which must be attributed to the inefficiency of the food marketing system.

In another country, it was observed that only the morning milk was collected from farms, as the truck did not pass in the afternoon, with the result that the afternoon milk had to be thrown away. In the same area, where the study was undertaken some 15 years ago, a modern grading plant for oranges had been started which supplied much of its output to a large integrated chain of retail stores. The quality of these oranges was far above average and reliable, and the higher price paid to the farmer did not result in a higher price being paid by the consumer because of the efficiency of the food marketing system.

A farmer cooperative, which started with some industrial activity such as grading and packaging of oranges, later integrated juice making and packaging facilities. It now exports part of its processed products such as juices and pulp. Slaughter-houses, which start to supply prepackaged meat to modern food outlets, can more easily integrate other meat-processing facilities once a certain size of demand for these is established.

As the latest development in improving food distribution is to maintain a maximum of freshness and quality from the producer to the consumer, the growth of the frozen food industry is of particular interest. Its impact not only stimulates the manufacturers, who specialize in this new type of product, but also the manufacturer of electrical cooling equipment. The benefits to the diet of the consumer derived from this new process, particularly in tropical countries, are enormous.

A technical innovation which has substantially contributed to the improvement of consumer goods distribution is simply the adequate size of stores. Adequate size, of course, means different things to different surroundings; $80\,m^2$, $200\,m^2$, $1000\,m^2$ and any mixture of different sizes can be the optimum, depending upon density of population, assortment, income distribution, mobility of population etc. In most less developed countries, sizes of retail outlets are far below the optimum. In industrialized countries, the latest developments show a mixed tendency. Some go in the direction of supersized stores, where up to 6000 different food items made by a large number of manufacturers (also medium-sized producers) are offered, and others develop in the direction of discount stores, where only 300 different food products are sold with extremely low margins. Both systems are now firmly established.

Discussion of problems

Problems of modernizing food distribution in less developed countries have been seen in the following two ways:

• The possible reduction of employment by increased productivity.

- The requirement for important investment in modern shops, warehouses and transportation facilities.

The reduction of employment through modernization of distribution has not been proven. While many inefficient sales outlets have disappeared, new employment has been created with the modern chains in different areas. Some studies appear to indicate that the proportion of the population employed in food distribution does not differ between less developed and industrialized countries. Semiskilled labour takes the place of unskilled persons, salaried personnel (unfortunately perhaps) that of many store owners. Also, many retail store owners have maintained their entrepreneurial independence by adhering to one of the large and efficient retailer cooperatives or voluntary chains (wholesaler cooperatives with affiliated retailers) who offer the advantages of large integrated chains or consumer cooperatives in terms of national purchasing, advertising, public relations, financing, leaving each store owner free to make his own purchasing decisions or to change his affiliation. The obvious common advantages of such systems hold these voluntary associations together.

Voluntary chains, which have proliferated from Holland, are probably the best suited form since the critical mass, in terms of affiliated retailers, necessary for success is rather high. Some estimate that any group smaller than 250 is bound to fail. This is difficult to achieve with independent retailers since considerable promotion is necessary. Results are not seen very early in the process and there are examples of fraudulent attempts where retailers have had to pay a fee to adhere to some future system which then never materialized. Wholesalers, if well prepared, can work more easily together because there are fewer firms to bring together to cover a large captive audience of retailers from the start.

In recognition of this fact, international organizations have given specific attention to this form of organization and, following their initiative, the world's largest group, SPAR, with over 50000 retailers affiliated, recently concluded a know-how agreement with Mexican food wholesalers resulting in the foundation of SPARMEX.

It appears that the benefits to be derived from accelerating, or at least not stopping, the modernization of food distribution will highly compensate for the possible demands on the economic system as a whole. Any such drive should, however, be accompanied by compensatory measures. If labour is momentarily freed, additional employment should be created in the new industrial activities of food processing, the manufacture and application of packaging material and the production of refrigeration equipment. It could also, in part, be employed in the construction of new distribution facilities.

The total cost on a macroeconomic level would only be a once off compared to the continuous cost involved in letting an antiquated system of food distribution persist in absorbing a large amount of adult persons who could usefully be occupied in value creating activities and in frustrating much of the farmers' work through spoilage of this products, inadequate and irregular prices and demand.

The capital investment required in distribution will certainly deserve further study. If one assumed that $2-3\,m^2$ of wholesaling and retailing space are required per consumer, the building requirements and its respective cost can be estimated. In industrialized countries, the investment necessary will probably be somewhere in the order of US$1000–2000 per inhabitant, but considerably lower in less developed countries with a low cost of labour, using local raw materials. Subsidizing some of these activities should be considered.

In a highly industrialized country, such as the USA, the capital invested in the retailing and wholesaling is in the order of several hundred billion US dollars. In less developed countries the additional investment required would be smaller on a per capita basis but even higher for the total of the less developed countries combined. Such huge developments will, of course, only be possible in years and maybe in more than a decade. As they will absorb local labour, local raw materials and finished products, they will, however, not normally be a stress on the balances of payment. The employment of a force of semiskilled people in such labour-intensive activities would have a multiplier effect on the economy as a whole.

The construction of wholesale markets as promoted in many countries would only be part of the process. Such markets will have to be complemented by a substantially bigger investment in other retailing and wholesaling facilities.

It is rightly argued that the continuation of traditional local retail markets, particularly in rural areas, might, in some ways, be preferable to the modernization of retail stores. The experience shows, however, that, while such markets still continue performing their function, they lose importance where more efficient systems appear in the trade. There are strong economic justifications for such developments. Investment in food distribution has been one of the most lucrative activities in the post-war growth area of industrialized countries. Although these developments normally start in urban surroundings, rural areas and rural consumers, e.g. in Bolivia, have been observed to closely follow the pattern of purchasing and consumption of urban consumers. In the light of the development of unemployment in recent years, the lack of capital in the hands of small entrepreneurs and of the future trends in the area of automation which will further sharpen the contrast between employed and unemployed, formal and informal sector, a word must be added here about the need to develop new types of economic environments. Much hope is being placed in recent times on the potential of small and microenterprises and on the development, or integration, of the informal sector. One of the obvious targets for such efforts of conceptualization is the entire area of food production, processing and distribution. Home industries receive increasing attention, the World Food Programme, in cooperation with other international organizations, attempts to promote such activities, on all three levels, by mother clubs in rural areas. Community development is another area where innovation takes place. While these developments deserve full attention and every creative effort possible, there appear, as yet, to be no proven systems to carry all or even only a large share of the volume of food to be distributed with the same efficiency as the system referred to above, which combines, in its advanced form, farmer cooperatives or large farms selling on a regular contract basis to integrated distribution systems, or to efficient industries with modern processing facilities and quality control where their products are also sold to the integrated distribution systems.

A continuation of horticultural enterprises, home processing and local market offerings in almost any neighbourhood appears to exclude at least the large cities.

Whatever the form that might finally prevail, the waste as it presently exists, in the form of spoiled merchandize on the way from the farmer to the consumer, in terms of pseudo-employment of labour, of badly utilized transportation and of warehousing facilities, should be reduced substantially and such reduction would more than compensate for the economic cost of an improved infrastructure in food distribution.

Entrepreneurship as a prerequisite for modernizing distribution systems

It can be observed that the moving forces behind the modernization of consumer goods distribution in industrialized countries are limited to a far smaller number of people, than for instance the universe of professionals which presently deals with the subject of industrial marketing. In western Europe, for instance, one could estimate that there are only 2000 distribution professionals against perhaps 100 000 marketing professionals. It may be assumed, however, that the overall impact of this entrepreneurial innovative group on the respective economies far exceeds the influence of the business-oriented marketing professionals in industry whose role is becoming increasingly limited towards microeconomic objectives*.

Considering the practical possibilities that exist for entrepreneurial persons in governments and in the private sector of less developed countries for acceleration of modernization of their distribution sector, these are two main aspects:

● The acquisition of professional knowledge and skill in this field – the complexity of which is often underestimated.
● The development of initiative and sociopolitical, i.e. also financial, support for implementation purposes.

In both respects, technical cooperation may be helpful. Although the provision of long-term experts will be difficult because of the limited number of professionals so far available, short-term experts and consultants may provide expertise in a concentrated form. Fellowships to specialized schools, such as the London School for the Distributive Trades, Credoc in Paris, or organizations like the NRMA in the US (and there are many others), could be combined with study tours to distributive organizations, documentation centres, research institutes and specialized consultancy organizations in this field. Also some governments and semigovernmental bodies can provide substantial background material in this area.

The documentation that has started to develop on this specific subject is large and comprises statistical comparisons as well as training courses for retail shopowners, models for the determination of where to put new wholesale depots or retail outlets and laws issued by governments (for instance Argentina) for the improvement of distribution facilities.

With regard to the promotion of an awareness of the modernization programmes themselves, short symposia, *ad hoc* consultancy assignments, the publication of newsletters and magazines, can be planned and carried out in collaboration with international consultants and experts.

Whether the initiative comes from the universities where chairs on distribution could be created, or from the governments who want to stimulate initiatives in this area as Spain successfully did 20 years ago, or from private entrepreneurs of whom there exist a number of outstanding examples, it is important that it is well planned and then executed with the determination to achieve the desired practical results.

Technical cooperation between less developed countries in this field has already started on a moderate scale. For an acceleration of the required process, intensified technical consultation between countries would carry very promising results. These

---

* To illustrate this, the fight for bigger market shares between industrial companies may have a stimulating effect on the economy as a whole; the organization of productive distribution systems, however, has a more immediate impact.

should include agreements to study the economies and social impact of innovative alternative forms, subjecting the results to rigorous evaluation with regard to their real potential for solving at least part of the food distribution problem in ways better than the above systems.

Conclusions

Many agencies of the United Nations system are concerned with the creation of an awareness for the urgent need to improve distribution systems, which is particularly obvious in those countries where urban centres grow proportionally fast.

As a link between industry, agroprocessing activities and agriculture on one side and the consumer on the other, distribution systems in less developed countries are the weakest link in the chain of economic development. Their strengthening will automatically benefit, more than proportionally, both industry and the consumer.

Modernization of the distribution system does not have to lag behind industrialization processes. On the contrary, it may even stimulate and accelerate tham as it probably did in the post-war era within the industrialized countries. Changes in this field may, however, require such strong personalities as that of a Duttweiler in Switzerland, who fully revolutionalized the sector, which, until the creation of Migros, had been completely antiquated.

As it attacks vital problems of procurement and economic growth at their roots, the strengthening of distribution systems can be considered as even more important to a country's overall industrial development than the improvement of marketing capacity in industry; the latter is recognized by many countries as being the key to successful industrialization programmes.

Independently of all that has been said above, alternative forms, which may be even more revolutionary than the deeds of Duttweiler and others, should be developed, evaluated and, if seen as useful, vigorously promoted in competition with the earlier concepts.

Chapter 3

Food imports of less developed countries

Howard Wagstaff

Introduction

The cereal imports of less developed countries have increased nearly six-fold since the mid-1950s. Trade and production data cited here and elsewhere in the chapter are based on *FAO Production and Trade Yearbooks* unless otherwise stated. Data also obtained from *FAO World Grain Statistics* (until 1973/74). Excluding Argentina, they accounted for 1.5% of world cereal imports in the 1930s, 20% in the early 1950s, and 40% in the late 1970s. A quarter of a century ago, the world's foodgrain exports were purchased almost entirely by industrialized countries, with the UK by far the largest importer. But by 1975–77, 70% of inter-regional trade in wheat was purchased by less developed countries, the volume of their imports having increased 5.5 times since the early 1950s compared with an increase of only 30% for the industrialized countries. In value terms, the total food imports of all less developed countries in 1972 rose by 180% over the same period[2]. These trends are persistent, and are a reflection of increasing imports in all the developing regions of the world. *Figure 3.1* shows regional trends in wheat imports.

The great majority of less developed countries now import some cereals at least in some years. Although India and Pakistan have both recently had years of net surplus, for the first time in more than three decades, production remains variable, and given the size of India's population a small percentage import requirement represents a significant purchase in the international market. For the Far East as a whole, the trend of grain imports is still upwards.

The trend towards greater reliance on imports, then, is clear. It is the basis of various projections of future import requirements by the less developed countries. For example, the United States Department of Agriculture world grain–oilseeds–livestock (GOL) model projected a net import requirement of 49 million metric tons in 1985 on a continuation of current trends and policies or 71 million metric tons with higher income growth, compared with 32 million metric tons in 1973/74–1975/76[3]. However, the meaning of this trend is far less clear. There are some who would instinctively see the 'gap' between total demand and domestic production in poor countries as confirmation of their gloomiest forebodings – the threat of worsening hunger consequent on population growth. On the other hand,

This chapter first appeared as an article in *Food Policy*, 1982, Vol. 7, No. 1, pp. 57–68.

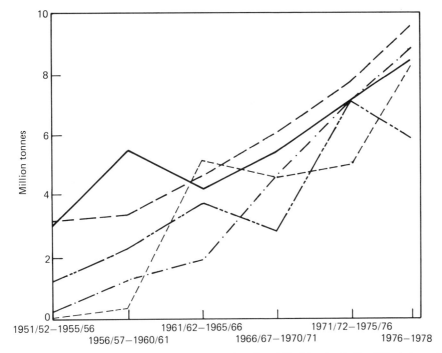

Figure 3.1. Net imports of wheat in developing regions (——) Far East (excluding China); (— —) Latin America; (— – – —) Africa (excluding Near East); (– · -) Near East; (– – – -) China. [From the *FAO Trade Yearbooks*]

it may be possible to view the growth of less developed country imports with at least a measure of optimism. Import growth often arises from an accelerated rate of economic change, rising domestic incomes, and higher expenditure. Although balance of payments problems may occur, changes would in this case be a cause for hope rather than despair. While this is generally acknowledged with respect to other imports, greater self-sufficiency in food is widely held to be imperative for less developed countries.

Food imports and economic change

Under what conditions, and to what extent, is it possible for imports to substitute for domestic food production in the course of economic development? It has sometimes been suggested that, at least in the early stages of development, such substitution is generally impossible.

In those countries which have markedly increased their reliance on imports over the last two decades, what else is happening to the economy?:

- Have those countries experienced a decline (or a below-average increase) in domestic food production per head? Or has the effect of imports been to permit an above-average rate of increase in consumption per head, while domestic production at least matches population growth?

- Has the increase meant that food imports absorb an increasing proportion of export earnings? Or have export earnings expanded at least as fast as the food import bill?
- Where are these countries placed in the 'league table' of gross national product per head, and how do their rates of growth of GNP per head compare with other developing countries?

There is a converse set of questions about those countries whose food imports have not increased. Does the relative absence of imports signify success in domestic agriculture, or is it a reflection of the lack of means to import? And if there are countries which have experienced a definite acceleration of food import demand, has this mainly reflected rising total demand, or the stagnation of domestic agriculture? This chapter assembles some evidence on these questions as they relate to less developed countries in the period from the early 1960s to the late 1970s.

Food energy supplies and domestic food production

A summary of the experiences of 94 less developed countries over the period 1961–65 to 1975–77 based on FAO data, is presented in *Table 3.1*. The early 1960s are chosen as the beginning of the present phase of rapid import growth by less developed countries. Regular estimates of food supplies per head based on national food balance sheets have been published since then. In 66 cases representing two-thirds of the population of less developed countries, food energy supplies per head rose. However, in only 36 countries did food production per head increase. Furthermore, there are another 11 countries where food energy supplies per head were just maintained, despite falling per capita production. In total, there were 59 countries where food energy supplies are estimated to have risen by more than the index of food production.

The two series of data cited here are compiled separately and were not originally designed to measure degrees of self-sufficiency of import reliance, although these are implicit in the food energy supplies estimates derived from national food balance sheets. Whereas the production data are published as an index and used directly in *Table 3.1*, the estimates of food supplies per head are published as independent three-year averages and have been converted to index form for use in these comparisons. No reconciliation of the production estimates implicit in the two series has been attempted, nor indeed would this be possible on the basis of published information. Moreover, the original units of measurement are different, since the production index is not weighted by food energy coefficients. There is

TABLE 3.1. Changes in food energy supplies and domestic food production per head, 94 less developed countries, 1961/65–1975/77

Direction of change	Food production per head		Food energy supplies per head	
	No. of countries	Percentage of population	No. of countries	Percentage of population
Rising	36	(50)	66	(66)
No change or falling	58	(50)	28	(34)
Total	94	(100)	94	(100)

Source: *FAO Production Yearbooks:* Indices of production per head, and food balance sheets.

nevertheless a strong implication that where the index of production per head increases less rapidly (or decreases faster) than food energy supplies per head, food imports are playing an increasing role. This applies in over half the cases where supplies per head have been maintained or have increased.

This conclusion applies particularly to Africa and the Middle East. Production per head declined in countries representing nearly two-thirds of the region's population, but in about 90% of these cases, food energy supplies per head are estimated to have been maintained or increased. In Asia and Latin America, the more usual case has been constant or increasing production per head, with food energy supplies per head estimated to have risen slightly faster. These observations suggest several further questions. Can any generalizations be made about the circumstances in which food supplies per head have risen? To what extent have increases in food consumption per head been associated with increases in domestic food production per head, to what extent with increases in GNP per head, to what extent with overall export growth, and to what extent with staple food imports?

These questions naturally involve comparisons across countries of changes over time. Asking questions about food supply in general also points to the use of aggregate measures of food production and availability. This results in the choice of methods unfamiliar in a number of respects. Time-series analysis might, in some circumstances, help to elucidate the factors influencing food supply within a single country, or in a series of case studies. What is sought here, however, is not the detail of specific cases but the grounds (if any) for generalizing about the recent experiences of less developed countries. Thus, a cross-sectional analysis is required, but the data must nevertheless pertain to changes over time.

For 66 countries (those for which trade data were compiled in the World Bank's *World Development Reports*)[5,6], changes in food energy supplies per head were regressed on changes in domestic food production, growth in GNP, export earnings, and cereal imports (all on a per capita basis), which is a proxy for total staple food imports. Changes in per capita food energy supplies, domestic food production, and GNP were expressed in percentage points. For the latter two variables, the original data are in index form, and it was desirable to express the food supplies variable in the same units. Changes in export earnings were measured in US$ per head adjusted to 1977 prices, and changes in cereal imports were measured in kg per head of population. This type of analysis cannot identify causes, nor suggest policy prescriptions. It can, however, offer some cautions against unwarranted assumptions. Nearly half of the variance in changes in food energy supplies per head was found not to be associated with any of these economic variables, singly or in combination (with all 4 independent variables $R^2 = 0.56$). This is not surprising since, apart from the many sources of error in these estimates themselves, the distribution of income is of vital importance in determining the composition of extra food production and imports. Taking single variables, there was a greater tendency for changes in food energy supplies to be associated with changes in GNP per head ($R^2 = 0.34$) than with changes in food production, exports, or cereal imports per head ($R^2 = 0.21$, 0.24 and 0.18, respectively). Moreover, the regression coefficient of percentage changes in food energy supplies per head or percentage changes in food production per head (either as above or in equations incorporating other variables) was only 0.27. It is the negative aspect of this result which is of interest. It is *not* true that changes in food energy supplies per head have corresponded closely with changes in domestic food production per head.

Introducing changes in total export earnings per head in addition to changes in food production per head, with changes in estimated food energy supplies per head as the dependent variable, only raises R^2 to 0.35. Moreover, between countries, changes in food imports do not appear to be associated with changes in export earnings. A cross-sectional analysis of 37 less developed countries in the period 1961–65 to 1972–74 showed an insignificant (and in fact slightly negative) correlation between the two. Again, in the 66 country analysis, the correlation between changes in cereal imports and changes in total export earnings was not significant ($r = 0.05$). These results suggest that export earnings have not, in general, been the effective constraint on grain imports of less developed countries, although specific relationships between food deficits and trade prospects require detailed study at the country level[4]. In this reference the authors identify a group of countries including Tanzania, India, Bangladesh, Ghana and Sri Lanka which 'do not have a prospect for financing food imports with increased agricultural export earnings'.

Cereal imports

The countries identified in *Table 3.2* imported an average of at least 100 000 metric tons of cereals in 1975–77, or at least 50 kg per head (or both). In addition, their cereal imports per head of population increased by at least 20% in the period

TABLE 3.2. Change in food production and food energy supplies per head, 1961/66 to 1975/77: in less developed countries with increasing cereal imports per head

Countries with an increase in cereal imports per head of 20% or more, 1961/65–75/77*	Average change in food production per head (%)[†]	Average change in food energy supplies per head (%)[†]	
		Countries listed	Region as a whole
Africa Egypt, Morocco; Mozambique, Somalia, Tunisia; Cape Verde, Gabon, Gambia, Mauritania	0 (−3)[‡]	+ 12 (+9)	+6
Latin America Brazil, Chile, Columbia, Peru; Ecuador, Haiti, Jamaica; Barbados, Guadeloupe, Neth Antilles, St Vincent	+1 (+12[§])[‡]	+10 (+6[§])	+6
Far East Bangladesh, Republic of Korea, Sri Lanka, Vietnam; Kampuchea, Lao, PNG	−1 (−2)	+4 (+4)	+1
Oil exporters Iran, Iraq, Algeria, Nigeria, Venezuela, Indonesia, Libya, Saudi Arabia	−1 (−5)	+28 (+33)	+7[¶]

* And importing at least 100000 cereals in 1975/77 or at least 50 kg per head (or both).
[†] The first figure in each case is the simple average for the countries listed. The figures in parenthesis are averages weighted by population.
[‡] For those countries with under 2 million people indices of food production per head are not available and hence excluded from these averages.
[§] Brazil is predominant in these weighted averages. In Brazil, the production index rose by much more than food energy supplies, reflecting a shift towards livestock products.
[¶] Average of all less developed countries.

1961–65 to 1975–77. Indices of food consumption and food production per head for these countries based on FAO data are compared with regional averages for less developed countries, and with non-importing countries. Changes in the percentage of imports accounted for by food are examined, and their characteristics in terms of GNP noted.

On average, food production per head has fallen for importing countries, whereas it has risen slightly in every developing region taken as a whole. In only 13 of the 31 listed countries for which data are available has domestic production risen. The increases in imports are in this sense a reflection of relative stagnation of domestic agriculture. However, it is also clear that imports have, in a majority of cases, more than made good this shortfall. Food energy consumption per head has (with important exceptions) tended to rise faster than the averages for the respective regions. There are, however, some clear differences between regions, and sizes of country.

In Africa, food energy supplies increased in all but two of the food importing countries identified. In a continent where there are now few countries not importing at least some cereals, it is notable that those with zero or negligible net imports (i.e. less than 10 kg per head) are with few exceptions those whose food energy supplies per head did not increase (i.e. Kenya, Niger, Chad, Upper Volta, Uganda). Generalizing, it can be said that Africa is a continent of increasing import reliance in foodgrains, and that the absence of imports in certain cases has been not so much a sign of agricultural success as that of stagnating consumption per head. Exceptions are Rwanda and the Central African Empire, where imports are negligible, but food energy supplies per head are estimated to have increased.

The position in Latin America is less clear. First, income levels are higher, so that improved food supplies are less directly manifest in higher food energy consumption per head. Changes in consumption patterns are more important. While the generalizations for Africa tend to hold true for medium-sized and small countries in Latin America, the larger countries with increasing net imports (Brazil, Chile, Columbia, Peru) do not show an increase in total food energy supplies per head, although the balance is shifting towards livestock products.

In the Far East, experiences are varied. What characterizes the region's cereals imports is the variable demand of a few large countries (India, Pakistan, Bangladesh, Indonesia). Although near to self-sufficiency, just a small percentage of total requirements represents a significant fraction of the volume of inter-regional trade. Fluctuations are therefore at least as important as the longer term trends. A further factor vitiating comparisons over time is the devastating effect of wars in Vietnam, Kampuchea and Bangladesh. What can be said is that, even in the Far East, cereal imports do not arise only from the exigencies of agricultural failure. The most rapid increase has been in the Korean Republic, where growth of livestock production has been rapid, industrial growth more rapid, and demand for feedgrain has added to total cereal demand at a faster rate than domestic crop production could meet. In Sri Lanka, growth in food production has been similar to the regional average and in this case imports partly reflect a shift towards wheat consumption in place of rice.

Import reliance and GNP

Although increasing import reliance has occurred among countries of greatly different sizes and income levels, it is also apparent that the tendency is greater among middle income countries (*Table 3.3*). Net cereal imports as a proportion of apparent utilization in middle income countries rose from 13% in 1961–63 to 23% in 1977–79. For low income countries, the proportion remained constant at about 4%[6]. There has, however, been an increase in the rate of growth of cereal imports of low income countries in recent years. As a group, they accounted for about one-quarter of the total increase of net imports of both wheat and total cereals by less developed countries (including China but excluding the major less developed country exporters, Argentina and Thailand) between 1971–72 and 1976–78,

TABLE 3.3. Increase in cereals net imports of low and middle income countries, 1960/63–1977/79*

Country or country group	Annual average net imports (million metric tons)		Increase (million metric tons)	Annual rate of increase (%)
	1960/63	*1977/79*		
Low income	5.6	8.7	+3.1	2.7
Middle income	12.7	44.7	+32.0	7.9
China	4.0	8.7	+4.7	4.8
Total	22.3	62.1	+39.8	6.7

* Excluding major less developed country exporters (Argentina and Thailand). From World Bank[6].

compared with only 8% over the whole period 1960–63 to 1977–79. The oil-importing countries have in the more recent period accounted for one-quarter of the total for wheat, and one-third for cereals as a whole, the rate of increase for total cereals being 17% per year. Of the countries identified in *Table 3.2*, 12 were 'low income', whereas 20 were non-oil 'middle income' and a further eight were oil-exporting countries. There is thus a clear indication that increasing import reliance tends to occur in the middle income phase of development for many countries. At this level, the evidence is that food consumption increases can be sustained even when domestic food production per head is stagnating or falling. More generally, import growth is a reflection of increasing utilization per head and is partly related to income growth. In the cross-sectional analysis of 66 countries described above, there is a positive correlation ($r = 0.4$) between changes in cereal imports per head and the growth rate of GDP per head.

Total grain utilization between 1960–63 and 1977–79 increased faster in middle income countries (+89%) than in low income countries (+54%). Several factors contribute to this. First, population growth rates (*Table 3.4*) have been higher in

TABLE 3.4 Average growth rates of population and GNP per head by level of GNP per head, 1960–77

GNP (1977 US$)	No. of countries	Population growth rate (% per year)	Growth rate, GNP per head (% per year)
< 150	15	2.3	0.8
150 < 300	20	2.6	1.7
300 < 600	18	2.7	1.6
600 < 1050	18	2.8	3.3
1050 < 1500	12	2.4	3.0
1500 < 3000	12	1.1	5.5
≥ 3000	23	0.9	3.6

Data from World Bank[5].

the middle income group (which includes many Latin American countries). Second, growth rates of GNP per head have been higher (which has increased the income disparity among less developed countries). Third, the demand for cereals for livestock feed becomes a significant factor, and this may lead to a proportionately greater increase in consumption (measured in cereal equivalent) than at lower income levels (this is not apparent from the conventional measurement of income elasticity of food expenditure). Time-series data are limited, but if utilization were to follow the relationship to GNP per head about 4% per year, compared with 2.5% per year at under US$150 per head implied by cross-sectional data, then with the growth rates shown in *Table 3.4*, the rate of increase in food utilization in cereal equivalent would be greatest between US$600 and US$1050 per head (about 4% per year, compared with 2.5% per year at under US$150 per head and 1.2% at over US$3000 per head, in 1977 prices).

TABLE 3.5. Trends in grain production, imports and utilization in selected countries where the rate of increase in imports has risen

	Period	*Rates of change (% per year)*[*]		
		Production	*Imports*	*Utilization*
Countries where the rate of increases of production and utilization have both fallen				
Morocco	1947/48–1959/60		Net export	
	1959/60–1965	+ 2.6	Net import; + 0.3	+ 3.7
	1966–78	+ 0.8	+ 18.0	+ 1.9
Ghana	1961–69	+ 4.4	+ 2.4	+ 4.1
	1970–78	− 2.2	+ 11.0	+ 1.1
Haiti	1961–71	+ 1.5	− 0.7	+1.4
	1971–78	− 4.1	+18.0	− 0.6
Republic of Korea	1950–66	+ 4.3	+ 8.5	+ 4.8
	1966–78	+ 2.1	+ 13.4	+ 3.8
Countries where the rate of increase of production has fallen, but the rate of increase of utilization has risen				
Gambia	1961–74	−	+ 2.3	+ 4.0
	1974–78	− 11.9	+ 48.0	+ 5.4
Mauritania	1962–70	− 1.4	+ 3.2	+ 0.7
	1970–78	− 7.1	+ 14.5	+ 5.6
Mexico	1961–69	+ 7.0	− 219 000 metric tons p.a.[†]	+ 4.7
	1969–78	+ 3.1	+ 387 000 metric tons p.a.[†]	+ 5.1
Countries where the rates of increase of production and utilization have both risen				
Ecuador	1961–71	+ 3.0	+ 1.3	+ 3.8
	1971–78	+ 4.4	+ 23.0	+ 6.4
Honduras	1961–74	+ 0.9	+ 4.4	+ 1.5
	1974–78	+ 4.6	+ 27.4	+ 6.7

[*] Estimated by semi-log regressions using annual data. Author's calculations, based on FAO data.
[†] Net export in 1960s. Change therefore given in absolute terms.

For a number of less developed countries it is possible to identify a point when grain imports accelerated. *Table 3.5* presents comparisons of rates of growth of production, imports and utilization in nine such countries. There is a definite indication that a falling rate of increase in grain production (or accelerated decrease) has usually accompanied an acceleration of imports. Whether the availability of imports has actually hindered domestic production, or whether the increase in imports is simply an unavoidable response to the reality of lagging domestic production, is an important question calling for further research. Meanwhile, it should be noted that in five of the total nine cases examined, the rate of increase in grain utilization accelerated, suggesting that increasing per capita demand often plays a significant role in the increase in import growth.

Reliability of international supplies

Imports have played a substantial role in allowing consumption per head to rise, and their increase has not generally absorbed a rising share of export earnings in the long run. Domestic agricultural policies are beyond the scope of this chapter, but the trend of rising imports appears unlikely to be curtailed in the coming decade as long as international supplies are available. This raises the crucially important question of the reliability of supplies.

The most sensitive issue here is again cereals, as the basic staple. The world's growing cereal imports are supplied almost entirely by just five exporters – USA, Canada, Argentina, Australia and France. The two North American countries alone account for three-quarters of net exports into regional trade. Although this predominance is not new, it has increased. The number of minor exporters has decreased, and the only other countries which are consistently net exporters now are Sweden, Hungary, Uruguay, Thailand and Burma. This reliance on so few sources of supply makes it difficult to view the widespread growth of imports with equanimity, whatever other arguments may be adduced for the benefits of trade. The geographical concentration of the world's exportable surpluses carries a number of obvious risks, political as well as environmental.

The possible political consequences of reliance on a market dominated by the USA have frequently been alluded to in discussions of international food problems, not least because the CIA itself had referred in the early 1970s to grain shortages giving the US 'a measure of power which it had never had before'[7]. However, the 'food weapon' may not be as powerful as some UK hawks might like to imagine. Despite its predominance, the US does not have a monopoly in the grain export business and the size of its contribution still does not prevent the other countries making their separate deals. During the 1980 US embargo on grain to the USSR (a misnomer, since the USA honoured its 8 million metric ton long-term contract), Canada, Australia and Argentina continued their sales: the *Financial Times* reported on 29th July 1980 that: 'Canada has dropped out of the US-led embargo on grain sales to the Soviet Union from a practical standpoint', recognizing that, 'the Australians made record sales to the Russians while participating (*sic*) in the embargo'. The *Financial Times* had noted on 3rd July 1980 that: 'Argentina, which exported no wheat to the Soviets in 1978–79, sold them 2 m metric tons during 1979–80. The Canadians sold them 3.8 m metric tons in the same year and reportedly will sell them 5 m metric tons next year. The Australians, under an agreement concluded before the embargo was announced, exported 3.9 m metric tons to the Soviet Union this year, 11 times more than in 1978–79'.

The problem of international food insecurity arising from concentration of exports in North America must therefore be considered to be more serious on several counts than a study of past yield fluctuations alone would imply. Some of these risks are in principle reducible at source, were different policies to be pursued, but they are without any control by importing countries.

The prospects of more countries joining the ranks of cereal exporters, over the next decade or two, and thus reducing the risk inherent in concentration, appear remote. If one is sufficiently sanguine to take a very long-term view, it is possible to identify many countries (first in Latin America, then in Africa, and even the Soviet Union and some European countries) with high ratios of cultivable area to projected population, which it may be tempting to think of as 'potential' exporters. Yet at present these countries are increasing their imports. Without radically different patterns of development this will continue. On one hand, less developed countries with low overall growth rates have (almost by definition) low agricultural growth rates. On the other hand, middle income countries with higher overall economic growth rates are generating new demands faster than domestic agriculture will supply. These demands include feedgrains for livestock (if only for a privileged minority benefiting from development). In neither case will food exports emerge from less developed countries. As far as the industrialized countries are concerned, Europe's net imports may decrease, but this will not add to the number of exporters, and in some respects it may further reduce global stability. Inter-regional trade would tend to become an even smaller fraction of total consumption, yet individual countries would continue to rely upon the international market to absorb variations in production and consumption.

Conclusion

For many less developed countries, an increase in per capita food energy supplies has depended at least partly on imports, particularly of cereals. This has in most cases been possible without a long-term increase in the share of export earnings spent on food. This import tendency has been greater among middle income countries, often reflecting rising incomes. Thus, the economic constraints have not been sufficiently severe to compel food self-sufficiency.

However, viewed in a global perspective, this appears precarious in view of the small number of net exporting countries, with the USA alone playing such a major role. There seems to be no immediate prospect of this changing. The degree of insecurity in international food supply inherent in this export concentration can therefore be mitigated only by such measures as a diversification in the holding of grain stocks. Despite the experiences of the early 1970s, most importing countries (including the EEC) have not recognized the responsibilities involved in this. Additions to grain stocks have occurred only accidentally, as in the case of India's recent large harvests, or in the case of periodic soft wheat surpluses in the EEC feedgrains market. Thus, while the importance of international trade continues to increase, its basis becomes no less insecure, and the need for renewed efforts to manage and coordinate national grain stocks policies to provide a buffer against production variability remains as urgent as ever.

References

1. SINHA, R. P. (1976) World food security. *Journal of Agricultural Economics* **28,** 123
2. UNCTAD (1977) *Handbook of International Trade and Development Statistics*. Geneva, UNCTAD
3. USDA 1973/74–1975/76 (1978) *Alternative Futures for World Food in 1985*. Washington DC
4. VALDES, A. and HUDDLESTON, B. (1977) The Potential of Agricultural Exports to Finance Increased Food Imports in Selected Developing Countries. Occasional Paper No. 2. Washington DC: International Food Research Institute
5. WORLD BANK (1979) *World Development Report,* pp. 144–145. Oxford, Oxford University Press
6. WORLD BANK (1980) *World Development Report,* p. 23. Oxford, Oxford University Press

Part III

Food marketing infrastructure

The first chapter of this section assumes that the building of an adequate food marketing infrastructure is a necessary condition of intensive agricultural development. For a 1982 discussion on this in Rome the introductory speaker painted a picture of the agriculture he foresaw in the tropical regions of the future. Land for individual farms would be restricted because of the pressure of the population, but it could be cultivated vertically. Fish would be bred in drainage ponds below ground level, the ground surface would be cropped continuously with plants rooting at varying depths, above which would be shade-seeking bush crops; beyond these would be mango trees and coconut palms with pepper vines trained up their trunks. Flying above it all using pollen to make honey would be bees. This is not already more widespread because the infrastructure is lacking; such an infrastructure for input supply and marketing would mean intensive cultivation of land to produce enormous yield and remunerative work for many people using skills that give considerable personal satisfaction. For all this, the infrastructure must exist, together with marketing system and services to supply fertilizer and other inputs at the right time, plus the smooth and profitable absorption of the marketable output.

The second chapter in this section briefly reviews ongoing projects in market centre improvement in the less developed countries in 1983, and discusses major issues of improving market centres as they have arisen in recent years in projects involving contact with the FAO. It is hoped that the analysis of issues and the lessons learned will contribute to improved planning of future programmes and projects in this field and will encourage other specialists to present their experiences. To this end, this chapter analyses the issues involved in developing food market centres as focal points for promoting effective agricultural and food marketing systems.

The adoption of horizontal and vertical integration in food retail systems in less developed countries has long been the recommendation of researchers in the field of food marketing. In the third chapter, it is suggested that such proposals may not achieve the desired results for the poorer consumers in low-income Asian countries. An alternative approach, based upon the strengthening and improvement of traditional methods, is suggested as a more appropriate course of action in those countries.

Chapter 4

Building food marketing infrastructure for economic development

John C. Abbott

Introduction

In the last two decades, the goal of the marketing improvement adviser in the developing world has been to build a marketing infrastructure better suited to the needs of small farmers. This goal is generally achieved by offering them easier access to favourable markets and to fertilizer and other inputs, to bring into the commercial economy the large numbers of family producers who continue to farm along semisubsistence lines. The development instruments were better transport, market and storage facilities, provision of market information and advice, and implementation of guaranteed minimum prices for major agricultural products through marketing board and cooperative purchasing systems.

Now some of these programmes and structures are coming under question. Many of the new facilities are not used as intended and the cooperative and government marketing and supply systems have proved less than effective. In 1972, the cooperative system was dismantled in socialist Tanzania. In 1981, the State Agricultural Marketing Board of Senegal was summarily abolished. There is wide concern over the slow pace of development. In the 1970s, many social scientists began to question whether governments actually promote development – as was generally hoped and expected in the preceding decades. Reappraisal of the usefulness of the approaches that have been followed and consideration of practicable alternatives seems, therefore, to be in order.

Literature review

For a broad coverage of food, agricultural and input marketing in the less developed countries, the *FAO Marketing Guides* series are the most comprehensive and convenient source, together with Abbott's chapter in *Agricultural Development and Economic Growth*[1,13]. Bauer[7] is the apostle of minimum aid. His analyses of government marketing policy in Cyprus and West Africa are among the first detailed criticisms of government bias against private marketing enterprise[5,6]. Jones[19] and the Stanford school have maintained a continuing focus on free market systems. Harper and Kavura[15] have assembled case studies of small-scale enterprises.

Accounts of misplanned packing, processing and storage investments tend to be played down in the reports of the agencies concerned. Mittendorf's review of 70 plants set up in less developed countries that failed[21] is an effective indictment of construction without due consideration of marketing issues. He has also carried out additional studies on the planning of marketing facilities and their role in development[22,23]. Scherer[27] and Von Oppen[32] have analysed the response to extending the assembly market network in Brazil and India, respectively. Behavioural studies of market users by sociologists are numerous. Illustrative are those of Mintz for the Caribbean[20], Dewey for Indonesia[11], and Epstein for Papua New Guinea[26]. Prolific in geographical writings on marketing is Bromley[8].

On the convenience of alternative forms of marketing enterprise to serve small farmers, Abbott's paper based on lectures presented at a rural development course in Sri Lanka provides coverage in some depth[4]. Protagonists of cooperative systems for small farmers are many; critics have been dubbed reactionary. Hunter[17] brought a more sober view into the literature. Hyden has analysed factors bearing on their performance under African conditions[18], Daines et al. provide a framework for evaluating credit assistance to marketing enterprises[10]. Problems in operating market news services in Latin America were reviewed at an FAO meeting in Lima[12] and Schubert has set out a systematic approach to their establishment[28].

Policy for the implementation of a national supply and price stabilization system was developed by Creupelandt and Abbott[9]. This was further elaborated in the FAO guide on rice marketing[13]. Sharp critics of stabilization in practice are Harriss[16] and Subbarao[30]. George is the authority on the Kerala two-price system to help low-income consumers – considered the most effective by the World Food Council in 1981[14]. A cogent advocate of self-targeting is Timmer[31]. *Accelerated Development in Sub-Saharan Africa*, issued by the World Bank[33], brings out clearly the handicaps to marketing performance set by some government policies. The ignorance of marketing prevailing among general economists was demonstrated in Abbott's review of national development plans[2]. Spinks wrote his courageous 'Attitudes towards marketing in developing country governments' in 1970[29].

Systematic review of international aid for marketing was initiated at a 1976 OECD/FAO meeting on critical issues in marketing development. It was pursued in *Technical Assistance in Marketing: a View over Time*[3]. In marketing development programmes in Latin America the Michigan State University group has played a formative role.

In this chapter it is proposed to review experience of marketing infrastructure development in the light of two hypotheses. These are:

- The university teachings of developed countries, the visibility of their institutions and the attitudes of their aid agencies have been a significant distraction.
- This distraction has been the more potent because of the social and informational gap between those who are actually engaged in agricultural marketing in many less developed countries and those who take policy decisions. Let us now look at what can happen in practice.

Infrastructural requirements

On the essential components of a marketing infrastructure there is general agreement. These are:

- Transport, storage and communication facilities.
- Assembly, domestic distribution and export marketing facilities.
- Enterprises offering convenient access to physical inputs and services and ready to purchase, sort, pack, hold, process and sell agricultural output to the best advantage.
- Institutions to provide finance, market intelligence and advice, and ensure satisfactory conditions for trade, and to reduce market risks to producers and consumers by cushioning the effect of seasonal and interseasonal fluctuations in supply.

How to build up the necessary infrastructure is more controversial. Evolutionists say that it should grow of its own accord through local initiatives and in response to demands for services. This is very much the view reflected in the writings of Bauer[5-7]: 'If a country cannot develop without external aid then it is unlikely to develop with it!' However, left to such a process growth can be very slow. There is the risk that the absence of some strategic element, a major transport obstacle unbridged, excessive trading risks and cost, lack of initial capital, deters provision of all the others with stagnation as the consequence. On the other hand, attempts to implant preconceived institutions and procedures developed in other parts of the world to suit different sets of conditions and the pouring in of external funds to build up physical facilities based on developed country models can be wasteful and disappointing. Where the capital has been borrowed from outside it can also tie up future foreign exchange earnings to repay commitments that never gave the returns that were expected.

Transport facilities

The direct and indirect benefits from the building of strategic highways between rural areas of high productive potential and consuming centres in Latin America and south-east Asia have been amply demonstrated. Studies in Ethiopia in the 1960s showed that motor vehicle transport of grain over rough traditional tracks cost five times that of transport over a paved road. The traditional fresh fruit resources of Linsing County in China went largely unused in 1977 for lack of transport capacity.

Aid and development agencies find a natural satisfaction in building roads in less developed countries up to the standards of their own – but, if afterwards, the roads will not be maintained much of the original investment is wasted. There is one country where major roads have been built and rebuilt two or three times at 10 to 15-year intervals under successive aid programmes. In a recent rural development project for a central African country this reality was recognized. Crops and fertilizer would be moved during the dry season with transport and storage arrangements designed to accommodate this. Similarly, helping a country maintain a steady supply of spare parts and effective repair facilities gives much better returns than furnishing successive fleets of new vehicles to specialized enterprises and projects. A suggestion that transport vehicles from an external source be included in a loan project to expand fertilizer distribution beyond rail head points in India was rejected because it would carry foreign exchange implications for their servicing.

Some expensive lessons have been learnt over the last decades. Air and refrigerated transport can bridge gaps in the movement of perishables to better-off consumers. However, in the less developed countries, improvements of feeder roads and elimination of specific obstacles such as streams without culverts, easy access to rubber tyres for bullock carts and spare parts for old motor vehicles, pay off much better than the introduction of radically new transport equipment. Fostering growth of a public carrier system with agencies established to organize return loads is an economical strategy for maximum transport capacity utilization. Importers of grapes from Afghanistan were able, in the 1960s, to arrange by telephone from Delhi to an agency in Amritsar, for trucks to meet the grapes when they arrived at the northern border.

Storage

The bulk of the storage for food and agricultural products and farm supplies constructed under development programmes has been put into public hands. This has occurred for a combination of reasons:

- The prevailingly large scale of the storage units built in developed countries because of the economies of scale it offers under their conditions. These reflect high manpower costs and easy transport and communication facilities – factors operating in the reverse direction in many less developed countries.
- The impact of this on decision makers from less developed countries who are not equipped to assess its suitability for their own conditions, reinforced by the professional training of foreign advisers, generally with an engineering background.
- The desire of financing and aid agencies to see the project executed within a given period of time and managed by a 'responsible' body. Designation by the government of some public body is the easiest and apparently safest way out of this dilemma.
- Biases against private marketing enterprise on the part of influential advisers coupled with a natural reluctance to favour some particular private enterprise – this latter reflecting a lack of familiarity with procedures that could be employed to allocate opportunities to build storage on credit. The words of one eminent European economist assigned to a World Bank mission on storage construction in a central American country were 'Do you want me to recommend that these stores be given to the very people who have been exploiting the farmers? and to which of them should the stores go – to those who have become the richest at the farmers' expense?'
- An underlying preference on the part of ministers and other government officials for keeping important new facilities under their own control – more to build up their own importance and provide opportunities for patronage, than to prevent their going into hands that might not always operate them in the public interest as usually stated in the project document.

Construction of storage for public bodies with aid and development money carries risks that are not implicit. Because their decisions tend to be taken centrally and in response to allocations of blocks of funds that must be spent, public organization investments in stores and other fixed facilities are often wasteful. They are built too elaborately. Capacity is concentrated in units that are too large for the output of the area within easy transport access using the means available. Fertilizer stores constructed for the government extension service in Iran cost three times per metric ton capacity more than those put up by private distributors. Because of their size and location, private traders taking over wholesale distribution of fertilizer from the Development Corporation in Bangladesh did not want its stores. For a decade, advisers with a marketing orientation campaigned against the building of big silos where small-scale multi-use hangars were much more appropriate. Even these can go wrong when built to meet standardized precepts set up under a big loan programme. Of those built in the late seventies for farmers bringing stocks to rural assembly markets in northern India, in practice hardly any were being used by farmers in 1981. The credit and handling procedures for this were just too cumbersome.

Packing and processing plants

The degree of waste in development-inspired packing and processing plants may be even greater than with storage. The motive for establishing most of these plants was to introduce some new technology, i.e. a technology that was in use in developed countries but seemingly untried in the less developed country concerned. Here the risk of failure is multiplied. Firstly, the technology might be unsuitable because of contrasting capital to labour cost ratios, inadequate supply of suitable raw material, differences in consumer demand, and problems of equipment maintenance and quality control. Secondly, the enterprise designated to manage the plant incorporating the new technology would be subject to the same considerations as those set out for development storage.

Projects where access to aid funds led to the purchase of mechanized sorting and packaging machinery that was never used are numerous. A 4000 metric ton capacity mechanized potato grading and storage plant built in 1964 in Jamaica used for one year only is but one example. This was constructed with Netherlands aid funds as a gesture of good will because Jamaican potato growers were purchasing Dutch seed; but it has made no contribution to development. Marketing organization in the channels concerned had not reached a comparable state of development. Step-by-step advances on a smaller scale through demonstration and continuing supervision would have been preferable.

Among some development advisers there is a view that the establishment of some physical facilities, e.g. a plant to pack or process an agricultural product, will stimulate an expansion of output in the area around. The subsequent appearance of a marketing organization able to use the plant, finance purchasing of the raw material and find outlets for the finished product is assumed. Such projects have been particularly favoured by agencies with aid targets to meet and seeking something concrete to show. A review of 70 canning, slaughtering, storage and related plants established in Africa and subsequently failing, evidences the risks of disappointment if there is not a more thorough consideration of the marketing component.

The scope for using advanced technology in packing and processing for export marketing is more clear. Here the need to meet standards of quality and presentation set by developed country governments can be a determining factor. In this the pacesetter was for a long time the USA; abattoirs were built over central America to meet its standards, dried fruit has been fumigated etc. The European Common Market now has a similar role.

As with development storage, there has been widespread reluctance to set up these plants in collaboration with enterprises already experienced in marketing the product concerned. The preference has been for management by a cooperative of the farmers in the area served – even where no such cooperative has existed hitherto. Otherwise the plant has been assigned to a new government enterprise again without prior trading links and experience. A third way out of the dilemma is for a plant to be assigned to public or municipal ownership with the objective of providing a service to existing traders for a fee. All of these alternatives adopted to meet government/aid agency preferences prejudice the ability of a new plant to operate successfully as compared with direct operation by an enterprise with established supply sources and sales outlets for the product handled.

Commonly stated as a justification for the focus on public and cooperative enterprise has been the reluctance of private enterprise to take on the risks of innovation. Perhaps this should be restated as reluctance of the governments and aid donors to give private enterprises the resources and incentive to take the risks and to let them begin on a small scale. The precept of a local businessman in a lecture at an FAO marketing training programme in Africa some years ago on how to start a new processing and marketing enterprise, was 'wait until some cooperative or government-initiated plant has gone bankrupt then take it over at a low valuation'.

Market facilities

With urban populations in less developed countries rising at a rate of 6, 8 or more per cent per year, there has been a corresponding need for expansion in wholesale and retail market facilities. Relocating and rebuilding wholesale and retail markets can result in lower costs for market users by reducing congestion, transport and handling time, and physical and quality losses. By raising market transparency and expanding market access it can increase competition so that savings are passed on to consumers, also to producers so stimulating additional output with further benefits to consumers.

Many national sponsors of new markets and associated international advisers build too expensively and too solid: where a simple shed is required for protection against sun and rain elaborate concrete boxes are erected. In addition to wasting money that would be better spent on 'soft ware' services and staff training, these structures are difficult to modify later as needs evolve. This tendency is particularly Latin. In South America high rates of inflation have led politicians and associated European advisers to build as fast and as big as possible.

Governments elsewhere have seen wholesale and retail markets as a municipal responsibility and they have featured only rarely in requests for external aid. In this area of development, advisers from the northern countries have been on the side of the angels. In their home environments wholesale markets have a declining role; funding has been local and economy in investment a prime consideration.

The rural market is, for many small farmers of Asia, Africa and Latin America, their first convenient link with the marketing system. The price paid at this market is an important determinant of income and incentive for the small farmer. Such a market is also often the farmer's main purchasing point for inputs such as fertilizers, insecticides and tools, for his basic household goods and daily necessities. The availability, choice and pricing of consumer goods at rural market centres is an important factor in motivating small farmers to produce for the market.

Furthermore, rural markets are not only a point of social gathering but an important information centre where ideas are exchanged and innovations introduced. Yet the role of the rural assembly market as an instrument for change and progress has been neglected until very recently. Affording access to large numbers of rural people the rural market can be an economical natural integrator of a range of development activities. Yet many governments and development agencies would have nothing to do with these markets. A suggestion to the Secretary of Agriculture of Sri Lanka that he site in traditional markets used by farmers some of the 500 new agroservice centres his government was establishing brought the following reply: 'but my people have specifically put them elsewhere because they do not want them to be mixed up with the traders'. Yet expansion of the network of regular markets and improvement of related access roads and facilities is an obvious development approach offering high returns in the quite short run.

In Brazil and India, surveys have shown that increasing the density of organized rural markets attended regularly by wholesalers has stimulated a significant expansion of farm output within two or three years. This response, moreover, came almost entirely from the smaller farmers because they were the ones formerly handicapped by distance from outlets for their produce where pricing and services would be competitive.

Marketing enterprises for development

To fill gaps in existing marketing channels or to supply new inputs and product outlet needs, many governments have tended to set up new cooperative and state marketing systems with external assistance.

For enterprises to market farmers' produce and provide supplies as needed, governments can choose between the following broad systems:

- Independent private firms operating within some institutional framework such as rural assembly markets, an auction market or exchange, possibly with some mechanism for cushioning extreme price fluctuations.
- A specialized enterprise bringing processing technology and marketing expertise, economies of scale and market outlets in distant locations.
- Development company, land reform organization or similar body, providing all services under official supervision.
- Farmers' associations or cooperatives.
- A state trading agency or marketing board.

We must then remember that we are interested in the small farmer with his particular sets of problems and handicaps for an efficient marketing service. For the small farmer the main consideration may not be how effective the marketing system is at the sales end, i.e. in expanding the quantities moved, obtaining marginally higher prices than competing sources of supply, expanding its share of the total market, and the like. It may be whether he is treated fairly at the local buying stage, how far the marketing system helps and protects him against larger rivals in the same production area, how far the system helps him to match their level of quality of output and to get access to the techniques and inputs needed to achieve this. So a review in depth of alternative marketing systems should also take into account the support they give to the provision of needed inputs – improved seeds and other plant materials, pesticides and practical advice on crop husbandry, crop protection and processing where some processing is necessary at the farm, and credit to help cover cash outlays until sales proceeds come in.

Independent private firms selling to wholesalers

This system has the important advantage of self-supporting continuity in the structure. If one private enterprise goes out of business others will compete for its market share. With open entry, farmers with produce to sell will never lack an outlet for long. The weakness of the small buyer in serving the small farmer often lies in his limited capacity to provide technical and financial support. He may not himself have the knowledge and contacts to provide extension support, improved plant materials, advice in a specialized field or access to sufficient finance to cover the growers' seasonal needs for production materials and labour. He also faces risks (over his resale prices and crop loan repayment) against which he tries to protect himself through his target margin.

Processing and marketing enterprises

A processing and marketing enterprise supplying inputs, technical advice and credit to farmers under a contract that also offers a sure outlet for specific produce is very effective in stimulating output and promoting development. Because of the ease with which organized labour can put pressure on an employer growing a crop that must be harvested at a specific time, many processing/marketing enterprises prefer to buy from farms run with family labour rather than to operate their own large plantations. This approach favours small-scale production of cash crops since the firm will generally be prepared to provide the technical and financial assistance the farmer needs to produce a crop meeting the firm's requirements. Repayment of advances is secured by the ability to deduct from the payment to the grower for his crop when it is delivered. The adverse feature of such an arrangement is dependence on the one outlet. The process of shifting to another outlet or to another crop if conditions become unattractive may be painful.

Development authorities or companies providing services under official supervision

Typically, these are established or authorized by governments to take charge of the planting, handling and marketing of a particular crop within a designated area. Often this is an area of new settlement by smallholders. It reflects recognition from the start that these new farmers will need continuing assistance in all aspects of the production, harvesting, processing and marketing process.

The Gezira Board in Sudan and the Kenya Tea Development Authority are notable examples. Both these organizations have focused primarily on the provision of production inputs, finance and processing facilities and in assuring a market outlet to small producers on equitable terms. Generally, they have left market development to others. Their sales policy has been to offer consistent qualities of product at open auction or by tender and to keep regular customers satisfied.

Commercial companies operating under government sponsorship and control have played a comparable role for coffee and cotton production and marketing in francophone Africa. In the Ivory Coast, this approach has attracted much outside investment in processing and other facilities. Pursuing an aggressive export policy, these companies have also been successful in expanding the Ivory Coast's share of the world market for various crops and in establishing new positions on foreign markets, for fresh pineapple, for example. They draw on large, medium and small producers, however, and how far they give special assistance to the smaller growers is not clear.

Farmers' associations or cooperatives

Spontaneous collaboration by small farmers to economize on transport costs to a known but distant market or to increase their bargaining power in negotiating terms with a local trader has the advantage of requiring no elaborate procedures.

The success of this approach depends very greatly on the managerial capacity that can be generated locally and the cohesion of the group in face of opportunities for individuals to benefit occasionally by going outside it.

Farmer cooperative organizations have made, in general, slow progress in less developed countries in spite of the massive national government and external support they have received. Some of the main reasons include overestimation of the economies of scale of cooperative marketing at assembly level, difficulties in finding qualified and reliable managers willing to work for modest salaries, and political interference. Bureaucratic procedures which discourage genuine cooperative initiative from below also contribute in preventing many cooperatives from becoming competitive with existing private traders in price and services offered to small farmers.

State trading corporations and monopoly marketing boards

In various tropical countries marketing boards have demonstrated their ability to undertake major marketing operations. They have achieved a high standardization of quality and packaging and brought benefits from large-scale transport, processing and sales. Generally farmers can count on receiving a pre-announced minimum price on delivering their produce to an official buying station. This price may, however, be set at a low level to cover rising costs of board operations. Export boards sometimes become a convenient mechanism for taxing farmers. Maintained over a period of years, discrimination against the producers of a particular crop in this way can discourage its production. The declining share of groundnuts from northern Nigeria in the export market for oilseeds during the 1950–60s and of cocoa from Ghana is attributed in part to such discrimination.

It may be questioned whether a marketing board, set up primarily to concentrate export bargaining power or stabilize prices, will concern itself very much with services to small farmers? Several such boards have declined to enter into the provision of fertilizers, or the handling of credit repayments. Many have little concern for what happens before produce arrives at their buying stations, leaving the small producers dependent on local assembling agents and other intermediaries.

The most favourable conditions for organizing marketing specifically to help small farmers seem to be (*a*) where they are, or can be, concentrated within one fairly compact area or (*b*) where they can be helped to raise a product of high unit value.

Credit, information and advisory services for marketing

Access to credit for the purchasing of supplies, and the assembly, transporting and holding of stocks is an essential service for marketing. Without it marketing operations can hardly proceed. Governments are very much aware of the need to finance cooperative and public marketing enterprises, either directly or by guaranteeing credit lines at a bank. Rarely, however, do the credit needs of private enterprise receive any special consideration. The contribution this could make to development is not recognized.

Additional credit can help greatly in expanding marketing operations and so intensify competition to the benefit of producers and consumers. Certainly the need to put up 40% of the cost of fertilizer stocks because of bank finance restrictions was considered the main constraint on private fertilizer distribution in India a few years ago. A World Bank loan for seed development in Ecuador concentrated its finance on a government-sponsored seed production and distribution company. The comment of a review carried out seven years later was that this company had been slow coming into its operation and could not compete with imports because of its high costs. The development of other national seed supply enterprises had been impeded by lack of finance.

At one time it was thought that setting up a market news service where none existed was the first and minimum step in any programme to improve marketing infrastructure for producers and consumers. By making available trustworthy information on prices in strategic markets, on quantities sold and on indications of trends, it would increase market transparency. All participants in the market would be helped in bargaining for an equilibrium price.

Some such services were suppressed by the same governments that had established them; they revealed that actual prices exceeded those used in official cost-of-living indexes. Others died for lack of user support. The need had been seen in developed country terms. Coverage and presentation were not adapted to local requirements. Small farmers, in particular, could not use them. To attract listeners in Peru one such radio market news service had to be put over with a musical accompaniment. Others have appealed only with an extension-type personalized interpretation.

Provision of practical advice on marketing to the farmers (and local produce buyers and handlers) is another valuable service. In various countries attempts have been made to introduce the US model – a nucleus of qualified marketing specialists preparing material for use by general extension staff at the field level. In practice, marketing extension seems to be done best under production and marketing contracts with the purchasing enterprise supplying the field staff and advice that is specific. Farmers growing peas for Hindustan Lever grasped the concept of the optimum maturity point within a very short time. Thereafter, they were insistent in calling for their peas to be collected at this stage. The advice given to farmers under general extension programmes tends itself to be general, with the agent a postbox for government policy rather than someone who can work out the best marketing strategy for individual farmers in their particular situation.

Stabilization of supplies and prices to producers and consumers

In most countries where the basic foods are grains originating from harvests once or twice a year, some market stabilization mechanism has been established. Generally, a public agency is designated to buy at a guaranteed minimum price at harvest time. In this way it protects producers against excessively low prices that would discourage future production. The stock acquired, usually averaging 15–20% of the normal quantity marketed, is then held for release onto the wholesale market later in the season when prices tend to rise to levels causing hardship to consumers.

Stabilization of prices to reduce producers' market risk is generally an effective generator of expanding output. Production economists still see the market risk as the greatest deterrent for the small farmer in India, for example. The relative decline in production of pulses and oilseeds there as against rice and wheat for which minimum prices are assured, is attributed largely to this.

Operation of a price stabilization system requires a very cool head. General awareness that the government is fixing the base price can attract intense political pressure. Only too easily the price can be forced up to an uneconomic level, or the intake specifications eroded to the point that heavy physical and quality losses are incurred on stabilization stocks in storage.

An organization undertaking such a stabilizing role will normally require some subsidy. Its terms of reference preclude its taking profit opportunities open to private traders operating in parallel. To help small farmers it may have to open seasonal buying stations within easy transport access. Its stores may not always be used to capacity. The main handicaps in practice of such a mechanism are bureaucratic procedures and arbitrary political intervention.

In less developed countries the price at which basic grains and pulses can be sold retail in free markets, if there is to be a continuing incentive to producers to expand domestic output in pace with growing populations, is often above that which their lowest income consumers can afford to pay. Measures can be taken to reduce distribution costs. Assistance to small retailers in low income areas to form voluntary chains and participate in group buying arrangements is being provided in some Latin American countries. They may still not reach that category of consumer for whom the cost of domestically produced food is still too high even after marketing charges have been brought down to the minimum necessary to cover costs.

To assure supplies of basic foods to very low income groups supplies must be made available at a price below free market level. This is generally done either by importing from lower cost world market or concessional sources the bulk of the supply, as in the case of Jamaica, or by pooling low cost imports and higher priced domestic production as in Colombia and other countries. In Latin America the low-priced grain is often retailed through a state-sponsored system on the model of CONASUPO in Mexico. Experience in India is that such distribution can be done much more economically through private retail shops on a contract basis – for a retail margin of about 5%. This is feasible because the low price grain serves as a loss leader for other products carrying a higher margin, and the retail shop labour is on a family basis.

To minimize leakage, whether or not a ration card, stamp plan or other device to identify eligible purchasers is used, the product sold should be self-targeting. This means that its nature, quality, variety, or proportion of brokens in the case of rice, should be such that while equal in nutritional value to the product offered on the free market there is little scope for resale at a higher price.

Decision making on marketing policy

Policy decisions on such vital issues as the marketing of the agricultural output of a country and the food supply of its people should be based on objective analysis of alternatives. To be useful, such an analysis must take account not only of what would be desirable, but of what will be feasible with the human and financial resources available. In an environment where traditional values and allegiances are still very strong, full allowance should also be made for these.

Few of the less developed countries have had the nucleus of qualified marketing specialists and accumulated body of information on performance at the practical level needed to provide realistic advice to their policy makers. India and Pakistan inherited agricultural marketing departments from the British. They carried out field surveys that were a basis for policy and legislation. Few other countries had them. Nor was there much interest in establishing them in other less developed countries after they achieved independence. The political leaders had already made their decisions, before they came into power, on how their country should be run. These reflected the education they had received in the universities of metropolitan countries. In none of these was marketing a subject at their formative time. Economics was taught in theory with government policy the focus. In class and student discussions, the relative advantages of free enterprise, socialist and marxist economic systems were debated in principle. How they worked in practice was of lower order.

This kind of thinking came naturally to people who in their own country, for social reasons, would normally have little contact with the realities of marketing. Staff of the new government departments reflected the same set of values. Often they were reinforced by traditional respect for authority. Information on facts running contrary to the policy that had been established might not even be transmitted to superiors in the government hierarchy.

Some reaction against enterprises and institutions dominated by the former colonialists could be expected. Ironically, in Africa it is the successor governments that have clung to colonial institutions such as the monopoly marketing board and asked them to take on responsibilities that were beyond their capacity or no longer desirable. Deep rooted, however, in many countries is a popular resentment of the immigrant who is both more skilful in marketing and more diligent. In face of a barrage of research conclusions favouring abandonment of the wholesale monopoly of the Kenya Maize and Produce Board, the Africans still maintain it. Once released to private traders they fear that the marketing of their basic foodgrain would soon be dominated by local Asians.

Training of additional personnel in marketing research analysis and policy formation, and in marketing operations, will eventually ease these constraints. Unfortunately, because of the carryover of Oxbridge academic traditions, still very little marketing teaching is offered in universities of less developed countries. In the United Kingdom, for example, since 1950 agricultural marketing has been taught mainly in terms of policy issues for government, with enterprise marketing handled quite separately. Practical visits organized for the overseas student would be to marketing boards and cooperatives – because they were accessible. Visits to private enterprises are more difficult to arrange. In the USA, marketing teaching has been available much longer and access to business courses easier. Illustration, however, of economic analysis and marketing procedure has been largely irrelevant to conditions of less developed countries.

Aid influences

In marketing, financial and technical assistance from the USA have had the major role. Funds accruing in local currency from the sale of food supplies on aid terms has provided capital for road and bridge construction, storage building and the establishment of market and processing facilities. Specific assistance has been given to farmers' cooperative marketing projects as a means of introducing new marketing methods and equipment. Recognition in a number of less developed countries of the need for government marketing units to provide information, advice and facilitating services owes much to the American model, likewise the introduction of marketing teaching into national university programmes.

British assistance to the less developed countries has focused quite strongly on promoting cooperative marketing systems, publicly sponsored enterprises and marketing boards. During the 1950s marketing boards were set up in various Caribbean islands, and in other Commonwealth countries along models prepared by an overseas development specialist. Some of these, involving the handling of perishable crops grown for local consumption, may be judged a disservice to the countries concerned.

At this time French aid took another form – providing a protected market for the export products of the Communauté countries. Government marketing enterprises and cooperatives sprang up there in the seventies reflecting a wider range of external support. Scandinavian marketing aid has been consistently for cooperatives – a combination of idealistic intention and domestic experience.

FAO has tried to be neutral in the politics of marketing. This has been the tone of its policy statements and of its training and advisory material. It has attracted criticism at different times from United States delegates to its Program Committee on one side and from eastern Europeans on the other. In aid projects financed by the United Nations Development Program it has had to back up predominantly government programmes because this was the aid requested. The international development banks are in the same position. For convenience in administration and to find favour for lending achievement, their priority may go to expanding loan totals as against effective return to the borrower per US dollar spent.

Recapitulation

The marketing infrastructure needed in many of the less developed countries must be sensitive and complex. Production systems and consumption patterns are less standardized in various ways than in some more developed economies. Marketing must respond in detail to the requirements of very small producers and to very poor consumers. Reconciling the interests of these two groups is a critical issue. High skills in management and decision making will be required for large numbers of small and medium-sized enterprises. In such an intricate structure, a government is likely to be more successful providing a broad frame of support than performing in detail.

Some of the reasons why the effort to build an effective infrastructure for marketing in the less developed countries has not gone as well as was hoped, seem to be:

- The influence on policy makers in the less developed countries of teachings originating from political and social conditions in Europe and North America, reinforced by the conspicuous operations of large-scale public and cooperative enterprises in the developed countries during the post-war period, and the guidance of advisers coming from these backgrounds.
- A preference of new governments to establish institutions that would be fully under their control as opposed to working with enterprises that had their own independent base.
- The reluctance of aid agencies to reject project proposals of doubtful realism for fear of appearing politically biased or of losing business, and in some cases the outright inflation of loan projects in pursuit of self-determined targets.

References

1. ABBOTT, J. C. (1967) The development of marketing institutions. In *Agricultural Development and Economic Growth.* Ed. by H. M. Southworth and B. F. Johnston. Ithaca: Cornell University Press
2. ABBOTT, J. C. (1968) Marketing issues in agricultural development planning. In *Markets and Marketing in Developing Economies*, Ed. by R. Moyer, S. C. Hollander and R. D. Irwin. pp. 87–116
3. ABBOTT, J. C. (1978) Technical assistance in marketing: a view over time. *Proceedings of the 17th International Conference of Agricultural Economists,* Banff, 1979. Farnborough, Gower Publishing Co.
4. ABBOTT, J. C. (1982) Consideration of alternative marketing organizations to serve small farmers. *Agricultural Administration* **9**, 285–299
5. BAUER, P. T. and YAMEY, B. S. (1955) *Aspects of Governmental Intervention in Cooperation and Agricultural Marketing in Cyprus.* Nicosia, Cyprus Federation of Trade and Industry
6. BAUER, P. T. (1963) *West African Trade.* London, Routledge and Kegan Paul
7. BAUER, P. T. (1981) *Equality, the Third World and Economic Delusion.* Cambridge, Mass., Harvard University Press
8. BROMLEY, R. J. (1974) *Periodic Markets, Daily Markets, and Fairs: A Bibliography.* Melbourne, Department of Geography, Monash University
9. CREUPELANDT, H. and ABBOTT, J. C. (1969) Stabilization of internal markets for basic grains: implementation experience in developing countries. *Monthly Bulletin of Agricultural Economics and Statistics*, Vol. 18, pp. 1–9. Rome, FAO
10. DAINES, S. R. *et al.* (1980) *Agribusiness and Rural Project Analysis Manual.* Washington DC, AID
11. DEWEY, A. G. (1962) *Peasant Marketing in Java.* New York, Free Press of Glencoe
12. FAO (1970) *Market Information Services in Latin America.* FAO, Rome
13. FAO (1973) *Marketing Guide Series:* No. 1 Marketing problems and improved programmes, (1973). No. 2 Marketing fruit and vegetables (1970). No. 3, Marketing livestock and meat (1977). No. 4, Marketing eggs and poultry (1961). No. 5, Agricultural marketing boards: Their establishment and operation (1966). No. 6, Rice marketing (1972). No. 7, Fertiliser marketing (1977). Rome, FAO
14. GEORGE, P. S. (1979) *Public Distribution of Foodgrains in Kerala – Income Distribution Implications and Effectiveness.* Washington DC, International Food Policy Research Institute
15. HARPER, M. and KAVURA, R. (1982) *The Private Marketing Entrepreneur and Rural Development.* Rome, FAO
16. HARRIS, B. (1980) *Going against the Grain.* Hyderabad, ICRISAT
17. HUNTER, G. (1970) Cooperatives: effects of the social matrix. In *Cooperatives and Rural Development in East Africa.* Ed. C. G. Widstrand. New York, Africana Publishing Co.
18. HYDEN, G. (1983) *No shortcuts to Progress.* Berkeley, California; University of California Press
19. JONES, W. O. (1972) *Marketing Staple Foodcrops in Tropical Africa.* Ithaca, Cornell University Press

20. MINTZ, S. W. (1956) The role of the middleman in the internal distribution system of a Caribbean peasant economy. *Human Organization.* pp. 18–23. New York, Summer 1956

21. MITTENDORF, H. J. (1968) Marketing aspects in planning agricultural processing enterprises in developing countries. *Monthly Bulletin of Agricultural Economics and Statistics,* Vol. 17, No. 4 pp. 1–8. Rome, FAO

22. MITTENDORF, H. J. (1976) *The Planning of Urban Wholesale Markets for Perishable Food.* Rome, FAO

23. MITTENDORF, H. J. (1982) Rural market centres: potential development centres for small farmer development? *Indian Journal of Public Accounting* **28,** 101–119

24. OECD/FAO (1976) *Critical Issues on Food Marketing Systems in Developing Countries.* Report of an OECD/FAO joint seminar, Paris

25. RILEY, H. and STAATZ, J. (1981) *Food System Organization Problems in Developing Countries.* New York, Agricultural Development Council

26. SCARLETT, E. T. (1981) *Urban Food Marketing and Third World Development.* London, Croom Helm

27. SCHERER, F. (1977) Rural markets as service centres for small-scale farmers. *Working papers presented for the International Expert Consultation on Marketing and Rural Development,* 1977. Feldafing, Federal Republic of Germany, German Foundation for International Development

28. SCHUBERT, B. (1982) *Agricultural Market Information Services.* Rome, FAO

29. SPINKS, G. R. (1970) Attitudes toward agricultural marketing in Asia and the Far East. *Monthly Bulletin of Agricultural Economics and Statistics,* Vol. 19, pp. 1–9. Rome, FAO

30. SUBBARAO, K. (1983) Agricultural marketing and public policy. In *Review of Agricultural Economics Literature on India,* in the press

31. TIMMER, C. P. (1980) Food prices and food policy analysis in LDCs. *Food Policy* **5** (3), 183–199

32. VON OPPEN, M. (1982) *Efficiency and Equity Effects of Market Regulation.* Hyderabad, ICRISAT

33. WORLD BANK (1982) *Accelerated Development in Sub-Saharan Africa.* Washington DC, World Bank

Chapter 5

Role of government in improving food market centres in less developed countries*

Hans J. Mittendorf

Introduction

During the last decade, many of the less developed countries have become more and more aware of the crucial role played by an effective marketing system in agricultural and small farmer development. The strengthening of market centres, important places of transaction within the overall marketing system, is considered a focal point for improvement.

Role of market centres in less developed countries

Market centres are defined as those physical areas within the overall marketing system where agricultural and food products are concentrated for sale. For analytical purposes one can distinguish markets in two different areas, namely rural and urban, each showing specific types of characteristics (*see Figure 5.1*):

- Rural areas, where they may be assembly and retail outlets and of permanent or periodic nature.
- Towns and large cities, which may function as:
    (i) Regional wholesale markets in larger rural towns, where part of the produce is sent on to other markets.
    (ii) Terminal wholesale markets in large cities, mainly for perishable food such as fruit, vegetables and fish for consumption in the city.
    (iii) Consumer food retail markets.

The functions of assembly, wholesale and retail are often not clearly distinguished; at lower levels of development they are often combined to a different degree in trading enterprises. The specific role of a market centre can be defined by an analysis of the functions performed within the overall context of the agricultural and food marketing system, the flow of commodities and the linkages of the various enterprises and subsystems.

---

* The views expressed in this chapter are those of the author and are not necessarily those of the Food and Agriculture Organization.

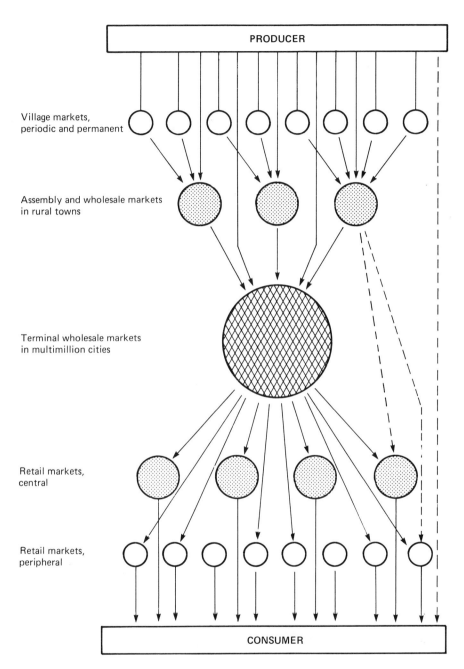

Figure 5.1. Food marketing channels and market centres in less developed countries. → Regular flow;
− − → bypass flow

In less developed countries, a large part of the agricultural commodities and food passes through different types of market centres. Markets are important points where supply and demand are balanced and where the process of price formation takes place. They are, consequently, important centres in the coordination of the production/supply/marketing process. The efficiency of the pricing process influences to a great extent the incentives provided to farmers and the stability of agricultural markets. Furthermore, markets are important centres of communication where information is exchanged among the participants, feedback is given in the marketing system and where innovations so essential to the development of the marketing/production system are disseminated.

A further function of market centres is the financing of the production/marketing process. Because institutional credit is not easily available to farmers and traders, a considerable part of the short-term credit required for crop production and marketing is provided by traders, particularly wholesalers/moneylenders located at markets, above all wholesale markets.

The role of market centres within the overall marketing system for agricultural and food products varies from country to country, within countries, and from commodity to commodity. Furthermore, according to the stage of development of a country and its marketing system, the role of market centres varies. In general, it would appear that the mass of small-scale farmers operating in a less monetized economy depends to a large extent upon rural market centres as sales outlets. Semisubsistence farmers often sell produce on markets where the produce has to be sorted, cleaned, graded and assembled. Larger and more market-oriented farmers prepare their produce for marketing at farm level and are therefore often able to send it directly to wholesalers, millers or processors without it passing through rural markets. Since the marketable surpluses of small farmers fluctuate in terms of quantity and quality and according to season, market centres are convenient places to facilitate the balance of supply and demand, with regard not only to the fluctuation of quantity but also to that of quality.

The role of market centres depends upon the type of commodity handled. Perishable commodities, such as fruit, vegetables and fish, which cannot be stored, livestock, and products with no easily standardized description of quality, are more likely to pass through market centres which facilitate inspection, grading and pricing. On the other hand, dry produce, such as cereals and legumes, which can more easily be stored and graded and for which the marketing time is less critical, tend to bypass market centres as development takes place, with particular reference to farmers who have become more market oriented and have relatively large quantities for sale.

The role of market centres is changing in the course of economic development. Empirical evidence shows that these centres as physical exchange points are more important at the lower development stage where farmers are less market oriented and general communication systems less developed.

The role of market centres tends to decline with the development of vertically coordinated and integrated marketing systems. Where farmers are market oriented they can contract directly with the wholesalers, who then plan and implement their operations with retailers. However, there are many different forms and degrees of vertical coordination of the marketing system, affecting the quantities of produce either passing through the market centre or bypassing it. The important point to stress here is that the planner of a new market centre has to have a clear understanding of the likely changes the marketing system will undergo during the course of the coming twenty years – this usually being the lifespan of a new market centre structure. The planner has to make assumptions about both the quantities of produce passing through the market centre and those quantities bypassing it; this again requires some sensitivity analysis of marketing costs and margins of competing marketing channels.

Review of market centre projects in various regions

In the last decade, many less developed countries have become aware of the need to improve their market centres. Although the general objective has been to improve market infrastructure and market facilitating services, the priorities have been different from region to region and country to country.

South America

Many countries have given priority to the improvement of the obsolete, congested, terminal wholesale markets which constituted a major bottleneck in marketing development. During the last two decades more than forty large-scale central wholesale markets have been built, of which Brazil alone built thirty; others are in the planning or implementation stages (*see Table 5.1*).

Rural markets are often mentioned as focal points for small farmer development, but few projects appear to have been implemented systematically with government assistance. COBAL (Companhia Brasileira de Alimentos) initiated about twenty rural assembly markets for fruit and vegetables during the 1970s. At the end of the 1970s, the Dominican Republic initiated a rural service centre programme, as did Jamaica in 1980 (parish markets), supported by an international financial assistance programme. Projects on rural markets have also been proposed in Honduras and Ecuador.

There have been a large number of investments in retail markets in many countries of Latin America, particularly in large cities. One large-scale programme of retail market projects was implemented in the municipality of Mexico City in the 1970s.

Africa

African countries south of the Sahara are still less urbanized than, for instance, Latin America. The role of terminal city wholesale markets in Africa is consequently less developed than in the multimillion cities of Latin America. Nevertheless, a number of cities such as Nairobi, Dar es Salaam and Abidjan have established, or are planning, new specialized terminal wholesale markets while many other cities with less developed wholesale trade envisage improvement of existing retail/wholesale markets located in the cities. A major issue in cities of Africa south of the Sahara is to find an adequate combination of wholesaling and retailing facilities in one enterprise. An artificial physical separation of wholesaling and retailing activities might create, under many conditions, operational problems for the predominating combined wholesale/retail activities.

Rural markets are important points as market outlets for small-scale farmers; improvement programmes have not yet, however, been formulated at national

TABLE 5.1. Growth of large cities and situation of wholesale markets in less developed countries, April 1985

Region and City	Population (Millions)			Status**	Region and City	Population (Millions)			Status**
	1960	1980	2000*			1960	1980	2000*	
Africa					*Central America*				
Abidjan (Iv. C.)	0.2	1.0	2.9	p	Guadalajara (Mex.)	0.8	2.8	6.2	n
Accra (Gha.)	0.4	1.4	3.9	p	Guatemala, Ciudad de	0.5	1.0	2.2	p
Addis Ababa (Eth.)	0.4	1.7	5.8	n	Mexico City (Mex.)	5.1	15.0	31.0	n
Ado-Ekita (Nig.)	–	1.1	3.8	–	Monterrey (Mex.)	0.7	2.1	4.6	n
Alexandria (Egy.)	1.5	2.7	4.8	o					
Alger (Alg.)	0.9	1.3	2.6	p	*South America*				
Cairo Giza Imbaba (Egy.)	3.8	7.4	12.9	p	Bogota (Col.)	1.3	4.9	9.6	n
Casablanca (Mor.)	1.1	2.2	4.5	o	Brazilia (Bra.)	0.1	1.6	4.9	n
Conakri (Gui.)	0.1	0.8	2.3	o	Buenos Aires (Arg.)	6.9	10.0	12.1	n
Cotonou (Ben.)	–	0.7	2.5	o	Belo Horizonte (Bra.)	0.7	3.0	6.5	n
Dakar (Sen.)	0.4	0.9	2.3	p	Cali (Col.)	0.5	1.4	2.6	n
Dar-es-Salaam (Tan.)	0.2	1.0	4.6	n	Caracas (Ven.)	1.3	3.3	5.7	n + p
Ilorin (Nig.)		0.6	2.1	–	Curitiba (Bra.)	0.4	2.1	5.2	n
Jos (Nig.)	0.7	2.7	7.7	–	Fortaleza (Bra.)	0.5	1.6	3.3	n
Kaduna (Nig.)	–	0.6	2.2	–	Goiania (Bra.)	0.1	0.9	2.5	n
Kampala (Uga.)	0.1	0.8	3.0	o	Guayaquil (Eca.)	0.5	1.0	2.3	p
Katanga (Zai.)	0.2	1.1	3.1	–	Lima-Callo (Per.)	1.8	4.7	8.6	p
Khartoum (Sud.)	0.4	1.4	4.0	–	Medellin (Col.)	0.8	2.1	4.0	n
Kinshasa (Zai.)	0.6	3.1	8.0	p	Port Alegre (Bra.)	0.8	2.5	5.0	n
Lagos (Nig.)	0.1	1.2	5.0	p	Recife (Bra.)	1.0	2.5	4.7	n
Luanda (Ang.)	0.2	0.9	2.8	–	Rio de Janeiro (Bra.)	4.5	10.7	10.0	n
Lusaka (Zam.)	–	0.8	2.3	–	Salvador (Bra.)	0.7	1.7	3.3	n
Lourenco Marques (Moz.)	0.2	0.8	2.7	–	Sao Paulo (Bra.)	4.4	13.6	25.8	n
Mushin (Nig.)	–	0.7	2.8	p	Santiago (Chi.)	2.0	4.0	5.6	p
Nairobi (Ken.)	0.2	1.3	5.3	n					
Rabat-Sale (Mor.)	0.3	0.9	2.3	–	*East Asia*				
Harare (Zim.)	0.1	0.9	2.8	–	Ansham (Chi.)	0.9	1.4	2.4	–
Tripoli (Lib.)	0.2	1.0	2.7	n	Changchum (Chi.)	1.0	1.5	2.5	–
					Cheng (Chi.)	0.8	1.4	2.5	–
Caribbean					Chengtu (Chi.)	1.2	1.5	2.4	–
La Habana (Cub.)	1.4	2.0	2.8	–	Chinchow (Chi.)	0.3	1.1	2.3	–
Port-au-Prince (Hai.)	0.2	0.8	2.2	o	Chungking (Chi.)	2.3	2.9	4.4	–
San Juan (P. Ri.)	0.6	1.4	2.1	–	Hangchow (Chi.)	0.8	1.2	2.0	–
Santo Domingo (Dom. R.)	0.5	1.6	3.4	–	Harbin (Chi.)	1.6	1.9	2.9	–

City			
Hofei (Chi.)	0.4	1.2	2.5	—
Kaoshiung (Chi.)	0.5	1.5	3.3	—
Kunning (Chi.)	1.0	1.4	2.3	—
Kwangchow (Chi.)	2.0	3.4	5.7	—
Lanchow (Chi.)	0.8	2.7	5.5	—
Loyang (Chi.)	0.3	1.2	2.8	—
Luta (Chi.)	1.6	1.9	3.0	—
Nanking (Chi.)	1.5	2.2	3.6	—
Paotow (Chi.)	0.7	1.3	2.3	—
Peking (Chi.)	4.7	11.4	20.9	—
Shanghai (Chi.)	7.7	14.2	23.7	—
Shenyang (Chi.)	2.6	3.4	5.3	—
Sian (Chi.)	1.4	2.0	3.3	—
Taipei (Chi.)	1.0	3.3	6.8	—
Taiyuan (Chi.)	1.1	1.8	3.0	—
Tientsin (Chi.)	3.5	5.1	8.1	—
Tsin (Chi.)	0.9	1.4	2.4	—
Tsingtao (Chi.)	1.2	1.6	2.5	—
Wuhan (Chi.)	2.3	3.2	5.0	—
Hong Kong	2.7	4.4	6.0	n
Pyongyand (D. P. Kor.)	0.6	1.3	2.2	—
Pusan (R. Kor.)	1.2	3.1	5.4	p
Seoul (R. Kor.)	2.4	8.4	13.7	n
Taegu (R. Kor.)	0.7	1.6	2.6	p

South Asia

City			
Bangalore (Ind.)	1.2	2.2	4.6	p
Bangkok-Thonburi (Tha.)	2.2	4.7	10.0	p
Bandung (Indo.)	0.9	1.6	3.1	—
Calcutta (Ind.)	5.6	8.8	16.4	p
Chittagong (Ban.)	0.4	1.4	4.3	—
Crimbatore (Ind.)	0.4	1.2	2.8	—
Dacca (Ban.)	0.5	3.0	10.5	n + p
Danang (Vie.)	0.1	1.8	6.5	—
Delhi (Ind.)	2.3	5.4	11.5	n + p
Dhambad (Ind.)	0.2	0.9	2.3	—

City			
Greater Bombay (Ind.)	4.1	8.4	16.8	n
Hanoi (Vie.)	0.5	1.1	2.5	—
Ho Chi Minh Ville (Vie.)	1.6	2.5	4.7	—
Hyderabad (Ind.)	1.3	2.5	5.2	p
Jaipur (Ind.)	0.4	1.0	2.2	p
Kanpur (Ind.)	1.0	1.7	3.3	—
Khulna (Ban.)	0.1	0.8	2.8	—
Kuala Lumpur (Mal.)	0.4	1.1	2.4	n + p
Jakarta (Indo.)	2.7	7.2	15.7	n
Ahmedabad (Ind.)	1.2	2.5	5.1	—
Madras (Ind.)	1.7	5.4	12.7	—
Madurai (Ind.)	0.4	1.1	2.6	—
Manila (Phi.)	2.3	5.5	11.4	n
Nagpur (Ind.)	0.7	1.2	2.5	—
Rangoon (Bur.)	1.0	2.2	4.8	p
Singapore	1.3	1.8	2.4	p
Surabaja (Indo.)	0.9	2.4	5.4	—
Tiruchirapalli (Ind.)	0.3	0.8	2.0	—
Ulhaswagar (Ind.)	1.0	1.2	4.5	—

Western South Asia

City			
Ankara (Tur.)	0.6	2.2	4.4	n
Aleppo (Syr.)	0.4	1.0	2.1	—
Baghdad (Iraq)	1.0	5.1	11.3	n + p
Beirut (Leb.)	0.5	1.9	3.4	p
Damascus (Syr.)	0.6	1.4	3.2	n
Izmir (Tur.)	0.6	1.1	2.2	—
Jeddah (S. Ar.)	0.2	0.8	2.0	—
Karachi (Pak.)	2.0	5.0	11.6	p
Lahore (Pak.)	1.4	3.0	6.6	p
Lyallpur (Pak.)	0.4	1.2	3.1	—
Rai (Iran)	—	0.7	2.7	—
Rawalpindi (Pak.)	0.4	0.9	2.1	—
Riyadh (S. Ar.)	0.2	1.0	2.5	p
Sahiwal (Pak.)	—	0.4	2.7	—
Teheran (Iran)	2.0	5.3	11.1	p

* Forecast

** Present status of wholesale markets: o = obsolete; p = new market planned; n = new market has been built or being built; = no information available.

Source: UN Urban, Rural and City Population, 1950–2000, as assessed in 1978, prepared by the Population Division of International Economic and Social Affairs of the UN Secretariat, ESA/P/WP.66, June 1980; regarding status of wholesale market, compiled by the author.

level, although at local level improvements are continually being made. Rural service centres as focal points for small farmer development have been established in rural development projects in Nigeria supported by international financing agencies. There are many proposals to build new retail markets in African cities since many women try to enter the retail trade to earn a decent income for their family. The issue that arises under these conditions is to what extent an investment in retail facilities, and in what form, is viable, i.e. how far women retailers can pay a cost-covering rent.

Near East

New terminal wholesale markets have been built in Dubai, Amman, Kuwait and Baghdad; others are planned for Beirut and other cities. Rural markets appear to attract less attention, apart from in a few less developed countries such as Yemen. The Government of Jordan established, at the end of the 1970s, packing stations for vegetables in the Jordan Valley, mainly for exports. Considerable investments have been made in retail markets and shopping centres in the oil-producing countries where funds are more amply available.

Asia

Terminal wholesale markets have been, or are being, built in a few cities, such as Hong Kong, Manila, Bombay and Seoul; others are planned (*see Table 5.1*). Considerable investment has been made, or is planned, in regional assembly wholesale markets (mandis) in India which serve mainly as assembly markets for surplus grain in the northern part of the country. The Government of China considered, at the beginning of 1984, a plan to improve market centres, mainly for fruit and vegetables.

Governments of Asia which participated in the FAO/DSE Asian Rural Market Centre Development Programme, 1978–80, have prepared programmes for rural market centre development consisting of investments in infrastructure and in strengthening of marketing support services (market information, marketing extension, marketing training) at rural market centres. Many countries in the region consider rural marketing centres important focal points in small farmer development.

Retail markets are continuously being built in towns and cities as demanded by the growth of urban population. Many governments are involved in market centre development programmes and projects. A number of Asian countries have focused on the regulation of marketing activities by providing some seed money to improve facilities.

The review of market centre programmes and projects outlined above shows that many governments are interested and involved in such development work. In spite of the considerable progress made in recent years, many problems have developed in the course of the planning and implementation of market centre projects, which should now be analysed. The following information is based mainly on FAO's technical assistance work in this area during the last two decades, also making use of information available in projects supported by agencies other than FAO.

Problems encountered in market centre development

Conceptual framework for analysing market centre performance

In evaluating the performance of market centres within the overall marketing system, one may distinguish between two levels of efficiency: (*a*) the market centre providing the basic infrastructure, services and environment to facilitate the marketing operations of the traders, and (*b*) the efficiency of the marketing operator to meet the service requirements of his customers. The marketing centre environment refers to conditions offered by the market for the most efficient physical handling of produce and transaction process. This refers in particular to the design and layout of the market (traffic flow, type of building), to supporting services, such as postal services, telephone, banking services, market information etc., as well as to the rules and regulations promoting efficient marketing operations.

With regard to the efficiency of the marketing activities performed by the trade at the market centre, one may distinguish among the following criteria:

- *Pricing efficiency*, namely the degree to which prices reflect the relevant factors determining the true market value of a product and the assessment of the relationship of prices to related prices at leading wholesale markets and to government price policy, where relevant.

- *Operational efficiency*, defining the degree to which the prevailing operational procedures such as unloading, stacking, cleaning, sorting, weighing, packing, transporting, measure up to optimum standards obtainable in given conditions; market charges should be sufficient to maintain the market in good working order so as to meet the service requirements of customers (farmers, consumers, traders), but should not discourage use of the market.

- *Innovative efficiency*, expressing the degree to which marketing enterprises and the market authority act as a force for the innovation of the production/marketing system through the systematic dissemination of appropriate technology, new techniques and practices by intensive extension and advisory work.

- *Credit efficiency*, defining the degree of efficiency at which short-term credit is provided upstream as well as downstream through the trade to participants, including farmers in the marketing system.

The adequate vertical coordination of the marketing system and government marketing policies and support programmes is another important criterion in the analysis of the performance of marketing activities (*see Figure 5.2*).

Any market improvement programme has to start with a clear analysis of the nature of the marketing problems, taking into account the criteria mentioned above and outlining alternative solutions in terms of costs and benefits considering the marketing system as a whole – and its linkages. Experience has shown that many strategies formulated for marketing improvement so far have been based on weak assumptions lacking a clear analysis of the problems and alternative solutions, which has consequently jeopardized the success of the proposed marketing projects. The problems encountered in improving market centres have been manifold and should now be discussed.

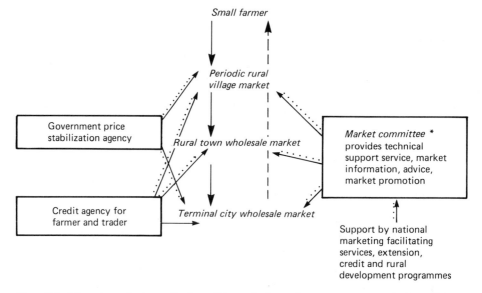

Figure 5.2. Adequate vertical coordination of the marketing system, government marketing policies and support programmes. → Flow of agricultural procedure; – – – – flow of agricultural inputs, consumer goods, market and technical information, credit; · · · · · · marketing facilitating services. *Represented: government, farmers, traders

Planning market centres

Markets in rural areas

In analysing marketing problems at the farm level, a clear distinction has to be made between the availability of adequate physical facilities, their functions and the performance of the marketing operators, namely farmers and traders with a particular view of small farmer development, which is a major government objective in most of the less developed countries. Furthermore, one has to identify whether the problems are of a macro- or microeconomic nature. Government price policies, with particular reference to price levels, minimum prices and price stability, are to a large extent of a macroeconomic nature and are not the subject of this chapter. The focus here is more on the scope and limitations of intervention at rural market centres with the overall objective of improving farm sales. The problems encountered in the past in this connection are featured in the following selected cases, with the overall objective of learning from these lessons for future programmes. As far as the type of market centres are concerned, the following may be distinguished:

- Retail markets.
- Retail/trans-shipment centres.
- Collection centres.
- Packing and grading centres, in particular for fruit and vegetables.

These centres may operate on a daily, weekly, biweekly, monthly or seasonal basis with a variety of facilities of a permanent or temporary nature. In general, experience so far has shown that interventions have focused mainly on physical facilities (hardware) with little attention being given to operational aspects (software) and to see the physical facility in the context of an overall marketing system consisting of competing marketing enterprises and channels. Furthermore, the dynamics of a marketing system and the changes it undergoes over time have often been ignored. A few cases should illustrate the problems encountered.

Major efforts have centred on improving fruit and vegetable marketing and the recommendations have often been to establish some sort of collection centre to facilitate marketing. With this objective in mind, the government of Korea built seven collection centres for fruit and vegetables in the 1970s, including grading, input supply and market information services. The collection centres have so far hardly been used since farmers have preferred to send their produce directly to the next wholesale markets, thus saving time, which is most important for highly perishable produce and costs.

In Kenya, at the end of the 1960s, simple vegetable packing sheds were established with government and outside technical support. Farmers were well trained in packing of vegetables and a person from the cooperative department of the government was trained in marketing. The scheme worked reasonably well for two years under the supervision of an expatriate expert. When he left, the scheme discontinued and farmers started to sell to competing private traders at a nearby rural market that offered better services.

The lesson learned from this experiment was that the physical facility, the packing shed, was of minor significance. An existing competing private trading system was more attractive to the small farmer than a cooperative marketing system initiated by the government, which was unable to compete with the private trade.

In Jamaica, in the early 1980s, a number of parish markets (combined retail/wholesale markets) were established. A number of them were designed incorrectly, lacked air circulation, adequate layout, and were overcapitalized, with the result that traders refused to enter the market. The reason for the failure was inadequate prior evaluation of local marketing practices and the lack of participation of local traders in the design and establishment of the new markets. The same thing happened in India, where a number of new collection centres/wholesale markets remained unused for a considerable time since traders refused to enter them.

In Barbados, at the beginning of the 1980s, a small collection centre was established for small-scale farmers. Although some sort of feasibility study was carried out, the volume traded in the first two years was less than 50% of that anticipated since a considerable number of farmers continued to market vegetables directly to retailers and consumers, which was less risky than selling at the collection centre at uncertain prices.

The list of such unsuccessful market intervention, with the provisions of physical facilities to improve marketing at rural level, could be extended further. The main conclusions to be drawn from these many experiences can be summarized as follows:

- Any intervention in marketing of farm products or inputs requires a comprehensive approach, the marketing system being viewed as a whole, taking into account competing channels and depending on the active participation of market users.

- Marketing problems at farm level can often be solved by strengthening organization and management rather than by investment in physical facilities, provided the minimum infrastructure (roads, telephones, mailing services) exist.
- Improvement of physical facilities, such as drainage, water supply, toilets, hygiene, requires modest funds and should be achieved by strengthening the management of market centres (setting adequate fees, providing for repairs and amortization) and the participation of the users. There appears to be great scope for encouraging market users to improve their market centre facilities by encouraging self-help, providing incentives and a minimum of technical support.
- International assistance should be provided more as technical assistance than as capital assistance to achieve the above objectives by emphasizing self-help and self-reliant approaches than outside assistance. There is more self-help spirit in the less developed countries than is usually recognized by governments and aid agencies.

Wholesale food markets

Wholesale markets play an increasingly important role in many of the less developed countries in the distribution of food, in particular in urban areas, and particularly of perishable produce such as fruit, vegetables and fish. Many problems have been encountered in the planning and execution of wholesale market projects which are highlighted below.

Need for a wholesale market   The first question to be asked is whether there is, in fact, the need for a wholesale market. In the course of development, a distinction should be made between three phases of wholesale market development (*see Figure 5.3*):

- A transitional stage to specialized wholesaling as occurring in many parts of Africa and low-income countries of Latin America. A specialized wholesale trade has hardly developed at all and, if it exists, is often combined with retailing. Under these conditions, there is no need for a specialized wholesale market; an area may be reserved for wholesaling activities in connection with a retail market. Since wholesale activities often take place in the early morning, the space could be used for retailing activities later in the day.
- Traditional wholesale structure, as in central European and North American cities 50–100 years ago, now present in many large urban centres of Latin America, Asia and the Near East. A specialized wholesale trade in agricultural perishables has developed on a larger scale of operation and investment in wholesale markets is justified.
- Supplementary role of wholesale markets to buying by chain stores direct from packing stations in producing areas, as in North America and highly developed countries of north and central Europe. Large retail organizations have developed; independent retailers are grouped in buying cooperatives or voluntary chains, which permit centralized purchasing in large quantities direct from producers or producer groups thus bypassing the wholesale market. The wholesale market performs only a supplementary function for highly seasonal and less standardizable produce.

The structures of the wholesale and retail trade, as well as the changes they undergo in the course of development are an essential factor in the planning of

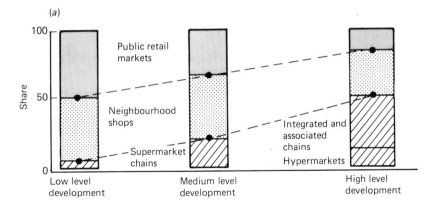

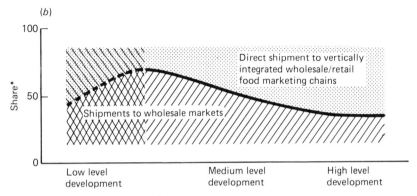

Figure 5.3. Changes in food retailing and wholesale in the course of economic development in less developed countries. (*a*) Retailing (increasing role of food chains and declining role of public retail markets); (*b*) wholesaling (declining role of wholesale markets and increasing direct shipments to food chains). *Share of food passing through wholesale markets and direct shipments to food chains

new wholesale markets. There are a number of cities of Africa, Asia and Latin America where wholesaling is less developed and where investment in specialized wholesale markets is justified.

Size of the wholesale market   A careful assessment of the type and quantity of commodities likely to pass through and bypass the market is essential to estimate the required size of the market. Experience has shown that parallel marketing channels bypassing the market have often been underestimated with the result that a part of the new market buildings has not been utilized. In the final analysis, the size of the market buildings has to be based on firm commitments of the wholesalers to rent or purchase the stalls. Adequate provision should then be made for the reservation of land to be made available for future extension. The estimation of the minimum size of the wholesale market for the first year of operation has to be finally based on the economic analysis of the type of individual wholesale stall proposed and the ensuring of an economically self-supporting project, which may exclude a number of marginal wholesalers who are not able to pay a cost-covering rent.

Do less developed countries need one or more wholesale markets?   While it is argued in many advanced countries that one central wholesale market, with exclusive rights to conduct wholesale transactions, is advisable, in many multimillion cities of the less developed countries, which depend predominantly on small traders with less motorized transport, it has to be studied whether one or more wholesale markets is more beneficial. Transport costs and time required for the retailer to travel to the wholesale markets are decisive factors. Under some conditions, one central wholesale market providing price leadership with a number of satellite redistribution markets and/or secondary wholesalers focusing on distribution, as in the large markets of Japan and Latin America, may facilitate distribution for small retailers. There may also be the opportunity to arrange wholesaling activities early in the morning, followed later in the day by retailing activities. This would make better use of the same building.

Size and shape of stalls   The degree to which the size and shape of the stall facilitates maximum use of the space for transaction purposes determines, to a large extent, the economics of the wholesale market investment. A common error in the past has been for less developed countries to adapt the type of building and stall designed to suit the more advanced requirements of Europe and North America, with the result that the turnover per square metre of sales and store area of a market stall has been inadequate to cover the capital costs of the investment. It is therefore essential to tailor the size and shape of the stall to the structure of the existing trade in the market. This necessitates a count of the existing traders and of the area used by each of them for sales and for storage (*see Table 5.2*). This

TABLE 5.2. Structure of fruit and vegetable wholesale trade according to the size of floor space of the store occupied (an example)*

Average size of floor space occupied $(m^2)^\dagger$	Number of stalls		Total floor space		Average size of the stall (m^2)	Proposed module‡
	Actual no.	Percentage total	Actual (m^2)	Percentage total		
<20	20	8	240	2	12	Open shed
20–30	20	8	520	4	26	
30–40	30	12	1050	8	35	
40–50	40	16	1680	13	42	
50–60	60	24	3420	26	57	
60–70	50	20	3450	26	69	
70–80	20	8	1600	12	80	
80–180	6	2	960	7	160	
>180	1	0	200	2	200	

* This is a hypothetical case to illustrate the type of information needed to complete the final column on the different types of module, i.e. wholesaling units proposed for different sizes of wholesaling enterprise.
$\dagger$ The area of the ground floor utilized daily for short-term storage and sales of produce, including space for walking but without office space and storage room for empty crates.
$\ddagger$ The modules proposed should meet best average size of wholesalers floor space requirements.

information provides the basis for defining the most suitable and economic modules of stalls proposed for different types and sale of wholesaling enterprises. Easily movable walls provide flexibility to meet traders' changing space demands. Open-shed buildings are particularly useful for the sales of small farmers and traders who can rent space on a daily basis.

The proposed modules with the turnover of produce assumed per square metre is the basis for calculating the rents and thus the economics of the investment.

Type of building   Although it has been stressed repeatedly that economically viable projects can support only low-cost simple buildings, architects are often inclined to propose sophisticated and costly structures which wholesalers are unable to pay and cannot be amortized in a reasonable period of time. A simple shed-type market building, providing protection against sun and rain, with a firm clean floor, will in most cases be adequate for small-scale wholesale traders who predominate in many of the less developed country markets.

Layout   The layout of markets has not only to take into account local trading patterns but also economics of alternative trading operations. Each square metre of investment proposed has to be considered in terms of alternative solutions. This refers, in particular, to size of area foreseen for parking, and for the movement of personnel and of vehicles. The analysis of markets built during the last two decades shows the considerable scope for savings which could have been made in investments if architects had been more economically minded.

Location   New wholesale markets should not be located too far from consumption areas in view of the transport costs and time incurred by the small retailer, who predominates in less developed countries. If transport time is, say, more than 30 minutes and retailers cannot go regularly to the market to purchase, the risk may arise that wholesalers will be reluctant to move to the new market since they fear losing their customers. In such a case a secondary wholesale distribution trade may develop in multimillion cities to serve small retailers.

Often there is not much choice of site since most of them in the urban development plan are already earmarked. It is therefore, in practice, most important to speed up a decision by the municipality and reserve a suitable site for a new wholesale market.

Ownership   Various forms of ownership are known, e.g. municipal, state, private, mixed corporations (state, municipal, province, users) or cooperative. In view of the large amount of funds required to finance a wholesale market, large markets are often financed by a multiple source of funds. It is essential that wholesalers be encouraged to participate in the financing of the market and adequate incentives have to be provided for them to put their own funds into the market. This also ensures their moving to the new market once it is completed.

In a number of cases the question has arisen of whether market stalls should be offered for sale. Some argue that facilities in markets should remain the property of the public to ensure orderly marketing, in particular pricing, an argument often used in India. Others feel that individual ownership of market stalls may not be in conflict with competitive pricing procedures if the necessary action is taken to provide an environment for competitive pricing. Competitive pricing can be ensured by promoting standardized grading, accurate and timely price information, by the provision of additional land to expand the wholesale market, if there is a real need, and by the promotion of alternative marketing channels. It is, therefore, the opinion of the author that private ownership of wholesale stalls is not in conflict with social objectives, provided measures are taken to ensure full competition.

Management and rent policies   The recruitment of qualified managers, the need for continuous training, for formulation of functional rules and regulations and their proper application, the need for financial autonomy and proper accounting procedures, including monthly balance sheets for the wholesale market, cannot be overemphasized. Regular meetings have to be held with market users for the discussion of grievances and market operation aspects. The provision of technical and commercial assistance and of market information to market users and related groups is another important responsibility of management. This includes the promotion of a proper product mix meeting retailers' requirements, for instance the inclusion of grains and staples.

Furthermore, the management of wholesale markets should take an active interest in the improvement of assembly, transport and retailing operations in order to ensure full vertical coordination of marketing operations. It may therefore be appropriate to include, under the responsibility of wholesale market managers, the supervision and development of public retail outlets, for instance retail markets and street markets, and assembly functions.

Policies on rents of market stalls are always a major issue. Low rent policies or the absence of a rent policy at all are a major obstacle to new investments in wholesale markets. Rents paid by wholesalers in many old wholesale markets are often so low as to make it difficult to cover administrative, cleaning and repair costs, not to mention capital costs. This has, in many situations, led to a distortion of the market situation and to a serious discouragement of new investments. The concept of fees covering costs must be advocated for a number of reasons and considerable efforts are required to convince wholesalers that they should pay adequate fees in a new wholesale market, on the grounds that it offers considerable opportunity for increasing productivity and for more efficient organization.

In a number of countries, issues of raising fees in new markets have been complicated by the fact that wholesalers were not involved in the design of the new wholesale market, which has often resulted in inadequate stalls from the functional point of view and, furthermore, expensive buildings for which wholesalers have not been prepared to pay. In such cases the organization responsible for designing the building would have to pay for the excessive costs and not the wholesaler who has to look for the most economic operational methods in order to be able to compete with parallel marketing channels bypassing the wholesale market.

There have been other instances where market fees have been used to a large extent as government revenue with inadequate attention being given to maintenance and extension.

Private ownership of stalls (or building of sheds by traders) on the understanding that traders accept basic market regulations facilitates the financing of the market facilities.

Financing   Since municipalities do not, in general, have the funds to pay for wholesale markets*, a search for additional sources has to be made. Since such wholesale markets are of national importance for marketing development in view of the crucial role they play in price formation and marketing development, central governments often take an interest in financing them. If wholesale markets are well designed, taking into account the points made above, projects can achieve economic and financial viability provided capital expenditure is kept at a minimum.

---

* An exception may have been the mandi markets in India that, at the beginning of the 1980s, were financially strong since fixed market fees generated ample income.

That this has often not been achieved in the past is an indication of the scope which exists for improving the planning of wholesale markets to reach economic solutions. Needless to say, a sound feasibility study outlining alternative solutions is the basis for appraising the project viability. The financial analysis of the project should be done, not only for the project as a whole, but also for different categories of user, to ensure their being able to repay the capital plus operating costs. If the volume of trade per square metre of sales area is sufficiently high, the rents to be paid for the stall may not amount to more than between 2 and 4% of the turnover of the trader. Thus, if the wholesale projects are well conceived, there should not be a great need for subsidization of investments. As explained above, different forms of ownership are feasible, offering various options for financing. In order to encourage the participation of wholesalers in financing, one form of financing would be the establishment of a mixed corporation. Shares could be issued per square metre of sales area to be purchased by wholesalers. Twelve shares per square metre amounted, for instance, to US$39 in CORABASTOS, Bogota, Colombia, in July 1982.

Transfer of wholesalers and protection of wholesale markets   In a number of wholesale market projects there have been considerable difficulties in moving wholesalers from the old premises to the new markets because they were not convinced of the benefits to be gained from doing so. The reasons why the traders did not find the new wholesale market attractive are very varied. They included unsuitable and/or too expensive buildings, markets too far from customers, rents not economic from the users' point of view. Many wholesalers preferred to stay in the old market which hindered those who wanted to move as they feared there would be no customers at the new market. The transfer time of wholesalers to the new market has, therefore, become in many market projects a critical point in the project life. A number of lessons have been learned. First, it cannot be stressed too much that the *active participation* of the users in the planning of a new market on a continuous basis is an indispensable condition for the success of the new market. This requires the effort, time and patience of the project management to ensure that wholesalers understand fully the technical aspects of the new market, as well as the economic implications, as early as possible. Secondly, an attempt has to be made to arrange the transfer of those wholesalers who have posts at the new market at a date by which time the old market would be closed. Considerable promotion and objective information work is needed to ensure that retailers come to the new market. It is important to make provision at an early stage for the transfer of the associated services, such as restaurants, repair shops, hotels, to the new market. It is often argued that a special law is required to 'protect' the new market against wholesale trading being carried out in other facilities outside the market. If there are other such facilities which, from the hygiene point of view, are suitable and which do not create any external costs (using public roads for parking, for instance) there is no reason to forbid their operation. For this reason, any legal measure proposed to protect the new market should be reviewed carefully to ascertain whether it restricts competition. This should, however, not speak against any temporary measures (say, for a few years) to establish legal measures to permit the market to be established and facilitate the transfer of the wholesalers from the old to the new market. In this connection, it is helpful to prepare at an early stage a rehabilitation plan of the old market areas, taking alternative economic uses of the old site into account.

Government role

In view of the important role played by markets directly in small farmer development and indirectly as an important link in the overall marketing system, governments have to take an active interest in monitoring market centre development. Past experience has shown that there has been considerable waste of resources in the management and extension of the market centre network. Since it can be expected that considerable funds will be required in future to improve the existing market centres and expand their network, it is most timely that governments provide a minimum of supporting services to stimulate effective development in this area. Government services might include those discussed below.

Assistance in planning   The analysis of the problems faced in the planning of market centres as outlined above indicates that technical knowledge of marketing and market centre planning is required to formulate economically viable projects. Less developed countries could set up a small group of economists and marketing engineers specializing in market centre building, as was done in Brazil, USA and India. Market centre planning has to focus in future much more on a broader concept of developing marketing systems, in which full attention is given to the views of the participants in the marketing system than to mere aspects of physical planning. This refers in particular to rural market centres which should be considered as focal points of service centres for small farmer development and less from the physical infrastructural point of view.

   Market centre planning has to follow a vertically integrated approach by paying adequate attention to rural wholesale and retail marketing and ensure that the marketing system as a whole is improved.

Management   The management of markets has to be recognized as a professional job. Governments should promote their proper management and support development through training, incentives, regulatory measures and supervision and provide the necessary authority to market managers.

Operation   There are a number of indirect support measures necessary to support the operation of market centres, namely proper market information and forecasting, and marketing extension and advisory services. Although these should be organized in close collaboration with the markets, responsibility for organizing and financing these services is with governments.

   In view of the urgent need to improve market centres and ensure a coordinated approach at national level, consideration has been given to institutionalizing some of the major support services in a national market authority, already proposed by India and Jamaica. Such a market authority would have a promotional and regulatory function in providing technical assistance in planning new markets, improving those already existing, in training of personnel, in particular managers and other personnel employed at markets, and in providing for rules and regulations. Such a national market authority could help in making better use of scarce resources of personnel as well as capital.

Training   Training of personnel at all levels is essential, not only for planning but, in particular, for operation in order to ensure that the new facilities are well utilized.

Further reading

1. ABBOTT, J. C. (1984) *Marketing Improvement in the Developing World.* Rome, FAO
2. BROMLEY, R. J. (1974) *Periodic Markets and Daily Markets and Fairs: a Bibliography.* Monash Publication in Geography No. 10. Monash University, Melbourne, Department of Geography
3. BUCKLIN, P. L. (1979) *Problems with Evolution of Urban Wholesale Food Markets in Developing Countries.* Berkeley, Oct. 1979. Mimeo
4. CHAGAS, A. (1983) *Operational Aspects of Retail Markets in Jamaica (UTF/JAM/007).* Rome, FAO
5. DE BALOGH, P. G. (1983) *Rural Parish Markets in the Agricultural Marketing System.* Rome, FAO
6. DE BALOGH, P. G. (1984) *Terminal Report – JAMAICA, UTF/JAM/007, Marketing Experts.* Rome, FAO
7. FAO (1979) Rural markets – a critical link for small farmer development. *Country Reports and Case Studies on Rural Markets in 10 Asian Countries.* No. RAFE 37, p. 2/9. FAO Regional Office for Asia and the Pacific, Bangkok, Thailand
8. FAO (1980) *Improvement and Development of Rural Markets in West Africa.* Results of investigations on selected rural markets in West Africa and on a follow-up Expert Consultation, Accra, Ghana, p. 60
9. FAO (1981) *Terminal Report – Mexico, AG:DP/MEX/77/006.* Sistemas de Commercializacion de Productos Alimenticios, Rome
10. FAO (1983) *Guide to Improving Rural Markets.* Provisional working document. Rome
11. FAO (1984) *Establishing Small Packing Facilities for Fruit and Vegetables in Rural Areas.* In draft
12. FAO/DSE (1980) *Rural Markets – a Critical Link for Small Farmer Development.* A report on the FAO/German Foundation for International Development – Asian Regional Evaluation Workshop on Rural Market Centre Development Programme. p. 90. Bangalore, 28 April–2 May
13. FAO AND REPUBLIC OF KENYA (1983) *Seminar on Planning and Operation of Markets.* Nairobi, Kenya, Feb. 28–March 4
14. GROSSKOPF, W., LORENZL, G. and STRECKER, O. (1983) Agrarmarkt-entwicklung als Aufgabe wirtschaftlicher Zusammenarbeit. *Forschungsberichte des Bundesministeriums fuer Wirtschaftliche Zusammenarbeit,* Bd 48. Cologne
15. HERTAG, O. (1984) *Development of Public Markets in Uganda.* Report to the Government of Uganda. Rome, FAO
16. INSITUTO INTERAMERICANO DI CIENCIAS AGRICOLAS (1974) *Centros de Acopio.* La Reunion Nacional sobre Instrumentos de Commercializacion. Merida, ICA
17. LOS CENTROS DE SERVICIOS RURALES INTEGRADOS EN LA REPUBLICA DOMINICA NA (1982) *Commercio y Desarrollo,* April/June 1982, Mexico Ano V, Vol. 1, pp. 87–91
18. LUCCIONI, J. (1982) *Organization of a Network of Markets of National Importance to the Government of India,* FAO/UNDP
19. MANUAL FOR MARKET PRICE COLLECTION (1980) *Azadpur Market, Manual No. 1,* New Delhi
20. MARKET PLANNING AND DESIGN CENTRE, NEW DELHI (1983) *Evaluation of Agricultural Produce Market Yards.* Report No. 22, in collaboration with FAO and Birla Research Institute
21. MITTENDORF, H. J. (1978) The challenge of organizing city food marketing systems in developing countries. *Zeitschrift fuer auslaendische Landwirtschaft,* **17**, 323–341
22. MITTENDORF, H. J. (1982) Improvement of wholesale markets in developing countries: an essential instrument for development. *Financing Agriculture* **XIV**, p. 8
23. MITTENDORF, H. J. (1982) Rural market centres: potential development centres for small farmer development. *International Journal of Public Administration* **28**, 101–119
24. PERCY, P. F. (1983) Marketing Development for the Transmigration Settlement Areas, Working Document Project UNDP/FAO/INS/78/012. Jakarta, FAO
25. REPORT NO. 20 (1983) Manual of Survey and Data Processing Techniques for Planning of Agricultural Markets. New Delhi
26. REPORT NO. 21 (1983) *Proceedings of the Second National Workshop on Agricultural Markets,* Lucknow (UP) 19–22 Oct. 1982, Vol. I, II
27. RILEY, H. and STAATZ, J. (1981) *Food System Organization Problems in Developing Countries.* Agricultural Development Council, Report No. 23
28. SCHERER, A. (1983) *Terminal Report – BRAZIL, AG:DP/BRA/016.* Centre for Human Resource Development in Agricultural Marketing, FAO
29. SMITH, R. H. T. *et al.* (1979) Market-place exchange, spatial analysis and policy. Papers presented at the Meeting of the International Geographical Union, Working Group on Market-place Exchange Systems, Zaria, Nigeria, July 1978. Geographisches Institut der Johannes-Gutenberg-Universität, Mainz, p. 136

30. SOUTHWORTH, V. R., JONES, W. O. and PEARSON, S. R. (1979) Food crop marketing in Atebubu District, Ghana. *Food Research Institute Studies* **XVII,** No. 2 157–195
31. STEPPE, H. M. (1983) *Terminal Report – INDIA, IND/71/625.* Market Planning and Design Centre, FAO
32. WHALE, M. (1982) *Financial Management and Accounting in the Parish Markets.* Kingston, FAO
33. WORKING PAPER NO. 3 (1981) *An Evaluation of Selected Agricultural Product Markets in Bihar.* New Delhi

Chapter 6

Improving food retailing in less developed Asian countries

Louis P. Bucklin

Introduction

Over the last 30 years, much of the literature on the improvement of food retailing in less developed countries has placed heavy emphasis upon the transfer of relatively capital-intensive technology originating in industrial nations. The small-scale, limited-line food retailer, and the lengthy, poorly coordinated distribution chain that serves him, have been identified as inefficient market elements. The literature holds that a modern system of vertically integrated supermarket chains would provide substantial benefits through scale economies, the adoption of self-service, and the bypassing of clogged wholesale food markets.

Here, an alternative approach to this 'high-technology' solution for less developed Asian countries is suggested. This alternative calls for the recognition, at least for the medium term, of the permanence of much of the small retailer system. Improvements in their operation and business skills can be obtained gradually through the upgrading of the public market, or 'bazaar', facilities and the management of these facilities. The fundamental argument behind this concept is that the supermarket, even in its more rudimentary version, is ill-equipped to service the low- and middle-income consumers in less developed Asian countries. Hence, if gains in food distribution are to be obtained, they must be secured through improvement in domestic or intermediate technologies.

The high-technology approach

Perhaps the earliest study to identify clearly the high-technology approach to the improvement of food retailing is the Galbraith and Holton report on Puerto Rico[3]. After a detailed investigation of the costs of small-scale retailer operations, and the reductions in gross margin perceived possible through expansion of product line and volume, the authors concluded:

> On *a priori* grounds it would seem that development of an integrated chain store operation on a large scale in Puerto Rico is the most promising single project for improving distribution efficiency . . .

This chapter originally appeared as an article in *Food Policy*, 1977, Vol. 2, No. 2, pp. 114–122.

The core of the problem is the small average volume of Puerto Rican food stores. A firm thoroughly aware of the economies of maximum sales per outlet and of how to achieve the same volume large enough to realize those economies could take great strides toward the rationalization of food distribution. . . . Direct buying and efficient servicing of retail outlets from central warehouses would bring still further economies of operation. Thus a chain organization modified to fit Puerto Rico's needs could be a very powerful force for improvement of efficiency in food distribution on the island. Every effort should be bent to encourage the development of such organization.

At a later stage, research conducted in Latin America by Michigan State University's Latin American Studies Center has done much to reinforce this approach. The differences in the costs between traditional marketing systems and integrated chain store operations were dramatically depicted for a number of countries. In the La Paz study, for example, it was held that 'the effect of large-scale retailing . . . would be to reduce by at least 3.4% the price of the foods carried. . . . If savings through reduced acquisition costs were passed on completely to the consumer, an additional reduction in 5% in the price of food would be gained'[7]. The actual ability of a supermarket to affect local prices was caught in a study of Recife, Brazil, where the entry of a low-margin supermarket created a domino effect in the market, causing other self-service stores and neighbourhood shops to reduce their gross margins as well[8].

The technology incorporated in this approach is characterized by Slater as the 'market integration thesis'. Specifically, both horizontal and vertical integration are required[6]:

Horizontal coordination implies larger-scale retail outlets selling several products – including necessities to low-income people – and following 'modern' practices of charging low margins for high-turnover staples and higher margins for low-turnover luxury goods.
The vertical coordination of the marketing system reduces the intermediaries' risks associated with transactions. The capital available to the intermediary is expanded because of the dependability of the order placed by the horizontally integrated larger-scale retailer. The vertical coordination of the higher levels of the marketing system with horizontally integrated retail operations also creates a set of producer expectations that can result in fuller utilization of presently available productive capacity.

A summary statement, emanating from an overview of the group of Latin American studies, provides this recommendation[4]:

Efficient food distribution can be achieved through the development of a variety of competitive wholesale–retail chains. The emphasis should be on governmental programs encouraging a competitive balance among the following types of wholesale–retail chains: (1) private chains – vertically and horizontally integrated chains of retail stores served by a single wholesale warehouse . . . (2) retailer-owned cooperative chains . . . (3) voluntary chains . . . (4) consumer-owned cooperative chains . . . and (5) government-owned retail chains . . .

The total impact of these recommendations on government policy in less developed countries through the world is difficult to ascertain. In Korea, consultants recommended the adoption of various parts of the market integration thesis. The failure of an attempt to form a cooperative chain of independents led the government to develop an ambitious programme to expand rapidly the number of corporate supermarkets. In 1974, the government initiated a five-year plan for the modernization of the distribution sector. They used various financial supports totalling US$9 million to implement the plan and urged several business tycoons, at present eight corporations, to invest in the distribution sector and thus to set up supermarket-type chain stores. The corporate chains are to receive about US$38 000 as a long-term, low interest rate (8%) loan for establishing each chain store[5]. The programme would result in almost tripling the number of supermarkets in the country.

Consumer cooperatives in various countries have also become involved in supermarkets, either already in operation or in the planning stage. In Manila, a US consultant was called upon to recommend and develop a plan for a specific location. In Singapore, a cooperative sponsored by the labour movement was planning to expand a small initial system of five stores after recovering from an early brush with bankruptcy.

Role of the supermarket in Asian cities

Despite this interest in the supermarket, there is a limited incidence of this type of institution in Asian cities, with the exception of Japan. As shown in *Table 6.1*, the extent of diffusion is quite limited, although there are several chains of formidable size, even by Western standards. In some instances, the sparse numbers, such as in Singapore, are related to a government policy that restricts the development of supermarkets by non-nationals. In other instances, such as in Colombo, government controls over food distribution inhibit the willingness of entrepreneurs to risk the development of such a store.

For the most part, however, the lack of penetration relates more to the general low levels of income and the lack of patronage of such markets by the low- and middle-income groups. The supermarkets, such as those in some parts of Latin

TABLE 6.1. Incidence of supermarkets and per capita income for major Asian cities, about 1973

City	Per capita income (US$)	Supermarkets	
		Number	Market share (%)
Tokyo	3700	–	>20
Singapore	1050	9	–
Kuala Lumpur	1000	11	–
Hong Kong	724	70	–
Seoul	500	35	5
Manila	400	32	–
Bangkok	300	35	4
Delhi	198	0	0
Colombo	180	0	0
Djakarta	142	<10	–
Dacca	130	0	0
Bombay	110	0	0

From unpublished data, FAO.

America, are located in the wealthier neighbourhoods and cater for upper-income nationals and foreign residents. This pattern of development is rooted in the character of this institution. Supermarkets are largely merchandisers of packaged and processed foods, e.g. canned, boxed, dried, bagged. In the developing world, particularly in those cities with the very lowest income levels, only a small proportion of food is consumed from processed products. A typical diet in Korea shows that less than 10% of the total is consumed in processed form. For lower-income cities, and for the lowest-income brackets in those cities, the proportion of processed food consumed must be close to nil.

The consequence is that supermarkets in these low-income Asian cities have little choice but to focus their efforts upon higher income populations. Of course, although many (but not all) carry fresh foods, these are typically handled in such a way that costs are increased relative to those in other types of retail institutions[8]; for example, the produce may be bagged and meat refrigerated. Hence, they may not be priced competitively with fresh foods available elsewhere.

Whether supermarket operators can shift their product orientation to one that primarily emphasizes fresh foods is a tantalizing proposition, but one for which the odds appear sharply adverse. The handling of both produce and fresh meat are more labour intensive than groceries. Even among the high-income classes, supermarkets have rarely been able to employ self-service operations for meat. Items are not always cut to order, and they are specially weighed and wrapped upon demand. In the same vein, produce must be specially cared for, pruned, and carefully priced to avoid holding some items too long. Refrigeration and wrapping to avoid spoilage, however, have added costs and resulted in a reputation that supermarket products are less fresh than those in the marketplace.

Beyond this, the search for economies through backward integration in fresh foods has been frustrated to a large degree. Supermarket chains do exist, but few have the volume of business to develop their own warehouse system. Managerial interests and capabilities in this area appear significantly limited. This development has been slow for processed goods because of the role of importer warehouses in the channel. More important, however, is the lack of product specialization and grading in rural wholesale markets which makes efficient field purchasing extraordinarily difficult. Farmers have not shifted to large-scale specialization as they have in the USA. They and the first handlers in the system seek buyers who will take all their produce, not just one quality level. As a consequence, the assortment function of the central wholesale markets remains an exceedingly critical one.

A final dimension of the supermarket's role, and one perhaps peculiar to Asian markets, concerns its participation in the sale of the principal food product, rice. Surprisingly, few supermarkets carry more than a small quantity of high quality, packaged rice. Their abandonment of this market to the independent rice dealer appears to be due to government regulation of the rice-marketing system. This has favoured the independent rice dealer. Also, the gross margins of about 6% that are sometimes to be found are unattractive to the supermarkets, reducing their incentive to sell the product.

At the same time, many consumers, especially those in the higher-income brackets, typically purchase rice in quite large quantities. This makes delivery by the rice dealer both economically and logistically desirable. The supermarket is thus unable to offer any significant advantage in the sale of *the* major Asian food product.

In sum, therefore, the technology of the Western supermarket is not well suited at present to serving the needs of the low-income food buyer. This is not to say that they can make no contribution, however. Supermarkets play an important role in improving standards for food retail service and introducing new products to the market. In some places they have an impact on processed food prices, but this typically extends only to neighbourhood grocery shops – not to the fresh food markets. Consequently, alternative approaches must be sought if progress in aiding the very poor is to be achieved.

The Asian bazaar

While there are many thousands of provision shops throughout Asian cities, and a seemingly inexhaustible supply of street hawkers, 50% or more of the food purchases appear to be made within the confines of the bazaar[2]. The bazaar is a food market in which many, tiny and highly specialized retailers function. Most such markets are chaotic, crowded, noisy, and colourful. By Western standards, however, they are dirty, insanitary, and often highly unattractive. Food is typically sold from open stalls, unprotected from flies and other pests. Quality ranges widely, items are unsorted, and haggling a way of life.

Entrepreneurs put in long hours of work, starting early in the morning with purchases at the central wholesale market. They typically take responsibility for immediate delivery to their stalls. While timing varies among countries, in tropical areas the mornings are devoted to the sale of the day's purchases with the entrepreneur seeking to minimize the degree of food carryover. Afternoons are given over to the cleaning and removal of the day's accumulation of rubbish by the market personnel.

The persistence of this institution is due to the efficiencies such markets bring to the sorting and rapid turnover of perishable products. In a world where heat and rough handling shorten product shelf life drastically, and grading continues to be shunned, the central retail market remains a remarkably efficient institution. Despite its manifold deficiencies, it serves to match heterogeneous supplies and demands while maintaining rapid turnover. The agglomerative power of the market is so strong that permanent shops selling fresh produce have difficulty locating any great distance away.

To the casual view, most bazaars appear to be highly similar. However, the review of markets in different countries reveals substantial differences. These occur not only with respect to such obvious aspects as size, degree of intermixture of wholesalers and direct selling producers, but in the standards of service provided for the consumer. Indeed, just as patterns in the development of Western retail food stores can be identified, so can an evolution be shown in formation of bazaars.

At the crudest level, such markets may be little more than open-air street fairs where food is displayed on makeshift fixtures or directly on the roadway. At more advanced levels, stalls emerge in permanent form, array themselves along tortuous paths, and invade nearby buildings in a haphazard fashion. In the more advanced stage, the buildings housing the stalls become large, specially constructed facilities. Some may be multistoried with parking facilities. Fixtures become more elaborate, wood is replaced with tile, ice is used everywhere to preserve foods, and some overnight refrigerated storage is found. The shops increase in size and tend to use modern materials and fully enclosed facilities.

In sum, food bazaars vary dramatically from their stereotype. While most retain the informality and atmosphere of a fair, they have the capacity of catering to both the wealthy and the poor. The continual upgrading of these facilities, as a consequence, represents at least one means for improving the food marketing system of less developed countries. Given the difficulties involved in broadening the customer base of supermarket chains, it may well be the most feasible approach to aiding the low-income buyer.

Bazaar problems

Policy makers seeking to improve the traditional bazaars, however, also face a wide range of barriers. These can be placed in three categories. They are:

- The derivation of capital necessary for maintenance, modernization, and expansion of the bazaar system.
- The design of more efficient and attractive facilities.
- The improvement of the efficiency of the food enterprises within the bazaar.

Capital

In all Asian cities the inability of the food retail system to keep pace with consumer needs derives partly from the rapid rate of population expansion. More fundamentally, the difficulty is rooted in the failure of such systems to generate capital that can be made available for the necessary expansion and modernization.

In most Asian cities, with the exception of Seoul, the majority of the bazaars are operated by municipal governments. In such markets, the political pressures wielded by the many small-scale merchants serve to keep stall space rentals low. Rentals scarcely cover stall replacement, let alone the economic value of the land. Increases, when they can be achieved, scarcely match inflation. Beyond this, collection rates lag for a variety of reasons, with a significant number of merchants in arrears.

Where markets are owned by private parties, some of these drains on capital are obviously closed. However, it is not clear that the capital so generated is funnelled back into the system. The nature of the incentives for private owners to take such action may be limited by a number of factors. Inhibitions may also lie in the difficulty of obtaining space for new facilities, given the high value of land in all Asian cities.

Design

Without doubt, the efficiency of the public markets and bazaars built in recent years is substantially superior to older facilities. Space is greater and better organized and congestion is reduced through the straightening and widening of traffic lanes. Concrete floors and drainage systems offer time savings and the opportunity for easier removal of the refuse that accumulates.

Despite such gains, however, it is apparent that the design of most of the newer markets reflects more of the historic housekeeping approach to operating the bazaar than one of total channel efficiency. Scant attention, for example, is typically paid to designs that would stimulate the attractiveness of the facilities or enhance the flow of products from the central wholesale market. Most continue to be dark and dreary concrete buildings, dank and musty from the incessant flow of water and the daily buildup of rubbish generated during the day which has no place to go but on the floor. For central wholesale market produce to reach the stalls it must be off-loaded from trucks and portered some distance to the various points of sale.

Other dimensions of design which appear to be resolved from past practice and political pressure are the location of the bazaar, its size relative to the population and competing centres, the number of storeys, the mix of retail tenants, location within the building of such tenants, and the design of the fixtures. Rough rules of thumb exist, but the rationale behind such rules can seldom be described in any economic terms.

Enterprise efficiency

With the evolution of the bazaar, there tends to be growth and change in the character of the firms operating in the market. Firms get larger, develop more enclosed space, adopt the more extensive use of ice, install telephones, use adding machines, and add some refrigerated space. The confines of a given market, however, seldom provide a great deal of incentive for rapid innovation and change.

One major reason is the limitation on the size of the individual stall space. Market policy appears generally to limit the space, sometimes to an area of less than a square metre. This maximizes the available space for the typically overwhelming demand by squatters or hawkers outside the markets, but makes it impossible for the individual entrepreneur to undertake innovations that would be economical with greater scale. In an important sense, the general lack of sufficient space for all retail activities in the city inhibits the development of individual retailers.

Another reason is the absence of any significant level of cooperation among the merchants of the market. Each operator performs all the functions of running the business: the buying, the transporting, the trimming, the selling. Opportunities for cooperative activity would appear, at least superficially, to be substantial. These are occasionally realized in the sharing of a truck for bringing fresh produce into the market, yet even when these cooperative ventures exist they seem to have little impact upon the long hours of work necessary to operate the stalls.

A final reason for slowness in innovation is the lack of knowledge of the availability of new techniques. Many entrepreneurs are not well schooled in their business and lack access to new ideas. There may also be substantial resistance to change because of capital costs, uncertainties, and preferences for the old ways. Where the desire to change exists, credit for the capital required may be unavailable because money is poorly handled, accounting is not well understood, and bankers have alternative, less risky places to loan their funds.

Efforts to change

Despite the various barriers to increasing the rate of development of the bazaar system, there have been a few significant efforts to change. Where, for example, the control of these systems has been removed from the hands of a moribund city bureaucracy, which saw its work as one of caretaking, rather than marketing, attempts have been made to introduce new management.

In the Philippines, a private corporation has been awarded a long-term lease to manage, repair, and expand the number of public markets. The company has already introduced substantial new capital to modernize markets that had seen little improvement in many years. However, much opposition to the approach was being registered by independent merchants fearful of exploitation by the new firm[9].

In Singapore, the construction of new markets has become the responsibility of the Housing and Development Board. The ambitious programme of Singapore's Government to resettle the population in new and improved housing, requiring the construction of complete 'new towns', has included the formation of shopping facilities as well. Part of these has been devoted to the more traditional bazaar. These stand as competitively successful beside Western-type facilities.

Perhaps the most interesting development is in Jakarta, where a series of government corporations, divorced from the city–state bureaucracy, have been established to construct and operate wholesale and retail markets. Different corporations have been formed for various wholesale markets and one for the retail.

The formation of this corporation has resulted in the development of a planned approach to the construction of new markets. Objectives have been established to provide 0.15 ha of market space for each 5000 inhabitants. Five existing markets were totally rebuilt, but covered only 40 ha and it was estimated that an additional 110 ha were needed just to serve the existing population[1].

A final example worthy of mention is the construction of a new bazaar by private enterprise in Manila. Established in a huge, high-roofed building (which conceivably might have seen prior service as a factory), with many windows to allow fresh air and light, a bright, colourful, and well laid-out facility was developed. The aisles were broad and clean; the stalls large, painted in attractive colours, and well lighted; the produce stacked upon the tables in tempting display. More important, the market was jammed with shoppers while, virtually next door, a huge modern supermarket – the equal of any in the USA – was largely empty, its gleaming produce and meat counters patronized sparingly. Clearly, here was an example that the competitive impact of a bazaar remained potent and that the development of attractive facilities would do much to retain the patronage of even the most fastidious consumer.

Conclusions

In Asian countries, for the most part, the consumption of processed and packaged foods has been limited by the very low incomes of large elements of their populations. For food distribution, the bazaar or public market has retained a substantially higher share of the public's expenditures. The economic and strategic advantages of the supermarket for serving this public are limited. As a consequence, a superior use of public funds suggests that policies be directed toward improving the quality of food service by upgrading existing bazaars and public markets rather than by subsidizing the growth of institutions which primarily serve the relatively rich.

The research that has been conducted upon the feasibility of such policies is regretfully minimal. There have been no known cost–benefit analyses, no evaluation of the improvement of facility appearance upon patronage, no examination of the sociology of the market vendors to accept direction and change, and no examination of the incentives necessary for the introduction of private enterprise to the role of market builders or for stimulating their vigour to improve existing facilities.

Some insightful thinking was done in the Recife study about the opportunity for public market reform. The authors stated:

> The renovation of the appeal of public markets and fairs and the institutionalisation of the operators themselves . . . is very worthwhile from the standpoint of lowering the prices of food . . .[8]

But no quantitative estimates of costs and benefits were undertaken. In the summary of the Latin American Studies Center's work in less developed countries, however, no mention of the opportunities for improving food marketing system operation by this means was made, and it must be assumed that the ideas were discarded[4].

Since the high-technology solution of the vertically integrated chain store seems likely to be one of dubious value for the low-income population for much of the foreseeable future, alternative procedures must be sought. The revitalization of the existing public markets through modernization and the provision of entrepreneurial services to its retailers warrants a far closer look than it has been given. The entrepreneurial unit becomes the bazaar itself and management the focal point for innovation. Evidence exists that change is possible and that, when well managed, a vigorous and highly competitive institution can emerge.

References

1. BIROWO, A. T. et al. (1975) Food marketing systems in Manila. In *Food Marketing Systems in Asian Cities*, pp. 273–274. Bangkok, FAO
2. FAO (1975) *Development of Food Marketing Systems for Large Urban Areas*, p. 25. Rome, FAO
3. GALBRAITH, J. K. and HOLTON, R. H. (1955) *Marketing Efficiency in Puerto Rico*. Cambridge, Mass., Harvard University Press
4. HARRISON, K., HENLEY, D., RILEY, H. and SHAFFER, J. (1974) *Improving Food Marketing Systems in Developing Countries: Experiences from Latin America*, pp. 50–55. East Lansing, Michigan, Latin American Studies Center
5. LAK OH, S. (1975) Urban food marketing systems in Seoul. In *Food Marketing Systems in Asian Cities*, pp. 133–134. Bangkok, FAO
6. SLATER, C. (1970) Market channel coordination and economic development. In *Vertical Marketing Systems*, p. 139. Ed. by L. P. Bucklin. Glenview, Illinois, Scott, Foresman and Company
7. SLATER, S., HENLEY, D., WISH, J. et al. (1969) *Market Processes in La Paz, Bolivia*, p. 211. East Lansing, Michigan, Latin American Studies Center
8. SLATER, C., RILEY, H. et al. (1969) *Market Processes in the Recife Area of Northeast Brazil*, pp. 3–6. East Lansing, Michigan, Latin American Studies Center
9. TIONGSON, F. A. (1975) Food marketing systems in Manila. In *Food Marketing Systems in Asian Cities*, pp. 162–163. Bangkok, FAO

Part IV

Basic economic and social development affecting food marketing in world markets

In recent years, governments in less developed countries have become more involved in the marketing of basic foods within their countries, but the policies adopted and the structures and approaches used have reflected many weaknesses and omissions The support given by academic institutions and international advisory and funding organizations to policy markers has often been too narrow, or only partially appropriate. In the first chapter, the author reviews recent work on marketing and suggests some major priorities for attention in the immediate future, and some new directions that could and should be explored.

Food marketing environment in Morocco is explored in the second chapter. Although part of north Africa, Morocco is not a barren desert but has a thriving agroindustry and an important export trade in citrus fruits, vegetables, canned juices and condiments. Government involvement in food marketing exists alongside private enterprise. Both sectors advertise to promote products and induce changes in consumer buying and nutritional habits. Examples of advertising campaigns, product launches and government regulations are discussed in this chapter, according to a general framework applicable to other less developed countries.

Chapter 7

New directions in food marketing policies in less developed countries

Vincent Tickner

Introduction

During the last thirty years, the systems for the marketing of basic foods consumed by the majority of the population in the less developed countries (LDCs) of Africa, Asia, Latin America, the Caribbean and Oceania have changed considerably. Many of these countries have experienced a rapid growth in their urban populations, expansion and changes in the structure of agricultural production, and changes in the modes of processing and transport of agricultural products. This has often necessitated considerable modification of the food distribution system, particularly where those systems had previously been predominantly oriented towards subsistence or local markets. Faced with a need to guarantee at least a minimum of food to a larger, comparatively low-income urban population, governments have gradually taken a stronger interest in food marketing.

Formerly, under colonial control, government involvement in agricultural marketing was largely focused on export crops. Because of the economic pressures of the world trading system and the limited options open to them for acquiring foreign exchange, many governments, even after gaining political independence, have continued to give disproportionate attention to such crops. During the last fifteen years, however, a number of governments have realized that the development of sufficient production of basic foods and their distribution for local consumption is of major importance in generating genuine economic development. Their policies have gradually begun to focus on efforts towards greater food self-sufficiency and the integration of basic food production into the market economy.

Weaknesses in government orientation

The evolution of government involvement in this sector has varied from one country to another, but certain themes, approaches and weaknesses have occurred in many of them. These weaknesses have been both structural and attitudinal. The structural weaknesses reflect the influences of the organizations that have been

This chapter is a revised version of an article in *Food Policy*, 1978, Vol. 3, No. 4, pp. 299–307.

created in the past, and the attitudes and orientations implicit within them. Such structural weaknesses are often not peculiar to the departments involved with marketing, but apply to other sectors as well. In addition, there are attitudes towards the marketing sector that reflect the kinds of contact experienced by policy makers and officials with the trading system, and reflect the influence of external groups and attitudes on the policy making structures.

First, government involvement in the sector has often been initiated for other objectives, which have not been particularly related to the efficiency of the distribution system itself, such as the securing of an urban food supply, reducing imports, stimulating production, raising tax revenue, or sustaining low consumer prices. Such objectives may originate from a variety of sources or from the short-term objectives of different political groups. These groups can sometimes provide an important stimulus but at other times can cause disruption to more long-term policies. Often, such policies need to be regularly reviewed and integrated to ensure effective policy making.

Increasing the internal food supply is still for many countries an important objective, not only to reduce food imports to help balance of payments problems, but also to generate a more effective use of the country's own resources. In addition, efforts to stabilize the prices and flow of food supplies have often played an important role in securing adequate food distribution to all sections of a community.

Policies have often favoured urban consumers more than the rural community, because of the often stronger political influence in urban areas. Marketing policy, in particular, often gains its initial major impetus from the needs of the urban population (for a review of 'urban bias' see Lipton[10]).

Attitudes

One characteristic of many LDC government policies has been the tendency to treat all private intermediaries as 'baddies'. Diatribes against the exploitative practices of 'middlemen' have been a regular part of political statements in many countries in recent years, despite efforts to make people more critical of who the middlemen are, and what they do (the article by Spinks[14] develops this point). Rarely is a precise indication given as to which middleman, performing which functions for which commodities, is the 'baddy'. When the Ivory Coast government called for a study of the food marketing system in Abidjan in the late 1960s, their attitude (treated as axiomatic) was that the Dioula, the main trading community, were making excessive profits from basic food trading. The study undertaken, however, showed that although some of the Dioula may have been making excess profits from some products, where basic foods were concerned competition with other traders limited their profit margins to a reasonable level (see Chateau et al.[4]). Such attitudes have often stemmed from an ignorance of the functions performed by the intermediaries, of fluctuations in supply, and of particular trading difficulties.

Such attitudes can develop because many of the people involved in policy making and its implementation in government departments have had little or no regular contact with different intermediaries, or knowledge of the functions they are performing. There is often little mobility from trading families into administrative or academic jobs, and people in such jobs have rarely had much social contact with trading communities, particularly where the latter are, as in many cases, ethnically based.

On the other hand, not all intermediaries are without fault; some are definitely exploitative, and most place personal or family gain above other considerations. Nevertheless, indiscriminate efforts to control such exploitative practices lead only to poor policies which impede the working of the system without providing a viable alternative. Greater differentiation of intermediaries is necessary.

This attitude has often led many governments to a 'control' orientation, where an alternative of stimulation of the private sector might have resulted in a better use of private sector resources. Many policies have been directed to controlling market prices or to controlling the activities of traders by licensing, quota allocations or restricted movement. Quite often the sharpest traders manage to invalidate such efforts through evasion, or bribery of poorly paid government officials. In Bangladesh in 1974 some private traders overcame restrictions on the storage of foodgrains through a sophisticated communication network linked to the storage of grain in boats, which were scheduled to arrive in consuming areas at a time when prices were most advantageous.

Another attitudinal weakness has been a rather uncritical adoption of marketing systems from other societies. Ideas have been introduced of the 'rationalization', 'regulation' or 'standardization' of the marketing system which reflect theoretical frameworks of marketing efficiency or development not necessarily appropriate to the country concerned, or which do not take into consideration the wider social influences of such policies. Some policies have reflected an ignorance of the dynamics of changing marketing systems, and of the needs and perspectives of different economies of scale. An awareness of the likely future needs of a food marketing system can enable a government to intervene more effectively by introducing structures which will gain in importance and influence as the marketing system changes. This is often applicable to storage or processing needs, for example.

Many of the policies affecting food marketing have been introduced without full consideration of their economic and social consequences, such as impact on employment. Knowledge of employment structures, occupational mobility and the possibilities of employment generation within the food marketing system are negligible in most countries. Similarly the impact of different policies upon migration or income distribution is almost never considered; the coordination of marketing policies with regional planning and developments in agroindustries, food processing and transport systems has also often been poor. Feeder road construction has helped the marketing system in some cases, but in others an improved telephone system, or improved provision of appropriate rural vehicles, would have helped more.

The full impact of alternative marketing policies on food production is rarely analysed. Where the producers are market conscious (and they often are, more than government officials give them credit for), poor market policies or the lack of them can have a considerable impact on the producers' activities. Improving production without simultaneously improving the distribution system for the incremental production can lead to wasted produce, discouraged producers and a decline in subsequent production. Such a case occurred in parts of the Limpopo valley in Mozambique in 1977: some producers had been encouraged to increase production and were supplied with the necessary inputs, but upon harvesting the produce, found it could not be marketed for lack of transport facilities and an adequate marketing structure. Accordingly, their incentive to produce more was much reduced. The International Fund for Agricultural Development (IFAD) recognized fully this fact when, in their annual report for 1979, they stated:

> If improvements in productivity are not accompanied by appropriate policies and better access to markets, agricultural prices tend to fall and destroy all incentives for higher production.

Structures

In addition to weaknesses brought about by governmental attitudes, the *structure* of government departments initiating and implementing policy has frequently been a significant handicap on development of integrated and effective marketing policies. There is often a range of government departments, from finance or planning to commerce, transport and agriculture ministries at the national level, as well as different local authority administrations, all of which initiate and implement policies affecting marketing. The peripheral importance often attributed to food marketing policies has meant that responsibility has been delegated to small subdepartments of these bodies, which have only marginal influence and limited resources, and limited opportunity for interdepartmental contact and coordination. Only in a few countries have food supply ministries or coordinating commissions been set up to coordinate varied departmental approaches and objectives, and provide an overview of developments in the sector.

One particular area of difficulty is the use of the food marketing system as a source of government revenue. The full economic and social costs of introducing a taxation element into policy making are rarely fully appreciated by the initiators. Some forms of taxation lead either to tax evasion or avoidance by private intermediaries, or to unproductive antagonism between such intermediaries and the government which inhibits possibilities for further cooperation. Part of the problem is that in many rapidly growing urban areas local government is confronted with numerous social and economic problems, and limited budgets; the marketing system, through such mechanisms as market fees and trader licences, becomes an important source of immediate revenue. The full cost of the long-term deterioration in local government–trader relations caused by introducing such taxation elements is often forgotten by decision makers in their preoccupation with short-term revenue gains.

Decision makers may also be handicapped by a dearth of relevant, reasonably objective analyses of the trading system, and by poor links with academic or research departments that might supply such analyses. Officials usually have little opportunity to spend time exploring the workings of the trading systems themselves, or establishing closer contact with intermediaries or their organizations.

Policy implementation

The methods used by governments intervening in the market system in the recent past have varied between efforts to control, direct, improve or provide facilities for private trade, and direct participation in the distribution system by nationalization or the creation of statal or parastatal organizations to perform specific trading functions.

Indirect involvement

In countries where the government has adopted a *laissez-faire* attitude towards the private sector, intervention has been predominantly through indirect controls on the market. A major tool in this form of control has been price policy. Governments have tried to control prices by direct legislation, by releasing of government food stocks at strategic times, or by restricting the possibilities of private trade to create or exploit irregularities of supply. Often the primary preoccupation of agricultural marketing departments has been the monitoring of price changes in order to intervene in an attempt to stabilize prices. Direct legislation to control prices or speculative practices has often been difficult to enforce, and can lead to bribery of officials and evasions of the system (such as through black markets), or can result in such disincentives that supplies are reduced. Releasing government stocks can influence the market, but stock policies often lead governments into uneconomic policies that cannot be sustained without considerable financial loss. This is particularly so where the costs of storage and administration are excessive, or where decisions on stock releases are subject to arbitrary external influences. A major preoccupation for some governments in the last few years has been the desire to create 'buffer stocks', partially to regulate the market. Unfortunately some of the methods used to build-up stocks have often disrupted the trading system and production patterns, without achieving the desired stabilization.

The innovations of recent years have usually been of a concrete, tangible nature, such as the construction of feeder roads, marketplaces, rural trading centres, storage facilities, chain stores, supermarkets or slaughterhouses. Unfortunately, the reasons for selecting projects have often reflected the influence of interested parties, and integration of the new projects into the existing system is usually only loosely planned. Concrete projects are desirable to governments as they provide visible proof of action, and superficial cost–benefit analyses are easier to carry out. These same considerations seem to have influenced financing institutions to give more support to such projects. In addition, construction and engineering firms are often eager to point out a 'need' for a project where they might obtain a sizeable contract. In some cases, such innovations have helped the marketing system; but, in others, where the full impact on the transport and marketing systems or on other sectors has not been fully assessed, they have been poorly integrated into the marketing system or have even reduced its effectiveness. For example, a new wholesale market for food products was planned for Abidjan in the early 1970s, but the feasibility study for the project ('Les halles d'Abidjan', AGRIPAC, Abidjan, 1972) only marginally touched upon the impact of the scheme on the intra-urban transport system and retailer supply from the wholesale market, and only very belatedly did the authorities enter into a dialogue with the people who were expected to use the market. AGRIPAC, the government parastatal organization involved, has subsequently been trying to integrate the wholesalers (who have continued to bear the brunt of supplying fast-growing Abidjan) into the project; but in 1975 Mr Assi, of AGRIPAC, was still referring to them disparagingly[2]:

   . . . The wholesalers, the majority of whom are aged illiterates of little stability, handicapped by too small a capital accumulation, [who] cannot . . . assume the risks of development and reorganization of their commercial activity. (Author's translation.)

With such patronizing attitudes it remains to be seen how the situation will work out.

Mittendorf's guide[12] attempts to draw attention to some of the major considerations necessary for planning wholesale markets in less developed countries, and to some of the pitfalls encountered in the past. Nevertheless, although this chapter recognizes the need to integrate such wholesale markets into the overall marketing system and to consult potential users both before and during implementation, it reflects a unilinear approach to the development of marketing systems that assumes an inevitable place for wholesale markets in many developing economies, while acknowledging the decreased importance of such markets in the most highly industrialized countries. Our continued use of the term 'marketing', as opposed to 'trading' or 'distribution', reflects the emphasis given to markets in our thinking.

Another reason for support of this type of concrete project is an overemphasis on making the places of exchange static. This may partly be a reflection of the static lives of sedentary government officials, but it also reflects an attitude that if things are settled in a specific location they are more observable and manageable than if they are mobile. The lifestyle of the trader who moves from place to place, linking supplies and demands, does not fit with a bureaucratic approach. As a result many governmental efforts try to fit the dynamic marketing system into a too-static mould, with resultant tensions. This goes far to explain the antipathy of some policy makers towards small-scale traders and hawkers, whose tangible assets are small, whose mobility is considerable, and whose political power is slight, although some of the functions they perform provide a valuable service. With the 'informal sector' coming more into vogue in recent years, such intermediaries have been considered more positively, but there have still been comparatively few concrete projects to develop their potential.

Some other areas of tangible support, however, which could be of considerable assistance to the marketing system, have been neglected. Some examples are aid in the purchase and maintenance of vehicles or boats, aid for establishing or renovating private storage facilities for producers or traders, or the improvement and extension of telephone and radio systems to help the speed of communication, so important for some types of marketing. (The publication of the ITU's *Appropriate Modern Telecommunications Technology for Integrated Rural Development in Africa* (AMTT/IRD), November 1981, has drawn telecommunication needs in the context of rural development more into focus, but still few projects are specifically oriented to the needs of the marketing system.)

Intangible assistance, such as the dissemination of market information to producers and traders, training in more complex marketing skills, the organization of trading cooperatives, or provision of credit to disadvantaged smaller traders, have also been neglected. Programmes for disseminating market information to producers have often been ineffective because the back-up services have been poor, or the data have been imprecise or outdated. Some imaginative uses of the radio, with adequate back-up, could achieve successes in this field. Training schemes for improving marketing or accounting skills have often reflected styles of trading prevalent in other cultures which may not be particularly appropriate for the country concerned, or which are designed to channel marketing procedures along lines which are more amenable to taxation. It is hardly surprising that such 'skills' have not always been warmly received by shrewd traders. Few efforts have been made to upgrade the level of marketing by private traders. In the early 1980s the FAO has been making more efforts to strengthen agricultural marketing training, not only for government and parastatal officials, but also for private intermediaries. This could be achieved by stimulating existing organizations that represent traders, or by encouraging the formation of new ones. The role of traders' organizations could be broadened not only to facilitate possibilities for training traders in new techniques, but also to offer a mechanism for continuing dialogue between private traders and the government.

The availability of government credit for traders and other intermediaries has often been restricted for some of the reasons given above. Instead, credit has been made available to producers and producer cooperatives to enable them to increase production. Such credit, particularly if it is short term, often does not enable producers to hold stocks and intervene effectively in the marketing system to combat exploitative practices. The problems of small producers needing to sell their products cheaply at harvest time, and to buy back the same products later in the year, are still acute in certain areas, such as among small farmers in Bangladesh. There has also been little effort to look for particularly disadvantaged groups within the trading community that could benefit from credit facilities (aiding them could increase the potential for competition).

The conflict in Guinea in 1977 between women traders and government officials showed what adverse results can be caused by confrontational, repressive, ill-informed and poorly thought out government intervention. (For some time the women traders in Conakry and other towns had been harassed by economic police and price inspectors, who had often forced prices down below economically viable levels. This had resulted in traders' smuggling and selling goods from back rooms, which had led to further clamping down by the economic police. The police were so successful that traders ceased operating, and goods became scarce on the markets. In August 1977, however, the women organized, marched on the Presidential palace and lodged complaints, and then marched on the economic police's headquarters and started destroying records and secret files that had been kept on a number of traders; *see* Hennessy[6].)

Direct involvement

The desire to offer a viable alternative to a free market system has been the reason why a number of governments have tried to participate directly in the marketing system. This has usually been done through statal or parastatal organizations. Many of the first examples of these were formed to market export crops. Some expanded to include food products for the local market, as in Malawi or Togo, and some new ones were established for locally consumed products (such as rice, maize, fruits or vegetables), but were modelled on the export-oriented organizations that had different needs and objectives. In many cases such organizations have become overstaffed, bureaucratic, inefficient organizations with high overheads that have not fulfilled expectations. Their establishment has often been marred by underestimation of what is needed for their efficient and economic operation and of the skills and staff required, and by poorly thought out timing and programming of their involvement in the sector.

The structure of government employment and promotion practices, and the experience, attitudes and aspirations of government employees have rarely been conducive to efficiency or to positive competition with private traders. Some of these weaknesses can be, and have been, overcome by vigorous and able management, but often the tendency has been to set up yet one more inefficient, ill-prepared organization, when other types of intervention might have achieved more. Sometimes such organizations end up being involved in a costly competition with the private sector, because they are unable to perform the necessary marketing functions as efficiently as (even if less exploitatively than) private traders. In some circumstances, however, parastatal involvement has proved very necessary when the private sector has been unable to adapt to changed circumstances. The establishment of the Dairy Marketing Board in what was then Southern Rhodesia was a direct consequence of the collapse of private traders to market effectively.

Academic influence

The orientation and approach of academic research has often done little to supplement the meagre and only partially relevant information at the disposal of government policy makers noted above. Some of the most comprehensive research has been undertaken by American research teams from the Food Research Institute in California, and Michigan State University. Those at the latter have been involved in a number of studies of food marketing systems in Latin American countries during the 1960s and early 1970s. They have provided some of the most comprehensive work available, and have looked at some of the wider issues. However, their orientation is very much towards ways in which government can *assist* private trade to develop, rather than towards ways in which government can *influence* private trade to develop in accordance with the government's own wider objectives, or towards developing alternative governmental organizations. Similarly, employment, income distribution and wider social implications have often been given very superficial treatment. For a brief outline of the major experiences culled from their work (*see* Harrison *et al.*[5]).

Until recently, most of the economic studies in the marketing sector have focused upon prices, profit margins, distribution costs or marketing channels, and often reflect a bias in favour of private trading systems. An overemphasis upon prices and profit margins that does not fully take into consideration the functions performed or the risks involved, has led to unworkable pricing policies. Also, much of the work on marketing channels has been comparatively superficial, establishing the major types of intermediaries, but not always analysing clearly the functions performed by each type for different products, and with what degree of efficiency, nor establishing the quantities of produce passing through alternative channels. At the same time such considerations as the nature and mode of operation of the trading organizations, occupational mobility, income distribution, employment, and relations with other sectors of the economy have been largely neglected. Despite the present trend in the International Labour Organization (ILO) and some other institutions to focus on employment in the 'informal sector', there have been hardly any attempts to focus on the employment aspects of food traders, processors and transporters within the 'informal sector'.

Apart from economic research, other academic disciplines have been slow to enter the field, although their contribution could be considerable. Part of the problem appears to be the demands of academia. Many academics tend to veer towards subject areas that are much more static and more manageable than trying to analyse or even collect data on the 'mobile' marketing system. It is easier to confine oneself to interviewing in a village or an urban market, than trying to interview itinerant traders, transporters or other intermediaries.

Anthropology has been one academic discipline that in its early development was more prepared to look at dynamic aspects of a system, but which moved in the 1930s to analysis of more static aspects. Only in recent years have anthropologists tended to move back into the more difficult area of change and dynamic structures. Some anthropologists, such as Polly Hill[7], have made positive contributions in attempting to link disciplines, to develop anthropology in a more practical way. Nevertheless, anthropologists' skills could be used much more actively in analysing such questions as the ways in which largely subsistence producers respond to marketing systems, and how they move into market economies, or the ways in which intermediaries build up and sustain their trading contacts. Similarly, sociologists and social psychologists until recently have made little advances into the activities of intermediaries. Rural sociologists appear to be growing in numbers, but very few have turned their attention to the organization, social structure and mobility of the different types of intermediaries. Almost no social psychologists have devoted attention to these areas, or to the attitudes and motivations of intermediaries.

Geographers have tended to be more adventurous in moving into the area, and have made some very positive contributions. However, in some cases they have focused on certain aspects that are methodologically of more interest to geographers than to planners, such as the 'central place theories' of market development. For a bibliography of the work done in this area, see Bromley, Hodder and Smith[3]. Where geographers could play a greater part is in clearly establishing the spatial and locational factors influencing marketing development, and their implications for future policy.

Another area in need of study is that of the politics of food marketing and of government marketing organizations. Some work has been done on the latter (for example, see Abbot and Creupelandt[1]), but analysis of political influences on government policy towards the food marketing sector has been poorly covered by political scientists. Economists, such as Uma Lele[9], have tended to work up to a point where they virtually say that economic objectives cannot be achieved until political differences have been resolved. Political scientists, however, have not proceeded to analyse the often numerous and conflicting political pressures on food marketing policy.

International organizations

International bodies such as the Food and Agriculture Organization (FAO), International Bank for Reconstruction and Development Programme (UNDP) have been involved for some time with marketing research and improving marketing systems, but the marketing sections of their organizations are often small, overworked, and have limited budgets. In the FAO, the allocation of funds for marketing work out of its Regular Programme Budget is less than 1%; for the UNDP it is less than 2%[8]. The 1984/85 budget for the FAO still only budgetted 1.9% of its Technical and Economic Programmes towards marketing support, although the recent trends towards alleviating postharvest food losses have led to some additional financing under this heading. Despite limited resources the FAO Marketing and Credit Service has tried to tackle a wide range of activities from food security to training and support to national centres and organizations. Currently the emphasis of the FAO has been on women and marketing, private trader efficiency, the effect of energy costs, pricing policies, handling losses and training. The importance of these international organizations lies in their ability to coordinate different research programmes around the world, to act as fora for the dissemination of techniques and ideas for marketing improvements, and to provide technical assistance. More recently they have shown signs of moving beyond more technocratic approaches to include wider perspectives. A number of commodity-specific international institutes that have been established during the last fifteen years, such as International Rice Research Institute (IRRI) or the International Maize and Wheat Improvement Centre (CIMMYT) have gradually become more involved with postharvest problems of processing and marketing, but their contributions could still be greater, particularly with commodity-specific marketing problems.

The role of the large financing institutions in marketing improvements has, until recently, been very slight and limited in outlook. The Inter-American Development Bank (IDB), over the two years ending in June 1976, provided funding of only US$9.6 million for agroindustry and marketing, less than 1% of its total funding for agricultural and rural development projects[8]. Most of this funding was either for agribusiness investment, or else for physical facilities, food processing, grain storage and marketplaces, rather than for improving the marketing system as such.

The World Bank (IBRD) has made little investment in marketing projects in recent years, and the emphasis has been more on tangible projects, as mentioned above, rather than on more intangible assistance to marketing systems or training programmes. This partly reflects the financial bias in the assessment and selection of projects, and the peripheral treatment of marketing issues in the past. Although there are Sector Policy Statements by the World Bank on rural development, agricultural credit and land reform, there are none on marketing improvements.

The creation of the International Fund for Agricultural Development (IFAD) in 1977 augured well for more support to agricultural development. As was seen from the 1979 Annual Report, IFAD has shown a more active concern with marketing aspects, and the 1981 Annual Report claimed that more than a third of the IFAD projects then envisaged explicitly involved an improvement of the storage facilities or of the marketing of the envisaged incremental production from the project. It is difficult from published reports to estimate the proportion of resources actually going to marketing-linked aspects in these integrated projects, and a substantial part of the investment seems to have been directed towards feeder road construction. Only one project, in Lesotho, was specifically directed to agricultural marketing and credit, and IFAD so far appears to have contributed little to innovations in the sphere of agricultural marketing approaches.

Another new organization created in 1975 was the International Food Policy Research Institute (IFPRI) in Washington DC. IFPRI has conducted a number of valuable technical studies in the following years, but its emphases have been on production and consumption projections, the impact of food subsidies, food distribution systems, international stockholding and food security, investment in agricultural research, and international foodgrain markets, particularly focusing on Chinese and Soviet foodgrain imports. Some work on pricing policies has been undertaken, but little direct focus has been given to agricultural marketing problems.

Bilateral assistance programmes have rarely been any better. In 1976, it was declared that only 8 out of 8000 people employed or supported by the UK Overseas Development Ministry were marketing experts[13]. Sometimes it is maintained that the lack of funding is because of the lack of demand for assistance in this area. This is partly a 'chicken and egg' problem; governments that are not particularly aware of their marketing systems are not inclined to look for assistance to solve them, and as the financing institutions do not have clearly established units for dealing with requests on marketing issues or for researching marketing needs, little is achieved.

The importance of financial specifications in the organizing of funding for specific projects, and the desire for the projects to be comparatively easy to monitor, have had a marked influence on the development of marketing projects, and have contributed to keeping the scope they cover within fairly narrow limits, that have left other crucial areas neglected.

Few international consultancy firms specialize in food marketing in the LDCs. For those that do, their expertise in internationally traded commodities is usually greater than their experience in internal food marketing. They are often called in as adjuncts to engineering, storage and transport projects that may be linked to food marketing and processing. Involvement in the improvement of the food marketing system or its integration with transport systems is usually treated as secondary rather than as an integral part of such projects, resulting in partial analyses of the marketing system that can be harmful.

What is to be done?

This chapter reveals the complexity involved in improving food marketing systems, and the comparatively minor steps that have up to now been made in this direction. Slowly, governments, academia and international organizations are becoming more aware of this complexity and of the needs for greater energy and resources in some of the areas outlined above. The FAO's *Agriculture Toward 2000* only envisaged an increase in investment for storage and marketing from US$3 billion in 1980 to US$4 billion in 1990, compared with a 50% increase for agriculture overall from US$16 billion to US$24 billion, yet the same study envisaged that up to 2000 marketed production would need to be tripled, rising from 35% of total production in 1980 to 54% by 2000. This implies a need for massive infrastructural investments in marketing as well as the need to improve substantially marketing systems.

The most important points to be recognized by governments in the less industrialized countries are: (*a*) that food marketing is an important area for concern, and that governments need to intervene more in the food marketing systems, but (*b*) that they also need to be more fully aware of their capabilities, the existing workings of the system in which they wish to intervene, and of the wider social and economic implications of different types of intervention. There is also considerable scope for innovation and lateral thinking, based on a detailed understanding of the system.

There is a need to improve national research into the marketing system within each country, and for more international research to explore the similarities and differences between systems, and to develop new lines of research, particularly in disciplines other than agricultural economics. International advisory bodies need to devote more attention to the sector, and to alternative approaches that take the wider aspects of marketing policy into consideration, and that stimulate technical and training support.

Most important is that the work of advisory organizations, and funding and academic institutions should become more linked to the policies being undertaken by individual governments. As Hans Mittendorf of the FAO has said[11]:

The rate of implementation of many recommendations made during the last twenty years on marketing improvement in developing countries underlines the need to improve the orientation of applied marketing research, and to aim at realistic targets.

Unless this is done, much time- and resource-consuming research may be wasted and/or only partially applicable, and many problems will still remain.

References

1. ABBOT, J. C. and CREUPELANDT, H. C. (1966) *Agricultural Marketing Boards: Their Establishment and Operation.* Rome, FAO
2. ASSI, M. (1975) La reforme de la distribution des produits en Cote d'Ivoire. Paper presented to the FAO Conference on Food Marketing Systems for Large Urban Areas in French-speaking African Countries, Dakar, Senegal, December 1975
3. BROMLEY, R. J., HODDER, B. W. and SMITH, R. H. T. (1974) *Market-place Studies.* University of London, School of Oriental and African Studies
4. CHATEAU, J. P., PREFOL, B., SERVANT, M. A., *et al.* (1972) *La Commercialisation de Produits Vivriers – Étude Économique,* 3 volumes. SEDES/Ministère du Plan, République de la Côte d'Ivoire, December, 1972
5. HARRISON, K., HENLEY, D., RILEY, H. and SHAFFER, J. (1974) *Improving Food Marketing Systems in Developing Countries: Experiences from Latin America,* Research Report No. 6. Michigan State University, Latin American Studies Research Center
6. HENNESSY, C. (1977) Market women revolt in Guinea. *New African,* November 1977, p. 1131
7. HILL, P. (1970) *Studies in Rural Capitalism in West Africa.* Cambridge, Cambridge University Press
8. KRIESBERG, M. (1976) Aid by international organisations to improve food marketing in developing countries. Paper presented at OECD/FAO Joint Seminar, Paris, October 1976
9. LELE, U. (971) *Food Grain Marketing in India.* Ithaca, NY, Cornell University Press
10. LIPTON, M. (1977) *Why Poor People stay Poor – A Study of Urban Bias in World Development.* London, Maurice Temple Smith
11. MITTENDORF, H. (1974) Facilitating services for agricultural and food marketing in developing countries. Paper presented at the International Conference on Marketing Systems in Developing Countries, Tel Aviv, Israel, January 1974
12. MITTENDORF, H. (1976) *Planning of Urban Wholesale Markets for Perishable Food.* Rome, FAO
13. OECD (1977) *Critical Issues on Food Marketing Systems in Developing Countries,* p. 60. Paris, OECD
14. SPINKS, G. R. (1972) *Myths about Agricultural Marketing.* Teaching Forum No. 15, Agricultural Development Council, New York, March 1972

Chapter 8

Food marketing environment in the less developed country of Morocco

Lyn S. Amine and S. Tamer Cavusgil

Introduction

Food marketing is an extremely important activity in less developed countries. However, little documentation exists with regard to this activity in north Africa. Notable contributions on food marketing in the Middle East have been made by Kaynak[10,11], Kaynak and Cavusgil[13], Goldman[7,8], and Yavas, Kaynak and Borak[16,17] with special attention to Turkey and Israel. More recently, Tuncalp and Yavas[15] offered new insights into supermarket acceptance in Saudi Arabia. The contributions which relate specifically to Morocco include Cavusgil, Amine and Vitale[6], Amine, Vitale and Cavusgil[3], and Amine and Cavusgil[1].

The objective of this chapter is to contribute to the growing literature on north Africa and the Middle East, with special emphasis on food marketing. An ideographic or case study approach is used. In order to facilitate future nomothetic analysis across several countries, a general framework will be adopted (developed by Kaynak[12]). This approach avoids the pitfalls of simple descriptive research by structuring the data in such a way that future comparative analyses and generalizations will be more feasible. The following themes are discussed:

- A general profile of the food industry, identifying the different types of companies and institutions operating in the market.
- An analysis of functional relationships between these different groups.
- Competition and cooperation.
- Marketing performance.
- Environmental impact.

A profile of the food marketing environment

Situated at the western end of the Mediterranean, Morocco is geographically and politically part of the north Africa group called 'Maghreb', along with Algeria and Tunisia. While Algeria's reputation in world trade is for petroleum exporting and Tunisia is famed for its tourist resorts, Morocco is the principal world exporter of phosphates.

This fact is of great relevance to agroindustry there, since Morocco is not a barren desert, but a well-irrigated and fertile producer of many foodstuffs for both internal consumption and export. It has a naturally rich subsoil and temperate climate, both critical factors for successful agriculture. It also has a ready supply of manual labour among a population estimated at 20 million, with 55% under the age of 20 years and 70% living in rural areas. The growing population also represents an attractive home market for food producers. Moreover, as a European Economic Community Associate, Morocco enjoys an important export trade opportunity through its physical proximity to the European Community and its historical links with France.

Knowledge of these characteristics is important in understanding the type and number of food industry companies and institutions, and the balance of power which exists between them. For example, state-owned monopolies are responsible for directing the production and export marketing of large revenue-earning products such as citrus fruits, vegetables, canned juices and condiments (OCE) and fish products (CODIMER-ASMAK)[14].

State participation is also found through 'offices' – monopolies which regulate and coordinate the import of sensitive foodstuffs, such as sugar and green China tea, both used in the preparation of the national daily beverage, mint tea (ONTS). Another state monopoly exists in the cigarette industry (Régie des Tabacs). Although not a food stuff, tobacco is grown locally and so constitutes part of the country's agroindustry.

Rivalling these state-owned institutions in market presence are several very large private food marketing companies originally set up by French entrepreneurs and still carrying a French (rather than Moroccan Arabic) name. Following the end of the French Protectorate in 1956, a policy of 'Moroccanization' was enforced, designed to transfer ownership and control of business to Moroccan hands and actively promote the employment of local nationals.

Smaller in size and less influential in the marketplace, but equally as successful in their respective market niches, are a plethora of local firms. These firms are usually the result of either wholly Moroccan entrepreneurship or Moroccanized joint ventures between local nationals and foreign parent companies and/or private investors. The differences in relative age and administrative traditions between these two categories of companies have important effects on competitive performance, as will be demonstrated later.

All these companies are located in Casablanca, the commercial capital of Morocco. Food marketing, as with all marketing activities, converges on this port as produce is brought in from the countryside, processed and then exported or redistributed. Outside this centre one finds only a handful of food marketing units, usually cooperatives run by local producers.

This review of food marketing institutions demonstrates clearly that members of the industry differ widely along several dimensions: size, age, administrative tradition, reputation, market share, consumer loyalty, and innovativeness. The following section discusses functional relationships between the state, producers, marketers and consumers.

Functional relationships

Typical of many less developed countries[8,17], consumers in Morocco shop for food on a daily basis, spreading their purchases over several retail outlets and several shopping trips per day. For example, bread (if not baked at home) is bought fresh each meal-time from the neighbourhood grocery store. These tiny 'mom and pop' stores ('épiceries') usually offer credit to their loyal customers who buy basic dry goods, bread, butter, milk, yogurt, and household products there. Lack of refrigeration facilities results in small inventories, rapid turnover, and usually two deliveries of fresh foods per day. Meat and fish are normally bought at specialized markets with individual booths for retailers, licensed and inspected by government officials who control prices, cleanliness and quality of the food. Fresh produce (fruit and vegetables) is sold in open markets where consumers use their shopping skills to inspect items and then bargain for the price. Other specialized items associated with foreign tastes (such as pastries, delicatessen, and candies) are sold in retail stores typical of Western markets.

Consumer shopping behaviour in Morocco is not at all different from that of other countries in north Africa and the Middle East[2]. Common behaviour patterns concerning haggling, daily shopping, and strong brand/store loyalty in this region are due, partly, to the general stage of development of marketing and distribution systems. Typically, demand far exceeds supply. Local producers very often escape the constraints of quality control, customer service, and even advertising, content in their knowledge that the consumer may have no other choice. This is especially the case in Morocco, as well as Tunisia, Egypt, Iran, and Turkey where naissant, local industries have traditionally been protected from foreign competition through import controls. In such cases, concern for 'marketing' as opposed to plain selling, and social issues such as pollution control, recycling of waste materials, employees' health and protection, and consumerism are totally irrelevant to everyday business life. The booming housing industry in Morocco means that Lafarge Cement Industries continue to allow great volumes of smoke to emit constantly from their plant chimneys on the perimeter of Casablanca. They claim that the city's incremental sprawl has created a problem where formerly none existed, at a time when the urban population was more distant.

In Morocco, an ethnic subgroup, the Berbers from the area around the Atlas Mountains (Soussi), controls the retail food sector. These people are efficient tradespeople but their social status is much lower than for the people of Fez who dominate the wholesale textile sector. The Berbers use their own language as a barrier against would-be newcomers to the sector. A global company such as Nestlé which manufactures and markets a full line of foodstuffs in Morocco is only able to do so by accepting the prevailing business customs and employing Berber salesmen who find natural acceptance at the retail level.

This profile of consumer food shopping behaviour demonstrates some important aspects of functional relationships between producers, distributors and consumers in Morocco. Two consumer priorities are freshness and variety. These priorities result in major problems for the members of the fruit and vegetable sector, namely logistical problems and waste. With a population of about 3 million people, Casablanca acts as a natural magnet for food producers. Wholesale produce dealers are particularly concerned since early morning shipments from outlying rural areas have to be sorted, graded and displayed in time for the morning shopper. Storage and refrigeration facilities are not available, so any supplies not sold to the evening shopper are thrown away or given to the poor at the end of the day. Because of the obvious risk of deterioration in the heat, consumers strongly reject any attempt to sell them the previous day's supplies.

Inherent in this method of market supply is, of course, the risk of waste. It is not unusual to see in open markets, city streets and country roads, heaps of tomatoes or oranges abandoned and rotting. Market inefficiencies at the level of production and distribution hurt both the producer and the consumer and, in the long-term, the country itself due to lost exports. The OCE (the government monopoly which buys produce for export in both fresh and canned form) also contributes indirectly to market inefficiency by taking first priority in choice and volume of produce allocated to exports (90% of production). Thus local canning plants experience uneven levels of production due to shortages in supplies of raw materials. Also consumer markets often receive only the 'rejects' – misshapen, bruised or mismatched produce, albeit fresh and wholesome.

This is a clear example of subordination of the domestic market to higher priorities such as national economic development through growth of exports sold for hard currencies. However, Morocco's relationship with its principal trading partner, France, is currently undergoing enforced change. The beneficial French duty-free import quota system has been replaced by new European Economic Community arrangements requiring Morocco to participate in a more competitive system based on price. Here Moroccan canned foods are at a disadvantage due to high production costs caused by irregularities of supply, uneconomic plant size, and expensive locally produced cans (representing almost 25% of the product's total cost).

Fortunately the articulation of functional relationships between the state, marketing companies and consumers in other segments of the domestic market works more smoothly as the following discussion will show.

Competition and cooperation

The Moroccan Government is well aware of the economic and social importance of the food industry to the country. Cooperation with producers takes many forms. For example, credit policies have been liberalized to assist farmers in purchasing tractors in order to promote mechanization. It is estimated that 70 000 tractors are needed for the land to be efficiently exploited; however, in 1979 only 20 000 were in use. Yet despite obvious inefficiencies and suboptimization, the agroindustry produces a wide range of foodstuffs: processed cereals, edible oils, refined sugar, fresh and canned fruits, and vegetables and related products.

Other examples of government cooperation in food marketing include free television advertising (aimed at bringing about changes in consumption behaviour) and sponsorship of educational programmes, e.g. a daily 30-minute early evening programme on modern farming methods. Social marketing campaigns have been used to promote various objectives:

- Increasing local consumption of oranges.
- Introducing the concept of sugar in individual serving-size sachets, in place of the traditional 'sugar-loaf' or French-style cube sugar.
- Promoting consumption of fish in inland areas (in order to increase the overall size of the domestic market and improve nutrition through a cheap source of protein).

However, not all campaigns have produced the desired effect. One unfortunate example concerns an infant weaning food, Actamine 5, promoted jointly by the government and a local food marketing company with the backing of UNICEF and the US Agency for International Development[3]. In order to depict the protein content of the baby food, a weighing scale was shown with Actamine 5 on one arm and a variety of protein-rich foods such as meat and fish on the other. The largely illiterate population (70%) took this to signify that Actamine 5 was made of fish. Not unexpectedly the product was withdrawn from the market.

Competition in the food marketing sector can become very intense, particularly when the position of an established market leader is challenged, as in the case of the yogurt Danone (marketed as 'Dannon' in the USA). Produced under license by the Centrale Laitière, this French product enjoyed the immense advantage of having entered the Moroccan market first. Hence the brandname is used locally to signify the generic product type, yogurt. In 1981 another French producer of yogurt, Yoplait, entered the market.

Within one month of launch, stocks of Yoplait were sold out. Innovative advertising and new flavours resulted in large-scale consumer trial. Production could not meet demand and Danone's market share plummeted from 90% to 40%. Danone's retaliation focused on increased production to fill the gap left by Yoplait's underproduction, rapid introduction of comparable new flavours, increased frequency of TV advertising promoting Danone as 'the real thing', and a not-so-praiseworthy campaign of tied deliveries at the retail level ('milk and yogurt, or no milk'). By the end of the first year, Danone retrieved a 70% market share as consumer curiosity for a newfound alternative diminished and the tendency to request a 'danone' guaranteed sales for the leader.

Marketing performance

In reviewing the performance of the food marketing sector objectively, several negative aspects become immediately apparent:

- Underutilization of production capacity – in the canning industry rates range from a high of 70% (juices) to a low of 35% (vegetables)[4].
- Persistently low wages and standard of living among rural workers – in 1980 the legal minimum wage was 9.80 dirhams (DH) per day (US$1.96) compared with 1.96 DH per hour in industry and commerce (or 15.68 DH per 8-hour day, equal to US$3.14).
- Inefficient distribution methods – resulting in unnecessary waste and/or periodic gluts and fluctuating retail prices.
- Lack of effective market supervision and data collection.

While manufacturing firms are well documented in number, type and volume of production, probably due to the more permanent nature of their premises and equipment, distributors appear to defy any type of accurate survey. Even the taxation system is not able to offer reliable data, as many traders are illiterate and do not keep any accounting books.

For example, the wholesale market for staple foods is characterized by a chaotic variety of small, medium and a few large-size traders whose sheer number (guesstimated at around 300) has so far defeated both government and private firms' attempts to identify and enumerate, even though most operate within the city of Casablanca. Lack of statistics makes accurate control of weights and measures, price, quality, collection of sales taxes, and inspection of premises difficult if not impossible. Periodic shortages in supply lead to speculation, widespread hoarding, and the creation of blackmarkets.

Positive aspects of performance are somewhat more diffuse in character:

- Clearly the government has recognized the need to develop the country's immense national resources through agrarian reform and increased investment, as expressed by the priorities listed in national five-year economic plans.
- Considerable effort is being made to regulate the food market by means of the various 'offices' and the use of regulatory mechanisms; for example, regional quota systems are applied to regulate supply and demand. Also, a Compensatory Fund operates to stabilize staple food prices and 'flying teams' attempt to exercise control by spot checks on retail prices.
- Marketing infrastructure is well developed with a variety of publicly and privately owned manufacturing, marketing and transportation companies. Advertising is carried out by five ad agencies located in Casablanca. University institutes specializing in business, agricultural science, packaging etc. provide technical and managerial training. Metallic packaging (canning), along with paper, cardboard and plastic packaging industries achieve a current capacity utilization rate of 67%.
- Advertising on television, although censored, is an effective means of mass market communication with a population intrigued by novelty and eager to experiment with new products.

Environmental impact

At the macro level, food marketing in Morocco is impacted by the changing conditions associated with an enlarged European Community. Future membership of Spain and Portugal, competitors in food marketing, may force the country into a more radical attempt to diversify export markets. Some evidence of this trend was seen in 1974 when Morocco negotiated a straight barter deal with Russia, exchanging citrus fruits for Russian, petroleum products, timber and industrial plant[9]. Similarly, growing links with Kuwait and Saudi Arabia augur well for future foodstuff exports.

Internally, climatic variations can severely affect a year's harvests leaving farmers with little other source of alternative income. Annual shortages of butter and milk, due to low levels of animal feedstuffs during the hot summer months, are controlled by government-imposed quotas on consumer purchases at the retail level.

Among food marketers a major preoccupation is the danger of adulteration either through environmental factors (heat, dust, infestation etc.) or through employee negligence. In a market where prepackaging is limited to a narrow range of products and many foodstuffs are hand delivered (e.g. bread) or sold door-to-door (e.g. eggs and honey) or by street vendors (e.g. figs, fish, couscous), adulteration is a common source of consumer dissatisfaction[5].

A final environmental factor of considerable importance is the political climate. The food rioting of 1981 in Morocco came about in reaction to a heavy-handed political manoeuvre to raise funds at short notice for the long-drawn-out war in the western Sahara (which has since been settled in Morocco's favour against Algeria).

Conclusion

Morocco's progress towards a modern economy is well under way, but underutilization of national resources remains a major problem. The food marketing sector vividly exemplifies this problem. However, it also provides evidence of a dynamic market environment characterized by a mix of public and private companies and government institutions actively involved in competition and some cooperation in social marketing.

As in many other less developed nations, government can play a significant role in the modernization of the food marketing sector in Morocco. Government support is needed in: (a) encouraging entrepreneurship; (b) providing incentives to the distributive trade as well as producers; (c) investing in the distribution infrastructure in order to modernize the physical distribution of goods – especially in the rural sector; (d) encouraging the establishment of large-scale enterprises at the retail and wholesale level in order to improve efficiency and bring about the necessary technological innovations; (e) creating healthy competition for private distributive enterprises. Other functions can be conceived for the government. However, it is clear that planned and deliberate intervention of the government can speed up the process of modernization in the food marketing sector in Morocco.

References

1. AMINE, L. S. and CAVUSGIL, S. T. (1983) Mass media advertising in a developing country: the case of Morocco. *International Journal of Advertising* 2, 317–330
2. AMINE, L. S. and CAVUSGIL, S. T. (1986) Marketing environment in the Middle East and North Africa: forces behind market homogenization. In *Advances in International Business,* Vol. 1. Ed. by S. T. Cavusgil. Connecticut, JAI Press
3. AMINE, L., VITALE, E. and CAVUSGIL, S. T. (1983) Launching a weaning food in a developing country: the Moroccan experience, *European Journal of Marketing* 17, 44–54
4. BMCE (Banque Marocaine du Commerce Extérieur) (1981) *Monthly Information Review* 37, Jan.–Feb.
5. CAVUSGIL, S. T. and KAYNAK, E. (1982) A framework for a cross-cultural measurement of consumer dissatisfaction. In *New Findings on Consumer Satisfaction and Complaining,* pp. 80–84. Ed. by R. L. Day and H. K. Hunt. Bloomington, Ind.: Indiana University
6. CAVUSGIL, S. T., AMINE, L. S. and VITALE, E. (1983) Marketing supplementary food products in LDCs: a case study in Morocco. *Food Policy* 8 (2), 111–120
7. GOLDMAN, A. (1974) Outreach of consumers and the modernization of urban food retailing in developing countries. *Journal of Marketing* 38, 8–16
8. GOLDMAN, A. (1982) Adoption of supermarket shopping in a developing country: the selective adoption phenomenon. *European Journal of Marketing* 16, 17–26
9. KAIKATI, J. (1981) The international barter boom: perspectives and challenges. *Journal of International Marketing* 1, 29–38
10. KAYNAK, E. (1980) Government and food distribution in LDCs. *Food Policy,* 5 (2), 132–142
11. KAYNAK, E. (1980) Transfer of supermarketing technology from developed to less-developed countries: the case of Migros-Turk. *The Finnish Journal of Business Economics* 29, 339–346
12. KAYNAK, E. (1980) Future directions of research in comparative marketing: a theoretical perspective. *The Canadian Marketer* 11, 23–28
13. KAYNAK, E. and CAVUSGIL, S. T. (1982) The evolution of food retailing systems: contrasting the experience of developed and developing countries. *Journal of the Academy of Marketing Science* 10, 249–269
14. KOMPASS MAROC 1979–80: *Register of Moroccan Industry and Commerce* (1980) Kompass Maroc-Véto, Casablanca
15. TUNCALP, S. and YAVAS, U. (1983) Supermarkets gaining rapid acceptance in Saudi Arabia. *Marketing News,* (Feb. 4), 5
16. YAVAS, U., KAYNAK, E. and BORAK, E. (1981) Modern retailing institutions in developing countries: determinants of supermarket patronage in Istanbul, Turkey. *Journal of Business Research* 9 (December), 367–379
17. YAVAS, U., KAYNAK, E. and BORAK, E. (1982) Food shopping orientations in Turkey: some lessons for policy makers. *Food Policy* 7 (2), 133–140

Part V

Food marketing strategies, facilities and procedures

The purpose of the first chapter is the examination of a food marketing system in an underdeveloped, but oil-rich, country: Libya. The country, described, in the early 1950s, as 'a hopeless case for economic development', emerged, less than a decade later, as one of the major oil producers in the world. This contrast provided an excellent opportunity for the study of pre- and post-oil discovery conditions of its food marketing system. The chapter is divided into four main parts: the first covers the general pre-oil discovery conditions, and focuses on the country's dual economy along with related characteristics of the food marketing system. The second deals with a developing surplus economy, and its impact on agriculture and food distribution channels, the third with the impact of a new dimension (military takeover in 1969) on the conduct of events in the 1970s, and the fourth with an empirical study of a sample from the food manufacturing industry which illustrates the way food manufacturers dealt with marketing, its various functions and techniques. This chapter deals with entirely different marketing institutions and practices which emerged as the products of the country's new ideological considerations, rather than through natural marketing development processes.

An important problem facing public policy makers is how best to measure market performance. Economists have traditionally used criteria such as the existence of monopoly forces, entry barriers, and externalities in production and consumption. Responding to the growth of the consumer movement, policy makers are assigning a relatively high priority to the development of programmes designed to protect the consumer interest and these depend on the availability of information that provides a basis for comparing levels of consumer satisfaction across a range of products and services, for identifying problem areas, and for effectively allocating limited consumer protection resources. Given the number of alternative foods on the market and the central role of food consumption in everyday life, the second chapter examines consumer satisfaction with food products.

The third chapter describes the characteristics of food distribution systems and practices in less developed countries, with particular reference to Latin America and the Middle East. The author also examines the characteristics of the environmental factors which have an influence on food distribution, and explores the relationship between the environmental factors and the specific characteristics of food distribution systems of less developed countries. The intention is to show how structural and operational changes can be induced in the distribution systems of less developed countries.

Opinions have been polarized on the role of food prices in economic development. The analysis of structuralists argues that food prices are irrelevant to long-term development, but neoclassical theorists believe that food prices may be a critical factor. The last chapter in this part attempts to reconcile these views, reports on the differential impacts of food prices in Indonesia and discusses the role of food prices in the policy process.

Chapter 9

Food marketing system in an oil-rich Arab country: the case of Libya

Ben Issa A. Hudanah

The pre-oil discovery conditions: The 1950s

At the time of its independence in December 1951, Libya had a land area of 679 000 square miles (mainly desert), a total population of just over one million, 20% of which was urban and the rest evenly split between rural and nomadic population, illiteracy rate at a record level of over 90% and a very low per capita income. These generally poor conditions suggested that the country had no chance for sound economic development.

Faced with difficult geographical and climatic conditions (large Sahara desert, meagre supply of ground water, aridity, high temperatures and frequent droughts), along with hostile population, the successive foreign forces which dominated the country throughout its history had concentrated their economic activities in the major coastal cities, namely Tripoli and Benghazi and their surrounding fertile lands. The rest of the country was left, until recently, with little knowledge, if any, of the twentieth century realities.

The geographical set up of the country, along with the regional concentration of modern economic activities in the coastal cities had, therefore, created a classical case of what is known as 'a dual economy'[11]: an economy with both a primitive and a modern sector. Obviously, a dual economy had to be coupled by 'a dual marketing system', where different marketing institutions and practices emerge to serve different consumer's wants and needs in both sectors of the economy (*see Table 9.1*).

With the exception of foreign nationals and a number of rich Libyan families, Libyan consumers, on average, had little income to spend. It was estimated that 65–80% of family income was spent on food in the 1950s[1].

Typical of many emerging nations[3,9,15], urban consumers in Libya purchased food items on a daily basis from various small and specialized shops. Their dietary items were mainly based on cereals, fruits and vegetables, whereas, in the rural areas of the country, foodstuffs were produced and preserved for later consumption. Examples are dried beans of all kinds, palm tree dates, olives and cereals.

Although vegetables and fruit were produced in large quantities in the agricultural areas surrounding the city of Tripoli, such food items were not distributed to the interior markets for economical reasons. Other items such as tea,

TABLE 9.1. Major characteristics of the Libyan dual marketing system prior to oil discovery

Terms of reference	Modern sector of the economy	Primitive sector of the economy
Actors of exchange	Small industrial units, intermediaries and final consumers	Farmers, itinerant retailers, craftsmen and final consumers
Subjects of exchange	Domestic produce and variety of imported goods	Mainly agricultural produce and handicraft goods
Means of exchange	Monetary and credit forms	Monetary and bartering
Forms of exchange	Mainly horizontal involving intensive use of middlemen	Mainly vertical excluding middlemen
Types of outlets	Variety of retailing shops supplied by wholesalers, import agents and domestic producers	Periodical open markets and small itinerant retailers using their own means to get resupply from major cities
Channel length	Rather long with numerous distribution levels	Mainly direct, involving one distribution level
Forms of promotional activities	Advertising and intensive personal selling	Word of mouth advertising and personal selling
Supportive marketing facilities	Various means of transportation, communication, banking and insurance services	Primitive means of transportation
Type of markets; consumer buying habits	Relatively large urban markets. Buying more frequently small quantities	Small village and oasis markets; buying infrequently, relatively large quantities

sugar, rice and the like, which were not domestically produced, could easily find their way to remote market places; clearly, participants in the food distribution system avoided the involvement of perishable items in their distribution operations.

Village traders did not compete against each other; they tended to settle for the notion of 'live and let others live'. Similar retailers' attitudes were reported in other less developed countries (LDCs)[14]. It was a common practice for those retailers to travel, on a rotating basis, to Tripoli to arrange for a truck load of commodities for their resupply.

Food distribution in urban areas of the country was dominated by a large number of small shops with little capital investment, no refrigeration facilities, minimal sanitary conditions, poor layout and long working hours. These characteristics are common to Middle Eastern countries and widely reported in the marketing literature[15].

Small retailers usually got their supply of fresh vegetables and fruit on a daily basis from large open air markets where farmers and wholesalers display their goods in quantities. Fresh items were often hidden in a corner for regular customers. When a desired item is not available or not in good condition, the shopkeeper would go out of his way to make it available in an hour or so for a favoured customer.

An unknown number of peddlers and itinerant traders, believed to be over 500 in Tripoli city alone, sold a wide variety of food items ranging from ice creams to fresh fish, and played an extremely vital role in food distribution. Their role proved important for the following reasons: (*a*) a large number of workers were paid their wages on a daily basis, and this required a similar base for food purchases; (*b*) socially, women were strictly kept indoors; thus, while men were at work, women could buy daily needs from these traders; (*c*) lack of storage and refrigeration facilities further emphasized the practicality of buying 'from hand to mouth'; (*d*) those traders offered fresh items at significantly low prices which was in the interest of the poor families.

The oil takeover: The 1960s

Libya became an oil exporting country in 1961. Three years later, the following direct impacts on the overall economy were observed: (*a*) the country's balance of payments showed a surplus for the first time since independence; (*b*) oil brought in 50% of the country's national income; (*c*) in 1964, oil was already accounting for 99% of the country's exports – a rate no other commodity has ever achieved anywhere in the world; (*d*) by 1965, oil revenues constituted 57% of total government earnings.

These dramatic events have led the way to the following two major inter-related developments which are worthy of mention here, for their implicit impact on the country's food production and related marketing system:

* The national economy became based on a single commodity (oil), hence ending the leading role of the agricultural sector.
* The rapid influx of oil revenues into the country quickly eliminated the problem of non-availability of capital as a factor hindering economic development. Thus, the public sector had a direct role to assume in speeding-up the process of development.

Government efforts over the 1960s, however, were rather a mere reaction to events than a planned course of action for future events where government planning efforts existed; they were along the traditional path of the pre-oil era. Development efforts were concentrated on urban cities with little attention paid to the problems of rural areas. The result was the widening of the gap between the two sectors of Libya's dual economy.

Despite large government earnings from oil, the country's economic system remained basically one of 'free enterprise', and government efforts were limited to stabilizing prices, the provision of agricultural and industrial credits along with managing the state-owned tobacco monopoly and a few tuna and sardine processing firms.

Food distribution and consumption

As Libya became more dependent on imports for the supply of most food and non-food products, its distribution channels became more import oriented. Lack of functional specialization, more concentration of wholesale businesses in coastal cities and profit making through the creation of false market situations (food shortages) were clear evidences of channel reorientation.

At the wholesale level, it was rather difficult to identify the characteristics of the participants accurately. Import agents, in some cases, acted as wholesalers or distributors, and non-importing wholesalers often got engaged in retailing. Intermediaries thus assumed different functions at various levels in the distribution system depending on profit potential. Their operations had one common practice. They all searched for suppliers and they all waited long hours for customers. Evidence of promotional activities was practically non-existent.

Although imported foodstuffs were dealt with by various participants in the distribution system at different levels, domestic agricultural produce could hardly find its way to wholesalers or food distributors except for dried items such as legumes, seeds and cereals. Lack of conditioned storage facilities, dispersion of small population over a wide geographical area, unfavourable climatic conditions and inadequate transportation network had discouraged wholesalers and food distributors from spreading their operations to cover remote areas with a wider range of commodities including perishable items. This situation often led to oversupplied urban markets with resulting impact on prices, i.e. in some cases farmers had to accept unrealistically low prices for items that are badly needed in other parts of the market.

At the final consumer level, improved income turned the percentage of undernourished people from close to 100% in 1951 down to 13% by the end of the 1960s[8].

Patterns of consumer's income expenditures tended to follow J. Engel's law: 'the poorer the family, the greater is the proportion of its expenditure on food'. This was confirmed in a study undertaken in 1969[5]. It was found that low income groups spent 48.2% of their income on food compared with 37.2% and 26.4% for middle and high income groups.

The public sector takeover: The 1970s

Following the military takeover of September 1969, the country was shifted from a path of relatively slow evolutionary process of development to a high speed revolutionary one. The new leaders lost no time in taking the following actions:

- As a result of expelling the Italian nationals from the country in 1970, the Italian firms, industrial enterprises and distributive institutions were all taken over by Libyans. A law was also enacted the same year which restricted the practice of domestic and foreign trade to Libyan nationals.
- A national supply corporation (NSC) was established in 1971 with monopolistic rights to import and regulate the distribution of certain sensitive items of foodstuffs (sugar, coffee, tea, olive oil, rice, flour and tomato paste). The establishment was also authorized to buy cereals from farmers with the aim of stabilizing prices and quantities supplied. This early move indicated government intention to play a significant role in both domestic and foreign trade.
- Self-sufficiency in food was declared in 1970 as a 'primary objective' to be achieved by 1980. Consequently, actions were directed to: (a) the initiation of large agricultural projects to be operated by the public sector, (b) the stimulation of the private sector to invest more in food production activities and (c) the distribution of newly developed farms to poor farmers at nominal prices.

While oil production was cut down by 40% in 1970, oil prices were pushed up to balance government earnings from oil revenues. However, the major increase in oil prices in 1973 provided sufficient funds to finance government development projects. The country's basic infrastructure was widened in terms of transportation network, communication and harbour facilities. Education, public health, electricity supply and housing conditions were drastically improved all over the country and, hence, narrowed the gap between urban and rural areas.

The industrial base of the country was also enlarged by some additional government factories, but the food manufacturing industry remained basically in the private sector. Patterns of government investment showed agriculture as the most dominant single development effort in the 1970s. Agricultural development and agrarian reform cost some 1.5 billion Libyan dinars (LD) over the 1970s compared with LD27.3 million over the five years between 1963 and 1968. Large agricultural projects were undertaken, practically, wherever water resources could be found (in some cases, regardless of soil fertility).

Typical of many of the less developed countries, marketing considerations did not seem to have any impact on project planning. The two main factors Libyan planners emphasized in dealing with a project were: project total cost and requirements and potential project output. The omission of marketing considerations created certain marketing difficulties.

Project management considered transportation and other logistical costs of their output as pure marketing problems to be dealt with by government marketing institutions, whereas, it was later found to be practically impossible to incorporate logistical costs of agricultural produce from remote projects in the pricing formula. In some cases, agricultural output from remote projects (cereals) were buried in sand for more than a year in a project area (a primitive but effective form of storage under dry weather conditions) or sold in nearby village markets at production cost prices.

Despite some positive results of government efforts in food production[8], the country had to import some 60% of its food requirements in 1979 compared with 80% in 1976[6]. The objective to reach self-sufficiency in food production by the year 1980 was not, therefore, achieved.

In order to examine the marketing organizations and related marketing practices, a total of 21 firms (all in the private sector) presenting three sections from the Libyan food manufacturing industry were studied[10].

The general characteristics clearly reflect a cautious approach on the part of the Libyan entrepreneurs to manufacturing operations. They had neither adequate basic formal education nor industrial experience. The elements of uncertainty related to their recent entry to manufacturing businesses made them reluctant to fully utilize existent market opportunities.

Marketing practices of firms

The marketing practices of the Libyan food manufacturing firms were reported to be, generally, in line with what is widely revealed about their counterparts in the emerging nations[12,16], i.e. minimum appreciation and utilization of the modern concept and techniques of marketing. Where differences in marketing practices existed, operational as well as environmental conditions specific to Libya were responsible causes. The impact of the National Supply Corporation (NSC) on various sections of the Libyan food manufacturing industry is an illustrative example. NSC, the largest single food distributor in Libya, monopolized importing and distributing operations of sugar, flour and olive oil. For the firms involved in macaroni making and confectionaries, the NSC was their only supplier of items which are heavily used as raw materials. As for the tomato canning firms, the NSC bought and distributed all of their tomato paste production.

Relieved from the bulk of their distribution efforts, some of the tomato manufacturers began to divert their efforts towards motivating their suppliers (tomato growers) to produce quality and more consistent raw materials. (Their counterparts elsewhere would be concerned about motivating customers to buy.) Incentives used included the provision of credits, technical information, free quality seeds, advance agreements on prices and the supply of packaging materials and containers at cost price.

Given that government protective policies against foreign competition were also applicable, managements of firms had no difficulties in marketing their produce. Consequently, marketing was not perceived as a major function that warranted specialists: marketing functions were performed in a non-specialized way at the various levels of their organizations. A closer examination of the use of individual marketing techniques and functions in the Libyan food manufacturing industry is provided below.

Product development

Operating under general conditions characterized by low market competition, limited industrial experience and little marketing education, the Libyan food manufacturers were engaged in strictly import-substitution type of industry, where markets are taken for granted. Product imitation, rather than product innovation, prevailed as an easy answer to the complexities of establishing product lines and related product mix. Market test of a product was irrelevant, and product quality adjustment was done in response to government regulations, rather than to the satisfaction of changing consumer's wants, needs and tastes.

Most firms had two or three product lines. The average depth of a product line was determined by the different package sizes most demanded by the market, thus ignoring other product item differentials which address specific market segments.

Pricing

The limits within which prices were set and manipulated in the food manufacturing industry did not allow pricing to be a major factor in formulating overall marketing strategies. At the firm level, once prices were set, they became rigid and any future adjustment was subject to government approval. On the other hand, the trading mark-ups were strictly fixed by government agencies for all links in the distribution channels. As a consequence, pricing became, for most firms, a mechanical 'cost-plus' decision.

Promotion

Capitalizing on their previous acquaintances with wholesalers and distributors, managers of firms were personally involved in contacting their customers. Their use of salesmanship was minimal (an average of three salesmen per firm). Only 8 firms engaged advertising, one way or another, in their marketing operations. With the exception of one, those firms used mainly poster and occasional messages in newspapers.

Such a low level of utilizing various tools of promotion was not unexpected. In a market where demand exceeded supply of various commodities, the direction of contact between buyers and sellers is reversed, i.e. it would be the buyer who makes the initial contact for a possible transaction.

Distribution

Unlike the practice of bypassing several links in the distribution channels common to manufacturers in less developed countries[12], food manufacturers in Libya had to deal strictly with one link in the distribution channels. While 10 firms dealt strictly with wholesalers, 6 firms dealt strictly with retailers and the remaining 5 dealt with both links. This was also reflected in the way their total sales were distributed between various levels of distribution. Fifty-five per cent of all sales of the firms under study were made to wholesalers, 26.1% to the NSC, 18% to retailers and 0.7% to others (unidentified) (*see Figure 9.1*).

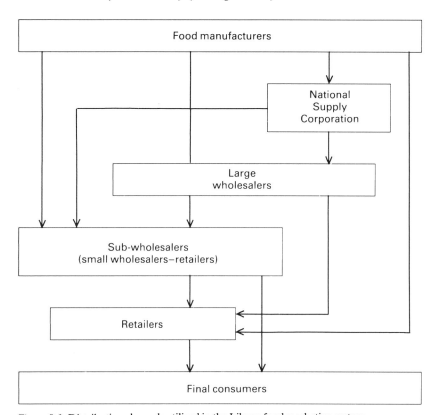

Figure 9.1. Distribution channels utilized in the Libyan food marketing system

The Libyan food manufacturers clearly under-rated the potential value of optimizing their distribution networks through carefully selected channels. They accepted 'the way it has always been done' as a criterion for channel selection, and their choices of individual middlemen were based on rather vague terms. Most firms emphasized 'financial strength' and 'business morality' as the most important two factors determining the selection of a middleman. However, when asked to elaborate the terms, the respondents forwarded statements such as:

'We do not use formalities without regular customers like contracts or any other forms of written agreements.'

'We do not want to run after our customers to make them pay us.'

These statements clearly reflect the personalized nature of business deals known to the Libyan society.

Customer services extended to middlemen were kept at a minimal level. All forms offered short credit terms to their regular customers, and 17 out of 21 offered free delivery to their customers provided that points of delivery were within the city boundaries.

Marketing research

If taken to mean the application of scientific method to marketing planning, problems and decisions related to both customer satisfaction and business objectives, then marketing research was, and still is, far from being adopted in the Libyan food manufacturing industry. Even when 13 firms out of the 21 claimed to have been engaged in marketing research activities, further investigation proved that their perception was much less than what the term 'marketing research' actually implied. What they envisaged as the scope of marketing was the occasional inquiry about new products in the market, their related prices, general consumer preferences based on wholesalers and retailers assessment of the market. None of the firms involved had an administrative unit for marketing research, or actually assigned the task to outside agencies.

Lack of competition, excessive governmental protective measures and the import-substitution nature of the industry provided guaranteed domestic market. Consequently, the firms involved were not pressurized to enhance the quality of their marketing decisions.

Marketing planning and strategies

The way individual marketing functions were dealt with in the Libyan food manufacturing industry suggested that marketing planning and strategies would have insignificant contribution to the overall planning efforts of individual firms. Indeed, only one firm claimed to be familiar with written marketing plans and budgets. The total fund allocated to total marketing efforts of this exceptional firm was divided as follows: 50% to product efforts, 30% to distribution, 15% to marketing research and 5% to sales efforts.

Various justifications given by the firms for poor or non-existent marketing planning efforts were revealed in the following quoted statements:

'You do not make plans to sell when your customers call on you frequently for more deliveries.'

'Our business is very small.'

'Get me more fresh vegetables and we will do the processing and sell them tomorrow.'

One respondent went on further to state: 'An Egyptian dealer offered me a contract involving 100 000 tons of macaroni annually. I turned it down, I have neither production facilities *at the moment*, nor can I be sure of producing this much *consistently* every year if I get the production facilities needed.' Note that in none of these statements were sales difficulties mentioned. Most interesting is that there was no mention of difficulties in acquiring production facilities either.

What this situation tells us is that managements of firms were aware of existing marketing opportunities, both in domestic and foreign markets. What they did not know was how to base their production efforts on market opportunities in a single comprehensive overall plan. Most firms kept records of growth rates of their sales and production, but only four had planned for specific annual rates of growth of their production and none did so for sales. In other words, both production and marketing activities of firms were an uncoordinated series of tactics usually in response to environmental conditions. Under such circumstances, production levels of individual firms were far from being maximized in relation to market potential and firm's resources.

In an attempt to measure the respondent's perception of relative importance of four major policy areas of marketing planning and strategies, respondents were asked to place their judgements on a 100 point scale. The same technique was used earlier in the USA and repeated in Peru[12]. Product efforts in the Libyan case averaged 70 points compared with 41 and 35 for the USA and Peru, respectively. While distribution efforts came second in importance (14 points) for Libyan respondents, their counterparts in the USA and Peru perceived sales efforts as second in importance, giving them an average of 28 and 25 points, respectively. Libyan respondents perceived sales efforts as third and marketing research efforts as fourth in importance and allocated 9 and 7 points for the respective facets.

The outlook for the 1980s

The world oil surplus which began in 1981 reduced the country's earnings from LD22 billion in 1980 to some LD10 billion in 1982[7]. However, recent development plans indicated that the scale of agricultural development efforts would not be affected by declining oil revenues, i.e. LD18.5 billion are allocated to the 1981–85 development plan. The aim is to reduce the country's dependence on oil earnings, with agricultural and manufacturing industry taking the lead by the end of this century. A huge project was also announced at the end of 1983 aiming at the creation of an artificial river to bring gas and water from the desert to the fertile soil of the coastal area. The project involves a network of over 3000 kilometres of concrete pipes, to be completed by the mid-1990s.

The nature and the scope of this project indicated a change in planning orientation, i.e. the existence of ground water in remote and less fertile soils no longer justified project locationing as was the case in the 1970s.

The entire marketing system of the country was subjected to major structural changes at the end of the 1970s. The aim was to implement related ideological teachings of Qaddafi's *Green Book* (private trade is an exploitative phenomenon); as a consequence, private trade was prohibited and various public marketing institutions were established.

- A giant national marketing company (NMC) was established in 1979 with initial capital of LD50 million. Its aim was to build three different chains of retailing outlets comprising supermarkets, department stores and specialty shops throughout the country to replace the existing network of private retailing outlets. By April 1980, the NMC was already operating eight prefabricated supermarkets in Benghazi and 12 in Tripoli city. The new supermarkets were identical (total area $2200\,m^2$, $1000\,m^2$ display area, 50% of which was for food items, plus some $50\,m^2$ for refrigeration facilities).

- Various specialized importing companies were established in 1979, to replace private importing traders and enterprises. The imports of food products are handled by three specialized establishments: the National Supply Corporation (NSC), the National Company for Meat Supplies (NCMS) and the General Food Company (GFC). By the end of 1979, all private wholesaling and importing businesses were ordered to close down and their licences were suspended.
- By the end of 1981, the NMC had completed the building of its network of retailing outlets; consequently, the General Peoples Committee for Economy ordered all retailing businesses to close down and hand over their stocks to the NMC. The whole country's foreign and domestic trade is now dealt with by specialized institutions and three chains of retailing outlets called 'People's markets'.

The new supermarkets and department stores did not differ significantly from those known in Europe except for: (a) they are not privately owned, (b) they are not based on profit objectives and (c) consequently, their pricing policies aimed at covering total cost, and no promotional activities were involved.

Domestic food production, from farms and manufacturers, was sold directly to the NMC, which in turn distributed to its various retailing outlets. Early results indicated certain inadequacies in this arrangement in dealing with farm produce:

- Perishable products naturally require immediate handling, whereas farmers had to go through long formal procedures to sell to their only customer (NMC).
- The NMC set grades of farm produce and fixed their related prices.
- Farmers who were used to selling for immediate cash had to accept receipts payable in banks.
- Farmers had to use their own transportation to take their commodities to market centres where representatives of the NMC operate. They had to follow official working hours and wait for their turn.

The flow of agricultural produce from one region of the country to another required a fleet of trucks and drivers, none of which the NMC had in the transitional period. This resulted in (a) irregular supply of fresh farm produce to various regional markets with resulting impacts on price levels, (b) the NMC, being obliged to buy all farm produce, was unable to distribute all of it rapidly and, consequently, large quantities of perishable produce were frequently wasted and (c) blackmarketeers stepped in and profited from undersupplied markets.

Uncoordinated operational rules between farmers and the NMC tempted the former to adopt a strategy based on selling the bulk of their produce at the beginning of the season for relatively higher prices. This strategy further aggravated the situation described above.

Finally, consumers were also affected by some inconveniences related to the new retailing outlets. The flexibility provided by the next-door grocer was replaced by impersonal establishments, operating in formal hours, taking no special orders, and too far away to be visited frequently.

Consumer reaction to the new situation was rather adaptive. Food items were bought in bulk, more time was devoted to shopping trips, and larger fridges and deep freezers were bought. Consumers also emphasized the habit of shopping in groups, and relatives, friends and neighbours provided a network of help to buy items in short supply by reciprocating favours. Realizing these shortcomings of marketing arrangements and related inconveniences at the consumer level, farmers are now allowed to market their own fresh farm produce to final consumers in open market places provided that no intermediaries are used. Farmers' marketing operations are not limited to specific regional markets, although this marketing arrangement gave them an opportunity to utilize undersupplied markets in various regions; it restricted the scope of their marketing operation by disallowing the use of marketing intermediaries. Thus, a farmer's marketing operations are determined by what he, or his family members, can handle along with their farming activities.

Conclusion

Detailed examination of food distribution and related marketing activities in Libya over the last three decades reveal that:

- The domestic market which looked too small, in terms of population and income levels in the early 1950s, is relatively more promising for the 1980s. The effective market economy has been enlarged, and improved accessibility to remote small markets has contributed to the development of a rather integrated national market.
- The domestic market and related environmental conditions which favoured small industrial units, based on regional markets in the 1950s and 1960s, could now support larger production enterprises aiming at market opportunities on a nationwide basis. The ability to relate production plans to market potential in Libya's food manufacturing industry is, therefore, essential. Empirical evidence suggested that such ability was lacking, thus, marketing education is most needed.
- Libyan consumers have become increasingly affluent; consequently, market demand is becoming more sophisticated. This placed a premium on skilled management to detect the subtleties of demand of different segments of the market. Import substitution may no longer be a satisfactory approach to establishing product lines, and the food manufacturing industry would have to get involved in marketing research and research and development activities. So far, both tools have not been significantly utilized in order to enhance planning decisions.
- The disregard for the potential formative role of marketing in government agricultural projects proved costly. Some of these projects would have to be reassessed with regard to production cost and marketing considerations. However, depending on how effectively the basic utilities of marketing are handled, recent agricultural development plans would eventually raise the food self-sufficiency ratio to some 60% by the end of this decade.
- The structural changes introduced in the distribution system at the beginning of this decade are too recent to assess in terms of effectiveness. Initial results, however, indicated mishandling of some basic marketing principles. Farm produce appears to be most affected for its high sensitivity to lengthy formal procedure.

Insofar as food producing and marketing are concerned, the Libyan case suggests that, in an oil-rich country, where availability of capital and consumer's ability to buy are no longer problems in the context of development, the agricultural sector and related food manufacturing industry may not be flexible enough to respond to growing consumer demand for foodstuffs. Where such a situation arises, governments might be tempted to assume a wider role in performing the tasks of development. Furthermore, when the flow of vital supply commodities in the market is inadequate, the pretext is set for governments to extend their role to the distribution and, hence, to the marketing system.

References

1. ATIGA, A. (1972) *The Impact of Oil on the Libyan Economy.* Beirut, Dar Al-Taliha (Arabic publication)
2. BANKS/CARLIP/DEWITT/OVERSTREET (1982) *Economic Handbook of the World:* 1982, pp. 319–323. New York, McGraw-Hill
3. BENNET, P. (1968) *Government's Role in Retail Marketing of Food Products in Chile,* p. 34. Austin, Bureau of Business Research, University of Texas at Austin
4. DEPARTMENT OF CENSUS AND STATISTICS OF LIBYA (1968) Statistical abstract. Libya, DCSL
5. DEPARTMENT OF CENSUS AND STATISTICS OF LIBYA (1970) *Report on the Second Phase of the Household Sample Surveys in Tripoli and Benghazi: Household Expenditures.* Libya, DCSL
6. EUROPA (1978–79) *The Middle East and North Africa,* 25th ed., pp. 529–558
7. EUROPA (1983) *The Europa Yearbook 1983. A World Survey.* Vol. II, pp. 843–854. London, Europa Publication Ltd
8. FAO (1978) *The State of Food and Agriculture.* Rome, FAO
9. GOLDMAN, A. (1974) Outreach of consumers and the modernization of urban food retailing in developing countries. *Journal of Marketing,* **38,** 8–16
10. HUDANAH, B. (1975) Market structure and marketing practices of the Libyan food manufacturing industry. PhD Thesis, Cranfield Institute of Technology, England
11. THE INTERNATIONAL BANK FOR RECONSTRUCTION AND DEVELOPMENT (1960) *The Economic Development of Libya.* Baltimore, Johns Hopkins Press
12. GLADE, W., STRONG, V., UDELL, J. and LITTLEFIELD (1970) *Marketing in a Developing Nation.* Cambridge, Mass., Heath Lexington Books
13. SADDIK, S. M. (1973) An analysis of the status of marketing in Egypt. *European Journal of Marketing,* 77–81
14. SLATER, C. *et al.* (1969) *Marketing Processes in the Recife Area of Northeast Brazil,* Chapter 5, p. 46. East Lansing, Michigan, Latin American Studies Centre
15. STEWART, C. F. (1961) The changing Middle-East market. *Journal of Marketing,* **XXV,** 47–51
16. YAVAS, U., KAYNAK, E. and BORAK, E. (1982) Food shopping orientations in Turkey: Some lessons for policymakers. *Food Policy,* **7** (2), 133–140

Chapter 10

Consumer satisfaction/dissatisfaction with food products

John A. Quelch and Stephen B. Ash

Introduction

The value of consumer satisfaction as a measure of market performance is already widely recognized by marketing practitioners who view the satisfaction of consumer needs as one of the principal goals of marketing activity. If both policy makers and marketers can agree on the usefulness of satisfaction data as a performance measure, the probability of cooperative efforts between these two groups to correct the causes of dissatisfaction with particular products or services is likely to be enhanced.

Interest in consumer satisfaction studies also stems from the growing recognition of the limitations of conventional complaint data as a measure of consumer dissatisfaction within a population, and as a means of giving priority to problem categories of products and services to guide policy interventions[3]. Several studies have suggested that complaint letters tend not to be representative either of the types of problems confronting consumers or of the types of people experiencing consumer problems. For example, complaint letters suffer from 'big ticket' bias since they tend to focus on unsatisfactory consumption experiences with products that are unusually important to the consumer.

Volunteered complaints therefore tend to under-represent dissatisfactions with lower cost items or those which play a relatively modest role in the consumer's daily life. There is some evidence, as well, that writers of complaint letters or those who take some action to resolve their dissatisfaction are atypical of the entire population since they tend to be younger, better educated, more affluent, and more active politically than non-complainers[9].

The over-riding concern about complaint letters, however, is that they may simply represent the tip of the iceberg. The number of dissatisfied consumers may substantially exceed the number who complain, particularly if the consumer is unclear about how to voice a complaint.

Concern with the value of complaint data as a diagnostic tool, has increased interest in the application of the survey research technique to the problem of measuring consumer satisfaction. This chapter reports a portion of the results of one such survey conducted for the Consumer Research and Evaluation Branch of the Canadian Ministry of Consumer and Corporate Affairs.

An earlier version of this appeared as an article in *Food Policy,* 1980, Vol. 5, No. 4, pp. 313–318.

Research method

The data for this study were obtained as part of a nationwide survey of Canadian consumers in 1979. The survey instruments employed in this research were similar to those used previously in a local study conducted in Bloomington, Indiana[1]. In both cases, the instruments obtained data on consumer satisfaction, dissatisfaction and complaining behaviour on an aided recall basis. The data were gathered with self-administered questionnaires using the 'drop-off/pick-up' method to a national probability sample of approximately 3000 dwelling units.

A five-stage, stratified probability sample drawn from a national frame comprising 42 000 enumeration areas distributed across the five regions of Canada was used to collect the data. The sampling plan represented a compromise between a strict random sample and a conventional quota sample in that cost constraints required substitution of households at the block level. Although the exact *true* response rate cannot be computed with the modified probability sample drawn for this study, results have shown that the data compare favourably with Statistics Canada census information.

Usable questionnaires were furnished by 3123 adult Canadians, both males and females, 18 years of age and over. Of these, 1041 subjects answered a questionnaire covering four categories of consumer non-durables, food products, household supplies, personal and health care products, and clothing. The results reported in this chapter pertain to the food products section of this questionnaire covering 26 product categories. Interviewers were instructed to interview the household member primarily responsible for buying the types of products or services covered by a particular questionnaire. Thus, the household self-selected a primary decision maker who acted as a spokesman for the household in completing the questionnaire.

Food products

The initial task required respondents to indicate whether or not they had purchased each of 26 food products during the previous year. Those who indicated that they had used the product were asked to rate the frequency of purchase and their relative extent of satisfaction or dissatisfaction within the category. Subjects then indicated whether or not they had been 'highly dissatisfied' with any of the 26 categories during the past year and, if so, stated the one product which was 'the most unsatisfactory of all'. The remaining questions in the section provided additional data on this single most unsatisfactory product.

First, subjects were asked to complete a set of questions identifying their reasons for dissatisfaction. Then, those reporting dissatisfaction were asked to indicate what steps were taken, if any, to resolve their dissatisfaction. In line with the framework developed by Day and Landon[4], the action options were divided into two groups – personal actions and direct or public actions. Respondents who reported taking direct action were asked to indicate how satisfied they were with the way their complaints were handled. Subjects who reported taking no action when dissatisfied were questioned as to their reason for not doing so.

Baseline data

Certain limitations to the scope of the study should be noted. First, there is no historical dimension to the study. No conclusions can be drawn as to whether consumers are more satisfied with food products today than they were in the past. However, it is anticipated that this study will provide baseline data against which the results of future surveys can be compared. It may be noted, though, that differences in consumer satisfaction over time may not only be caused by objective changes in product quality or performance, but also by changes in consumer perceptions and expectations[6].

Second, no attempt is made to develop an overall index of consumer satisfaction which might serve as a social indicator analogous to the Consumer Price Index. The advantages and problems associated with development of such an index have been discussed elsewhere[7].

Third, the study does not permit a detailed diagnosis of the reasons for satisfaction or dissatisfaction with specific food products in terms of their attribute profiles. Handy[5] has previously defined consumer dissatisfaction as 'the gap or distance between the consumer's "ideal" attribute combination for a particular product or service and the attribute combination of the product or service offered in the marketplace which comes closest to his ideal'. In this study, detailed attribute-related reasons for dissatisfaction are not available. Problems associated with product attributes and performance are subsumed within a broader set of reasons for dissatisfaction covering the major dimensions of marketing practice.

Satisfaction

Responses denoting the frequency of use and level of satisfaction and dissatisfaction for each of the 26 food product categories are summarized in *Table 10.1*. The percentage of subjects purchasing each food product during the last year is first listed, followed by the percentage of purchasers buying the product 'often' as opposed to 'sometimes'. Next, the relative frequency with which purchasers checked each of four satisfaction/dissatisfaction scale responses is reported. The final columns in *Table 10.1* summarize the percentages of satisfied and dissatisfied subjects in each food category.

The information presented in *Table 10.1* is not available either from volunteered complaint data or from studies which ask consumers to recall a single unsatisfactory experience. The problem of 'big ticket' bias has been identified with both of these approaches and the suggestion is that recurring causes of dissatisfaction with less important items, such as food products, may not be brought to the attention of business leaders, consumer interest groups or policy makers.

Information on the rate of use of products permits the number of consumers expressing dissatisfaction with the category to be considered in relation to the total number of respondents reporting usage of the category within the recall period. For example, specialty, dietetic, and gourmet foods ranked twenty-fifth in terms of percentage of respondents who had purchased, but ranked tenth in terms of percentage of dissatisfied purchasers. Specialty foods would probably not figure on conventional complaint lists as a problem in the food products area because the absolute number of purchasers is relatively small. Although the number of users is

TABLE 10.1. Food products: purchase; frequency rating; satisfaction/dissatisfaction rating*

Category	Purchase (% respondents having purchased)	Frequency rating		Percentage purchasers				Percentage purchasers			
		Percentage purchasers buying often	Rank by frequency rating	Satisfied		Dissatisfied		Satisfied		Dissatisfied	
				Quite	Somewhat	Somewhat	Quite	Total	Rank	Total	Rank
Fresh bread, rolls, cakes, other baked goods	97.6	74.1	8	48.9	44.5	5.3	1.3	93.4	16	6.6	10
Frozen bread, dough, pizza, cakes, pie crust	55.1	17.4	25	32.3	54.9	10.6	2.2	87.2	21	12.8	6
Flour, cornmeal, rice	93.5	60.9	11	65.0	33.3	1.4	0.3	98.3	3	1.7	24
Macaroni and noodle products	92.8	60.0	12	64.7	33.5	1.5	0.3	98.2	4	1.8	23
Breakfast cereals	83.2	59.5	13	56.4	38.4	4.4	0.8	94.8	12	5.2	15
Syrups, molasses, honey	90.3	38.0	20	65.1	33.7	0.9	0.3	98.8	1	1.2	26
Sugar, salt, spices, seasonings	98.0	73.3	9	68.4	29.7	1.3	0.6	98.1	5	1.9	21
Cake/cookie mix, pudding, desserts, party food	86.4	38.1	19	49.9	45.0	4.2	0.9	94.9	11	5.1	16
Margarine, cooking oils, shortening	98.0	79.8	6	65.9	32.2	1.3	0.6	98.1	5	1.9	21
Peanut butter, jams, jellies, spread	93.1	55.3	15	60.5	36.3	2.7	0.5	96.8	8	3.2	18
Milk, cheese, yogurt, butter, ice cream, dairy	99.5	91.9	1	60.8	33.3	4.9	1.0	94.1	15	5.9	12
Eggs and egg products	97.4	88.9	3	58.7	36.0	4.5	0.8	94.7	13	5.3	14
Non-alcoholic beverages	98.2	82.0	5	60.0	36.7	2.6	0.6	96.7	9	3.2	18
Canned, frozen fruits, vegetables, soups	89.7	56.9	14	48.8	45.5	4.8	0.9	94.3	14	5.7	13
Cooked, canned or processed meat, poultry, fish, dinners	76.8	31.3	21	35.4	49.0	13.1	2.5	84.4	24	15.6	3
Pickles, mustard, ketchup, other dressings	96.7	53.5	17	61.7	36.8	1.2	0.3	98.5	2	1.5	25
Baby food, juices, formula	10.4	53.8	16	58.3	37.0	–	4.6	95.3	10	4.6	17
Fresh or frozen meats	96.5	84.8	4	40.0	46.1	12.3	1.6	86.1	22	13.9	5
Fresh, frozen, BBQ poultry	87.1	64.4	10	45.9	46.7	6.0	1.4	92.6	19	7.4	8
Fresh or frozen fish/seafood	82.9	43.4	18	43.0	50.0	6.0	1.0	93.0	18	7.0	9
Fresh fruits/vegetables	98.0	89.6	2	43.0	42.7	12.9	1.4	85.7	23	14.3	4
Specialty, dietetic, gourmet foods	24.7	23.9	23	42.6	50.8	4.6	2.0	93.4	16	6.6	10
Pet food	42.6	75.6	7	47.6	44.7	6.8	0.9	92.3	20	7.7	7
Alcoholic beverages	75.1	30.8	22	58.4	38.7	2.3	0.5	97.1	7	2.8	20
Restaurant meals	83.4	17.9	24	26.7	54.1	17.6	1.6	80.8	25	19.2	2
Take-out foods	70.0	12.1	26	24.8	54.6	17.2	3.4	79.4	26	20.6	1

*Based on 1000 responses

itself of significance to consumer protection agencies, this example pinpoints the weaknesses of setting policy priorities on the basis of volunteered complaint data.

From the standpoint of specific food product categories, the principal highlights of *Table 10.1* are as follows:

- Take-out foods and restaurant meals are the two categories with the highest percentages of dissatisfied purchasers. Several explanations may be applicable. First, the purchase in these cases often involves a complete meal rather than an individual food product which may serve as a component of a meal. The product is therefore more complex and there are, potentially, more 'parts' which could be deficient. Both financially and psychologically, the importance of the purchase to the consumer is likely to be greater: the consumer is, therefore, likely to be more sensitive to performance. Secondly, consumer expectations for meals eaten away from home may be higher than for individual food products since such activity is frequently regarded as a treat. If expectations are inflated or ill-formed due to a relative lack of prior purchase experience, consumers may be more prone to dissatisfaction. A third explanation centres on the fact that purchases of meals away from home involve the purchase of a service as well as food. Since quality control along these two dimensions has frequently presented a problem for service operations in the catering business, it would not be surprising if some of the dissatisfaction of purchasers of away-from-home meals stemmed from deficiencies in service performance rather than in the quality of the food.
- Processed dinners registered the third highest percentage of dissatisfied purchasers. Once again, the fact that TV dinners constitute complete meals rather than components of meals raises their importance to the consumer. For some consumers, expectations may also be inflated due to lack of prior purchasing experience. They may not expect to have to make a trade-off in terms of product quality for the convenience and time saved by a TV dinner.
- Among the ten food categories registering the highest percentages of dissatisfied consumers, no fewer than five categories include fresh foods. Given the efforts of nutritionists to increase consumption of fresh rather than processed foods, particularly fresh fruits and vegetables, the discovery of widespread dissatisfaction with fresh foods represents a significant finding. A previous study of 31 individual food products found that the highest level of consumer dissatisfaction was with fresh tomatoes[5]. Consumer dissatisfaction with fresh foods may be explained in several ways. In the absence of packaging for purposes of preservation, fresh foods are subject to wider quality variations than processed foods. Since the quality of fresh produce can deteriorate rapidly, dissatisfaction may occur if the consumer does not understand degrees of ripeness or overestimates the quantity needed at the time of purchase, or if the consumer lacks knowledge of appropriate storage and preparation techniques. In addition, fresh foods are subject to wide and frequent price fluctuations on a seasonal basis and as availability dictates.

In summary, *Table 10.1* indicates that an overwhelming majority of respondents were satisfied with each of the 26 food product categories, suggesting that consumers see far more good than bad in their consumption experiences. The results accord with those of an earlier study which concluded that 'consumers expressed a moderately low level of dissatisfaction with the food products they buy'[5].

The greatest frequency of dissatisfaction is paradoxically found at the two ends of the processing spectrum – with those fresh foods which have not been processed, and with those products involving the highest degree of processing which amount to complete meals. The least dissatisfaction is evident for processed food products of standard quality which leave the meal preparation function to the consumer.

Dissatisfaction

Subjects were asked to indicate whether they had had one or more experiences during the previous year with food products with which they were 'highly dissatisfied'. Giving the frequency of food product purchases, it may seem surprising that only 370 or 35.5% of subjects responded affirmatively. Of these, less than 25% stated that they had been dissatisfied with food products more than ten times in the past year.

To organize the analysis on reasons for dissatisfaction and action by dissatisfied consumers, subjects who reported being highly dissatisfied were asked to indicate the one food product category which was the most unsatisfactory of all.

Dairy products

The five categories cited most often were 'fresh or frozen meats', 'fresh fruits and vegetables', 'cooked, canned, or processed meat, poultry, fish dinners', 'milk, cheese, yogurt, butter, ice cream, dairy products', and 'take-out foods'. Four of these five categories also appeared in *Table 10.1* with the highest percentages of dissatisfied purchasers. The remaining category, dairy products, ranked twelfth in percentage of dissatisfied consumers.

Usage of dairy products is both widespread and frequent; the more frequently a product is used, the more likely it is, by chance, that the consumer may encounter an unsatisfactory item. Moreover, frequency of use generates clear expectations about the quality and performance of a product. Digressions from this norm are readily apparent and liable to lead to dissatisfaction. Quality deterioration can occur rapidly with dairy products and is clearly noticeable when it has occurred. The fact that dairy products were among the five categories most often cited as unsatisfactory reinforces the notion that consumer dissatisfaction is particularly likely to occur with fresh foods.

Among the 370 highly dissatisfied consumers, 18% reported that they suffered out-of-pocket financial losses arising from the purchase of the product. In three-quarters of these cases, however, the loss was reported as being less than C$25, as might be expected in the case of food products. A physical injury, presumably sickness, was reported by 5.6% of highly dissatisfied respondents.

Reasons for dissatisfaction

The 370 highly dissatisfied subjects were asked to check reasons for dissatisfaction with the one food product category named as the most unsatisfactory of all. Multiple responses were permitted. From a list of 15 reasons, respondents checked an average of 2.1 items.

The percentage share of mentions for each reason is reported in *Table 10.2*. Due to small cell sizes, share data are not provided on a product-specific basis.

However, a breakdown of the share of mentions for six fresh food categories versus the remaining categories is reported. In both cases, the most frequently cited reasons for dissatisfaction were 'the quality was poorer than I expected' and 'the product was spoiled, had a defect, or was damaged'. The second of these was significantly ($P < 0.05$) more frequently mentioned for fresh foods than for other foods, reinforcing the earlier suggestion that quality variations may partially explain the relatively higher level of consumer dissatisfaction with fresh produce.

TABLE 10.2. **Major reasons for consumer dissatisfaction with food products**

Reasons	Percentage share of mentions*		
	Fresh foods (N = 415)	Other foods (N = 365)	All foods (N = 780)
The product was spoiled, defective or damaged	27.7	16.1	22.3
The quality was poorer than expected	33.0	31.8	32.5
The amount was less than it was supposed to be	4.6	4.4	4.5
The product did not correspond to the advertisement	7.5	15.1	11.0
A salesman made false or misleading claims about the product	0.0	1.4	0.8
The package was misleading	6.5	4.9	5.8
The product was not delivered when promised	0.5	0.1	0.6
A different item than the one bought was delivered	0.5	0.1	0.8
The instructions of use were unclear or incomplete	1.0	0.1	1.0
The product was unsafe or harmful	2.9	4.4	3.6
The special discount price was as high or higher than the regular price of other sellers	3.4	4.7	4.0
An advertised 'special' was out of stock	7.0	5.8	6.4
I was charged a higher price than that advertised	1.4	0.1	1.4
The store was unwilling to provide a refund or exchange	0.5	0.1	0.6
Other reasons not listed above	3.4	6.3	4.7

* 780 mentions by 370 highly dissatisfied respondents.

Significantly fewer subjects were dissatisfied because of marketing practices such as selling techniques and advertising claims. As might be expected, complaints relating to the content of advertising held a lower share in the case of fresh foods which tend to be less heavily advertised. Stock-outs of foods advertised by retailers were mentioned as a source of dissatisfaction with similar frequencies for both fresh and processed foods.

Conclusions

The survey results suggest that the majority of consumers are, in general, satisfied with food products. However, the results showed wide variation in the proportions of dissatisfied purchasers across the 26 food product categories. A relatively higher frequency of dissatisfaction was found among purchasers of fresh foods and among purchasers of highly processed foods, both in the form of meals eaten away from home and in the form of TV dinners.

References

1. DAY, R. L. and ASH, S. B. (1979) Consumer response to dissatisfaction with durable products. In *Advances in Consumer Research*, Vol. 6, pp. 438–444. Ed. by W. L. Wilkie. Association for Consumer Research

2. DAY, R. L. and BODUR, M. (1977) A comprehensive study of satisfaction with consumer services. In *Consumer Satisfaction and Complaining Behavior*, pp. 64–74. Ed. by R. L. Day. Division of Research, Indiana University

3. DAY, R. L. and LANDON, E. L. (1976) Collecting comprehensive consumer complaint data by survey research. In *Advances in Consumer Research*, Vol. 3, pp. 263–268. Association for Consumer Research

4. DAY, R. L. and LANDON, E. L. (1977) Toward a theory of consumer complaining behaviour. In *Foundations of Consumer and Industrial Buying Behaviour*, pp. 425–437. Ed. by A. G. Woodside, J. N. Sheth and P. Bennett. Amsterdam, American Elsevier

5. HANDY, C. R. (1977) Monitoring consumer satisfaction with food products. In *Conceptualization and Measurement of Consumer Satisfaction and Dissatisfaction*, pp. 215–239. Ed. by H. K. Hunt. Cambridge, Marketing Science Institute

6. LINGOES, J. L. and PFAFF, M. (1977) The index of consumer satisfaction: methodology. In *Proceedings of the Third Annual Conference of the Association for Consumer Research*, pp. 689–712. Ed. by M. Venkatesan. Chicago, Il.: Association for Consumer Research

7. PFAFF, A. (1977) The index of consumer satisfaction. In *Proceedings of the Third Annual Conference of the Association for Consumer Research*, pp. 713–737. Ed. by M. Venkatesan. Chicago, Il.: Association for Consumer Research

8. PFAFF, M. (1977) The index of consumer satisfaction: management problems and opportunities. In *Conceptualization and Measurement of Consumer Satisfaction and Dissatisfaction*, pp. 36–71. Ed. by H. K. Hunt. Cambridge, Marketing Science Institute

9. WARLAND, R. H., HERMANN, O. and WILLITS, J. (1975) Dissatisfied consumers: who gets upset and who takes what action? *Journal of Consumer Affairs*, 148–163

Chapter 11

A comparative study of urban food distribution systems in Latin America and the Middle East

Erdener Kaynak

Introduction

Modern distribution, especially the distribution of food, is a vital requirement particularly in the rapidly growing urban centres of less developed countries. In these countries, it is generally observed that in the process of economic development, the creation of new production capacity receives the limelight. However, it is often overlooked that industry cannot exist or grow without equally modern distribution facilities. This chapter focuses on two aspects of modernization of food distribution which are both inter-related: the creation of vertically and later horizontally integrated distribution systems, and the appearance of innovations in food distribution, particularly in retailing.

The major premise of this chapter is that there are similarities between food distribution systems in the Latin American countries and the Middle East. The applicability of the comparative approach to the study of distribution systems requires recognition that the differences in distributive practices in various countries are as important as the similarities. Such contrasts are essential elements in a comparative analysis. For this reason, it is not adequate to simply describe distribution in one particular country. The critical element in comparative distribution in less developed countries is the manner in which experience gained in developed countries is interpreted, related and generalized[2,23]. Unfortunately, few studies of this kind have been undertaken in less developed countries; this made a comparative approach particularly necessary.

Distribution systems in less developed countries

The food distribution system in most less developed countries is still largely based on a traditional retail structure which consists mainly of small-scale groceries and of a large number of specialized retailers and public markets. It is pointed out that most of these retailers have rather small sales volumes, the efficiency of their operation is low and their sales prices are comparatively high, and the goods they handle are limited. Many of those found in small towns and neighbourhood areas of

An earlier version of this chapter appeared as an article in *Food Policy*, 1981, Vol. 6, No. 2, pp. 78–90.

cities are one-man shops, carrying limited stock of merchandise and undertaking no promotion. Large-scale retailing is substantially concentrated in the major cities[8,21,22,28].

In rural and underdeveloped areas of less developed countries, food retailing systems are normally dominated by small retailers, allowing consumers to purchase small quantities near their homes, frequently on credit. For instance, the retailing systems of Thailand and Sri Lanka continue to be a conglomeration of thousands of small retail outlets and public markets, the exact number being unknown. Each retail unit is highly specialized in its range of stock and restricted in its catchment area with the single proprietor still predominant[35,37].

These traditional types of food retail outlets are typically small, carry a poor range of food products of uncertain quality, and lack sanitary facilities. Understocking is common, and retailers offer few services, and only the most elementary accounting records are kept. These institutions generally are an important form of unemployment relief for developing economies. Entry into traditional food retailing is relatively easy because of the low investment and technical skills required. The result is a multiplicity of small food retail outlets characterized by poor management practices. These stores tend to operate with a minimum of space and the scale of operations in most cases is low. For these reasons, the retailer seeks high margin rather than volume[5]. A significant recent development in Turkey and in some of the Latin American countries like Colombia, Brazil and Peru is the gradual decline in the importance of small food retail establishments and the beginning of a trend toward greater concentration among large food retailing units in the last decade. In terms of size as measured by floor space, the relative importance of small food retailers in these countries has been declining as the importance of stores with $50\,m^2$ or less has declined. A trend toward greater concentration among large food retail establishments is evident[17,22].

The organization and structure of the market for food products in less developed countries are a function of certain economic variables such as the size of the market, the nature of the goods, the size of the production units, and the degree of specialization. These variables show a similar pattern throughout the densely populated less developed countries of the world, because they, in turn, are the products of a certain state of economic development. A definite type of food marketing structure whose basic uniformity is eventually ascribable to a certain relationship of factor supplies, i.e. low capital and low natural resources per capita, is to be found throughout this area.

In contrast, those developing economies possessing large natural resources per capita (the sparsely populated developing economies) have a distinctly different marketing structure[33]. Urban food distribution in Latin America and the Middle East is still largely based on a traditional retail structure which consists mainly of small-scale groceries and of a large number of specialized retailers and public markets. Most of these retailers have rather small sales volumes, the efficiency of their operation is low and their sales are comparatively high. One important fact to take into account is that approximately half of the amount of money spent by these consumers on food is paid for marketing services while the other half is received by farmers, livestock owners and fishermen[4,13].

Food distribution systems prevalent in developing economies adjust themselves to the characteristics of the trading community. Conditions vary from country to country. Even within a particular country there may be different groups of consumer classes requiring different retail arrangements[25]. An obvious distinction can be drawn between consumers residing in urban and rural areas; of course, each will require different retail systems. Traditional general stores that are successful in rural areas have competitive difficulties in urban areas. The style of stores prevalent in urban areas have certain difficulties in rural areas. Different classes and different types of customers have different outlooks and patronize different retail stores.

Some studies of domestic marketing and distributive systems in less developed countries describe the existing structure and prescribe that the system should look more like the North American model[26]. The criteria to support these normative models for less developed countries were the improvements in transaction and market structure productivity and efficiency which come from the economies of large scale distribution. These studies clearly recommended that large, modern, low-cost multiline, self-service supermarkets should be put into place alongside the traditional small, one or two person, single-line, high-cost shops[10,14,30].

Food distribution even in urban communities of the Middle East and Latin America appears to be through a highly fragmented system. This type of system is characterized by small, neighbourhood food stores carrying only one line, small sales volume per store and per worker, trade areas which are small and relatively fixed, owners that regard the number of customers and the amount they purchase as stable and inelastic, and owners who are passive and resist change[17,19,22]. The accepted view is that food distribution to urban low income areas of less developed countries is inefficient and that it functions in a fragmented food marketing system with little coordination. This results in high food marketing costs that cause high prices to consumers and low returns to farmers. Consequently, it is generally accepted that inefficient retailing practices are affecting the welfare of the population and the economic growth of these countries[29].

Is Western technology applicable?

The tendency of Western marketing scholars has been to compare the marketing institutions of any less developed country with a developed economy during one or more stages of its development. This is probably done without full recognition of the implications that it holds. Development processes can somehow be hurried along if institutions from developed economies are transplanted into developing economies without paying due attention to the varying environmental conditions prevailing in the recipient country. Understanding the environment in a less developed country helps in understanding the middlemen and the total distribution system because these marketing institutions are a product of their environment. In less developed countries, just as in developed ones, consumer buying habits are a major factor in shaping distribution channel activities. The channel members will capitalize on environmental change by introducing innovations which anticipate trends in the environment. Thus, when supermarkets were first introduced in some west European countries, they were accepted enthusiastically because enough of the market was ready to change from the practice of shopping at several small, limited-line stores.

Several European retailers have innovated: within relatively few years, they have moved from the stage of 'mom and pop' stores to a variety of retailing concepts as advanced as the ones in North America. In so doing, these innovative retail institutions simply telescoped time and leap-frogged several stages of institutional development[34]. Arndt[3] found a tendency for supermarkets to be more prominent and retail establishments to be larger in nations where the gross national product was higher. Temporal lags in the development of retail systems between countries tend to approach the same length as lags in the most important environmental factors. For the five environmental and retail structure syndicates studied, temporal lags in the range of seven to nine years emerged quite consistently. This result shows that the structure of retailing systems is a function of selected characteristics of the societies they serve.

Developed country practices

In Western societies, marketing innovations of this century are, to a large extent, a reflection of the changes in the retailers' environment: increase in discretionary purchasing power, growth of production capacity through technological progress, growth of private automobile ownership and transportation, the movement towards suburbia and changes in consumer attitudes. Institutional changes take place slowly; for this reason, retailing institutions, like product specialized stores, are a function of the environmental factors of the immediate past[36]. The factors which created the introduction of supermarkets in the USA were favourable in 1932 when the first supermarket was established in New Jersey. It was established to provide customers with low-cost food and variety of other products. In the depression of the 1930s, this form of self-service retailing was one of the mechanisms for cutting distribution costs to make consumer staples accessible to the unemployed. People were willing to give up the wide variety of services such as credit, delivery, and friendliness which the small food stores provided. Supermarkets spread quickly during the later years and by the 1970s they accounted for more than 70% of retail food sales. The growth of supermarkets in the USA was the result of several important environmental factors.

First, the US population has become highly mobile. With better roads, people began to move away from the centre cities to the suburbs where they enjoyed the benefits of single family dwellings. Car ownership, as a result of substantial increases in personal disposable income, increased quickly. Food shopping became a task for which people were willing to spend the extra time and effort to go to a single store where they could purchase most of their food and non-food needs for a period of a week or more. Because of the costs of the introduction of technology from manufacturers to retail food stores, large retail firms were required to perform the activities from production to wholesale and retail themselves. With the introduction of technology came better means of packaging, preserving, and handling food products. The small independent food store could no longer find economic reasons to exist[2,11]. However, in the last decade, with the dramatic change in the shopping behaviour of most Americans, the number of convenience store units has more than tripled and all indications are that this figure will only continue to grow, as many of the larger chains indicate that they plan to add units at a rate of about 10% a year for the next five years[12].

Less developed country practices

Marketing experts of less developed countries try to apply the marketing and distributive institutions of the West to their countries. These marketing institutions and techniques are conditioned by the immediate environment and the unique culture of Western countries. By making proper adaptation perhaps both less developed country planners and the distributive institutions may overcome certain difficulties which were encountered by the developed countries' planners during their implementation of the various marketing techniques and institutions in their home countries.

Too often, US and West European marketers are inclined to assume that effective marketing institutions and methods of the West would be equally successful in the less developed countries if introduced and implemented with Western 'know-how'. But, these institutions should not be adopted without considering their applicability. Furthermore, to improve the value of such adaptation, a better understanding of the evolution pattern and development of marketing institutions such as supermarkets in developed countries is needed. For this reason, proper implementation of the retailing institutions and methods of the West requires sound understanding of the historical development of these practices[18].

Food marketing practices of the last two decades in most less developed countries have shown that the mere transfer of marketing technology from the West is not sufficient. There is a strong need for a proper adaptation by paying particular attention to environmental factors which hinder or encourage the development of supermarketing practices in those countries.

Another concern is that mass marketing technology of the West is too big and too expensive. It does not create the jobs needed to absorb the rapidly expanding labour force in the less developed countries, and it is not appropriate for their small distributive institutions that make up so much of the economic activity in these countries. The customary Western marketing systems evidently do not bring about the desired reorientations of marketing technology. Using the final price to the consumer as an independent measure of performance, study findings point to the conclusion that the traditional food retailing structure is more suitable for their current needs than generally assumed. For instance, the high-margin, high-selling price factor was not verified. The indication is that low volume retailing firms in developing economies might be more efficient than theory would lead one to believe[1].

Barriers to change and development

The retailing system takes a great deal of the blame for the inefficiency of the food distribution system in less developed countries. This may be caused by conspicuous characteristics of the retail structure and of retailing practices: the numerous small shops and market vendors who handle low volumes with little investment, the poor sanitation conditions, the inaccurate measurement tools used, the low labour productivity and the high wastage. It was argued that the net result of this is the perception that the consumer is paying a higher price for his goods than he would if 'modern' distributive techniques were used.

Modern distributive techniques by these people are generally characterized as those used by mass retailers who handle large volumes and operate with high merchandise turnover with a selling area of more than 300 m^2 and include: self-service, prepackaged goods, refrigeration equipment for storage and self-service, check-out counters, mechanical handling methods and a sanitary selling environment[29].

Why is it that mass-marketing technology has spread from the USA and helped to deliver a high living standard to 30% of the world but has not been adopted adequately to serve the basic needs of the poor masses in rural and urban areas of less developed countries? From the consumer's perspective, modern food marketing has been inhibited by: a disproportionately high demand for staples; the lack of ready cash; the cultural pattern of daily buying at traditional retail outlets; the dependence on public transportation for shopping mobility and the lack of appropriate storage and refrigeration capability. From the retailer's point of view, small-scale retailing practices with their low volume, low investment characteristics and the lack of management training and motivation seem to pose barriers to modernization.

To overcome the deficiencies of the food distribution systems in less developed countries, the adoption of horizontal and vertical coordination and the introduction of modern large scale retail institutions into the distribution system of these countries has been recommended by some researchers[15,31,32]. The same people are not at all explicit, however, concerning how the introduction of supermarkets and resultant horizontal and vertical integration would correct those deficiencies of the food distribution systems of less developed countries. Studies of comparative marketing systems show that a number of barriers exist which deter the adoption of new marketing and distribution practices and structures. Academics have developed certain checklists for examining the market opportunities in different countries and the factors which serve as obstacles to identical strategies being used internationally[7].

The barriers to changing marketing and distribution systems from the way they existed to the way analysts recommended are usually called 'the environmental factors'. Economic, social, political, legal, cultural and physical conditions and variations result in differing local and national values and consumption patterns[24]. These environmental factors affect the food distribution system primarily through their impact on the food distributive institutions. The environment contains certain operating conditions which limit the scope of the institutions' activity and affect their organizational structure. Among the environmental factors studied, the most significant one is the consumer environment.

Studies have indicated that the structure of food distribution systems is a function of selected characteristics of the societies they serve. In North America, the retail innovations of this century are, to a large extent, a reflection of the changes in the retailers' environment. Retailing and marketing institutions are a function of the environmental factors of the immediate past period. Retailing practices may be said to be a function of the environmental factors of the same period. In less developed countries, the environmental factors affecting the operations of retailers are not the same as the ones in developed countries. For this reason, proper analysis of the different environmental conditions affecting any marketing institution and its operations need to be made before embarking on transferring any marketing technique or institution to less developed countries of the world[9].

It has been noted previously that not only is the overall pattern of the food distribution system and its operations in the Middle East and Latin America less advanced than that found in North America, but within each region the nature of the food distribution system and its practices tend to vary. Certain patterns of food distribution systems and institutions and their practices tend to correspond with the incidence and operations of certain factors which are operating in the environment within which food distributive institutions of all kinds are found.

Less developed countries are characterized by a continuous increase in income and population density. This constitutes an ever present source of pressure on food distributors for the appearance of new forms of marketing institutions in their food distribution systems to meet the ever increasing wants and needs of the food shoppers. That is the reason why the interaction taking place between the food marketing system and the surrounding environment is complex.

The new marketing institution, such as the supermarket, is subject to several limitations: the number of potential customers, their incomes, their social and economic make-up which influence the type of distributive institutions operated in a less developed country. Each of these sets a different limit on the number of units demanded for the new marketing institution.

Likewise, the number of units that could be set-up in a given part of Latin America or the Middle East is subject to a variety of limitations: available managerial talent, financial, resources, initiative and capital which are considered as input variables, each of which sets a different limit on the number that could be operated profitably. It must be pointed out here that the growth of the new marketing institutions is, to a certain extent, contingent upon easing the most restrictive limiting input stimuli.

As in any other distribution system, there has been a change and rapid development in the distributive systems of Latin America and the Middle East. This involves looking at all changes in the distributive environment (social, economic, and operational) as well as distributors' responses to them. Of course, such environmental changes are, to a large extent, beyond the control of the distributors. For this reason, such environmental conditions should be taken into consideration and the necessary adaptations be made while designing a distribution system for a less developed country. Among all the environmental factors, the most significant ones are the consumer and government environments. Certain characteristics of less developed country consumers and governments serve as a constraint on the development of modern distributive institutions such as supermarkets and that only when certain changes occur does it become possible for these institutions to develop and prosper.

Consumer environment of food distributors

In the rapidly growing cities of Latin America and the Middle East, the socioeconomic environment of food distributors is extremely heterogeneous. There are acute disparities of income, education and lifestyle among the residents of these cities which make it very difficult for both government officials and businessmen to design food distribution systems that can adequately meet the needs of all segments of the market[16,20].

Many of the food consumers in less developed countries in the lower income classes for instance remain tied to shopping in traditional general stores and public markets and do not generally patronize the modern food retail institutions because they are unable and therefore unwilling to pay any extra for the services offered by modern distribution systems. These low-income consumers simply do not have enough income. Limited storage capabilities in the typical house, and desire of the housewife to socialize with culturally rooted patterns encourage the high frequency of food shopping trips.

That is the reason why food distribution systems serving consumers in most parts of Latin America and the Middle East with these characteristics seem to be totally conditioned by them. The consumers being sparsely scattered, the distribution system serving them is fragmented. Consumers buy in small quantities and frequently. As a result of such shopping patterns and other factors, the retail distribution structure encountered in simple retail systems is characterized by a large number of small grocery stores carrying only a few lines of products. When private enterprise introduces supermarkets in less developed countries, it tends to place them in high and middle income areas simply because there is not enough buying power in low income neighbourhoods.

Thus, an institution, which in North America caters adequately for the basic needs of the masses, becomes exclusive in less developed countries, bringing the benefits of mass marketing to those who least need them[27]. There is not much concern on the part of these large food retail institutions operating in upper and middle-class areas with the needs and wants of consumers residing in the lower income brackets of an area. The effect of consumer environment of the food distributors is shown in *Figure 11.1.*

Food shoppers in Latin America and the Middle East are generally willing to devote more time to shop for food than those in developed countries. Furthermore, they are not able to make large purchases at infrequent intervals. This is true in general because of the small amount of cash they have to spend and, in particular

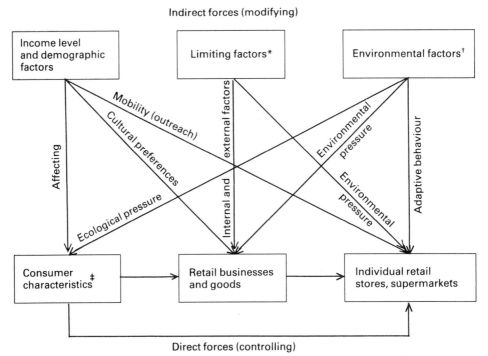

Figure 11.1. System approach to food distribution. Notes: *Capital, labour, financial resources, initiative, management talent, know-how, location and site. †Urbanization, government, competition, suppliers, consumerism. ‡Culture, population make-up, income distribution, social class, family make-up, education

for food, because of the lack of refrigeration. With limited means of transportation and because of the friendliness of the small food retailers, most of the less developed country consumers prefer to buy from stores within easy walking distance, i.e. within a one kilometre radius. Thus a food distribution system which is composed of a great many small food retail outlets, distributed throughout a community, is more appropriate to their needs.

Over the last two decades, much of the literature on the improvement of food distribution systems in less developed countries has placed heavy emphasis upon the transfer of capital intensive technology originating mainly in the USA. The small-scale, limited-line retailers, and the lengthy, poorly coordinated distribution chain that serves them have been identified as inefficient market elements. The literature holds that a modern system of vertically integrated chains would provide substantial benefits through scale economies, the adoption of self-service, and the bypassing of clogged wholesale food markets[6].

It is difficult to transfer capital intensive distributive techniques to the Middle East and Latin America with reasonable success. The USA, for example, has been an important nation for two centuries; it has abundant resources and expertise, and received its human capital through immigration. Today, most of the countries in the Middle East and Latin America are generally short on resources and lack of know-how. It is difficult to transfer US marketing technology, which is a product of historical and economic conditions, to a completely dissimilar environment.

For that reason, certain difficulties are inherent in transferring technology like supermarketing and horizontal integration from the USA to less developed countries. Making technology available is not the same as transferring technology[18]. At present, it is evident that there are a number of large food retail stores operating mostly in urban areas of Latin America and the Middle East. It seems that these countries, like most other less developed countries, are not ready for the food distributive innovations of the West.

Conclusions and policy recommendations

The marketing institutions like capital intensive distributive institutions; their operational methods and techniques can only be introduced into the Middle East and Latin America when the forces in the environment permit. There cannot then be an instance of the most appropriate or advanced retail institutions and techniques, since what is most appropriate will be different from one environment to another. A retailing system can be meaningfully 'advanced' or 'underdeveloped' depending only upon whether the environment in which that system operates is advanced or underdeveloped. If this is the case, the nature of the relationship can be speculated in more specific terms than simply advanced or underdeveloped. If we can identify the stages of socioeconomic development, then we should be able to predict in general terms the kind of retail pattern which is found associated with a given stage of development.

The policy implications suggested here are designed to institute change as an evolutionary process of the present food distribution systems rather than as a revolution in the food distribution institutions and their operational techniques. It must be pointed out here that changes in food distribution systems of the Middle East and Latin America will ultimately depend upon simultaneous changes in the infrastructure surrounding retailing systems. These changes may be the enabling conditions that will make the retailing changes possible.

The best way to design a kind of food distribution system for less developed countries will be by working on the existing food distribution institutions of the Middle East and Latin America which can be suitably modified for that purpose. Action programmes to improve the performance of the traditional food distribution structure could be undertaken by governments, community groups such as retailer or consumer cooperatives or by business enterprises. The existing small food retailers of less developed countries cannot grow to the large volume of sales by a programme of reducing prices to generate more volume to enable further price reductions. The reason for this is that these stores are perceived as charging high prices, offering low quality of goods, and having no desirable attributes other than locational convenience, the friendliness of the store personnel and offering some credit facilities. The operators of these small food stores must be able to sense consumer dissatisfaction and be able to discover the causes of such dissatisfaction. They must also be prepared to remedy them.

The pattern of change in food distribution is complicated because it involves the interaction of many different elements. Changes in product lines can bring about changes in sales size which, in turn, permit changes in operating methods and personnel utilization. However, it may be that the operating changes may have to occur first in time, to attract customer attention and thus make possible the changes in merchandise assortment and total sales.

An essential element in this process of change is the preservation of locational convenience and mass merchandising for food shoppers. The food store should carry a complete food line, but within each category of foods only the high turnover items. This model store differs considerably from the convenience store found in the USA where its main function is to complement services of conventional supermarkets. Convenience stores in the USA are used by consumers to make small unplanned purchases that were not included in the weekly shopping trip to the supermarket. In both Latin America and the Middle East, neither the length of the shopping trip nor the mode of travel are likely to change easily for the consumers of these two regions in the foreseeable future. Therefore, most food distribution innovations will take place within existing shopping areas. This requirement suggests a process of gradual adaptation rather than a revolutionary obsolescence and replacement of existing food distribution facilities.

References

1. ADAMS, K. A. (1970) Resources utilization by meat retailers in a developing economy. *Business Perspectives*, p. 16
2. APPEL, D. (1972) The supermarket: early development of an institutional innovation. *Journal of Retailing*, **48**, 39–52
3. ARNDT, J. (1972) Temporal lags in comparative retailing. *Journal of Marketing*, **36**, 45
4. BOYD, H. W. (1961) Marketing in Egypt. *Proceedings of the American Marketing Association*, pp. 419–424. Chicago, Illinois
5. BOYD, H. W. and SHERBINI, A. A. (1961) Channels of distribution for consumer goods in Egypt. *Journal of Marketing*, Oct., 26–33
6. BUCKLIN, L. P. (1977) Improving food retailing in developing Asian countries. *Food Policy*, **2** (2), 114
7. BUZZELL, R. D. (1968) Can you standardize multinational marketing? *Harvard Business Review*, Nov.–Dec., 102–113
8. CANAS, W. (1961) Food retailing practice in Chile. *Journal of Retailing*, **37**, 32–33
9. CRANCH, G. (1973) Modern marketing techniques applied to developing countries. In *Marketing Education and the Real World and Dynamic Marketing in a Changing World*, Series No. 34, p. 183. Ed. by B. W. Beeker. Chicago, Illinois
10. DOUGLAS, S. P. (1971) Patterns and parallels of marketing structures in several countries. *MSU Business Topics*, Spring, 38

11. DUNCAN, D. J. (1965) Responses of selected retail institutions to their changing environment. In *Marketing and Economic Development*, pp. 583–602. Ed. by P. D. Bennett. Chicago, American Marketing Association

12. EDITORIAL (1979) Convenience stores. *Progressive Grocer*, **58**, 133

13. FAO (1973) *Report of the Technical Conference on the Development of Food Marketing Systems in Large Urban Areas in Latin America*, pp. 8–17. Rome, FAO

14. GOLDMAN, A. (1974) Outreach of consumers and the modernization of urban food retailing in developing countries. *Journal of Marketing*, Oct., 8–16

15. GUERIN, J. R. (1974) Limitations of supermarkets in Spain. *Journal of Marketing*, **23**, 21

16. GUTHRIE, C. B. (1972) *Food Distribution in a Latin American City (Cali, Colombia)*, p. 278. PhD Thesis, Michigan State University

17. HARRISON, K., HENLEY, D., WISH, J. and HARRISON, K. (1974) *Improving Food Marketing Systems in Developing Countries: Experiences from Latin America*. Research Report No. 6, pp. 26–55. Latin American Studies Center, Michigan State University

18. IZRAELI, D. (1974) *Priorities for Research and Development in Marketing Systems for Developing Countries*. Working paper No. 209/74. Tel Aviv University, Tel Aviv

19. KAIKATI, J. G. (1976) The marketing environment in Saudi Arabia. *Akron Business and Economic Review*, **7**, 10–11

20. KAYNAK, E. (1975) *Comparative Analysis of Food Retailing Systems in Urban Turkey*, p. 461. PhD Thesis. Cranfield Institute of Technology, UK

21. KAYNAK, E. (1976) Food retailing systems in developing countries: the case of Turkey. *Hacettepe Bulletin of Social Sciencies and Humanities*, **8**, 41

21a. KAYNAK, E. (1977) Some theoretical foundations for the appearance of new retail institutions in developing countries. Presented at the Annual Meeting of the European Academy for Advanced Research in Marketing. Sixth Annual Workshop on Research in Marketing, pp. IX–I to IX–II. Saarbrucken, West Germany

22. KAYNAK, E. (1978) Changes in the food retailing institutions of urban Turkey: the Istanbul experience. *Studies in Development*, **18**, 53–71

23. KAYNAK, E. (1979) A refined approach to the wheel of retailing concept. *European Journal of Marketing*, **13**, 237–245

24. LANDE, I. M. (1967) Consumer marketing development in emerging economies. In *Marketing for Tomorrow Today*, pp. 251–253. Ed. by M. S. Moyer and R. E. Vosburg. Chicago, Illinois: American Marketing Association, Conference Proceedings Series No. 25.

25. LATIN AMERICAN STUDIES CENTER (1974) *Fomenting Improvements in Food Marketing in Costa Rica*. Research Report No. 10, Latin American Studies Center, Michigan State University

26. LIPSON, H. A. (1976) The impact of double digit inflation upon the modernization of the retail structure in developed and developing economies. In *1975 Combined Proceedings*, Series No. 37, p. 315. Ed. by E. M. Mazze. Chicago, Illinois: American Marketing Association

27. MEISSNER, F. (1978) Rise of Third World 'demands marketing be stood on its head'. *Marketing News*, 6 Oct., p. 1

28. MUNN, H. L. (1966) Retailing in Nigeria. *Journal of Retailing*, **24**, 26–32

29. PAIZ, R. E. (1974) *Experimenting with New Concepts of Retail Food Distribution in a Developing Environment*, pp. 1-1–2. Instituto Centro-amercano de Empresas (INCAE), Managua, Nicaragua

30. SLATER, C. C. (1965) The role of food marketing in Latin American economic development. In *Proceedings of the 1965 Conference, Marketing and Economic Development*, pp. 30–37. Chicago, American Marketing Association

31. SLATER, C. C., HENLEY, D., WISH, J. and HARRISON, K. (1960) *Market Processes in La Paz, Bolivia*. Michigan, Michigan State University

32. SLATER, C. C., RILEY, H. *et al.* (1969) *Market Processes in the Recife Area of Northeast Brazil*, Chap. 6. Michigan, Michigan State University

33. SOLOMON, M. R. (1948) The structure of the market in underdeveloped economies. *Quarterly Journal of Economics*, Aug., 519–540

34. SORENSON, R. Z. (1972) US marketeers can learn from European innovators. *Harvard Business Review*, Sept.–Oct, 89–99

35. WADINAMBIARATCHI, G. (1970) Food retailing institutions in Ceylon. *Vidyodaya Journal of Arts, Sciences and Letters*, **3**, 89–110

36. WADINAMBIARATCHI, G. (1972) The theories of retail development. *Social and Economic Studies*, **4**, 392–394

37. WIGGLESWORTH, E. F. (1966) Retailing trends in Thailand. *Journal of Retailing*, **42**, 41–51

Chapter 12

Food prices and food policy analysis in less developed countries

C. Peter Timmer

Introduction

Two very different views of the role of food prices in the economic development process have dominated thinking in academic and decision-makers' circles since the Second World War. General development economists, following the implications of the classical economic growth model developed by Arthur Lewis and others, argued that food prices should be kept low to keep real wages low and thus promote rapid industrialization. A variant of this argument emerged primarily in the Latin American context, where the structural analysts argued that food prices are irrelevant to the long-run development process since both producers and consumers are insensitive to changes in prices. Consequently, political leaders can feel free to manipulate food prices for whatever short-run political effect is desirable. Usually this manipulation takes the form of keeping urban food prices low to satisfy workers, politically active students, and the urban middle class. The basic article outlining the industrialization strategy through low food prices is by Lewis[14]. Most of the subsequent two sector models build on this Lewis restatement of the classical growth model. (*See,* for example, Fei and Ranis[5].) The structuralist perspective is presented in Grunwald[9] and a succinct review is contained in Weisskoff[37].

The second, or neoclassical, view holds that food prices are a critical factor in farmers' decisions about which crops to grow and how intensively to grow them, even in fairly traditional peasant economies. In the presence of new biological and chemical technologies that offer significantly higher yields for basic food crops when used properly, price incentives become the major factor in determining yields. As empirical evidence has been gathered over the last decade demonstrating a dramatic long-run response to price, this neoclassical view has increasingly been pushed on leaders of less developed countries who are urged to set their prices carefully. The empirical evidence is reviewed by Timmer[32]; more detailed discussions are in Timmer and Falcon[35] and Peterson[17]. The production-oriented neoclassical policy advice is most clearly argued in Schultz[26].

This chapter attempts to reconcile these two views of the role of food prices. It does this by examining the role of prices in the production sector, where the evidence for impact in both the short run and long run is quite persuasive. In other

This chapter was originally an article in *Food Policy,* 1980, Vol. 5, No. 3, pp. 188–199.

words, as far as it goes the neoclassical perspective is correct. But food prices play two important roles that neoclassical analysis has largely ignored on an empirical basis:

- The differential impact on levels of food consumption (and hence on nutritional status) by poor and rich households. Serious constraints on data and on modelling methodology have prevented significant empirical investigation of this important issue. The issue of the statistical base for the analysis of problems of hunger and malnutrition is discussed by Hay[10]. Consequently, this chapter will report in some detail the results of attempts to understand the differential impact of food prices in Indonesia.
- The mechanisms by which short-run and long-run food prices determine the distribution of household income levels.

When these two added dimensions of the impact of food prices are included in the neoclassical analysis, the policy advice to 'get prices right' becomes much more complicated than assuring farmers prices determined by world markets and realistic foreign exchange rates. Indeed, the income distribution and differential consumption effects of food price changes legitimize much of the short-run political concern over urban food prices, even if the advice based on the classical growth model or structuralist analysis is faulty on empirical grounds. The chapter concludes, then, with a discussion of the role of food prices in the policy process and the type of analysis modern political economies need to cope with the complex trade-offs in an inter-related multistaple food system.

The production sector

Direct roles

Traditional economic theory and more than half a century of empirical investigation confirm three important direct roles for prices in the production sector: in the choice of crops to be grown, in the choice of technologies used to grow the crops, and in the choice of input levels needed to produce output levels, i.e. of aggregate agricultural output.

The evidence is overwhelming that farmers are quite sensitive to changes in relative output prices between alternative feasible crops. Where permitted (and frequently even where they are not), farmers change the crops they plant in close correspondence to their relative profitability which, for given technologies and input prices, will depend directly on the relative farm gate prices. Krishna's review of estimated price elasticities for long-run acreage response reports values greater than one for cotton and jute in pre-war India and Pakistan, and values exceeding 0.5 for important food crops for much of the developing world[13]. Clearly, the composition of agricultural output is largely determined by the relative prices farmers receive for their produce, although the evidence from rich countries suggests that farmers move into major specialty crops, such as tobacco and sugar, more easily than they move out.

The type of technology used by farmers and within the food system more generally also depends on food prices. The issue here is the nature of the production process itself and particularly whether it should be capital or labour intensive. With low food prices in poor countries, few peasants are able to afford modern agricultural equipment; the level of food prices determines whether capital-intensive agricultural techniques are feasible without government subsidy.

The choice between capital and labour intensive farming depends on the relative factor prices, i.e. how expensive capital is relative to farm labour in the face of their differential contribution to output. Barker has shown that four-wheeled tractors make relatively small productivity contributions for much of Asian agriculture and need subsidies to compete with labour in most settings[1]. Similarly, the appropriate choice of rice milling technology in Java is neither hand-pounding nor large rice mills. Small rice mills are optimal under a fairly wide range of factor and output price conditions likely to prevail in Indonesia. (The evidence is presented by Timmer[29].) Again, prices are the crucial variables in the socially desirable choice once the technical productivities of the alternatives are understood. It must be emphasized, however, that improving technical productivities of inputs is at least as important for raising the profitability of food production as manipulating the relative prices of inputs and outputs.

The most debated role for prices is their influence in determining the aggregate level of agricultural output. Griliches found a response of total US agricultural output to agricultural prices relative to input prices, i.e. the parity ratio, of only 0.15, but argued that his figure was a lower bound to the true value[8]. Similar searches within a single country's historical evidence have proven equally low or inconclusive. However, recent analyses of combined time series (historical) and cross section data (from many countries) do reveal significant and substantial short-run and long-run responses of total agricultural output to relative prices.

Evidence from the Stanford Project on the Political Economy of Rice in Asia indicates a yield elasticity for rice production (with constant rice and other cropped areas) of 0.14 when varieties and cultivation techniques are kept constant, and 0.33 when these can also change in response to price incentives. (The overall project is described in Timmer[30]; the yield response evidence is reviewed in Timmer[31]. A much more detailed treatment of the empirical evidence is in David[4].) The strikingly positive relationship between the relative price of rice to fertilizer and per hectare rice yields for ten important Asian rice producers and the USA is shown in *Figure 12.1*.

Peterson has recently extended this type of analysis to include total agricultural output for 20 developed and 33 less developed food-producing countries. Despite significant problems in defining both output and prices for such a diverse group of countries, his results are significant and robust. The long-run price elasticity of agricultural output appears to be about 1.25[17].

Indirect roles

The long-run impact of prices on agricultural production depends partly on letting the direct effects discussed above accumulate and gradually take hold. But three areas of indirect impact also contribute to a more significant long-run price response: the rate of adoption of new technology, agricultural research directions and its social pay-off and the directions and effectiveness of institutional change.

The factors determining the rate of diffusion of new agricultural technology have been studied quite intensively for several decades. The profitability of the new technology relative to existing varieties or techniques is the most powerful factor explaining the speed and magnitude of its impact on national agricultural productivity. Given the risks of experimenting with new techniques and varieties in traditional agricultural settings, this price impact works more slowly than farmers' adjustments in fertilizer use when prices change.

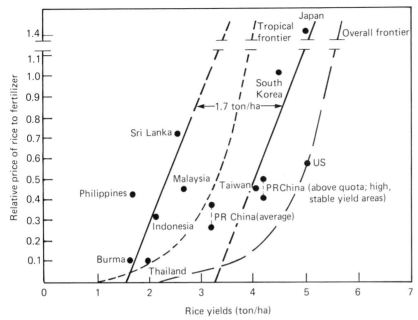

Figure 12.1. Relationship between rice yields and the rice price to fertilizer price ratio in selected countries, 1970

Vernon Ruttan has been the leading proponent of a long-run role for prices in the agricultural sector that is ultimately more powerful than any discussed so far. The induced innovation hypothesis grows out of the recognition of severe limits to agricultural growth from factors of production in abundant supply, such as labour, in many Asian countries. The nature of the agricultural production process is such that strongly diminishing returns are likely when any single factor is used very intensively. Consequently, few growth opportunities exist using traditional agricultural techniques for countries with unbalanced factor endowments (the most important presentation of this perspective is in Schultz[25]).

In response to food prices rising relative to the prices of the abundant factors of production, societies find it profitable to invest in research that supplements the availability of scarce factors of production, such as land in Asia, while being complementary to the abundant factors. Thus, Japan invested heavily in biological and chemical innovations to raise yields per hectare in the face of severe land constraints and rising agricultural land prices. The fertilizer-responsive seeds developed by Japanese scientists thus extended the productivity potential of Japan's scarcest agricultural resource while complementing its abundant labour supply.

In the USA, land was the abundant resource but agricultural wages were rising (relative to food prices). The response of both public and private agricultural research organizations was to discover mechanical innovations that saved scarce labour while complementing the land. The result was rapidly rising labour productivity as a major source of agricultural productivity growth, the mirror image of Japan's rising land productivity as its primary growth source. The induced innovation model was originally presented by Hayami and Ruttan[11] and an excellent summary appears in Ruttan[24].

Even the research institutions themselves seem to evolve in response to perceived social problems. No society has managed to transform its agricultural sector from a subsistence-based to a highly productive commercial sector without major public support for the research establishment that provides the scientific and technological base for such a transformation. The emergence of national and state agricultural research stations in the nineteenth and early twentieth centuries was a clear signal of the recognition of a social role in food production. Similarly, the emerging network of international agricultural research centres, including one for policy research, is attempting to generate a technical base for tropical agriculture that most less developed countries cannot yet afford or manage on their own. The emergence of these institutions in the absence of significant food shortages would be difficult to imagine. The theory of induced institutional innovation is developed by Binswanger and Ruttan[3]. It is interesting to note that the US Government did not support the development of international agricultural research institutes such as IRRI and CIMMYT until after the grain shortages and high food prices caused by the Indian drought in 1966 and 1967.

The consumption sector

Ample economic analysis and business evidence confirm that consumers substitute between various commodities as their relative prices change. This is increasingly true as the commodity becomes more narrowly defined and, hence, as the scope for substitution increases. Consumers may find it quite difficult to substitute between food and non-food items, although they shift quite flexibly between chicken and turkey when the relative prices shift significantly. But farmers do not grow food or non-food and the scope for consumption changes of particular commodities is extremely important for agricultural policy purposes. Traditionally this was the major reason for analysing consumption patterns, to determine how much and which crops farmers should be encouraged to grow.

The overall market changes in consumption induced by price changes are composed of changes from thousands and millions of individual households, and each household reacts to price changes according to its own circumstances. These circumstances depend on a host of individual factors including tastes, household composition, knowledge, and social background. Most important, consumption response to food price changes depends critically on the household's income level.

Understanding the extent to which consumers at different income levels change their food intake as food prices change is extremely important, for only with such information is it possible to trace the impact of food price changes on nutritional status of at-risk populations. The impetus to do this comes from economic planners concerned about guaranteeing basic needs and from nutritionists concerned about the nutritional status of populations at risk. This broader food policy analysis is just now receiving serious methodological and empirical treatment, but several diverse threads of research have been reported, including: Pinstrup-Anderson et al.[18,19] attempting to measure the consumption impact by commodity and urban income class of neutral supply shifts and of changes in income distribution; McCarthy and Taylor[15], and Taylor[27] attempting to incorporate a foodgrain sector explicitly in a consistent macroplanning model disaggregated into three urban and three rural income strata, and the author's attempts[33,34] to model the impact of foodgrain prices on the size of the calorie deficit in a Reutlinger–Selowsky[23] type analysis.

Policy impact is traced through one of three mechanisms: price effects, exogenous income effects, and endogenous income effects. Pinstrup-Anderson *et al.* have investigated the impact of a shift in food supply curves (a possible food supply policy) on the calorie and protein intake of various income strata of urban households in Cali, Colombia. This is the simplest of all possible policy effects to trace out because there is a single chain of causation from food supply policy through price effects to nutritional, i.e. consumption, impact on the urban households. Even so, the methodology requires a full own-price and cross-price elasticity matrix by income strata to translate food price changes into income-strata-specific consumption changes and a full set of market equations to translate neutral supply shifts into price changes.

Extending the analysis to broader policies (food marketing or economic development policies) or to other vulnerable groups (the landless rural poor or subsistence-oriented small farmers) adds entirely new dimensions to the complexity of the impact. Exogenous income effects via changed employment patterns or opportunities and endogenous income effects for farmers due to output or price changes must be added to the price effects. Income-strata-specific income elasticities will be needed to translate the income changes into consumption changes. Much more difficult will be the corresponding functional relationships that translate the policy changes into income-strata-specific income changes. For the exogenous income effects it will be necessary to specify any changes in employment and/or wages (by income class) caused by the policies under analysis. The endogenous income effects are especially difficult to specify because they depend on both output and price components. Both of these, but especially the output component, are likely to vary systematically by income strata.

More important, the translation of policy change into resulting effects on prices and incomes must necessarily be done in the specific political, social, and economic context of the change itself. For instance, any price changes due to a shift in supply will depend on whether the country is an importer or exporter, the state of the marketing sector, and existing institutional mechanisms of price formation. Similarly, the income effects of a marketing change will depend on the extent of open or disguised unemployment, choice of technique in processing and distribution, and mechanisms of wage formation. It is difficult to generalize about these in the absence of a significant number of reliable agricultural sector models able to trace through price and income effects by income class. No such models exist at present, although several models are able to trace these effects without disaggregating income.

McCarthy and Taylor[15] have constructed a fully integrated and consistent macroeconomic food policy model that traces through the nutritional (protein–calorie) impact of policy changes on three urban and three rural income groups in Pakistan. The complexity of such an undertaking is obvious and significant simplifications were needed to make the model computable. The translation of policy changes into income-class-specific income changes is one area where such simplification was necessary. Production in all sectors of the economy is presumed to take place according to Cobb–Douglas technology and income groups share in the resulting income generated according to the factor elasticities distributed by fixed weights. Useful as the assumptions are for computation purposes, they do considerable violence to reality. Much more sensitive techniques are needed for tracing income distribution impacts of policy changes even if they must resort to *ad hoc* and case-by-case analyses.

Regardless of the subgroup or type of policy being considered, at the heart of the analysis is a matrix of price and income elasticities that must be income strata specific. Obtaining this matrix for aggregated income classes requires a blend of complex theory and sophisticated data analysis that is only possible with restrictive assumptions about the separability of the impact of price changes for one commodity class on changes in demand for other commodity groups. This econometric approach builds on the pioneering consumption modelling of Ragnar Frisch and the availability of powerful statistical techniques for use on large computers[2,6,7,20,21,28].

The separability assumptions are fairly restrictive even in the context of highly aggregated commodities such as food, housing, clothing, and so on. But when important nutritional effects occur due to the substitution of equal money values of one quality of wheat for another, or the substitution of cassava for rice, then the level of commodity detail needed to accurately reproduce the impact of relative price changes forecloses the econometric approach even for combined income classes. Obtaining the full price and income elasticity matrix for disaggregated income classes requires innovations in modelling consumer reactions to price and income changes.

Research on Indonesian food expenditure data is pursuing this issue. It involves estimation of specific commodity demand functions using detailed cross-section household food expenditure surveys. The use of cross-section data to derive price elasticities has been limited for fairly obvious reasons. Households are sampled only once at a particular time when the prices they face are given. If the whole sample is taken during a brief period, e.g. one week, then the only price variation observed will be due to spatial differences.

These price differences will, by necessity, be faced by different households which may have different tastes. In such a situation it is difficult to infer causality to regionally different consumption patterns even when prices are different. However, the Indonesian Socio-Economic Survey V (1976) (Susenas) drew a large sample over enough geographical and temporal diversity to capture significant variance in the relevant variables. With three separate samples of 18 000 households drawn in each trimester of 1976, the sample is large enough so that cell means can be used as observations for analysis. This smoothes out most individual taste differences but leaves adequate variations in incomes and prices for statistical analysis.

Currently, the analysis deals only with rice, fresh cassava, and total calorie intake from rice, fresh cassava, and corn. Attempts to unravel the factors influencing shelled corn consumption alone have not been successful and data for gaplek, a form of dried cassava important to the poor, are not yet available for analysis. Since rice, corn, and fresh cassava are the three most important foodstuffs for most Indonesian consumers, accounting for about two-thirds of average calorie intake, whatever functional specification and approach is ultimately chosen must permit accurate estimation of the factors determining their use.

A summary of the important consumption elasticities for rice and fresh cassava is shown in *Table 12.1*, which indicates that the coefficients are large in absolute size and vary significantly by income class. Such income-class-specific price and income elasticities are critical for any food policy analysis that attempts to trace the nutritional impact of food price changes on the poor. The Indonesian statistical results are the first to allow this to be done with any confidence.

Rice income elasticities are extremely high for the first two income classes,

TABLE 12.1. Income and price elasticities of demand for food in Indonesia, 1976

	Income class				
	Poor (1)	Low (2)	Middle (3)	High (4)	Average
Per capita total expenditure (Rp/month)					
Value (TX)	1548	2513	3876	9085	5412
Range	<2000	2000–3000	3000–5000	>5000	6151
Proportion of Indonesian population					
Susenas sample	0.106	0.185	0.321	0.388	–
Population weight	0.154	0.237	0.324	0.285	–
Expenditure elasticities					
Rice: urban	0.997	0.759	0.533	0.070	0.265
rural	1.168	0.924	0.704	0.364	0.581
Fresh cassava: urban	0.839	0.522	0.230	−0.369	−0.047
rural	0.994	0.679	0.394	−0.046	0.410
Calories*: urban	0.740	0.584	0.435	0.130	0.261
rural	0.776	0.615	0.470	0.246	0.471
Price elasticities					
Rice	−1.921	−1.475	−1.156	−0.743	−1.105
Fresh cassava	−1.284	−0.818	−0.943	−0.780	−0.804
Calories*: urban	−0.561	−1.081	−0.943	−0.811	−0.514
rural	−0.329	−0.849	−0.711	−0.579	–
Cross-price elasticities					
Rice with fresh cassava	ns	ns	ns	ns	–
Fresh cassava with rice	0.996	0.709	0.787	0.685	0.765

* Calories from rice, shelled maize, and fresh cassava only.
ns = not significant.
Source: Timmer and Alderman[34]. The research was sponsored by the Ford Foundation and the Department of Nutrition, Harvard School of Public Health.

indicating that it is effectively a luxury product for the poorest 30–40% of the Indonesian population. Even high income populations increase their rice intake with higher incomes, especially in the rural areas. Substitution away from rice because of higher incomes is occurring for less than 5% of the Indonesian population.

Income elasticities for fresh cassava are also surprisingly high. They are about one for the bottom 10–15% of the rural population and remain positive for 50–60% of the population. Although the effective income elasticity of demand for cassava in the last decade has no doubt been negative due to the concentration of income growth among upper income groups, higher incomes among the bottom half of the rural population would be likely to generate significant increases in demand for fresh cassava. Graphical analysis of more aggregate data than used for the statistical analysis shows that virtually all gaplek is consumed by the bottom two income classes, and the income elasticity is probably negative even for these groups.

The most important aspect of the analysis is that it shows that very poor consumers respond to rice price changes one and half times more strongly, in proportional terms, than do rich consumers. For cassava consumption, poor households react half again as strongly as rich consumers to cassava price changes, even though cassava is relatively much more important as a foodstuff to the poor.

The cross-section evidence shows high price sensitivity for individual commodities and a functional decline in that sensitivity as household incomes increase.

Price elasticities estimated from cross-section data tend to capture the full adjustment of households to long-run regional differences in prices and to expected seasonal price movements, and hence are not likely to be accurate predictors of short-run response. However, the addition of geographical and seasonal dummy variables in analysis of covariance specifications helps to reduce this effect. For example, analysis of data for rural Java using separate intercepts for each province and each of the three survey rounds reported in the 1976 Susenas data results in a rice price elasticity just half the size of the coefficient obtained without separate intercepts. This relationship of short-run responses tending to be about half the long-run response is broadly characteristic of distributed lag models in agriculture, although such models are applied more frequently in supply analysis than in consumption analysis. Consequently the short-run response to rice price changes is likely to be about half the average coefficient of -1.105 in *Table 12.1*, i.e. between -0.5 and -0.6.

Substitution of one basic foodstuff for another as relative prices change promotes efficiency in an economy, encouraging consumers to buy the relatively more abundant, and hence cheaper, commodity. Does such substitution have any welfare costs? In particular, are some basic foods nutritionally better than their substitutes, and does any significant substitution of food in general take place when overall food prices rise and fall in real terms?

The first question is more difficult to answer than would first appear since the nutritional value of foods depends on what is relatively least adequately supplied in the diet. Although protein deficiencies have received much attention in the last thirty years as a focus of nutrition policy concern, most experts now view the primary nutritional problem in the less developed countries as inadequate energy intake from traditional foods. Protein tends to be supplied in adequate amounts from such foods when caloric needs are met, with perhaps the important exceptions of weaning and toddler children and in areas with high reliance on tropical roots as the main caloric source. (This point of view is presented in more detail in the National Academy of Sciences[16], especially the Nutrition Overview section prepared by Study Team 9. Further elaboration is contained in IBRD[12].) In most environments, substitutions which maintain or improve caloric intake, even if cassava is substituted for rice, will not result in serious deterioration of nutritional status if high protein foods such as legumes and fish continue to be consumed with starchy roots in their traditional pattern. Certainly, little nutritional harm arises from substituting equal calories of sorghum or millet for wheat or rice.

The second question is analogous to asking whether aggregate agricultural output is responsive to the terms of trade between agricultural and non-agricultural goods. Just as that question must be answered positively on the basis of long-run evidence drawn from cross-section data, so too must the consumption equivalent. On the basis of data from 16 less developed countries for an average of 10 years each, Weisskoff[37] estimated the overall price elasticity of demand for food at -0.87, a figure that is predictably much larger in absolute terms than the -0.16 that Houthakker derived with similar methodology for European countries. At the level of national aggregates, consumers do substitute food for non-food and this substitution is more responsive in poor countries than in rich.

The evidence is similar for cross-section analysis of consumers within countries, with an intriguing twist. The Indonesian data shown in *Table 12.1* indicate significant price elasticities for calories from rice, maize, and cassava (providing on average three-quarters of Indonesian caloric intake), but the lowest income group has a smaller absolute price response than the higher income groups. There is a real physiological constraint below which poor consumers cannot go, and nearly all the budget must be devoted to calorie purchases.

The final role of food prices in determining consumption patterns relates to the formation of long-run tastes. Although economists usually assume that tastes are given, the duality between equilibrium quantities and equilibrium prices that derives from formal planning models provides the framework for a new interpretation of mechanisms of taste formation that rely on natural climatic advantage and physical availability of particular crops as the basis for a society's basic food tastes. The dual of such factors is the (implicit) relative price of, say, rice to wheat, or potatoes to maize, and if these prices were consciously manipulated for long periods of time then tastes would similarly be changed. Japan's new taste for wheat products may be a case in point.

The policy process

Many food deficit countries urgently need higher real food prices as an incentive to millions of small farmers to raise their agricultural productivity through adoption of modern technology. But those same higher, incentive foodgrain prices will have a disproportionate impact on food consumption of the poor. Many of these people are already suffering from inadequate protein–calorie intake, and further reduction in their food consumption may mean serious malnutrition or death.

This dilemma has been resolved historically in two ways. First, foodgrain imports can be used to fill the gap between inadequate domestic production and consumption levels generated by low food prices. Second, in some countries, prices of the preferred foodgrain have been raised as an incentive to domestic farmers while secondary grains and root crops have been kept cheap, or subsidized, to protect the poor. The substitute opportunities increase policy flexibility to deal with this fundamental dilemma of modern political economies.

Policy analysis in multistaple-food economies is obviously much more complicated than in single foodgrain economies. The consumption picture becomes more complicated because of the need to know multiple own-price effects by income class, and cross-price effects also become important. Estimating cross-price effects by income class is extremely difficult with existing methodology and data sets. The Indonesia consumption project has been quite successful at estimating income class-specific own-price effects (*see Table 12.1*), but cross-price effects have been estimated successfully only for cassava consumption (which depends on rice prices as well as cassava prices). The production side is made more complicated by the substitute possibilities if they are produced domestically. Planning intensification programmes for rice, for example, when maize, wheat, or barley are alternatives, requires a complex balancing of output price incentives, input subsidies, credit programmes, and development of suitable seed and production technologies. Attempts to raise rice prices to increase production, while keeping maize prices low to protect poor consumers, may simply be frustrated by the production substitution options and the level of alternative technologies, unless dual price systems with extensive subsidies can be implemented.

The complications extend to the import and domestic marketing arenas. Planning foodgrain imports, especially if much of the grain will be available under food aid terms, is far more complicated if several grains are being imported (or some exported) and changes at the margin in their rate of substitution are being attempted. On the domestic side, the marketing structure for the preferred grain, typically rice or wheat, is usually much more fully developed than for secondary grains and root crops. The latter are usually viewed by government planners as inferior foods produced primarily for subsistence which deserve little government attention to production, marketing, or consumption issues.

A number of important countries with large populations now seem to be facing the prospect of inadequate internal or external resources to increase availability of favoured foodgrains fast enough to meet market demand at constant prices, not to mention the latent nutritional demand that would be forthcoming at significantly lower prices. In the absence of massive food aid transfers, these countries will have to seek foodgrain substitutes for the poorest parts of their populations until long-term investment in agricultural infrastructure, made profitable by higher incentive prices for the preferred foodgrain, begins to transform the domestic production outlook.

A differential price policy by commodity, even if it includes direct subsidies on those foodstuffs such as cassava and maize that are consumed primarily by the poor as a means of implementing the policy, offers the potential to target the nutritional impact without many of the associated enforcement costs and leakages of target-oriented programmes using more preferred foods. Such a strategy relies on self-enforcement. The desire, or necessity, of the poor to eat staple foodstuffs no longer attractive to the more wealthy presents an opportunity to deal with inadequate protein–calorie intake without subsidizing the consumption of the entire population and hence bankrupting the nation. Such a strategy calls for high political commitment to increasing the access of the poor to adequate food. It may also be the only financially feasible way of coping with protein–calorie malnutrition over the next several decades.

The analytical costs of such a multicommodity price policy are quite high. But these high analytical costs must be compared with the costs of subsidizing food consumption for much of the population or attempting to enforce target-oriented food distribution. The combination of high analytical and political costs is not attractive, but neither are the alternatives.

References

1. BARKER, R. (1967) Barriers to efficient capital investment in agriculture. In *Distortions of Agricultural Incentives*. Ed. by T. W. Schultz. Bloomington, Ind.: Indiana University Press
2. BIERI, J. and DE JANVRY (1972) *Empirical Analysis of Demand Under Consumer Budgeting*. Giannini Foundation Monograph No. 30. University of California, Berkeley
3. BINSWANGER, H. and RUTTAN, V. (1978) *Induced Innovation: Technology, Institutions, and Development*. Baltimore, Johns Hopkins University Press
4. DAVID, C. C. (1976) Fertilizer demand in the Asian rice economy. *Food Research Institute Studies*, **15,**
5. FEI, J. C. H. and RANIS, G. (1964) *Development of the Labor Surplus Economy*. Homewood, Illinois, Richard D. Irwin
6. FRISCH, R. (1959) A complete scheme for computing all direct and cross demand elasticities in a model with many sectors. *Econometrica*, **27,** 177–196
7. GEORGE, P. S. and KING, G. A. (1971) *Consumer Demand for Food Commodities in the United States with Projections for 1980*. Giannini Foundation Monograph No. 26. University of California

8. GRILICHES, Z. (1960) Estimates of the aggregate US farm supply function. *Journal of Farm Economics,* **42,** 282–293
9. GRUNWALD, J. (1961) The structuralist school of price stability and development: the Chilean case. In *Latin American Issues.* Ed. by A. O. Hirschman. New York: Twentieth Century Fund
10. HAY, R. W. (1978) The statistics of hunger. *Food Policy,* **3** (4), 243–255
11. HAYAMI, Y. and RUTTAN, V. (1971) *Agricultural Development: An International Perspective.* Baltimore, Johns Hopkins University Press
12. IBRD (1979) *Nutrition, Basic Needs and Growth.* Draft from the Health, Population and Nutrition Department
13. KRISHNA, R. (1967) Agricultural price policy. In *Agricultural Development and Economic Growth.* Ed. by H. M. Southworth and B. F. Johnston. Ithaca, NY, Cornell University Press
14. LEWIS, W. A. (1954) Economic development with unlimited supplies of labor. *The Manchester School of Economics and Social Studies,* **22,** 139–191
15. McCARTHY, D. and TAYLOR, L. (1986) Macro food policy planning: a general equilibrium model for Pakistan. *Review of Economics and Statistics,* **62** (1), 107–121
16. NATIONAL ACADEMY OF SCIENCES (1977) *World Food and Nutrition Study.* Washington DC: US Government Printing Office
17. PETERSON, W. (1979) International farm prices and the social cost of cheap food policies. *American Journal of Agricultural Economics,* **61,** 12–21
18. PINSTRUP-ANDERSON, P. and CAICEDO, E. (1978) The potential impact of changes in income distribution on food demand and human nutrition. *American Journal of Agricultural Economics,* **60,** 402–415
19. PINSTRUP-ANDERSON, P., DE LONDONO, N. R. and HOOVER, E. (1976) The impact of increasing food supply on human nutrition: implications for commodity priorities in agricultural research and policy. *American Journal of Agricultural Economics,* **58,** 131–142
20. POLLAK, R. and WALES, T. J. (1969) Estimation of the linear expenditure system. *Econometrica,* 611–628
21. POLLAK, R. and WALES, T. J. (1978) Estimation of complete demand systems from household budget data: the linear and quadratic expenditure systems. *American Economic Review,* 348–359
22. POWELL, A. (1974) *Empirical Analytics of Demand Systems.* Cambridge, MA: Lexington Books
23. REUTLINGER, S. and SELOWSKY, M. (1976) *Malnutrition and Poverty: Magnitude and Policy Options.* World Bank Occasional Papers, No. 23. Baltimore, Johns Hopkins University Press
24. RUTTAN, V. (1977) Induced innovation and agricultural development. *Food Policy,* **2** (3), 196–216
25. SCHULTZ, T. W. (1964) *Transforming Traditional Agriculture.* New Haven, CT: Yale University Press
26. SCHULTZ, T. W. (Ed.) (1978) *Distortions of Agricultural Incentives.* Bloomington, Indiana, Indiana University Press
27. TAYLOR, L. (1978) Price policy and the food people eat. Mimeo
28. THEIL, H. (1976) *Theory and Measurement of Consumer Demand,* Vols. 1 & 2. Amsterdam, North Holland Publishing
29. TIMMER, C. P. (1973) Choice of technique in rice milling on Java. *Bulletin of Indonesian Economic Studies,* **9** (2), 57–76
30. TIMMER, C. P. (1975) The political economy of rice in Asia: a methodological introduction. *Food Research Institute Studies,* Vol. 14, No. 3, 191–196
31. TIMMER, C. P. (1975) The political economy of rice in Asia: lessons and implications. *Food Research Institute Studies,* Vol. 14, No. 4, 419–432
32. TIMMER, C. P. (1976) Fertiliser and food policies in LDCs. *Food Policy,* **1** (2), 143–154
33. TIMMER, C. P. (1980) Food price policy and protein–calorie intake: issues and methodology. In *Development Issues in Indonesia.* Ed. by Gillis and C. P. Timmer. Boston: Harvard Business School
34. TIMMER, C. P. and ALDERMAN, H. (1979) Estimating consumption parameters for food policy analysis. *American Journal of Agricultural Economics,* **61** (5)
35. TIMMER, C. P. and FALCON, W. P. (1975) The impact of price on rice trade in Asia. In *Trade, Agriculture and Development.* Ed. by G. Tolley and P. Zadrozny, pp. 57–89. Cambridge, MA: Ballinger Press
36. TIMMER, C. P., THOMAS, J. W., WELLS, L. T. and MORAWETZ, D. (1975) *The Choice of Technology in Developing Countries: Some Cautionary Tales.* Harvard Studies in International Affairs, No. 32. Cambridge, MA: Center for International Affairs
37. WEISSKOFF, R. (1971) Demand elasticities for a developing economy: an international comparison of consumption patterns. In *Studies in Development Planning.* Ed. by H. Chenery *et al.* pp. 322–358. Cambridge, MA: Havard University Press

Part VI

Government food marketing policies and facilitating services

There are wide differences of opinion concerning the extent to which the government directly intervenes in the actual buying and selling of food products and thus takes on the functions of an intermediary. Although private sector intermediaries continue to be the central core of the food distribution system in less developed countries, there is a trend in recent years toward increasing government involvement. Patterns characteristics of food distribution systems in use differ from one area to another within less developed countries.

In the first chapter, food policy in Africa is examined, this being a derived policy, developed in an effort to solve the political and economic problems of persons other than farmers. Food policy is employed to obtain peaceful relations between governments and their urban constituents and to secure the allegiance of powerful elites. A major consequence is the transformation of social and economic patterns in the countryside.

Growing conflicts between multinationals' infant food marketing practices in less developed countries and these nations' consumer expectations have led to a significant public policy dilemma in recent years. The second chapter in this part examines the marketing strategy issues of this dilemma, explores the mechanisms of demarketing, and suggests a socially responsive framework for marketing infant foods in the less developed countries and its public policy implications.

Since the oil embargo of 1973, the Gulf States have emerged as an overwhelming financial power. However, apart from Iraq, the spiral in oil revenue has had little effect in promoting the development of agriculture. Historically, interest in agricultural development has been invariably linked to agricultural potential.

The final chapter in this part takes the opposite view, suggesting that agricultural development may be important even under harsh ecological conditions, and that the limiting factor is the lack of skilled manpower needed to cope with the management of complex enterprise systems.

Chapter 13

Government food marketing interventions: food policy in Africa

Robert H. Bates

Introduction

Food policy in Africa is derived policy, in the sense that choices made with respect to food production are to a high degree made to serve the interests of groups other than producers themselves.

Food policy is defined as those choices made by governments which affect prices in the markets determining the real incomes of farmers: the markets for the commodities they sell, the inputs they employ in farming, and the goods they purchase from urban manufacturers. A review of government policies shows that most African governments tend to take measures which lead to higher prices for manufactured items and to lower prices for food products. And while they attempt to lower the price of farm inputs, the benefits of these subsidies are captured by a privileged few. Food policies in Africa tend, in short, to be antithetical to the interests of most farmers.

Food prices and food production

Perhaps the best evidence of food price policy is to be found in the area of commercial policy. In striking contrast to the use of commercial policy to protect urban industry and manufacturing, the governments of Africa have often manipulated the relationship between domestic and world prices so as to reduce, as opposed to enhance, the domestic price of food. They have done so by maintaining an overvalued exchange rate and by failing to adopt a structure of protective tariffs that would compensate for the resultant lowering of the perceived price of foreign food supplies. They have also done so by allowing the importation of food when the domestic price exceeds the world price and by banning its export when the opposite holds true.

Examples of these measures are to be found everywhere in Africa; but some of the most apposite came as part of the 'anti-inflation' policy package in Nigeria. Thus a World Bank Mission to Nigeria in 1978 reported that imports of wheat had risen dramatically in the late 1970s. One reason, it noted, was that the price of

This chapter originally appeared as an article in *Food Policy*, 1981, Vol. 6, No. 3, pp. 147–157.

bread had been fixed since January 1974, and given rising urban incomes and the fact that bread prepared from wheat is a preferred good, the result was a rising demand for wheat. Moreover, the report continued, 'at current exchange rates, wheat can be imported much more cheaply that it can be produced locally. Wheat can (also) be imported duty free. . . .'[8].

Rice provides another example. Following the recommendation of the anti-inflation task force set up following the displacement of the Gowan regime, the Nigerian government reduced the duty on rice from 20 to 10%; with rising domestic prices, demand shifted to foreign sources and, given the overvaluation of Nigerian currency, imports rose by more than 700%. As the World Bank report concludes, 'the overvalued exchange rate is consumer biased. The massive importation of rice and wheat keeps the price of these and substitute commodities lower than would occur under restricted imports or a lower exchange rate'[8].

Not only do governments often encourage the importation of foreign crops when domestic prices lie above world market prices, but they also sometimes ban the export of food crops to prevent local prices from rising to the international price when the latter lies above the former. In December 1974, for example, the Government of the Sudan imposed an export duty of 20% on meat and meat products, thereby making it unprofitable for domestic producers to sell on the growing Middle East market and lowering the price to domestic consumers. In Kenya, both the Kenya Meat Commission and the Kenya Cooperative Creameries are compelled by government regulations to offer their products in the internal market at prices which lie well below the world price for meat and dairy products. While both agencies strenuously lobby to be freed of such controls, they are nonetheless compelled to supply the domestic market at prices below the world price and to suffer the resultant loss of profits[6,16].

African governments thus employ commercial policies to reduce food prices in domestic markets. They also seek to reduce prices by increasing domestic supplies. The dilemma for African policy makers, however, is that it is difficult to increase supplies without providing proper incentives for producers. But it is precisely the proper incentives (increased prices) which they seek to counter in the first place. In their attempts to increase supplies without increasing prices, African governments have turned to an alternative set of policies: direct government investment in food production and the public subsidization of farm inputs.

The determination of the governments to increase the supply of food to the urban populations is strongly underscored by their investments in food production schemes. One of the best examples is the system of state farms in Ghana. Begun in 1962, the programme of state farms had by 1966 expanded to include 135 state farms with a total of 20 800 workers. Between 1962 and early 1966, the state farms received approximately 90% of the development budget for agriculture. Hundreds of tractors were imported for these farms; one tractor was provided for every 60–70 acres put into production. The costliness of the effort is underscored by the magnitude of the losses incurred: over 17 million cedi over a five-year period[1,5,10].

A second example is provided by the Farm Settlement Schemes of the western region of Nigeria. Begun in 1960, the programme of farm settlements was designed to provide a series of 1500-acre farms, each with 50 settlers and a 'stable' of livestock and farm machinery. By 1971, the western region government had spent 16.4 million naira on these settlements and it has been estimated that 55% of the total capital expenditure for agriculture in the 1962–68 development plan period went into these production schemes[15] (see also Hill[7]).

The willingness of the governments of Ghana and the western region of Nigeria to pay the inflated costs of these production schemes underscores the magnitude of their determination to contain the rise of inflation in the urban areas by increasing the quantity of food available and to produce these increased supplies without depending on the traditional market mechanism: increases in food prices.

The subsidization of inputs

Another common approach to the problem of food supply involves not direct public investment, but rather the subsidization with public funds of the costs of private production.

Urban protest over increases in the costs of living leads to the promulgation of public policies to alleviate the rise in prices. It has also been noted that a central feature of these promulgations are statements of policies toward agriculture. Among the primary methods advocated in these pronouncements for increasing the supplies of food is the strengthening of the incentives for private producers, not by raising the price of their products, but, rather, by lowering their costs of production.

For example, the second and final report of the Wages and Salaries Review Commission set up after the civil war in Nigeria proclaimed that 'certain measures should be taken by the Government, as a matter of emergency, to lend special assistance to farmers so as to ensure the increased volume of foodstuffs necessary to contain and reduce the steep rise in the cost of living'[3]. The measures included a full range of subsidies for credit, fertilizer, and mechanical equipment, and the removal of 'hindrances to farming', such as import duties on mechanical equipment and inefficiencies in the transport system. In its white paper on economic policy, the military government which came to power following the 1972 urban disturbances over price rises in Ghana, also announced a public commitment to the sponsorship of commercial farming and pledged a full panoply of subsidies and fiscal concessions to support the growth of food supplies in that nation.

The specific nature of the subsidies offered in Ghana and Nigeria is not unique to these nations. They are common elsewhere. What is critical about these subsidies is that they tend to support (and indeed are intended to support) the development of commercially oriented, technologically advanced agricultural producers, capable of marketing large volumes of agricultural products. They are designed to secure increased food production by encouraging the adoption and use of 'modern' farm technologies by persons in the countryside.

Included among these measures is the subsidization of fertilizer. The 1972 white paper in Ghana announced a fertilizer subsidy of 87%. In Nigeria, a subsidy of 80% was applied until 1978, when it was reduced to 75%, but only after 100 million naira had been spent to reduce the price of this input. In the case of both nations, fertilizer is imported duty free. In Kenya and Tanzania, fertilizer is also subsidized, though at a much lower level (in the range of 40%); similar levels of subsidization are common throughout Africa.

As part of the policies to promote commercial farming, governments also provide subsidies for the development and distribution of improved seeds. In Ghana, for example, the government paid for one-third of the cost of new maize seeds and three-quarters of the cost of new rice seeds. In Nigeria, the government helped to finance the development of a new, if ultimately ill-fated, variety of maize.

In Kenya, Zambia, and elsewhere, the costs of developing and distributing new seeds have been subsidized by the government[2,4].

Public support is also given for the purchase of mechanical equipment. Thus, in Ghana, farm equipment is exempt from duty, and the overvaluation of the exchange rate lowers the perceived price of farm machinery imported from abroad. Moreover, by encouraging the incorporation of farming enterprises, the governments in Africa have extended into agriculture the provisions of corporate tax law which cheapen the relative price of machinery. Tax holidays are offered to those making major investments in food production or food processing, losses on investments can be carried forward indefinitely until they are written off against profits, interest payments can be written-off, and favourable forms of capital depreciation are allowed. In Nigeria, an additional capital allowance of 10% is offered for expenditures on plant or equipment used in farm enterprises. Similar provisions are allowed in Kenya.

To promote the purchase of these new inputs, African governments have manipulated the terms of credit. In Nigeria the government has made credit available to farmers at 5% below the opportunity cost for capital. In Ghana the government funded the Agricultural Loan Bank; operating under government regulations, the bank could charge but 6% for its loans. The poor recovery rate of the Bank, 63% in 1974, further emphasizes the concessional nature of the credit offered to investors in food production. Lastly, governments have encouraged commercial lenders to move into agriculture by absorbing some of the risks of these investments. Deeming agriculture a 'preferred' sector and guaranteeing loans made in that sector, the governments are able to lower the price of credit for those seeking to borrow to invest in food production.

Governments in Africa have also sought to cheapen the price of land. When the state itself enters agricultural production, it rarely pays for the land it uses. In the case of Ghana, for example, the Government Food Production Corporation simply seized the land without compensating those who had traditional rights to it; these actions sometimes led to violent conflicts between local villagers and the state corporations[12]. In Nigeria, the government's land decree of March 1978 reserves for the state governments rural land not under active exploitation. While the full implications of the land decree are as yet unclear, many observers are convinced that a prime purpose of the decree is to make it easier for the state governments to seize land for public purposes, including the implementation of large-scale agricultural schemes. In addition to the broadening of the application of eminent domain for purposes of state production, governments in Africa have also revealed an increased responsiveness to pressures on the part of potential private investors for legal regulation over the conditions of land sales – measures that would have the effect of lowering the price of land.

Such pressures have been reported in Ghana (see the discussion of the law reform commission in Nyanteng[11]). And it would appear that in the Sudan, state power over land rights in the savannah zones is being used precisely in the way that private investors would have it be used in the savannah zones of Ghana. Thus, in the Sudan, not only government corporations seeking land but also private investors seeking to engage in mechanized farming can obtain land from the government. By 1968 the government had allocated 1.8 million feddans to private individuals[9]. In many cases, the government used its legal powers to transfer land from traditional production activities, such as nomadic herding, to the mechanized production of food crops without paying, or requiring that the private investors pay compensation for the loss of rights to use the land for traditional purposes. In effect, therefore, the government exercised its power over land rights to confer a subsidized price for land.

In Kenya, the government has reformed land law in order to promote private investment. The government has sponsored the wholesale transferral of land from a jurisdiction governed by customary or traditional rights to one governed by private rights. The intention of this transformation, it would appear, has not been to artificially alter the price of land, but rather to institute a method of allocating rights in land (a private land market) which would enhance the ability of those seeking to make use of this resource to claim it, invest in it, and thereby develop the productive potential of the countryside[13]. In practice, however, state intervention to reform land rights has been exploited by those seeking to secure land at well below the free market price, as has been revealed in recent events and disclosures in that nation[17].

Implications for the countryside

In the face of protests by urban consumers, the governments of Africa have sought to increase food supplies without increasing food prices. They have attempted to do so partly by entering into food production themselves and partly by manipulating the prices and availability of inputs to strengthen the incentives for private investors to engage in the production of agricultural commodities. These policies have had major social consequences. They have encouraged the development of largescale mechanized farming. They have also promoted the movement into the countryside of powerful, urban-based, administrative and economic elites.

The reasons lying behind the more frequent adoption of new farm technologies are obvious; the lowering of the prices of 'modern' inputs would naturally promote their adoption. The relationship between the provision of subsidies and the entrance of the rich and powerful into farming are more complex and are best captured in the following argument.

By subsidizing the price of farm inputs, the governments create an increase in the demand for these inputs. Insofar as they are willing to supply them at a price lower than the market price, they reduce the supply of these inputs from alternative sources – commercial banks, private firms etc. The result is that the demand for these inputs exceeds their supply. The question remains: how are these commodities to be allocated among competing claimants for them?

One answer often is that they go to those who will pay the market clearing price for them. The result then is the economic corruption by wealthy persons of the public agencies engaged in the agricultural development effort. The growth and development of black markets is symptomatic of this consequence. A second answer is that the farm inputs go either to those who control the agencies which allocate them or to those whose political support is useful to the agency heads. The result then is the political corruption of the agricultural development effort. In either case, attempts to increase food production through the public subsidization of farm inputs leads to the entrance into rural production of the wealthy and/or politically influential, and thus to the transformation of the social structure of the African countryside.

Much of the evidence for this contention is indirect. Thus, it is commonly and almost universally found that the poorer, small-scale, village-level farmers do *not* secure farm inputs which have been publicly provisioned and publicly subsidized as part of the rural development effort.

The best information in support of this contention is contained in investigations into the apparent failure of small-scale farmers to adopt new agricultural technologies. Time and again these investigations reveal that the conventional explanations are wrong. The village-level farmers do in fact know about the advantages of new seeds and of fertilizers; they do want to employ them, and they are especially interested in securing them at their publicly supported prices. The reasons for the failure of the new technologies to 'diffuse' through the rural community, thus, most often have little to do with the attitudes of village farmers themselves, as is commonly claimed. Rather, the problem most often is that the inputs are simply not available.

While governments have sought to increase the production of food by supplying farm inputs at subsidized prices, the experience of local-level farmers has not been that these inputs are more readily available, but rather that they remain scarce. But the evidence also suggests that the governments' programmes have been enthusiastically responded to by others. Wealthier and more powerful people have found that governmental efforts to promote the development of agriculture have made opportunities more bountiful.

Perhaps the best evidence of these trends comes from the savannah regions of West Africa. With the rise of government efforts to promote the supply of inexpensive food for the cities, there has arisen in this zone a cadre of commercially oriented, mechanized farmers – a group whose existence is predicated on the provision of government subsidies and a large proportion of whose membership is made up of wealthy and politically influential members of the urban elite. An example would be the mechanized farmers of northern Ghana. Using political connections to secure land, publicly subsidized credit and forgiveness for debts, publicly subsidized and allocated fertilizer, and highly favourable terms for the importation and financing of capital equipment, influential members of the Ghanaian urban elite with close ties to the managers of the public bureaucracies have entered food production in the northern savannah areas.

The result has been a transformation of the pattern of agricultural production in the savannah zones. Rather than small-scale peasant farmers, the new entrants are large-scale commercial producers. Rather than hoes and oxen, they use tractors and combines. The consequences are most readily seen in the production of rice, one of the principal crops of the northern regions of Ghana. Whereas the traditional rice farms averaged six acres in size, the new commercial farms tend to average more than 50 acres. Furthermore, while most rice production originates from the small-scale producers, a vast disproportion of the farm inputs have gone to the 400–500 agrobusinesses whose owners have 'connections' in the public sector and so can obtain inputs which allow them to farm on a much larger scale. As one reviewer of the government's efforts to promote food production in the savannah regions noted[19] (for further detail see [14,18]):

> . . . a growing number of southerners – mostly civil servants and army officers – have been encouraged . . . to join the boom. Many of Ghana's most powerful citizens now have large rice farms, often managed by others, and use their influence to ensure themselves a high rate of profit.

In their efforts to promote the production of food for the urban areas, the governments of Africa have thus chosen to subsidize inputs to farming. They have allocated them through bureaucratic channels, and the result has been the entrance into rural production of those with privileged positions in the public sector. Insofar as these methods of promoting local food production are widely adopted, the result is the development in the countryside of large-scale producers – producers whose fortunes are as much determined by the influence they possess within the political system as by their economic acumen.

The evidence suggests that such policies have increasingly been adopted elsewhere in Africa and that the consequences are increasingly widespread. Another example would be the growth of mechanized farming in the Sudan, with its controversial effects on the environment and the threat it poses to pastoral production. Another is the spread of wheat and barley production southward along the Rift Valley of Kenya. The production of these crops is sponsored and financed by state grain corporations, which are themselves headed by persons of enormous political influence. A similar pattern appears to obtain in the middle-belt regions of Nigeria, where state corporations and private individuals of political consequence are investing in mechanized schemes for the production of food.

The policy responses of African governments to the problem of urban food supply thus appears to be leading to the entrance in the countryside of politically influential elites – elites who seek to augment their fortunes by engaging in food production, and who adopt farming technologies that fundamentally alter the social and economic patterns of the African countryside.

References

1. DADSON, J. A. (1970) *Socialized Agriculture in Ghana, 1962–1965*. PhD Thesis, Harvard University
2. DODGE, D. J. (1977) *Agricultural Policy and Performance in Zambia*. Institute of International Studies, University of California, Berkeley
3. FEDERAL REPUBLIC OF NIGERIA (1971) *Second and Final Report of the Wages and Salaries Review Commission, 1970–1971*, p. 17. Ministry of Information, Lagos
4. GERHART, J. (1975) *The Diffusion of Hybrid Maize in Western Kenya*. International Maize and Wheat Improvement Center, Mexico City
5. GORDON, J. (1970) State farms in Ghana. In *International Seminar on Change in Agriculture*. Ed. by A. H. Bunting. New York, Praeger Publishers
6. GRAY, C. S. (1977) Costs, prices, and market structure in Kenya. Mimeo, Nairobi, Kenya
7. HILL, F. (1977) Experiments with a public sector peasantry. *African Studies Review*, **20**, 25–41
8. INTERNATIONAL BANK FOR RECONSTRUCTION AND DEVELOPMENT (1978) Nigeria: an informal survey. Mimeo, p. 12
9. INTERNATIONAL LABOUR ORGANISATION, UNITED NATIONS DEVELOPMENT PROGRAM (1976) Mechanized (rainfed) agriculture. *Growth, Employment and Equity: A Comprehensive Strategy for Sudan*, Technical Paper No. 3. Geneva, ILO
10. NYANTENG, V. K. (1978) Some policies and programs related to small-scale farming in Ghana, Mimeo, The Hague
11. NYANTENG, V. K. (1979) Ghana: a country review paper. Mimeo, The Hague
12. OFOSU, S. B. (1972) *Case Study of a Farm Within the Workers Brigade*. Honors Dissertation, University of Ghana
13. OKOTH OGENDO, H. W. O. (1976) African land tenure reform. In *Agricultural Development in Kenya*. Ed. by J. Heyer, J. K. Maitha and W. M. Senga. Nairobi, Oxford University Press
14. PROJECT PAPER FOR GHANA MANAGED INPUTS AND DELIVERY OF AGRICULTURAL SERVICES PROGRAM FOR SMALL FARM DEVELOPMENT (1975) Washington DC
15. ROIDER, W. (1971) *Farm Settlements for Socio-economic Development: The Western Nigerian Case*. Munich, Weltforum Verlag
16. *The Weekly Review* (1978) 1 December
17. *The Weekly Review* (1978) 29 December
18. UNITED STATES AGENCY FOR INTERNATIONAL DEVELOPMENT (1975) *Development Assistance Program FY 1977–FY 1980*, Vol. 4, Annex D – Agricultural Sector Assessment. Washington DC
19. *West Africa* (1978) 9 January

Chapter 14

Multinationals' food marketing practices in the developing world: the dilemma of infant nutrition

Attila Yaprak

Introduction

During the last three decades, the world economy has experienced a profound transformation. Significant advances in marketing technology, relative stability in the international monetary system, and rising consumer demand, particularly in the less developed countries (LDCs), have propelled the multinational corporation (MNC) into an efficient agent in servicing world markets.

Recently, however, growing conflicts between MNCs' marketing practices and the expectations of LDCs' social forces have led to a more critical examination of the marginal benefits derived by LDCs from MNC operations. While earlier studies in this context have correlated MNC operations with economic growth, technological advancement, more efficient distribution of capital and employment, and upgrading of managerial and know-how skills[10,14,18], recent studies have raised serious questions about MNCs' socioeconomic contributions to LDCs[2,5,8,10,17,21,22].

Perhaps the clearest manifestation of this debate has evolved within the marketing function. At one end of the spectrum, researchers have argued that MNC marketing in LDC environments has led to progress in long-run consumer welfare. Enriched lifestyles, wider choice, more effective diffusion of marketing know-how and innovations, more efficient distribution of products, effective satisfaction of consumer needs, and enhanced product servicing have been cited as derived consumer benefits[10,11,14,15,18]. At the other end, other researchers have advocated arguments that MNCs approach, and operate in, LDCs with an ethnocentric vision and with little regard for long-run consumer welfare[2,5,9,11,17,21]. These charges have been advanced within all elements of the marketing function[21].

For example, product policies have been attacked for planned obsolescence, unnecessary product proliferation, and unsafe products. Blanketing markets with marginally differentiated products for which there is little consumer need, stimulating demand through aggressive promotional schemes, inadequate product servicing, and dumping obsolete products into LDC markets have been other sources of attack. Pricing practices have come under fire within the context of intracorporate transfer pricing procedures, manipulating price elasticities, psychological pricing ploys, unfair price/utility relationships, fictitious price discounts, and unreasonable channel margins. In the distribution dimension, the primary sources of criticism have been high-pressure selling techniques, inadequate in-store and after-sale servicing, and unfair retailing methods which tend to push unnecessary consumption. Manipulation of the distribution channel structure and exploitation of channel members through margin allocation schemes have strengthened these arguments[21].

The intensity of charges levelled at MNCs have perhaps been strongest in the communications domain of the marketing function. The underlying theme has been that MNCs promote (in LDC markets) a new form of 'social colonialism' by fuelling mass-consumption-society values and excessive unnecessary consumption, hence ultimately destroying the moral fabric of the LDC society. It has been argued, for example, that through advertising, consumers have been manipulated toward excessive consumption, and vulnerable groups have been subjected to subliminal seduction, deceptive advertising, and non-informative messages. In support of this view, the promotion of unnecessary style attributes, unreliable product information, and false or misleading claims in comparative advertising have also been cited[5,21].

Perhaps the most illuminating example of this dilemma has been in the arena of 'Third World' nutrition, reflected by the marketing of infant foods in LDCs. This chapter examines the marketing issues underlying this controversy, explores the mechanisms for demarketing infant foods, and proposes a framework for socially responsive food marketing in LDC markets.

The infant nutrition dilemma in LDCs

Malnutrition and/or undernutrition, coupled with inadequate and inefficient distribution channels, rapid urbanization, increasing number of women in the workforce, and the 'revolution of rising expectations' in the less developed countries have simultaneously propelled LDC governments, food MNCs, and international organizations, e.g. United Nations agencies, to commercialize high-nutrition but low-cost food products for consumption by nutritionally vulnerable consumers in LDCs[6,17]. While the initial intentions of all actors involved in this dilemma were clearly more than philanthropic, 'questionable' marketing practices of food MNCs paralleled by product misuse by LDC consumers may have led to 'commerciogenic malnutrition' in the developing world[17].

In this controversy, the food content and nutritional quality of the infant formulas marketed were judged to be nutritionally conforming to international product standards[15]. Intensive advertising practices of the food MNCs, however, had led LDC mothers who could ill afford artificial foods to abandon breast-feeding for bottle-feeding. The portrayal of healthy babies by MNCs with a particular brand of formula, their use of milk-nurses in nurses' uniforms, false images and sales pressures had seduced mothers into artificial feeding. Because these foods were sold in powdered form to preserve shelf-life and because they were relatively expensive, LDC consumers were tempted to overdilute the formula, often with contaminated water. Further, mass-media promotion, characteristic of food marketing, had been misleading to illiterate mothers in LDCs, and product labelling and artificial feeding education had been inadequate or deceptive. In addition, the lack of preservation capabilities of LDC retail outlets, and periodic shortages in supply often led to speculative prices, hoarding, creation of black markets, and even spoiled infant food. Marketing research, particularly postuse research, had also been insufficient or non-existent[17].

It could not, of course, be argued that infant food MNCs had been socially irresponsible over 'Third World' nutrition before they came under public pressure. They had, all along, supported prolonged breast-feeding; had argued at various United Nations forums, e.g. Protein–Calorie Advisory Group – PAG, World Health Organisation – WHO, Food and Agriculture Organization – FAO, and UNICEF, for the need for breast-milk supplements, and had articulated the necessity of breast-feeding substitutes due to undernourishment of the mother, death at childbirth, and work outside the home. They had further agreed to enforce the 1970 PAG guidelines which promoted: (a) emphasizing the importance of prolonged breast-feeding; (b) developing company guidelines for the marketing of breast-milk substitutes; (c) supporting the development of low-cost, protein-rich weaning foods; (d) enhancing worldwide public health through joint action. The industry had also committed itself to self-regulation in the mid-seventies through the establishment (in 1975) of the International Council of Infant Food Industries (ICIFI). Many rapidly adopted the marketing code of ethics developed by the ICIFI, and some even moved beyond this code by issuing stricter marketing policy guidelines, albeit in response to consumer boycotts launched against them[17]. For example, Nestle, through its 1981–82 code has[15]:

- Contributed to the development of the International Code of Marketing of Breast-Milk Substitutes and its adoption by most WHO members in 1981.
- Implemented the code's provisions in LDCs where host governments themselves did not introduce national measures.
- Issued to its distribution system (in 1982) new marketing guidelines substantially reflecting the code's provisions, eliminating (a) advertising and promotion of infant formula including generic promotions, (b) all gift promotions and sampling, (c) the mothercraft-nurse function, (d) baby pictures on all product labels, and (f) point-of-purchase promotion by retailers.
- Established the Nestle Infant Formula Audit Commission to enhance self-regulation.
- Embarked on new research on LDC infant nutrition (supported by the ICIFI, the WHO, and other public health organizations).

Although these codes have brought restrictions on many forms of promotion, they have not yet signalled a clearcut commitment to socially responsive marketing behaviour, particularly demarketing. For example, postmarketing reviews to determine the users, use conditions, and the socioeconomic correlates of infant food consumers in LDCs are still relatively non-existent. While it may be argued that the use of contaminated water is a consumer error, the illiteracy of the mother is not caused by the food MNCs, the poverty which tempts overdilution is not the fault of the industry, and the lack of product liability laws in LDCs is not within the control of MNCs, there may still be merit in fundamentally revising the concept and methods of marketing artificial food products with safer and more proper product use[17]. In this context, it would be imperative to adopt a responsive corporate marketing perspective toward the evolution of consumer expectations in LDC markets. Further, such a demarketing approach would emphasize both curbs on marketing practices and affirmative efforts to rectify past behaviour[17]. This approach would also appreciate the complex inter-relationships among industry, consumers, public pressure groups, international organizations, and LDC governments[12,17].

A framework for socially responsive food marketing in LDCs

The underlying assumptions for socially responsive food marketing in LDCs must, necessarily, include the understanding that the MNC is:

- A social organism within a dynamic environment, and therefore in a symbiotic relationship with the social forces in its ecology.
- A 'catalyst agent' of social change affecting, and in return being affected by, the evolutionary developments in the social currents surrounding it.

Effective adoption of this approach requires a fundamental change in corporate perspective: from ethnocentric to geocentric, from confrontation to voluntary adjustment, and from paternalism to accommodation. Further, in the operationalization of this approach, three capabilities must be developed. These include a geocentric philosophy of 'social posture', the abilities for 'social tracking', and, procedures for 'social pulsing'. These are discussed below.

Social posture

The adoption of a geocentric philosophy of social posture helps guide the MNC toward social responsiveness (a more pro-active anticipation and monitoring of social developments within the host country) in contrast to social responsibility (where the firm conforms to market forces by following guidelines rather than leading them, or adjusts its behaviour in congruence with currently prevailing norms and performance expectations)[20]. This difference may be significant as social responsiveness brings to the firm a clearer mandate for effecting social change (the firm becomes pro-active), rather than being affected by it, and subsequently responding (the firm is reactive). For example, the socially responsible behaviour of infant food MNCs in LDCs could have been more responsive had they conducted research on the possible cumulative effects of advertising, promotion, and use of infant formula under segmented (e.g. urban versus rural) use conditions. Such research, supplemented by postmarketing reviews, could have led to earlier detection and prevention of product misuse before the acceleration of the problem. Further, this perspective could have enhanced the industry's awareness of the problem's domains rather than its arrogant denial of the existence of any problem whatsoever[17].

Social tracking

Social tracking may also be significant as it facilitates more systematic detection, identification, and evaluation of the growth of consumer movements within the firm's environment. More importantly, it allows the firm the flexibility with which to accommodate, or collaborate with, the objectives and expectations of these forces. It may also contribute to the firm's remedy or relief positions in interacting with them. For example, infant food marketers could have taken more accommodating postures in dealing with their critics had they monitored, more carefully, the evolution of the moral and political conscience of these forces. Such tracking may have led them to changes in corporate policy and in competitive marketing behaviour. Education of consumers about proper product use and scientific research on nutrition could have led to more collaboration with their critics. In this context, Nestle disseminated to the world public in 1982 the results of its 1981 study conducted in three LDCs: Kenya, Malaysia and Mexico. The findings revealed that more than 50% of the mothers had introduced breast-milk supplements before their infants were four months old, regardless of whether infant formulas were commercially available. Further, many of the substitutes used were not generally preferred over the use of formulas[15]. These findings were in sharp contrast to the activists' claims that even a malnourished mother could adequately feed her child for at least the first four months of life; only 2% of the mothers were physiologically incapable of breast-feeding, and less than 6% of the mothers were unable to breast-feed because of the work outside the home[15].

In addition, Nestle currently has more objective research projects under way focusing on mixed feeding, timing of the introduction of breast-milk substitutes and supplements, and the scientific examination of the literature on infant nutrition in the 'Third World'. The findings of these projects can further facilitate Nestle's efforts in educating and informing LDCs' consumers and help reinforce more positive attitudes toward Nestle by its critics.

Social pulsing

Through social pulsing, the MNC attempts to raise operating managers' awareness of, and adaptability to, evolving consumer expectations in their LDC markets. This attempt emphasizes a rhythmic, two-way information flow, rather than a commanding, one-way one. Such continuous pulsing can help assure more efficient information exchange, and can facilitate flexibility in responding to changes. Possible strategic actions in this context may include substantial intrafirm modifications in product and promotion policies and voluntary guidelines for corporate marketing behaviour, and tangible interfirm efforts such as the establishment of industry-wide audit groups and procedures. Examples of intrafirm changes may involve adaptation of products to fit local needs and conditions, radical alteration of promotion and communication methods, and voluntary architecture of audit procedures. Nestle has implemented each of these tactics in the last three years. It has adapted its infant formula to local nutritional and preparation requirements, instituted the promotional modifications discussed earlier, and established the Nestle Infant Formula Audit Commission to review complaints about its marketing practices. Strategic modifications in the interfirm sphere include Nestle's active participation in the independent research/audit bodies such as the ICIFI, and the WHO.

Nestle's concerted efforts in adopting and implementing this pro-active management philosophy seems to have been a major ingredient in the toned-down allegations of its critics recently. Its sincere attempt to accommodate, and collaborate with, the expectations of these forces now appears to be leading to a more positive reflection of Nestle's corporate image and social impact.

Policy implications and conclusions

The debate over socially responsive marketing practices of food MNCs in LDC markets exemplified by the infant nutrition dilemma discussed in this chapter is likely to continue into the foreseeable future. It is also clear that movement toward effective resolution of this debate will necessitate harmonious interaction among the actors involved. Food MNCs, for their part, will need to continue their demarketing efforts through more socially responsive marketing activities in LDCs. For example, they will need to adopt more geocentric corporate objectives and behaviour, and will need to enhance their social posture, tracking and pulsing skills. In many, if not most, LDCs they will need to conduct more premarketing as well as postmarketing research to adapt more effectively to local nutritional and preparation requirements, to promotional restrictions, and to audit procedures. They will also need to increase their participation in efforts to enhance the nutritional education and needs of developing markets, even at the expense of no-growth or gradual demarketing in some countries.

Governments of less developed countries will also have to become actively involved. For their part, they will need to enhance consumer education, prudently regulate promotional activities of artificial food marketers, develop policies to prevent rather than treat malnutrition, and perhaps even restrict the marketing of some products in their countries. They will also need to act affirmatively in developing and enforcing antitrust policies, marketing audit procedures, and consumer protection statutes to prevent product misuse.

The critics will need to continue to monitor food marketing practices in LDCs to stimulate affirmative changes in corporate policy and competitive behaviour. They will need to positively press marketers to transform their policy objectives into responsive marketing practices. By praising marketers' positive self-restraint measures in addition to exposing their violations, they will continue to enhance more accommodating and collaborative postures.

Finally, international organizations, such as United Nations agencies, will need to continue their efforts in expanding nutrition research, in providing objective debate forums, and in suggesting guidelines for industry marketing ethics.

Without harmonious interaction among these actors, the dilemma of 'Third World' nutrition is not likely to approach resolution in the years ahead. With more accommodations among these groups, however, positive advances are more likely to occur.

References

1. ABBOTT, J. C. (1975) Food distribution: limitations on supplies and consumption. *Columbia Journal of World Business*, **10** (3), 8–14
2. ASHOUR, A. S. (1981) Self-serving practices of multinational corporations in less developed countries. *Management International Review*, **4** (3)
3. BARKSDALE, H. C. *et al.* (1982) A cross-national survey of consumer attitudes toward marketing practices, consumerism and government regulations. *Columbia Journal of World Business*, **17** (2), 71–86
4. BAROVICK, R. (1979) Guidelines for multinational enterprises. *Business America*, July 16
5. BODDEWYN, J. J. (1982) Advertising regulation in the 1980s: the underlying global forces. *Journal of Marketing*, **46** (1), 27–35
6. CAVUSGIL, T., AMINE, L. and VITALE, E. (1983) Marketing supplementary food products in LDCs: a case study in Morocco. *Food Policy*, **8** (2), 111–120
7. COOK, C. W. (1975) World food problems – an overview. *Columbia Journal of World Business*, **10** (3), 5–7
8. DAS, R. (1981) Impact of host country regulations on MNC operations. *Columbia Journal of World Business*, **16** (1)
9. DAVIDOW, J. (1980) Multinationals, host governments and regulation of restrictive practices. *Columbia Journal of World Business*, **15** (2)
10. GABRIEL, P. (1973) MNCs in the Third World: is conflict unavoidable? *Harvard Business Review*, July-August

11. JAIN, S. C. and PURI, Y. (1981) Role of MNCs in developing countries. *The Policy Makers View*, **4** (2)
12. KAYNAK, E. (1980) Government and food distribution in LDCs: the Turkish experience. *Food Policy*, **5** (2), 133–142
13. KAYNAK, E. and MITCHELL, L. A. (1981) Analysis of marketing strategies used in diverse cultures. *Journal of Advertising Research*, **21** (3), 25–32
14. KINSEY, J. (1982) The role of marketing in economic development. *European Journal of Marketing*, **16** (6), 64–77
15. McCONNAS, M., FOOKES, G. and TAUCHER, G. (1983) *The Dilemma of Third World Nutrition: A Report Prepared for Nestle SA*. Washington, DC, Nestle SA Coordination Center for Nutrition, Inc.
16. MELLOR, J. W. (1975) Food aid and long-run world food–population balances. *Columbia Journal of World Business*. **10** (3), 24–35
17. POST, J. E. and BAER, E. (1979) Demarketing infant formula: consumer products in the developing world. *Journal of Contemporary Business*, **7** (4), 17–35
18. REEKIE, W. D. and SAVITT, R. (1982) Marketing behavior and entrepreneurship: a synthesis of Alderson and Austrian economics. *European Journal of Marketing,*, **16** (7), 55–66
19. SANDERSON, F. H. (1975) Export opportunities for agricultural products. *Columbia Journal of World Business*, **10** (3), 15–28
20. SHETH, J. N. and FRAZIER, G. L. (1982) A model of strategy mix choice for planned social change. *Journal of Marketing*, **46** (1), 15–26
21. STRAVER, W. (1978) The consumerist movement in Europe. *European Journal of Marketing*, **12** (4), 316–325
22. THORELLI, H. B. and SENTELL, G. D. (1982) The ecology of consumer markets in less and more developed countries. *European Journal of Marketing*, **16** (6), 54–63

Chapter 15

Food marketing policy in the Arab Gulf States

Abdel Aziz El-Sherbini

Introduction

The Gulf States comprise seven Arab countries: Iraq, Saudi Arabia, Kuwait, Bahrain, Qatar, Oman, and the United Arab Emirates (UAE). As an indication of their rapid financial growth, their combined revenue from crude oil exports increased from US$5.5 billion in 1972 to more than US$72 billion in 1977. (Based on information in the *OPEC Annual Statistical Bulletin, 1977*. Estimates for Bahrain are obtained from other sources since it is not a member of OPEC.) Allowing for small production cuts, the group's 1979 crude oil revenue should have increased by at least 65% over the 1977 level.

Apart from Iraq, the spiral in oil revenue has had little effect in promoting the development of agriculture in general, and food production in particular. The ratio of planned investment in agriculture to aggregate planned investment is about 20% for Iraq, 8% for Saudi Arabia, and 5% for Oman. The ratio is much lower for the other four Gulf States.

For countries in the first group, there is no question about the mandate for agricultural development. Capital resources are abundant and some agricultural resource base is available. Essentially, the problems are of investment strategy and effective project implementation. There are two different issues for the second group. First, can agricultural development take place under the ecologically harsh conditions of this group? This is a 'technical' question. Second, should there be greater emphasis on agricultural development provided it is technically feasible? This is a 'socioeconomic' question.

Historically, interest in agricultural development has invariably been linked to agricultural potential. Thus, if potential was very limited, interest in development would be minimal. This paper takes an opposite view, suggesting that agricultural development may be important even under harsh ecological conditions. Other considerations need to supplement the conventional project analysis in these situations of abundant capital resources coupled with a limited non-oil resource base. The focus is on the group of four Gulf States including Kuwait, Bahrain, Qatar, and UAE.

This chapter was originally an article in *Food Policy*, 1980, Vol. 5, No. 2, pp. 97–104.

Socioeconomic profile

The group of four Gulf States has a distinctive socioeconomic profile reflecting significant implications of direct concern to agriculture and food policy. The first is a very high degree of urbanization seldom observed in less developed countries. This is shown in *Table 15.1*.

As can be seen, the four Gulf States are urban communities *par excellence*. Compared with the large rural sectors typically found in most of the less developed countries, these urban communities reflect significant ethnic diversity which has its roots not only in the indigenous population, but also in the large working class of foreign residents drawn from many countries. This combination of urban concentration coupled with ethnic diversity, has important food policy implications, particularly in terms of differing tastes, consumption patterns, and the variety of food requirements.

The second important feature is the very high share of the population in secondary and tertiary sectors. In addition to primary crude oil production, this concentration has affected the pattern of infrastructural development in the four Gulf States with the focus on roads, housing, drinking water and power, and has led to relatively heavy government expenditures on urban social services. Such specially designed infrastructure for urban development is of very limited use to the development of the non-oil primary sector, particularly agriculture and food production.

TABLE 15.1. Population distribution in group of four Gulf States (1978)

State	Total population (thousands)	Percentage urban population	Percentage in secondary and tertiary sectors
Kuwait	994.8	88.6	97.5
Bahrain	256.0	80.1	95.0
Qatar	170.0	88.0	–
UAE	558.0	83.9	95.4

Source: Economic Commission for Western Asia (ECWA), Population Division.

TABLE 15.2. Sectoral distribution of GDP in group of four Gulf countries (1976)

Sector	US$ million	Percentage GDP
Agriculture	195	0.7
Oil and mining	17 856	61.3
Manufacturing	2100	7.2
Others	3982	30.8

Source: ECWA, Statistics Unit.

The largely urban populations of the four Gulf States possess very high per capita incomes by international standards, ranging from US$2350 in Bahrain to US$13 500 in UAE. The weighted average per capita income for the group is presently estimated at US$10 585 per annum. This highly urbanized population with unusual purchasing power has led to an extremely effective demand for consumer goods, particularly food and beverages. Ironically, domestic food production has done very little to meet this buoyant demand. Agriculture plays a very minor role in the economies of this group illustrated by the meagre contribution of agriculture to sectoral GDP shown in *Table 15.2*.

Consequently, per capita food imports are the highest in the world standing at US$320 in 1975. This compares with US$147 for Europe, US$118 for all developed countries, and US$15 for all less developed countries[3]. It is also interesting to note that per capita food imports have spiralled to this high level in 1975 from only US$126 in 1970, reflecting a 50% increase per annum (in current prices).

Indigenous food production?

At first glance, environmental adversity appears as a formidable constraint to any sizeable food production in the group of four Gulf States. The region is characterized by hot and dry summers and mildly cold winters. Air temperatures fluctuate between 52°C in July/August to below freezing during December/January. The relative humidity ranges between 85% as a maximum average usually in January, and 12% as a minimum average in the summer months.

Rainfall averages about 150 mm annually mainly in the winter months. It normally falls in a light drizzle, accompanied by strong local thunderstorms in the early winter and late spring months. Furthermore, the low average rainfall, together with high evaporation rates, limits the amount of water that could reach the water table, and hence the local natural recharge of underground water is relatively limited.

In addition, the oil-producing Gulf States suffer from some degree of atmospheric and sea pollution which is often an inevitable consequence of large-scale oil production, particularly where effective environmental controls have not yet been introduced.

For all these reasons, policies relating to indigenous food production should be considered with caution. For one thing, agriculture must have irrigation to cope with the harsh conditions of that region. However, the main technical constraint is that the amount of arable land suitable for irrigated agriculture is far in excess of the amount of water available for irrigation. Thus, in determining land use, major consideration should be given to the most effective use of the limited water resources.

Food production policies should be considered in the two distinct contexts of crop and livestock sectors. Environmental adversity affects food production in these two sectors through different mechanisms. Therefore, the two contexts are considered separately.

Crop production

The potential for enlarged crop production under the harsh ecological conditions of the Gulf States is related to two technical questions: the first concerns the possibility of increasing water resources for irrigation purposes, and the second pertains to the improvement of irrigation system efficiency, i.e. reducing the amount of water required for crop irrigation without any significant loss of productivity.

There are several sources which can be tapped to increase the supply of irrigation water.

Underground water

It is evident that there is little surface water in the group of four Gulf States. The main source of natural water in the region is underground water. Plans for the utilization of underground water are not based on obtaining an equilibrium between the amount of the natural recharge of the aquifers from rainfall and the amount of water discharged by the wells. To obtain such an equilibrium in the use of groundwater, the available supplies would not be sufficient to meet the aggregate demand for water (urban and agricultural). Consequently, under present underground water use plans, the level of water in the aquifers will decline with time. Also the salt content of the water of some aquifers would increase with continuous pumping. However, there are various possibilities for artificially recharging the aquifers by such means as water from Shat Al-Arab, from the water produced by the distillation plants, or water carried by the returning oil tankers. The proposed technologies are hypothetical at this stage and require the initiation of feasibility studies which can only be carried out by a very high level of expertise.

Treated sewage water

This is an important potential water source for agricultural development in the Gulf region. Such a water resource is being utilized for growing crops in many parts of the world where solutions to health hazards and pollution problems have been worked out. Being a mixture of the distillation water and underground brackish water, its present salt content is about 2700 parts per million. Obviously, this source of water would increase with population growth. As an example, a major project to make use of sewage effluent water was started in Kuwait in 1977 for a total project area of 920 hectares. About 500 000 gallons/day are used to irrigate windbreaks in the project area, and 6 million gallons/day irrigated 263 hectares during the 1978–79 cropping season.

Refinery waste water

Some research is already underway to study the feasibility of using this water for irrigation purposes. This water has a relatively low salt content (500 to 1000 parts per million of TDS), but it has some phenol. It could be an important source for green tree planting.

Desalinated water

This is currently an important source of fresh water for urban consumption and gardening in most of the Gulf States. About 10–15% of the output of desalinated water is usually taken from the brackish underground water so that the salt content of potable water is within the range of 500–800 parts per million. Thus, the increasing production of desalinated water restricts the use of underground water for agricultural purposes. On the other hand, if desalinated water is to be used for agricultural purposes, water would have to be made available at a price of about US$1.50 per 1000 gallons, which would be a highly subsidized price. In the long term, any substantial use of desalinated water for agriculture would depend on the possible development of lower cost methods of desalination. As an example, the feasibility of using the process of reverse osmosis for desalination of brackish water is currently being investigated in some Gulf States.

As indicated, there is important potential for increasing water availability for irrigation purposes. There is also equally important potential for improving irrigation system efficiency whereby adverse climatic conditions can be modified to suit growth requirements of different crops. Cropping under cheap plastic structures and the use of water-saving drip irrigation systems alone or in conjunction with polythene mulching are examples of possible farming methods, some of which are currently used in the Gulf States. Progress is also possible in related fields such as chemical weed control in mulch and bare plantings, virus problems, designed and environmental control, use of plastics and other materials, handling, packaging, storage and marketing aspects, particularly in the field of protected cropping.

However, much work is still needed to improve irrigation system efficiency and specially designed farming practices in the Gulf States. This includes investigations on the design of multibay structures to improve environmental control systems using thermostatically controlled equipment. It also covers the introduction of new, more economical, drip-irrigation systems which are automatically controlled. More research is needed to produce more durable polythene sheeting to cover structures, as well as new mulching materials.

Modern nurseries, equipped with controlled environment as well as electronically controlled misting irrigation systems for the production of healthy seedlings throughout the year, form an integral part of successful protected cropping. There is also a need for the introduction of new adapted virus and nematode-resistant clones. Crop phasing and appropriate cropping patterns under the controlled conditions should be tested. Finally, there is need for nutritional studies on crops produced under protection to ensure their suitability for the adopted food policy.

Almost all of the proposed techniques for increasing water resources and farming efficiency are the product of 'Western' technology. Their massive use hinges largely on cooperation and trade with western European countries. They all have the twin features of high capital intensity associated with the need for highly skilled labour and managerial manpower. The former is no problem for the Gulf States; the latter is in short supply.

Livestock production

There is a general mistaken belief that harsh ecological conditions such as those prevailing in the Gulf States are technically unfit for livestock production. On the contrary, the results obtained from an intensive technical study undertaken recently in the UAE, indicated that European cattle breeds could be maintained successfully under high environmental temperatures[1].

The often disappointing results are mainly due to inadequate management and feeding, in addition to a lack of knowledge of the requirements of exotic cattle. Indeed, zero grazing systems in extreme climatic conditions have the advantage that energy expenditure and heat production due to walking are kept to a minimum.

Naturally, Western technology is essential in taking steps to mitigate climatic stress, thereby contributing to the successful maintenance of livestock. This relates to various aspects such as showering and cooling methods, and the provisions of shelters. Special-purpose technologies would also be required for feeding and watering the stock. When all such measures were taken, 'the herd remained remarkably trouble-free and tolerated the conditions of the Gulf littoral very well'[1].

In addition to dairy production, both egg and broiler meat production can be expanded without serious technical constraints. In effect, almost all the Gulf States have commerical poultry production already underway. Again, all these livestock and poultry enterprises are characterized by high capital intensity and call for skilled management and manpower.

The role of Western technology is very obvious. Furthermore, although the expansion of these activities would be import substituting, it would, nevertheless, increase the dependence of the Gulf States on imported feed needed for livestock and poultry expansion. However, 'feed' security would be generally less costly and a much lesser threat to these countries than 'food' security. Sources of supply are more diverse and accessible with some located in less developed countries. The logistics of transport, storage, and distribution are inherently less cumbersome and costly than for finished livestock and poultry products.

It is interesting to note that the above issues concerning the technical possibilities for increasing food production under the harsh ecological conditions of the Gulf States are not simply prospective horizons or remote opportunities. For instance, some effort has already been undertaken to counteract the depletion of underground water and recharging the aquifers in Bahrain. A few projects for the production of protected vegetables have been started on a relatively large scale in several Gulf States. In Kuwait, which is the most arid of the group of four Gulf States, a poultry and egg farm has recently been established with a production capacity of 70 million eggs per year. Local production of sheep meat in that country has been started and plans are underway to produce 250 000 lambs per year.

All these examples show that the technical constraints on agricultural production are *not* prohibitive. Indeed, one United Nations mission recently recommended a significant expansion of agricultural production in Kuwait to include the following:

- Complete self-sufficiency in eggs and broilers.
- 80% self-sufficiency in whole fresh milk.
- 80% self-sufficiency in fresh vegetables.

These recommendations indicate that the growth of agricultural production in the Gulf States is not simply of academic interest. There must be socioeconomic justifications for such capital-intensive and costly enterprises. Thus, let us now consider the socioeconomic issues.

Is agricultural development justified?

A petrodollar may be saved, invested, or spent on consumption goods and services including imported foods and other agricultural products. Agricultural development is related to the last two decisions. One is an investment decision: should funds be invested in agricultural development projects or in other ventures? The second is a 'buy-or-make' decision: should the Gulf States produce their food or should it be imported? Obviously, the two decisions are not mutually exclusive; the 'make' decision inevitably implies an investment decision. However, the relevant criteria underlying the two decisions are different.

Criteria for investment decision

Many investment options are open to the petrodollar holder. Investment in the development of domestic agriculture may be gauged according to the criteria below.

Returnability

This is based on the classical cost–benefit analysis. The internal rate of return for Gulf agricultural projects would, in most cases, be comparatively lower than alternative projects due to their high capital intensity, small volume, and low unit prices of agricultural commodities. But agricultural projects in the Gulf States would normally involve very important indirect benefits that are *not* 'internalized' in the cost–benefit analysis. For instance, the impact of windbreaks on the improvement of the environment and on public health (such as restricting the spread of trachoma) would not usually be internalized in assessing project returnability.

Diversity

Diversification is an important consideration in most investment decisions. A balanced portfolio of well-conceived investment is very desirable. The relation of domestic to foreign investments is an important aspect of this balance. Without greater attention to agricultural development, the potential for increasing the share of domestic investment will remain highly restricted. Furthermore, domestic investment will be minimal in direct-productive activities and will continue the focus on civil infrastructures and housing projects. The expansions of food production should open new horizons for direct productive investment and for balancing the relation between domestic and foreign investment.

Appreciability

Investment in agricultural development would appreciate with improved yields and rising food prices, provided good management is available to carry out the relevant projects. Conversely, investment in securities and liquid assets may be subject to erosion due to fluctuations in foreign exchange. Therefore, investment in land reclamation and other agricultural projects may entail long-term capital gains which would more than offset a relatively low rate of return.

Linkability

Much of the domestic investment of the Gulf States is directly linked to oil production, e.g. refineries, fertilizer plants etc. Indeed, much of the service sector is dependent on income flows from the oil sector. A cessation of oil production is, therefore, a menace to all linked activities. Agricultural development breaks this vicious circle and dampens the dominance of the oil sector. Moreover, it may generate its own linkages (backward and forward), thereby creating new activities that are linked to a permanent resource. The expansion of food production and processing enhances the proportion of intersectoral transactions to total output of the countries concerned and, therefore, should be helpful in restructuring their economies.

Criteria for buy-or-make decision

Whether to produce or import food is another critical decision which has a direct bearing on agricultural development in the Gulf States. The decision is assessed in the light of the criteria dealt with below.

Efficiency

According to this criterion, food should be imported if it costs less than when produced domestically. Food imports would appear to have an edge in this respect, although the comparative advantages of foreign supply sources seem plausible for such enterprises as poultry production where Western technology can be stimulated without much difficulty.

Security

Food security is now an over-riding objective for many less developed countries. A certain minimum level of domestic self-sufficiency is often advocated even at the expense of efficiency. The security may be against possible blackmail or boycott[2], or it may be a hedge against economic contingencies such as short supplies on world markets. Also, it may provide a buffer stock to accommodate domestic consumption while imported foods are in transit.

Stability

Prices of imported foods are not controllable by Gulf States. Their purchases are too small to exert any influence on world food prices. Thus, they must accept price fluctuations as exogenous or given. This is an element of instability which has adverse socioeconomic effects. In contrast, prices of domestic foods are controllable to a significantly greater extent since they are largely affected by indigenous forces.

Adaptability

Consumers in the Gulf States, as in other regions of the world, have distinctive tastes and consumption patterns. Consumers are often forced to adapt themselves to imported goods, rather than the other way around. Domestic production is in a better position to adapt output to local conditions, both quantitatively and qualitatively. For instance, imports usually involve the procurement of relatively large quantities in anticipation of, say, six-months demand. This requires storage and handling facilities such as a cold store chain. The associated costs of these services significantly inflate consumer prices.

Equity

The business of food imports is often concentrated in the hands of a few agencies. The 'spillover' effects of profits and earned income are very limited. In contrast, domestic production generates employment and income not only in the tertiary sector, but also in the primary and secondary sectors. Therefore, more equity in income distribution is realized. Parasitic incomes are characteristic of import businesses in many of the less developed countries. The expansion of domestic food production and marketing through producers' and consumers' cooperatives should go a long way in rectifying this situation.

Highly skilled manpower

The pace of agricultural development in the four Gulf States has been very slow. Attention has focused mainly on foreign investments and on domestic ventures directly linked to oil production, or indirectly dependent on income flows from the oil sector. This has been essentially a psychological bias, since the expansions of agricultural production is *technically* feasible with the assistance of advanced Western technology.

The criteria of investment returnability and project efficiency, though important in project analysis, are not very pertinent to agricultural development projects in the four Gulf States. Other criteria should be considered. They tend to support the hypothesis that agricultural development under such ecologically harsh conditions should be pushed to the maximum possible threshold.

The capital intensity of food production projects is not a limiting factor as in other less developed countries. Employment creation and labour intensity are not important considerations in the four Gulf states. The main limiting factor is management of complex enterprise systems and the need for highly skilled manpower to absorb and implement the advanced technologies required to initiate and sustain agricultural production under the harsh environmental conditions characterizing these Gulf States. Thus the problem at stake concerns neither the technical nor economic feasibility, but focuses mainly on the severe demands on highly talented managers.

References

1. ANSELL, R. H. (1976) Maintaining European dairy cattle in the Near East. *World Animal Review,* No. 20, 1–7
2. EL-SHERBINI, A. A. (1979) *Food Security Issues in the Arab Near East.* Oxford, Pergamon Press
3. EL-SHERBINI, A. A. and SINHA, R. (1978) Arab agriculture – prospects for self sufficiency. *Food Policy,* **3** (2), 84–94

Part VII

Developing efficient food marketing systems

The first chapter in this part provides a broad gauge approach to the analysis of food marketing systems – particularly in less developed countries. It offers a systematic way of looking at measures of efficiency, effectiveness, and performance in food marketing systems. Giving consideration to the development of 'bankable' projects in the marketing subsector, the chapter provides a simple account of calculating economic costs and benefits in proposed marketing projects or for assessing business firms. Kriesberg candidly recognizes the limits of economic analysis and the importance of judgement in assessing specific actions that may be needed to improve the functioning of food marketing systems in less developed countries.

The second chapter summarizes the main results from a study of food product development and marketing in 20 major Swedish food processing companies, data were collected taking into account both overall company policies and strategies and specific new food products developed and marketed by them during the period 1969–78. Altogether some 121 new food products, selected by company representatives to give a balanced picture of each company's total product development during this period, were included, with the aim of evaluating the success of different product development strategies used.

The last chapter aims at assessment of organization of food distribution in the field of agricultural production means and services. Each organizational solution in the marketing sphere should be adapted to objective market conditions, and, accordingly, the specific characteristics of the food market analysed have to be pointed out. Disproportions between the present organization of the food market and distribution system, on the one hand, and the characteristics of the food market on the other, should be underlined allowing the determination of possibilities and directions of improvement in the agricultural food distribution system. The main research effort was focused on the market of spare parts for agricultural machines, not an accidental selection since trade in spare parts is highly unsatisfactory.

Chapter 16

Food marketing efficiency: some insights into less developed countries

Martin Kriesberg

Introduction

In wealthy developed countries the poor represent a relatively small part of the total population. The economy can therefore readily support special feeding and food distribution programmes. In contrast, in many of the less developed countries the bulk of the population spends over half its income on food which is often inadequate both in quality and nutritional content. Since the poor are so many, the food must be distributed to them either via the commercial marketing system in urban areas, or via barter in the rural subsistence areas. It therefore becomes imperative that the marketing system perform efficiently.

There are many opportunities for improving efficiency. Take the case of fresh fruit and vegetables: in the process of getting the produce from the field to the consumer's table half the crop is often either completely lost or deteriorates substantially in quality. Therefore, even a relatively small reduction of waste per unit of produce handled, when multiplied by millions of units in the marketing channels, can significantly increase the availability of food for many. Furthermore, lower transportation costs, better storage and handling, and more efficient processing of commodities (including by-products) can also contribute to quality of foods and lower prices for consumers. Such improvements in food offer a very direct way of improving standards of living in populous low-income countries.

In short, gradual and systematic improvements in marketing systems in less developed countries tend to help lower food costs, boost purchasing power of wages, and can lead to more equitable income distribution.

Measures of efficiency, effectiveness and performance

Food marketing performs different functions for farmers, middlemen and consumers – the main participants in the system. Farmers see marketing as a means by which the portion of their product that they want to sell can be transferred to a purchaser at a price the farmers are willing to accept. Consumers are concerned

This chapter was originally an article in *Incomas Proceedings* (1974), Vol. 1. Ed. by D. F. Izraeli and D. N. Izraeli, Israel Universities Press, Jerusalem with permission of the publishers.

with buying the products they want in the forms, places and quantities they want, at prices they are willing to pay. Both farmers and consumers see the marketing system as serving their needs. They often fail to recognize the many functions that take place to accomplish this. Middlemen perform these functions, and consequently they tend to view the marketing system as a means of earning their livelihood as well as satisfying their needs as consumers.

Because marketing systems serve people with different interests, who want the system to achieve different ends, efforts to evaluate marketing must start with a clarification of objectives. Measures used and the outcome of our evaluation will be different if we judge marketing systems by how well they serve the needs of farmers, consumers or middlemen. Further delineation may be necessary as between different classes of farmers, consumers and middlemen.

Micro- and macroapproaches

Measures of performance by firms or cooperative groups are often at the 'micro' level, while measures of overall performance are at the 'macro' level.

For a transportation firm, a performance measure might be the cost per metric ton per mile of moving a particular commodity from the farmer to the silo in a city some miles away. The firm may use larger trucks with different on- and off-loading arrangements, and metric ton–mile costs may be lowered for the firm. These kinds of measures indicate how well a firm performs the function of transporting particular commodities within the domestic market; the results often show up in its profit–loss statement as well as its prices. One might also determine whether the transportation charges made by a firm are considerably in excess of its costs. Where this is the case, it might be evidence that the process by which transportation is utilized in the marketing system is not functioning well, even though the physical movement is being carried out with reasonable efficiency. The firm might be the only one able to provide the transportation service, or the only one having the financial leverage to make large profits. Artificial trade barriers may exist, such as local taxes on truck shipments from one part of the country to another. In a study on marketing efficiency in several African countries, Jones[2] uses these latter charges as measures of performance in marketing rather than actual costs for the physical movement of the commodities. It may then be found that a principal factor causing high transportaton charges is not the high operating costs of the firm, but public policies which restrict importation of additional trucks and sanction cumbersome local tax collection on trucking.

When a government economist or planning officer, concerned with the nation's overall development, evaluates marketing this evaluation is usually based on 'macro' measures of performance rather than the 'micro' measures as applied by a farmer or marketing firm. In a macromeasure of marketing performance, one looks at the entire marketing function or system rather than the operations of a particular firm or group of firms. Thus, transportation charges may be estimated for the moving of major commodities to markets to determine how well the transportation function is being performed within the country. Changes in roads and transportation equipment for a number of firms may lower costs and hence improve overall performance.

The analyst seeking to determine the sources of high transportation costs and/or charges may take either a micro- or macrolook at the problem. Ultimately, both types of analyses are necessary to bring about improvements. The macromeasures will be useful in determining where marketing costs are excessive and, hence, warrant remedial attention. Analyses at the firm level can provide the close insights necessary for bringing about changes in how the function is performed by such firms, thereby providing clues to help the firm, the industry, and perhaps the society as a whole.

Often societal and firm objectives are not the same and hence different measures of marketing performance are used. The government economist and the firm economist may well come up with different conclusions on the efficiency of the firm and of the overall system in which the firm operates.

Efficiency versus effectiveness

Efficiency in marketing systems relates to the amount or costs of inputs required to obtain a given level of output, e.g. a given amount and mix of marketing services or the movement of a given amount of product to markets at given distances. Effectiveness may be viewed as the performance of the marketing system in terms of objectives set for it. If an objective is to move larger quantities of foods to urban markets at reasonable costs, effectiveness might be measured in several ways, e.g. whether the cost per given unit of commodity is going up or down over time, and whether the cost in one country is significantly different from that in other countries with similar conditions and at a similar stage of development. When such measures are used, effectiveness and efficiency have similar meanings, i.e. performing marketing functions at reasonable cost.

But the effectiveness of a marketing system may be evaluated against other kinds of objectives. For example, the marketing system may do reasonably well in physically moving the grain produced for market from farmers to consumers who have enough money to buy their food needs through regular commercial channels. The same marketing system may be inadequate in meeting the objectives of getting the food to people who cannot afford to pay commercial prices. A market news service may disseminate information useful to producers in getting higher prices but the information may be of little use to consumers. But efficiency and effectiveness have essentially the same meaning, if the objectives sought are the same. Raising the question of effectiveness brings the issue of objectives into sharper focus.

Marketing performance

In performing its functions, the marketing system uses resources of labour and capital, and these have a price. Whoever performs the activity or provides the capital, whether a cooperative, a corporation, or a government agency, the marketing activity incurs a cost.

Three common measures used to evaluate marketing performance are: (*a*) the farmer's share of the consumer's food expenditure; (*b*) its counterpart, the gross marketing margin, sometimes called the farm-retail price spread; (*c*) what proportion of a consumer's income must be spent for food. These statistics are often misunderstood and, consequently, are misused. For example, the gross marketing margin may be low because marketing activities are being carried out at low cost. But, the margin may also be low because the marketing system is providing few services. In Brazil, in January 1969, for example, the gross marketing margin for beef was 36% of the consumer price; the comparable statistic for meat in the United States was 43% during that year[3]. Analysis showed that the Brazilian marketing margin for beef was low because the system provides few services.

Thus, objective measurements of prices and margins as reflections of costs become extremely important in marketing efficiency considerations. The costs of performing specific marketing activities must be evaluated on the basis of the prices of the inputs. This is not a particularly difficult compilation for inputs that have known market prices, such as labour, containers, raw materials and the like. Equitable charges for other inputs, such as management and capital, may not be as easily evaluated. Economists turn to concepts such as normal profit, risk factors and opportunity cost in such evaluations.

The proportion of incomes that consumers spend for food is not strictly a measure of marketing performance but rather of how well the entire agribusiness system is working. Since marketing costs are often 50% and more of total food costs, and since the marketing system influences the system and costs of production, this measure has some validity. Moreover, this measure takes on special importance where governments set national food policies in which some minimum standard of nutrition is sought. In such situations, the proportion of incomes that people spend for the minimum diet is a good gauge of how well the agroindustry system is serving the nation's objectives.

Input–output measures for specific marketing functions

Marketing efficiency can be measured by input–output or cost–benefit ratios. A change that reduces input costs without reducing consumer services or satisfaction would be viewed as increasing efficiency; conversely, a change that increases input costs and was not balanced by more consumer benefits would mean less efficiency in the marketing system. Marketing efficiency can be further divided between: (*a*) pricing, or economic efficiency and (*b*) operating, or technical efficiency.

Pricing or economic efficiency

Economic efficiency is concerned with whether the price of marketing services reasonably reflects the costs of resources used in providing them. Economic efficiency also means that the marketing process is responsive to consumer wants, e.g. more resources will go to provide more marketing services, if consumers are willing to pay the price that firms charge for the services. However, the usefulness of the measure depends upon four conditions:

- Consumers be provided with viable alternatives from which to choose in the marketplace.
- Prices of alternatives adequately reflect the costs of providing them.
- Business firms be relatively free to enter or leave the given marketing activity.
- There is competition among these in the marketplace.

If markets are operating efficiently, prices of a given food will be related over space and time, and among forms. Prices should only differ between geographical areas of a country by transportation costs from one point to another. The price of a storable commodity at one point in time should not exceed the price in a previous period of time by more than the cost of storage. Similarly, the price of the processed product should only exceed the price of the unprocessed equivalent by the cost of processing.

Operating or technical efficiency

A system may operate efficiently by economic criteria, but if it is not conducive to cost-reducing technological change it may contribute little to economic development. In contrast to pricing efficiency, operational or technical efficiency focuses on reducing the costs of services and moving the goods through market channels. Thus, the substitution of a less expensive, but more durable and lighter, packaging material increases the amount of finished product storable in existing cubic space and reduces damage and spoilage, thereby contributing to lower costs. Knowledge from diverse disciplines such as engineering, food technology, business management and economics is directed at increasing efficiency of food marketing operations.

Marketing firms, operating in a competitive environment, seek to improve operational efficiency . Although their goal may be to enhance a profit position, often the benefits derived from improved operations accrue to society in the form of lower unit costs. These may be passed onto consumers in the form of lower prices and/or shared with producers. The marketing firm that improves its raw material procurement practices (centralizing purchases, buying in larger quantities, taking advantage of unit freight rates) is likely to increase operating efficiency. Similarly, a firm that rearranges sales territories and distributes food with fewer but larger deliveries per customer per week may effect savings.

Physical loss of commodities as they move through the channels of distribution from producer to ultimate consumer is another aspect of operating or technical efficiency. Just as production efficiency is often measured by yields and physical output, so too may marketing efficiency be measured by losses incurred. If, for example, in a less developed country, out of every 100 bushels of corn that leave the farm, only 80, on the average, finally reach the consumer, serious barriers to efficient marketing exist in the system. Losses owing to poor handling methods and storage facilities reflect operational inefficiencies, but losses to theft or bribery should probably be considered as part of economic inefficiency.

Calculating economic costs and benefits in marketing

This section owes much to the kind of analysis used by IBRD and described by Gittinger[1].

Measuring the efficiency of a marketing system in its entirety would require development of a complex model and collection and processing of large amounts of data. In practice, analyses of marketing efficiency are limited to measuring the value of alternative improvements to a specific marketing function or facility or, alternatively, of evaluating what would be the result if a particular marketing improvement were not made.

Thus, a general analysis of the marketing system in a country like Iran might disclose serious pricing and operational inefficiencies affecting the marketing of fruits and vegetables. (The data on the Tehran market are based largely on a preliminary study of wholesale produce in markets in Tehran, conducted by the Agricultural Marketing Centre of the Ministry of Cooperation and Rural Affairs. The descriptions relate principally to the Anbare Ghalleh market, visited by the author in June 1973 as part of a mission to Tehran aimed at evaluating the joint UNDP/FAO marketing programme in Iran.) Closer investigation might point out the need for changes in the process of assembling and storing produce destined for the urban population of Tehran. As a result of the investigation, a proposal is drawn up for a new central market and supporting facilities and infrastructure. Now, the analysis becomes one of determining costs and benefits of alternative market designs and locations.

The methodology used to measure the value of any proposed marketing improvement is basically a quantification of the expected benefits and costs. The quantification is completed for each alternative under consideration. Then an internal rate of return appropriate to the country and project is calculated so that the alternative having the highest net rate of return may be determined. Assuming that reliable data are used in the analysis, some assurance is obtained about which alternative would be best (from an economic point of view) though not necessarily which alternative political leaders should choose.

The analysis must consider both direct costs and benefits as well as indirect ones. The former are more readily measured, while the latter may include social costs and benefits which often can only be estimates based on judgement and experience. However, estimates of the indirect costs and benefits need to be made since they can significantly affect inter-relationships and shift a decision from one alternative to another. Costs and benefits are calculated for the estimated life of the project. The present worth of the stream of costs and returns is computed to facilitate comparisons. Thus a benefit–cost ratio is:

$$\frac{\text{present worth of benefits}}{\text{present worth of costs}} = \text{benefit–cost ratio}$$

Using the hypothetical example of a central produce market for Tehran the following analyses might be made.

Direct benefits

Reduction in spoilage   Although turnover is high, commodity spoilage at existing wholesale markets indicated that 20% of all perishable fruits and vegetables, and 10% of all semiperishables, such as potatoes and onions, were lost through spoilage in the wholesale system. Spoilage rates are expected to fall to 15% for perishables and 6% for semiperishables in the new market. The reductions in spoilage of 5% and 4%, respectively, are anticipated from improvements in storage, handling, quality control and packaging, in addition to the substantial reduction in the time food is in process between farmer and consumer. To evaluate the savings in spoilage, the food saved is priced at its cost to the wholesaler. Volumes are based on surveys of the tonnage entering and leaving the market.

Reduction in costs due to decrease in spoilage   Another substantial benefit is that, with a lower rate of spoilage, a smaller inventory is needed for a given volume of sales – resulting in lower storage, transportation and handling costs. The present worth of the stream of savings is calculated.

Reduction in unloading and loading time   Congestion is observed at the existing traditional wholesale markets, especially at peak periods on principal market days and peak seasons for fruits. The situation is much worse during rainy periods. In addition to lost time due to inefficient unloading and loading methods, there is also time lost because of long waiting periods due to the small size of the facilities compared with the volume and number of vehicles serviced and the limited number of access points or gates to the market. Initial savings in loading and unloading time per truck entering and leaving the new market are estimated and the value of the stream of savings is also calculated.

Direct costs

Construction and equipment   A number of engineering proposals and studies are made and analysed. These studies are evaluated and an estimate is made of construction and installation costs, as well as the costs of operating the facilities.

Maintenance of facilities   The study of the present Tehran market shows total operating costs, including personnel, maintenance and utilities. The same cost basis is assumed for the proposed facility, and three-quarters of these costs are considered to be in addition to those existing in the older market facility. Increased operating costs include more use of electricity for producing ice and lighting, as well as water and sewage not available or utilized in the older market.

Internal rate of return

On the basis of the estimates of direct costs and benefits described above, an internal rate of return[1] is estimated. This is the value of the net flow of returns on investments during the life of the project discounted to yield its present worth. In less developed countries an internal rate of return of 15–20% should be possible for a wholesale market facility. Volume and growth rate statistics used in the calculations are based on the last five years of data for Tehran.

In the case of fruits and vegetables, an average annual growth rate of 9% was assumed, based on the population growth rate, per capita income growth, and the income elasticity of demand for fruits and vegetables. The volume of fruits and vegetables is then projected for each year for 10 years and 20 years, though the life of the facility may be greater. The same procedure, with some modification, is used for potatoes and onions, assuming a 4.5% average annual growth rate. The annual volume of fruits and vegetables for 1973 was estimated at 1.2 million metric tons and for 1990 at 1.6 million metric tons.

The value of reducing spoilage 6% below what it would have been in the old facility is estimated for 1980 and for 1990 at current prices, over the life of the project. In similar fashion, savings in labour costs are estimated. Construction, maintenance and operating costs are subtracted from benefits for each year to derive *net* flows, which are then discounted to present value to yield the internal rate of return. In the analysis, returns for different suppliers of capital (a farmer in a marketing cooperative or an external lending agency) are presented separately.

Indirect benefits

Reductions in costs   Initially benefits from reductions in costs and risks will be quite small, but should grow over the years. The design of the facilities assures a much larger operating scale per business unit than prevails in the existing market. The market is designed to handle future demand by increasing the number of operating areas and stalls. The augmented market news service will link other markets and interior points. All of these factors will reduce marketing risks and costs. Increased competition should also be generated and hence reduced margins; but the amount of net reduction is not known.

Indirect income effect   More direct marketing by farmers would give them a larger share of the total price that consumers pay, and hence larger incomes. The result should be increased farm production that would not have otherwise occurred without the new facilities. This stimulation of farmer production, due to increased opportunity for direct marketing, is referred to as the 'indirect income effect'.

Economies in retailer purchases   Benefits to larger retail markets will result in (*a*) an eventual reduction of perhaps 2% in purchasing costs of fruits and vegetables; (*b*) an increase of some 15% in participation of retail markets in sales of fruits and vegetables; (*c*) more uniform produce quality.

Health impact   Improved public health, due to improved hygiene, cleanliness and more stable supply, will result. Therefore, rough estimates of the effect on the health of increasing numbers in Tehran, if a new facility were *not* built, can be made.

Indirect costs

At least three indirect costs will be incurred:

- Reduction in wholesaler's sales directly to consumers, resulting from the suburban location of the larger market.
- Additional loading and unloading of trucks which will occur particularly in the early period until all facilities are in place and administration of the new facility is well organized.
- Displacement of some intermediaries who operated in the old market but could not make the transition. These might well be marginal operators who will have difficulty making a livelihood in other pursuits.

Employment effects

Labour productivity gains are estimated at 4% which could result in some unemployment. However, the increase in the amount of food flowing through the system is expected to be 9% per year. Increase in demand for labour needed to handle this extra volume of food will most likely balance the loss of employment resulting from productivity gains.

The construction of the market itself will generate significant short-term demands for labour. Because of their increased productivity workers employed in the new market will be able to earn more.

Backward and forward linkages

The project would have important backward and forward linkage effects. These should also be taken into account. The new wholesale market would encourage farmers' cooperatives to rent stalls and thus be in a better position to benefit from the existence of an efficient outlet for their produce.

On the retail side, a growing number of supermarkets and smaller retailers would share in the benefits of purchasing commodities in the new facility. The improved method of purchasing perishables would be of primary benefit to the small retailer and hawker whose sales consist of a high percentage of fresh fruits and vegetables.

Furthermore, the new facility would make it possible to improve market news services. Backward and forward linkages, in addition to competitive pressures, should broaden the benefits of the improved wholesale system. No attempt has been made to estimate how much of the benefits would go to different groups. Nevertheless, a consideration of which economic groups would benefit from the proposed new market and the extent to which modifications in the proposal could shift the benefits in one direction or the other, should be taken into account in an overall appraisal of market plans. Almost certainly, political leaders will make such estimates if the analyst does not, and their methods of estimating may be more subjective.

Limits of economic analysis

Economic analyses, which are attempts to quantify costs and benefits associated with changes to increase efficiency of marketing systems, do not take away the importance of judgement. Moreover, marketing functions are carried on largely in the private sector. Hence, proposals for reform or changes in marketing infrastructure need to take into account the impact on private traders. These factors need, therefore, be taken into account in reaching decisions on project and policy alternatives.

It is not enough to recommend changes solely on the basis of economic costs and benefits, nor solely on the basis that a proposed loan will be repaid under terms negotiated. Also to be included in the analysis are: the human and institutional capability for accomplishing reforms and operating new facilities; the likely effect on innovation, initiative and adoption of technological change; impact on employment and income distribution.

Human and institutional capability

Marketing activities are performed by individuals working within the framework of many varied institutions. The institutions give form and continuity to the individual actions and to the overall marketing process. Often marketing institutions in less developed countries lag behind other programmes, even where capital is readily available for marketing facilities, because trained personnel are not available to help staff them.

As marketing institutions become more complex (taking on more activities over larger geographical areas, involving more products and people as well as capital) the task of management grows more difficult. In most of the less developed countries, there has been little training in specific marketing functions or in the management of agribusiness firms performing them. The shortage of technical competencies in LDC marketing systems is in two areas:

- Lack of technically trained people to delineate problems and to determine implications of alternative policies at both micro- and macrolevels.
- Lack of individuals with operational and management capabilities to perform functions essential for efficient operation of both public and private marketing institutions.

Innovation and technological change

The capability of private as well as public institutions to carry out marketing changes called for should be fully taken into account in formulating individual marketing projects. Change and improvements in marketing are a continuous process, in which the private sector can be an important innovative element.

A system may be judged efficient because traders are charging reasonable prices for performing their marketing functions. But technological change may help integrate activities and reduce costs, thereby providing a different basis for measuring efficiency.

Indeed, the private sector in LDCs is often efficient in economic terms, but backward in its technology and institutional arrangements. New infrastructure may improve operating of technical efficiency as compared to existent facilities. But, institutional arrangement may impede reaching higher levels of efficiency.

These factors make it mandatory for the project formulator to look beyond the physical facility that is the basis for calculating economic benefits and costs in marketing changes. In addition to the analysis of a specific facility, he also needs to consider whether the associated policies and institutional arrangements will encourage further initiative and innovation in the marketing system. Will project-linked policies open up the market to additional entrepreneurs? Will credit and import policies encourage importation of appropriate new technology in the marketing system? Will traders have incentives to seek means of lowering their operating costs? These are some of the questions that should be examined as part of the non-quantitative aspects of economic analyses, so as to institutionalize desirable changes in marketing related projects.

Economic equity

Economic equity is difficult to treat in project calculations and in proposals for marketing improvement. Perhaps it can be made more susceptible of analysis if it is looked at in terms of employment and income distribution. Inequity is most directly felt by the unemployed, and by those who eke out a precarious livelihood by brief periods of employment.

Improved income distribution is effected most directly by providing jobs to those who lack them. Perhaps a retraining programme, or an enlargement of the project, or a phased development could moderate the effect of people put out of employment. New work situations, in which displaced people may find employment commensurate with their experience, might be explored with local authorities involved in carrying out the project as initially formulated.

In reckoning returns from a project or programme to improve food marketing, care needs to be taken to include the several groups directly affected – producers, consumers, and those in the middle, the marketing people. While it is difficult for a project analyst to weigh the trade-offs between marketing improvements which may hold down food costs for some 500 000 in a city like Tehran, against the loss of employment for 100 working in antiquated facilities, one would need to apply different weights to these numbers before placing them on a scale of benefits and costs.

One of the virtues of the kind of analysis suggested here is that questions are raised which focus attention on the range of considerations that should be dealt with in making investments to increase marketing efficiency in ways simultaneously stimulating to socioeconomic development, while also tending to improve equity in distribution of accrued benefits.

References

1. GITTINGER, J. P. (1972) *Economic Analysis of Agricultural Projects.* Baltimore, Johns Hopkins University Press
2. JONES, W. O. (1970) *Measuring the Effectiveness of Agricultural Marketing in Contributing to Economic Development. Some African Examples.* Stanford University Food Research Institute
3. STEELE, H. L., VERA-FILHO, F. M. and WELSH, R. S. *Commercializacao Agricola,* 1st ed., Appendix Table V-1 and Table V-3. San Paulo, Editora Atlas SA

Chapter 17

Developing and marketing new food products: the case of Sweden

Hary Nyström
Bo Edvardsson

Introduction

This chapter reviews the main results from an empirical study of food product development and marketing in 20 major Swedish food-processing companies[3]. Data for this study were collected both with regard to overall food company policies and strategies and to specific new food products developed and marketed by the companies during the 10-year period 1969–78. A wide range of food products are covered in the sample – dairy and fat products, cereals, meat and fish, fruit and vegetables being the main groups.

Personal interviews with leading company executives responsible for the new product policy and actual development work were carried out as a basis for the study and these interviews were supplemented with written material such as internal company reports and product specifications. The outcomes of different strategies were evaluated along three dimensions.

Technological success

Technological success is measured by the level of technological innovation, i.e. the extent to which technically developing a new product made necessary the use of new ideas and techniques. In other words this outcome measure is used to indicate the level of technological creativity which a company had to achieve to be able to solve the critical technical problems in connection with developing a specific product. Based on interview data for each product, the level of technological innovation was measured on a scale from 1 to 5, with higher values indicating greater technological success.

As in the case of market success all the assessments were made independently by the two authors when interviewing, and when different assessments were made the average of the two values was used.

Market success

Market success is measured by the competitive situation for a new product at the time of market introduction. The more unique a product was judged from a buyer's point of view, in comparison with the closest competing products on the market, the greater was the market success according to this definition. As in the case of technological success a scale from 1 to 5 was used, with higher values indicating greater market success.

Commercial success

Commercial success is measured by the estimated profit level of a new product, as judged by company executives. For products which had been on the market long enough to make possible such estimates, a scale from 1 to 5 was used to indicate the degree of commercial success. A product was judged to be a big commercial success (1), a small success (2), neither a success nor a failure (3), a small failure (4) or a big failure (5).

In our analysis, we look at three strategy dimensions of product development and marketing to see how related they are to success along these outcome dimensions. The first is technology use, the second research and development cooperation with the outside research community, and the third marketing strategy.

Technology use

Technology use refers to the extent to which companies work within established technologies to find new products or try to combine different technologies to achieve this purpose. Working within established technologies is called 'isolated technology use', while combining different technologies is called 'synergistic technology use'. A technology is viewed as a relatively well-defined and delimited area of technical knowledge, usually the basis for educational and professional specialization.

Synergistic technology use is, therefore, interdisciplinary and makes necessary the bridging of information and communication gaps between different specialists and separate specialized areas of knowledge. Isolated technology use is intradisciplinary and may be more easily carried out by individuals and companies, without going outside their established areas of specialization.

Our analysis shows that synergistic technology use was significantly related to greater technological and market success than isolated technology use (95% level) and also to somewhat greater commercial success. For the Swedish food-processing companies, it thus appears to have been a successful strategy to expand, rather than concentrate, technological knowledge in order to successfully find and develop new food products.

Research and development cooperation

The terms 'external' versus 'internal' research and development orientation are used to refer to the extent to which companies stress their internal compared to their external research environment in finding and developing new products. The more a company relies on its own knowledge and competence in idea generation and technical product development, the more internal its research and development orientation is. The more it depends on outside aid and assistance for these purposes, for instance by cooperating with universities, research institutes, consultants or other companies, the more externally oriented its research and development orientation is. Our data from the Swedish food-processing companies show that, as in the case of synergistic technology use, external research and development orientation was associated with significantly greater technological success than internal research and development orientation (95% level). With regard to commercial success, however, internal research and development orientation was associated with significantly greater profitability than external orientation (*Table 17.1*).

TABLE 17.1. Technology use, research and development orientation and marketing diversification in relation to technological, market and commercial success for 121 products from 20 Swedish food-processing companies

		Technological success, measured by the level of technological innovation	Market success, measured by the market situation at product introduction	Commerical success from low to high
Synergistic technology use	(54)	2.9	3.8	3.4
		S_1	S_1	NS
Isolated technology use	(67)	2.0	3.3	3.3
External orientation	(27)	2.7	3.5	3.1
		S_1	NS	S_2
Internal orientation	(94)	2.4	3.4	3.4
Diversified marketing	(45)	2.4	3.6	3.0
		NS	S_2	S_2
Concentrated marketing	(76)	2.5	3.4	3.5

Higher numbers indicate greater technological, market and commercial success.
Number of products within parentheses.
Source: Nyström and Edvardssson[2].
S_1: significant at the 95% level (*t*-test).
S_2: significant at the 90% level.
NS: not significant at the 90% level.

It thus appears to have been more profitable for the food companies studied to stress their own competence in product development, whilst utilization of the outside research community had evidently led to more unique products from a technological point of view. One reason for this could be the conservative demand situation which, according to our interviews, is highly characteristic of the food market. Customers, by and large, are not very willing to try unfamiliar food products. Since they are used to the products of certain companies, their brand names are probably often viewed as quality guarantees for the type of products mainly sold by these companies, and for which the companies usually have a special inhouse research and development competence. When developing such products, which are easier for a company to successfully market, outside aid and assistance is more seldom needed than when developing products outside a company's usual product line. This, then, could be one possible reason why internal research and development orientation is associated with more profitable products than external research and development orientation.

Marketing strategy

In our analysis we differentiate between two marketing strategies for each new product. The first, concentrated marketing, means that a new product fits into a company's established assortment and is also mainly directed towards the needs of existing customers. The second, diversified marketing, means that a new product either falls outside the existing assortment of a company or is heavily directed towards new customer groups.

Our data show that a concentrated marketing strategy was, on average, associated with somewhat greater technological success than a diversified marketing strategy for the new products studied, but the difference is not significant. A diversified marketing strategy, on the other hand, was associated with significantly greater market success on the 90% level. With regard to commercial success, a concentrated marketing strategy was clearly associated with greater success than a diversified marketing strategy (significant on the 95% level).

It thus appears to have been more profitable for companies to develop new products similar to their existing products and directed towards their existing customers' needs, than to diversify their assortment and market orientation. The implications of diversification for technological and market success is less clear from our data.

Company variables

In addition to strategic variables, our study of Swedish food-processing companies also looked at some relationships between company variables and product development success. The variables analysed in this connection were company size, research intensity and ownership.

TABLE 17.2. Company size in relation to technological, market and commercial success for 121 products from 20 Swedish food-processing companies

Size group*	Number of companies	Technological outcome (level of technological innovation)	Market outcome (competitive situation at market introduction)	Commercial outcome
The largest companies	6	2.5	3.7	3.4
The middle-sized companies	8	2.4	3.4	3.3
The smallest companies	6	2.3	3.3	3.3

* Size measured by average annual sales during the ten-year period studied.
Higher numbers indicate higher technological, market and commercial success.
Source: Nyström and Edvardsson[2].

Starting with company size, measured by sales, we found that larger food companies appeared to have employed more innovative research and development strategies during the period, while smaller companies appeared to have employed more innovative marketing strategies. With regard to product development outcome, larger companies were more successful than smaller companies, from both a technological and market, as well as from a commercial, point of view, but the differences are fairly small (Table 17.2).

Looking at research intensity, measured by research and development expenditure in relation to sales, we did not find any tendency for high research intensity to be associated with greater attempts by companies to develop new markets and technologies than low research intensity. Instead of mainly spending research and development funds on developing new technologies and markets, highly research-intensive companies appeared to give even greater priority to developing their established markets and technologies than less research-intensive companies. With regard to the outcome of product development more research-intensive companies, as might be expected, were technologically and commercially more successful than less research-intensive companies, but as in the case of company size the differences are quite small (*Table 17.3*).

TABLE 17.3. Research intensity in relation to technological, market and commercial outcome for 121 products from 20 Swedish food-processing companies

Research intensity*	Number of companies	Technological outcome (level of technological innovation)	Market outcome (competitive situation at market introduction)	Commercial outcome
Companies with high research intensity	6	2.7	3.5	3.4
Companies with intermediate research intensity	8	2.4	3.4	3.3
Companies with low research intensity	6	2.3	3.5	3.3

* Research intensity measured by average annual expenditure on R & D in relation to average annual sales. Higher numbers indicate higher technological, market and commercial succes.
Source: Nyström and Edvardsson[2].

Our analysis of research intensity points to the conclusion that highly research-intensive companies were able to find enough opportunities for new products within their established markets and technologies, and viewed exploiting such opportunities as more attractive than venturing into new areas.

Turning to ownership (*Table 17.4*) we first looked at differences in product development outcome between cooperative and private companies and then also at

TABLE 17.4. Ownership in relation to technological, market and commercial outcome for 121 products from 20 Swedish food-processing companies

Ownership	Number of companies	Technological outcome (level of technological innovation)	Market outcome (competitive situation at market introduction)	Commercial outcome
Consumer cooperatives	3	2.5	3.3	3.5
Producer cooperatives	4	2.5	3.6	3.5
All cooperatives	7	2.5	3.5	3.5
Swedish dominated private companies	7	2.3	3.5	3.3
Foreign dominated private companies	6	2.5	3.4	3.2
All private companies	13	2.4	3.4	3.3

Higher numbers indicate higher technological, market and commercial success.
Source: Nyström and Edvardsson[2].

differences between different types of cooperative and private companies. Seven of the companies were classified as cooperatively controlled and 13 as privately controlled, while three of the cooperative companies were consumer cooperatives and four producer cooperatives. Seven of the private companies were classified as Swedish controlled and six as foreign controlled.

In this analysis, it was found that the cooperative companies as a group had been technologically and commercially somewhat more successful in their product development than the private companies. When comparing producer cooperatives with consumer cooperatives, we found that producer cooperatives were more successful from a market point of view, while there was no difference from a technological and commercial point of view. Looking at the two types of private companies we found that Swedish-dominated private companies had been somewhat more successful in their product development from a market and commercial point of view, while the foreign dominated companies had been somewhat more successful from a technological point of view. Again, as in most of our data, we find that the differences are quite small, but the overall tendency is for cooperative companies to have been more successful than private companies.

Consumer outcome

In our study we also tried to assess the consumer implications of the companies' product development strategies, based on data provided in connection with the interviews (*Table 17.5*). Five aspects of consumer outcome, price, convenience, taste, nutritional value and medical value, were analysed. Price refers to whether or not new food products at the time of market introduction had a higher or lower price than the closest comparable competing products on the market. Our results indicate that price competition between new products and existing products had not been very intense during the period studied. A majority of the new food products (78%) had about the same price as the existing closest substitute, considerably fewer (16%) a lower price and very few (6%) a higher price. This is not surprising since one important reason why companies introduce new products is to avoid price competition by differentiating the product itself to make it, quality wise, more attractive to buyers than other products. From a consumer point of view the implication is that product development did not appear to have led to very many new products with either a higher or lower price than comparable products on the market.

The second consumer variable, convenience, refers to whether or not new products are easier to prepare, handle or store compared to the closest competing

TABLE 17.5. Consumer outcome for 121 products from 20 Swedish food processing companies

Consumer outcome	Measures of consumer outcome, number of products in each category				
	Price	Taste	Convenience	Nutritional	Medical
Favourable	20 (16)	40 (33)	49 (40)	31 (26)	17 (14)
Neutral	94 (78)	74 (61)	70 (58)	87 (72)	104 (86)
Unfavourable	7 (6)	7 (6)	2 (2)	3 (2)	0 (0)

Source: Nyström and Edvardsson[2].
Numbers in parentheses are the percentage.

products. Our data indicate that convenience is an important aspect of consumer outcome for new food products. Almost half of the products (40%) were judged to be superior to competing products from a convenience point of view and almost none (2%) inferior.

With regard to the third consumer outcome variable, taste, about one-third (33%) of the new food products were judged to be more attractive to consumers than other comparable products on the market and only a few (6%) were judged to be less attractive. After convenience, taste was the most frequently mentioned consumer attribute of new food products.

Our fourth consumer outcome variable, nutritional value, was assessed on the basis of fat, fibre, protein and sugar content, and from this point of view about one-quarter (26%) of the new products was judged to be beneficial from a consumer point of view and very few (2%) detrimental. Our fifth consumer outcome variable, medical value, was attributed to a relatively small proportion of the new products (14%) which were directly intended for medical treatment.

Summing up our analysis of the consumer implications of product development, as viewed by the companies themselves, we see that the most common aspect of consumer outcome attributed to new products was convenience. Somewhat less frequently mentioned was a taste advantage and nutritional value, while a low price or medical value was held to characterize only a small number of new products studied. Since the results are not overly favourable from a company point of view, and as far as possible based on measurable qualities, there is little reason for us to believe that company representatives have intentionally given us misleading information as to what they believe are the consumer implications of the new products they have developed.

Comparison with earlier studies

It is surprising that the results from this study of product development in food-processing companies point to quite similar conclusions as we have previously found in other much more research and technology intensive industries, such as pharmaceutical drugs, industrial electronics and industrial chemicals[1]. These earlier studies were mainly concerned with the technological success of different product development strategies and showed for instance, as in the present study, that synergistic technology use and external research and development orientation were clearly associated with greater success in finding and developing new products, than isolated technology use and internal research and development orientation. It thus would appear that these findings do not only apply to high technology, research intensive industries, usually focused on in innovation studies. Instead similar conclusions may be drawn from our study of a much less innovative industry, food processing.

References

1. NYSTRÖM, H. (1979) Creativity and Innovation. New York, John Wiley
2. NYSTRÖM, H. and EDVARDSSON, B. (1980) Technological and Marketing Strategies for Product Development, Report No. 164 from the Innovation Research Group, Institute for Economics and Statistics, SLU, Uppsala, Sweden
3. NYSTRÖM, H. and EDVARDSSON, B. (1982) Product innovation in food processing – a Swedish survey. R and D Management, No. 2, 67–72

Chapter 18

Distribution system of agricultural production means and services in Poland

Bogdan Gregor

Introduction

Production and trade services for agriculture represent a key element of the agrobusiness complex in Poland today. Weakness in this sphere is usually attributed to inadequate investment and the insufficient supply of agricultural production means and services. Simultaneously, there pass unnoticed other equally important weaknesses. Some drawbacks of the distribution system should be pointed out that are revealed, amongst others, in the excessively long route of food product flow from the producer to the end-user, which increases the social costs of the functioning of the system. Furthermore, uncoordinated activities of marketing institutions responsible for product supply, and lack of adjustment of agricultural marketing to spatially differentiated conditions of agriculture, are of equal importance.

The analysis in this chapter is based on information coming from both primary and secondary sources. Information of the primary type was collected through empirical research carried out in companies representing all levels of trade in spare parts for agricultural equipment or industrial sales, wholesaling and retailing. This was, for the most part, qualitative analysis. To be able to describe the characteristics of the present distribution system and determine its basic shortcomings, fieldwork was carried out. In addition to contacting channel members, the interviews also encompassed 27 farmers whom the author met in stores selling spare parts for agricultural machines[2].

Methodological problems of the distribution system's research in the market for agricultural production means and services

Distribution channels of agricultural production means and services operate within the framework of the agrobusiness complex. They form a system which is affected by numerous internal and external factors. These factors can be evaluated from different angles: that of the end-user, the microeconomic, the macroeconomic and the social.

Any decision concerning changes in the distribution system must take into account the viewpoints of all system participants. Nonetheless, the end-user's point of view is of utmost importance, as it is through the satisfaction of end-users that organizational objectives are achieved. It should also be added here that the end-users point of view is highlighted, and that there are differences between detailed preferences for the agricultural farm and the institution purchasing spare parts to provide repair services of agricultural equipment. As a rule, the end-user's viewpoint corresponds to the social viewpoint. In the long run, the producer of production means and further distribution links must not only increase adaptability to the market situation, but must also stimulate the preferences of end-users in this market. This statement produces two practical consequences.

First, needs and preferences of end-users must be treated as superior to that of producers and distributors. Accordingly, they would constitute a starting point in the construction of an effective planning and organization of distribution channels. It can be added, at this point, that there exists a high substitution between production and distribution/marketing costs and social costs as a result of a freeze of production means (inventories). Apart from this, a substitution between costs incurred by particular distribution links takes place, as well as interbranch substitution within the agrobusiness complex. Therefore, a narrowly understood profitability account of any organizational solution is of secondary and not of primary concern.

Second, each proposition of structural and/or operational changes in distribution channel organization and each economic method of calculation that provides a basis for this proposition, must include an element of risk connected with a deficit of the said products at a given place or time. Hence, monetary benefits resulting from reduced inventories of most production means may be eliminated by the above-mentioned risk. A thesis might even be developed here that, other things being equal, a mutual correlation exists between inventories of production means and the extent to which the product flow is determined by the information and, to some degree, negotiation flows. Accordingly, if appropriate information is not secured and appropriate conditions, in which this information will provide a basis for decisions concerning the flow of products (sales, deliveries), are not created, then reduction of inventories and their spatial concentration may produce such a large risk that it will undermine all benefits resulting from reduction of these inventories.

In order to take into account different points of view, different criteria of evaluation must be applied. In the case of the macroeconomic point of view, the criterion will be maximization of the utilization of economic resources. Practically it encompasses three more detailed criteria:

- Creation of conditions for market equilibrium at a given time and place. This implies, in practice, that from the macroeconomic viewpoint a desirable distribution system is one that, with other conditions unchanged, ensures continuity of sales and full range of products for all end-users (and not only the assortment receiving preference of a given branch).
- Manipulation of growth, intensity and specialization of agricultural production.
- The third detailed criterion which is most closely connected with the microeconomic point of view is the capital frozen in inventories of production means and measured by the index of average inventories for trade.

The end-user's point of view is expressed by availability of production means and services with regard to their quantity and assortment. A general preference is formulated in such a way that it is compatible with the apparent macroeconomic viewpoint of the state. One more point remains, however, and that is the so-called 'utility of purchase'. This utility, due to the character of the purchase, corresponds in most cases to the social point of view. Its quantification is, nonetheless, difficult due to subjective and objective variables that make up an evaluation expressed by the end-user. It can, furthermore, be added that, in as much as punctuality of delivery or repair, frequency of deliveries and their form are a result of distribution channel organization, other product characteristics affecting the evaluation of the end-user, such as quality and price, are loosely connected with organization of distribution.

Profitability of a given organizational solution to marketing of agricultural products provides a decisive criterion when one takes into account the microeconomic point of view, either fragmentary, of a given distribution link or, overall, of the whole marketing system. The cost accounting might constitute a basis for its estimation. It is not easy, in practice, not only due to lack of information, but also due to the need for application of the concept of hypothetical costs; thus costs will be incurred or will spring up at times $t^1, t_2 \ldots t_n$, as a result of organizational changes introduced in the period t_0. The problem would be quite simple if changes in size and structure of costs could be analysed just in the sphere of newly formed organizational structures and flows within agricultural distribution channels. In practice, however, each change in the agricultural distribution system produces the following changes:

- Changes in relations and remuneration of production factor, i.e. capital and labour, within the framework of particular links of the agricultural distribution system and between these links.
- Considerable degree of substitution in relation to organizational changes between costs incurred by particular distribution links – including also the producer and the end-user and trade links.
- Between the agricultural distribution system treated as a means of strategy and tactics of a company and other activities, e.g. promotion, prices, where there are substitutional and complementary ties. Hence, changes in the distribution system may be reflected in changes of prices or promotion. As a result, it is difficult to make provisions for it in cost accounting.

Besides the above-discussed profitability account, an additional criterion, in a way a qualitative one, can be provided by the capacity or effectiveness of task implementation imposed upon a given agricultural distribution link. Accepting the principle of management by objectives (these objectives are outlined in the company plans by the central plan), the question should be asked whether the company's capacity for implementation of these objectives will be increased or decreased as a result of introduced organizational changes. Only this, combined with the profitability calculation, allows an evaluation from the microeconomic viewpoint to be carried out.

Factors determining distribution of agricultural production means and services

Organization of the distribution system is determined by many factors. Basic importance should still be attributed to three inter-related factors. These are: (*a*) product, (*b*) characteristics of demand and preferences of end-users, and (*c*) market situation.

A product, according to Dietl[1], is any object of sale or purchase and this may be a physical object or a service. In the market for agricultural production means and services three kinds of products can be distinguished: (*a*) physical objects, e.g. tractor or fodder concentrate, (*b*) services, e.g. ploughing, sowing, threshing, (*c*) a physical object combined with a service, e.g. plant protection means and their spreading. The assortment of products is extremely wide. Particular products differ between themselves, as regards both their physical and chemical properties, frequency of purchase and time in which they are used. From the supply point of view, the division of products into investment goods, e.g. agricultural machinery, and those for running production, e.g. mineral fertilizers, is of great importance. The former are more seldom purchased and their unit price is higher. This justifies a rational concentration of trade in these products. Size of products that satisfy production needs of agriculture and specific characteristics call for considerable individualization of organizational solutions in the distribution system within the framework of each branch. In *Table 18.1*, characteristics of demand for the analysed products and their significance for organization and management of the

TABLE 18.1. Characteristic features of demand for agricultural production means and services and their bearing on programming, organization and management of the production sector of the agricultural marketing system

Characteristics of demand	*Consequences for the agricultural marketing sector*
Basic, direct and growing in time demand	Rational deconcentration (services) and concentration of marketing (selected production means)
Spatial differentiation of demand	Elimination of indirect links between buyer and seller of services (provision of services directly to a farm and shortening of flow routes for production means between industry and end-user)
Differentiation of volume and structure of demand between individual farms	Maintenance of optimal service level and storage base for trade in production means. able to satisfy demand in periods of demand intensification
Strong concentration of demand for products in time–time utility (seasonality of demand)	Deconcentration of management task and performance in the spheres of agricultural production and marketing – specialization
Time correspondence between needs, demand, and purchase (satisfaction of needs) – absence of phenomenon of delayed demand for most production means and services	Adaptation of agricultural organization and its forms of marketing; volume and structure of market demand to spatially differentiated needs and preferences of end-users of given food products
Direct relationship between demand, agricultural production process and socioeconomic situation of place, i.e. village	Horizontal coordination of activities of facilitatory institutions dealing with the agricultural marketing system
Complementarity and substitutionality of demand for production means and services	Basing of programme development of marketing activity on knowledge of real demand for agricultural production means and services
Differentiated elasticity of demand in relation to product type and/or end-user	Active pricing and subsidizing policy in steering marketing activity – its relationship with agricultural price policy

agricultural marketing are presented. Some of the salient characteristics of demand for agricultural products, as well as their anticipated consequences for the agricultural marketing sector are now examined.

Features which essentially differentiate demand for agricultural production means and services from demand for other products include: agricultural production conditions pose close relationships with type of consumers and/or end-users representing numerous differentiated and territorially scattered economic units, and offer extremely high seasonality of demand. Almost three million farmers are buyers of agricultural production means and services. Two macrosegments of the market can be distinguished: socialized and individual farming units with the latter amounting to over 2.8 million. Socialized farms, due to the large scale of production and its capital intensive character, declare a relatively high demand for production means and services. This allows the application of direct deliveries from wholesale or even industrial companies. It would, however, be wrong if both macrosegments were treated as homogeneous systems. They are highly differentiated and this is reflected by the volume and structure of demand.

Programming of development and organization of agricultural marketing must take into account the existing relationships between production means and services for agriculture. Complementary character of demand for certain production means and services is of special significance for the organization of supply. In some cases a joint demand is spoken about. This refers especially to plant protection means and provision of services connected with their sowing. It would thus be justified if a commercial offer (sale of plant protection means) were combined with an offer for services.

Problems encountered

The above analysis obviously does not encompass all the variables which must be taken into account while organizing distribution. Each system is linked with other elements of the economy and operates within a given system of economic management and control. All these form an environment of a definite fragment of reality.

A basic question arises here: is the distribution system of agricultural production means and services in Poland adapted to market requirements and, accordingly, does it perform its functions adequately? It is difficult to provide an explicit answer to this question as the situation may differ between different agricultural branches. There are, however, important prerequisites justifying a negative estimation of the present distribution system. Some of the salient characteristics of the system are now highlighted:

- Trade in agricultural production means is, to a large extent, subject to various forms of control. Priority is given here to farms belonging to the socialized sector. There are employed tied sales (possibility of purchasing production means for contracted deliveries). Sale of production means carried out along such principles is a derivative of the mechanism of aggregated rights to their purchase and not of real needs of agriculture and particular farms. Trade control largely reduces the economic role played by the market mechanism, paralysing one of its most important functions – the allocation function. As a result, production means do not reach, in optimal proportions, those farms in which they could ensure the most favourable final effectiveness of increments and thus promote the highest production and income effect.

- The agricultural distribution system is generally too developed in the vertical marketing system. Routes of product flows are, as a result, very long which raises the costs of functioning of the whole agricultural production marketing system.
- The system is characterized by an expanded network of storage facilities at all levels of trade. This is due to a conviction that only maintenance of adequate stocks can ensure proper (with respect to their volume and time) deliveries of agricultural production means. This leads, however, to splitting up of supply which, accompanied by a lack of knowledge about farm needs and mechanical distribution of means among particular regions, produced a situation where a surplus of essential products very often appeared in some areas and considerable deficit in others.
- There is a far-reaching unification of organizational planning efforts in the supply of agriculture products with production means, which hampers adaptation to needs and preferences of particular market segments.

Suggested solutions

Solutions adopted in the field of distribution are also determined by the market situation. Lack of equilibrium in the market for production means and services causes the capital factor in agriculture to be at its minimum level, and it is this factor which really determines economic effectiveness of the agrobusiness complex. Accordingly, it is also quite important to know who is receiving these means and how they are utilized.

Two solutions can be adopted here: the first is control of the product sales and the second free sale of products at prices ensuring the market equilibrium. Both forms of distribution have their merits and shortcomings. Sales control is aimed at purposeful activity. Some priorities can be represented by definite branches of agricultural production or groups of farms. It is a selective procedure since with a market for a definite product a certain group of farms not fulfilling these definite criteria is automatically excluded. The farmer, moreover, faces restricted selection of sources, especially size of purchases of production means, which reduces adaptability of production to changes in the price relationship. In order to pursue the sales control, it becomes necessary to possess a perfect knowledge of farm needs and their economic effectiveness. Unfamiliarity with these needs often leads to the wastage of a number of agricultural production articles in short supply.

Free sale of products, in the situation of market disequilibrium, is usually accompanied by price increase to a level ensuring some degree of balance of demand and supply. This type of activity is much less complicated than is the case with controlled sales; it also partly eliminates informal ties between supplier and buyer. The only selection criterion of farms in the market is a relatively high price representing an instrument forcing farms to utilize effectively the purchased products. The problem, however, is that in the case of some farms an income barrier will be encountered. Rise of prices for production means will, moreover, increase production costs and simultaneously decrease competitiveness of these products in relation to other production factors.

Evaluation and directions of improvements in the distribution system of spare parts for agricultural machinery

The distribution system of spare parts for agricultural machinery in Poland shows some of the most serious shortcomings. These are listed as follows:

- This system is excessively expanded (*see Figure 18.1*). All levels of trade are seen here: industrial sales, wholesale, and retail trade. This extends the route of flow of spare parts from the producer to the end-user. In most countries (especially in those that are highly developed) this system is very simple, with the producer of spare parts being separated from the end-user by one trade link at the most.
- Several organizational vertically integrated systems dealing with supply of agriculture with spare parts exist. These vertical systems sometimes perform mutually overlapping functions. Such a solution, accompanied by the shortcomings in coordination (mainly in the horizontal system) and ineffective information flow, can hardly be considered satisfactory.
- Excessive expansions of distribution channels and spreading of trade organization between several organizational systems lead to dispersion of supply, which consequently leads to a freeze of spare parts in the forms of inventories. It is estimated that inventories of spare parts amount to the level which is equivalent to the volume of their sales over a two-year period.
- Excessive expansion of the distribution system causes the marketing apparatus to show little elasticity. This is expressed by, among other things, the mode of booking orders (a need of ordering spare parts a long time in advance). The economic method of calculation often forces companies to simplification of the mode of purchases and product flows which is often contrary to binding regulations.
- Shortages in supply of spare parts mean that orders for spare parts submitted to producers are for much bigger quantities than are really needed. The channel intermediaries are aware of the fact that they will obtain only a part of the ordered goods. A similar situation is present in contacts between retail trade and wholesale or organizational sales. It often also happens that the confirmed order does not correspond to actual possibilities of delivery, that is due to the fear on the part of suppliers that they be penalized for a failure to materialize the contracted deliveries. Such activity undoubtedly leads to dislocations in the whole market.
- Influence exerted in this branch on the industry by the trade is insignificant. In the situation of the market disequilibrium, the producer holds mostly a superior position in relation to the buyer. At present the industry is not materially interested in production of spare parts. Their production is not competitive in relation to production of finished products from the point of view of profitability of production.

It is thus obvious that the present distribution system of spare parts does not properly fulfil its functions. Changes in the distribution system should, first of all, tend towards bringing about the following changes:

- Shortening of the flow route of spare parts from the producer to the end-user and substantial acceleration of circulation of products. There exist viable possibilities for elimination of the wholesale level from the channel with shifting of the centre of gravity towards industrial sales points. This concept calls for

204

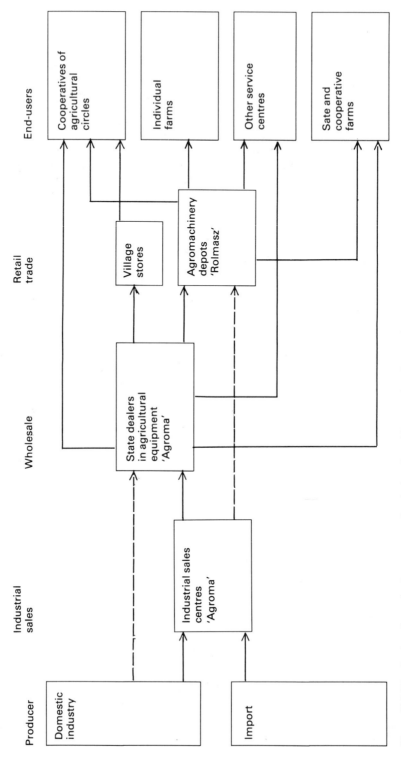

Figure 18.1. Distribution channels of spare parts of agricultural machinery and equipment (flow of products). → Indirect or long marketing channel; – – – direct or short marketing channel

development of transport base (substitution of storage facilities with transport facilities). In the case of parts for harvester combines and new types of tractors, e.g. Massey–Ferguson, the author proposes introduction of the service system. The producer could take over maintenance services of these machines: it is the most modern and most commonly applied solution in highly developed countries. It ensures the highest integration of activities of all links in the distribution channel, with the producer being relieved of the responsibility for the whole organization of a market for a given commodity. This solution promotes increased confidence on the part of the end-user towards the producer and supplier. Under these circumstances, the producer may perform the role of the market leader in three forms. The first consists in direct provision of services. The second encompasses opening of authorized stations. The third form is represented by franchising. Development of repair stations operating on principles of franchising, and run by agents being equipped by the producer with repair equipment, know-how, and spare parts, should be promoted.

- Consolidation and development of the role played by the information flow not only within the framework of a distribution channel but mainly between the channel and its environment. This particularly concerns information referring to supply (production possibilities) and demand (information from the end-user), and ensuring motivation of the producer and end-user. The information flow should constitute a variable determining the product flow. This information must provide a basis for decision making and, in some cases, information transmitters should be of directive character. This calls for essential changes in the negotiation flow as well as in the management systems. This view can be stated as: 'the management of a company should be identified with management of the information flow'.

References

1. DIETL, J. (1981) *Marketing: Selected Problems*. Warszawa: Panstwowe Wyndawnictwo Ekonomiczne
2. DIETL, J. and GREGOR, B. (1977) Selected Problems of Trade in Spare Parts for Factory and Agricultural Machines in the Light of Empirical Research. An unpublished report. Lodz, University of Lodz
3. DIETL, J. and GREGOR, B. (1978) Expertise concerning Projects of the Distribution System for Spare Parts for Agricultural Machinery and Equipment. An unpublished paper, Lodz, University of Lodz

Part VIII

Facilitatory services in food marketing

Marketing of agricultural products is often operated at the industry level through marketing boards. Also, in many countries agricultural cooperatives have marketing responsibilities at the industry level. Other examples of agricultural marketing at the industry level are institutions like CMA in West Germany and SOPEXA in France, which perform specific marketing functions for the industry. Changes in agricultural markets require adjustments of marketing functions and marketing institutions at the industry level. Developments in consumer behaviour, in the retailing and processing industry, and in agriculture itself make this adjustment of current interest in many countries of the world. The aim of the first chapter is the development of a framework for planning and implementing a marketing policy at the industry level with discussion of the criteria and consideration of the functions. The institutionalization of an agricultural marketing policy at the industry level is analysed, and illustrated by the Commodity Boards in the Netherlands.

It is widely believed that a strategy of intensifying food production and agricultural exports in marginal areas and secondary regions presents significant long-term potential. Can that potential be reached without thoroughly re-evaluating existing mixes of technology, institutional and economic policies? The second chapter reviews salient features of the problem of marginal area development, giving special attention to the nexus of technological, economic, social, and institutional variables, and the roles of policy and market systems are discussed from within this framework. An understanding of agricultural markets which is based on development experiences in more well-endowed regions, may be an inappropriate foundation for that in a marginal area development.

The final chapter examines implementation of food distribution policies in south India. Public policy for foodgrain distribution and consumption in the Coimbatore District of south India involves processing through state trading institutions, and distribution through fair price shops, Food for Work and Employment Guarantee Schemes. Policies are evaluated in terms of their objectives, and institutions for the implementation of policy are analysed in terms of the way in which they mobilize and distribute the resources of foodgrains, capital and labour.

Chapter 19

Food marketing at the sector level: the case of Dutch commodity boards

M. T. G. Meulenberg

Introduction

Agricultural marketing at the sector level is practised in many countries. Its application varies a great deal in responsibilities and activities both between products and countries. Generally, it is institutionalized in different ways, such as agricultural marketing boards, commodity boards, marketing agreements and marketing orders. Sector agricultural marketing is criticized since it benefits the farmer at the cost of the consumer, particularly when it determines production quotas and prices; it is also criticized for being too rigid in adapting to changing marketing structures.

The foregoing reasons underline the need for more research into sector agricultural marketing and some recent interesting contributions have been made[4-6]. In this chapter, the author has attempted to develop a set of criteria for sector marketing based on its general viability, what marketing functions should take place and on the institutionalization of marketing functions. Using this set of criteria an attempt is made to analyse commodity boards in the Netherlands.

A set of criteria for sector marketing

Some characteristics

Textbooks on general marketing usually use the marketing management approach to solutions of marketing problems, while those on agricultural marketing use the functional, institutional or commodity approaches and concentrate on price formation[8,9,11,13,15]. In this chapter, the marketing management approach is used as this is the most fruitful one for marketing agricultural products. As such, marketing management is described as[9]:

> . . . the analysis, planning, implementation and control of programs designed to create, build and maintain mutually beneficial exchanges and relationships with target markets for the purpose of achieving organizational objectives. It relies on a disciplined analysis of the needs, wants, perceptions, and preferences of target and intermediary markets as the basis for effective product design, pricing, communication, and distribution.

It has been argued that the implementation of marketing management in agricultural markets depends on the market structure, in particular on product homogeneity and size of enterprise, and on the dynamics of the market[12]. When agricultural markets are dynamic, i.e. changes in consumer, trade, industry and competition, there is a need for a marketing management policy involving the different elements of the marketing mix. Generally, agribusiness companies are better able to use the marketing mix if they are larger and if their products are differentiated. This is particularly true when market structure is oligopolistic with product differentiation or is monopolistic in nature.

Sector marketing of agricultural products is a special case of macromarketing. It concerns marketing by a large group of companies, but does not consider societal consequences of marketing operations to be a main issue, only a side condition. Before discussing sector agricultural marketing, the concept of 'sector' should be clarified. In this chapter, sector is understood as those undertakings in a country producing and marketing the same generic product. These may differ in size, product line and management, factors which influence the cohesion of the sector and, consequently, the usefulness of a marketing policy for the generic product. Since 'sector' is defined by communality in production and sales of a particular generic product, the sector can comprise undertakings in different stages of the marketing channel. For further information on the subject the reader is referred to the following recent publications[3-7]. Marketing activities for the generic product are characterized by national or state marketing programmes. They are institutionalized into marketing boards, marketing orders and agreements and into cooperatives or private organizations set up by groups of producers and/or traders. Most organizations aim at creating favourable farm prices and returns through specific marketing programmes. Marketing boards and marketing agreements often have as an objective the raising or maintaining of prices[5].

Various classification schemes for sector marketing institutions have been proposed. Abbott and Creupelandt[1] distinguished between trading and non-trading boards; Hoos[5] differentiated between export and domestic boards, which in turn were divided into trading and non-trading boards. There are also informal marketing organizations which can be valuable for marketing operations of individual sector members. There has been much criticism of these boards, orders and agreements. One such criticism is that these are monopolistic and, therefore, detrimental to consumers[4,5]. Another point of critique is that farmers and traders must cooperate with a marketing board. The point is also raised that such organizations are not innovative in production and marketing, as vested interests rather than the innovators have the stronger influence. These discussions point out the usefulness of research on marketing at the sector level. For instance, Hoos raises several questions: 'What should be the composition of the board?', 'Perhaps most crucial, a decision has to be made as to whether marketing boards should be established by legislation', 'Further, what is the best way to keep a board . . . vital and relevant?'[5]. The following section develops a frame of reference which may be helpful in answering such questions and this includes:

- Criteria for ensuring that a sector marketing policy is viable and feasible.

- Criteria for ensuring that a sector marketing policy is effective.

- Criteria for organizing such policies in a proper way.

Criteria for ensuring that a sector marketing policy is viable and feasible

To investigate whether a sector marketing policy is viable and feasible, certain essential and sufficient conditions are proposed. Essential conditions are those that must be fulfilled to make a marketing policy meaningful. Sufficient conditions are those conditions, some of which have to be fulfilled, which make the marketing process feasible.

Essential conditions are related to the common interests of sector members.

- Products of the various sector members have to be homogeneous for those product characteristics that sector marketing is concerned with. Lack of such homogeneity implies lack of a common basis for a marketing policy and the market interests of individual sector members differ too widely. A corollary of this condition is that a sector characterized by national brands is less suitable for a marketing policy than one characterized by local brands. Brands differentiate between products of different companies.
- There must be some overlap between markets of individual sector members. When individual members supply different markets, they have little interest in joining a marketing programme at the sector level. Presumably, agricultural producers share markets with other colleagues. This is also often true for food industries. However, food industries and food retail companies may be oriented towards different market segments and in that case they are not interested in a sector marketing for the generic product.
- Markets are dynamic and/or marketing operations of individual sector members are inefficient because of diseconomies of scale. If there is no change in consumers, competitors, distribution structure, government regulations and method and size of production, sector members have no impetus to join a marketing programme for a generic product. In reality such a situation could not exist, but those markets closest to this situation are less suitable for marketing programmes at the sector level.

Sufficient conditions have to be met in order to make sector marketing feasible. The following conditions are proposed:

- Companies within the sector are not able to handle marketing problems of the generic product individually. This condition seems obvious, but is worth considering carefully because of the concentration in the food industry and in food retailing. A corollary to this condition is that companies are more inclined to be sympathetic to sector marketing the more the market structure is similar to pure competition. Companies are also less ready to join a sector marketing programme, if they are already participating in large integrated vertical operations involving farmers, wholesalers, food industries and food retailers.
- The generic product is important to the income of individual sector members. If a generic product is not contributing substantially to the income of individual companies, there is no great incentive to join a marketing programme; companies might even leave the market and change to other products if there are structural market problems for the generic product.
- Marketing problems are structural. Producers of a product are more ready to participate in marketing programmes if marketing problems of the generic product are structural and consequently systematic action at the generic level is needed.

- The generic product of the sector in a country or state must be distinguishable from the same generic product of producers from other countries. Marketing programmes for a generic product favour all producers and if the foreign producers profit substantially from the joint marketing efforts of the domestic producers, the latter will be less willing to participate in sector-wide programmes.

If all essential conditions and a number of sufficient conditions are present, analysis of marketing at the sector level should then continue with the examination of the marketing functions to be performed.

Criteria for ensuring that sector marketing is effective

The elements for a marketing policy are those of the marketing mix: product, price, promotion and distribution. Functions for these marketing elements are: marketing intelligence, marketing research, consultation with and advice to relevant marketing parties, development of plans for improving marketing of the generic product, performance of marketing functions on some aspects of the marketing process, execution of a total marketing plan for the product. In this order of marketing functions, the responsibility of a sector marketing organization to the individual sector members becomes greater. Effective marketing of the generic product should contain a combination of functions which suits the marketing problems. For this the following specific criteria are proposed:

- The above order of marketing functions is hierarchical in the sense that each successive function is dependent on the previous ones except when these have become superfluous. This criterion suggests how marketing programmes should be built up. For instance, one cannot abstain from marketing research and yet advise the sector members on the marketing of the generic product; promotion requires market data, market research and consultation with sector members.
- Sector marketing functions should not overlap functions already being effectively and efficiently performed by the member firms themselves. A correlative of this criterion is that marketing organizations should adapt their programmes to policy changes made by individual sector members. Also sector marketing should extend to activities at a later stage in the suggested hierarchy of marketing functions as the market structure becomes more similar to pure competition.
- When products of sector members become more heterogeneous, marketing becomes increasingly concerned with only a section of the marketing mix. Since sector marketing is based on the homogeneity of products, heterogeneity of product forces marketing of the generic product to concentrate on general aspects in which the products of sector members are still similar.

    These criteria help in the evaluation of functions to be performed as part of a marketing programme. The next stage is an analysis of the institutionalization of the functions.

Criteria for the institutionalization of sector marketing functions

The different types of agricultural marketing organizations have been reviewed previously. The following are criteria for the institutionalization of sector marketing functions:

- Sector marketing, which serves societal objectives, will have to be institutionalized by public law. Marketing functions of this type imply a commitment of government to the outcome of the marketing operation. This can be realized only when the responsible organization has power over the market behaviour of all sector members.
- Institutionalization of sector marketing operations has to be in agreement with the views of both government and society on the desirable economic system. For instance, a centrally planned economy will often have a government-based institutionalization of marketing functions. However, in a free market society, it will be left to sector members to set up marketing programmes and to choose the type of organization.
- Institutionalization of sector marketing functions has to be flexible and should fit into the existing sector structure. This point is important for existing organizations. The size of the food industries and product differentiation is increasing and, in such market situations, organizations may have to shift activities, such as promotion, whole or in part, from the sector level to individual companies.
- Marketing organizations at the sector level should have sufficient authority to carry through an adequate marketing policy. Sector members should abide by plans developed by a marketing organization. For this the organization needs adequate authority. For instance, it needs the authority to make sure that all sector members contribute to collective promotional programmes. In the case of price formation the organization must be able to influence market supply. This is guaranteed if it is endowed with such authority by public law. It may also be so for a cooperative group in which all growers participate, like the Dutch auction system for horticultural products. Here too it is worthwhile to analyse the bases of power as distinguished by Stern and El-Ansary[16]: reward, coercion, expertness, legitimacy and identification.

The commodity boards system in the Netherlands

The Dutch commodity boards were established under the Industrial Organization Act of 1950 and embrace all companies participating in the marketing channel for a particular product such as milk. The act was based on the view that people of the same profession have the right to organize their own sector and to manage their own sector problems. Protestant political parties based this view on the concept of sovereignty in one's own socioeconomic business sphere. The Roman Catholic political party supported the view on the principle of subsidiarity: a central organization should not engage in matters which could be handled just as well, if not better, by a local one. Another argument put forward for the development of commodity boards was that of functional decentralization so that not all economic power would be in the hands of the government.

A great many commodity boards were set up in the mid-fifties. They are supposed to engage in improving market relations between the different companies in the marketing channel of the respective product, and are concerned with the markets and marketing of a specific agricultural product. A fundamental property of commodity boards is that both employees and employers are represented on them, in principle, on a parity basis. Although the ideal of worker participation was important for the advocates of the boards, consumers are not represented on them.

By the beginning of the sixties there were fourteen commodity boards in the Dutch agriculture and agribusiness. The authority of commodity boards was formulated in rather general terms in the decrees which established them. For example the Commodity Board for Livestock and Meat has the authority to regulate matters concerning:

- The exchange process between companies in the various stages of the marketing channel.
- The registration of companies and the collection of data from companies.
- The right to set up financial funds aiming at supporting the business of sector members.

It is important to note that no authority was granted to commodity boards to establish business and trading or the export and import of products. Also they have no authority to determine prices without government consent.

Before the establishment of the Common Agricultural Policy (CAP) of the European Economic Community, commodity boards were responsible for:

- Taking measures concerning supply and demand in the respective agricultural product in order to realize the target prices determined by government.
- Issuing orders to standardize market supply of particular products and packaging.
- Imposing levies on marketed products in order to finance promotional campaigns, and research and development projects.
- Collecting market data and doing market research.
- Advising government on marketing problems, agricultural policy and regulations, which influenced the exchange process in the market, like the Food and Drugs Act.

With the advent of the CAP, commodity boards lost some of their authority over regulations relating to agricultural policy and today they act as co-administrator with the government in the execution of CAP regulations. *Table 19.1* shows the difference in the economic importance of commodity boards between the various sectors of Dutch agriculture.

The development of Dutch commodity boards is further discussed on the basis of the criteria suggested earlier. It is not this author's intention to systematically describe the development of all commodity boards, but rather to show their strengths and weaknesses as sector marketing organizations[2,10].

Essential and sufficient conditions for sector marketing by commodity boards

Essential conditions for viable marketing as proposed earlier are present in the marketing of Dutch agricultural products. Products at farm level are homogeneous; markets of agricultural producers and processors are geographically the same, and markets are generally dynamic. In relation to product homogeneity, it seems useful to distinguish between agricultural products which reach the consumer after being processed and those which reach the consumer as a fresh product. Marketing problems of products like fresh fruit and vegetables are often those of the generic product. Some agricultural products, like dairy products, are differentiated by processing and brand. For these products the generic characteristics are also very important for market opportunities.

Since Dutch agricultural products are mostly sold in the west European market, there is no need for further discussion on whether the criterion of similarity of markets is met.

Changes in supply are caused by the increase in productivity as a consequence of both technical and product innovation. Changes in demand are the result of changing lifestyle and purchasing power of the consumer, of the increasing market power of retail chains which develop their own retail strategies concerned with the efficiency of their operations, and of the increasing competition caused by the internationalization of food markets and also because of oversupply.

TABLE 19.1. Total expenses of Dutch commodity boards in 1983 (in million guilders) and their distribution over various expense categories

Commodity board for	Total expenses (million guilders)	General expenses (%)	Technical and economic research (%)	Promotion and extension (%)	Market regulation and other objectives (%)
Arable products (Central board)	20.9 (=100%)	89.5	3.8	0.8	5.9
Grains, seeds and pulses	13.4	2.0	8.3	89.4	0.3
Potatoes	6.2	2.0	58.3	39.4	0.3
Feedingstuffs	3.9	3.3	83.1	2.5	11.1
Agricultural seeds	1.0	10.1	62.2	15.6	12.1
Dairy products	107.3	21.1	12.9	65.6	0.4
Ornamental horticultural products	45.0	12.8	23.9	55.8	7.5
Vegetables and fruit	14.5	42.4	3.3	15.8	38.5
Poultry and eggs	12.8	42.8	21.7	34.9	0.6
Livestock and meat	40.5	23.6	21.0	27.7	27.7
Margarine, fats and oils	4.9	93.8	0.3	0.4	5.5
Fish and fishproducts	11.4	39.2	1.3	21.4	38.1
Distilled spirits	1.8	83.6	–	6.2	10.2
Beer	0.09	97.7	–	–	2.3
Total	283.6	28.1	16.2	46.2	9.5

US$ = 3.06 guilders, ultimo 1983.
Source: Sociaal Economische Raad[14].

Sufficient conditions for a sector marketing policy are suggested earlier.

The criterion that companies should not be able to handle marketing problems of the generic product individually, is relevant to an analysis of commodity boards. At the time of their establishment, many sectors of agriculture in the Netherlands were characterized by features of pure competition. This was true at farm level and, at that time, also to a large extent, of the food-processing industry. Market structure has changed substantially since that time. A case in point is the market for milk, milk products and dairy products. The number of dairy factories decreased from 543 in 1955 to 138 in 1983. Over the same period, the number of companies decreased even more. In fact, today five large cooperative dairy companies dominate the industry. This concentration has not yet taken place in pig and poultry slaughtering. Concentration is also substantial in the sugarbeet industry, where, in 1982, one company processed 52.6% of the crop[17].

In many sectors of Dutch agribusiness, huge companies have come into existence. They need less support from the marketing programmes of commodity boards which have to take this development seriously. But even today many companies are not able to master marketing problems of the generic product individually. Large companies realize that structural marketing problems, like overcapacity and overproduction or unfavourable consumer attitudes to the generic product, can be solved only by joint action within the sector.

Using the criterion of economic dependency of individual firms on a specific generic product, it can be concluded that this dependency has increased as farmers have specialized. Also many food companies depend to a large extent on one specific agricultural product, like dairy companies on milk.

In the Netherlands, for many agricultural products marketing problems are structural in nature. These problems include overproduction of milk and some dairy products, a strong increase in flower production for which markets have to be developed, an overcapacity in the meat processing business requiring a restructuring of the industry, an overcapacity in bakeries and structural problems in the marketing of potato flour. These examples provide opportunities for commodity boards, particularly since both employers and employees are represented on them.

There is not always sufficient distinction between Dutch and foreign generic products. However, in export markets an indication of the origin of Dutch agricultural products is either required by law or is evident from the packaging. In the domestic market, foreign products are sometimes recognizable by an indication of origin. As many Dutch products dominate the domestic market, the Dutch companies especially benefit from the marketing policy. In this case, the criterion 'being distinguishable from foreign products' loses its relevance.

In conclusion it appears, on the basis of the criteria proposed, that marketing at the sector level is necessary and that commodity boards can contribute to it. However, in many sectors of Dutch agriculture it appears that private and cooperative companies are now more likely to have reservations about commodity boards than when they were first established. Larger companies and product differentiation have increased the ability of individual sector members to handle marketing problems themselves.

Criteria for the type of marketing functions needed for the generic product

Marketing activities of commodity boards include all the elements of the marketing mix. As such, commodity boards have been very active in market research and information: they collect market data, carry out market research and commission consumer research.

Commodity boards are centres for the exchange of views and for consultation with advice to the government about marketing problems; they are very well suited for this purpose since all groups operating in the marketing channel are represented on the board. The actual use of marketing elements varies between boards. No one board develops a total marketing policy for a generic product. They have little authority over *prices*; only for liquid milk and bread, have boards been granted authority by the government to fix minimum retail prices. *Promotion* is an important activity of some boards (*Table 19.1*). Although boards raise funds, promotional programmes are run by separate organizations, like the Dutch Dairy Bureau and the Flower Council of Holland. The same applies to *research and development*; the commodity board finances the research done by research institutions. The boards are empowered to promulgate decrees concerning *quality* regulations and *packaging*. Also they act as advisers to the government on both the Food and Drugs Act and a law on the quality of agricultural products.

This review of the marketing activities of commodity boards demonstrates that they cannot solve marketing problems of the generic product independently. Their main marketing task seems to be to support and stimulate marketing actions of sector members and, in addition, to execute marketing programmes on certain aspects of the generic product.

On the basis of the criterion on the hierarchy of functions, it seems that commodity boards have been consistent in the way they have developed marketing functions. The basic functions are collection of market data and market research. Boards consult systematically about marketing problems and frequently advise the government on marketing issues. Their actual marketing programmes relate to certain aspects of the generic product and are often executed in cooperation with other organizations.

Although there seems to be a consistency in the hierarchy of the marketing functions of the commodity boards, they have not been extended so far that boards are able to handle marketing problems on their own. The functions are spread over a number of special organizations and working parties, and this makes coordination sometimes difficult.

The criterion that the functions of a sector marketing organization should not overlap with functions of sector members is important today because of the concentration in the food industry and the retailing industry. Bigger companies prefer to spend money on research and development and on promotion of their own brands instead of spending it on joint projects, beneficial to the industry as a whole. This is becoming especially important in the Dutch dairy sector.

It should be pointed out that, from the beginning, the importance of commodity boards developed differently in different sectors of Dutch agriculture, because of the varying importance of other marketing organizations in their sectors. The cooperative auction system played a central role in marketing fresh fruit and vegetables and did not leave much room for the marketing functions of the Commodity Board for Fruit and Vegetables.

It seems likely that commodity boards are able to adapt to the expanding functions of the individual sector members. One problem could be that commodity boards might limit their functions too easily in order to stay on good terms with large sector members and, therefore, run the risk of being left with an inconsistent marketing programme for the generic product.

The last criterion is that of product homogeneity. Commodity boards have developed to a minor extent in sectors of the Dutch agriculture and agribusiness where product differentiation is substantial. There are small commodity boards in the margarine, fats and oils sector and in the beer and distilled spirits sector (*Table 19.1*).

It seems to me that on the one hand the marketing functions of commodity boards have become more general and somewhat reduced, because of concentration and product differentiation in food processing, wholesaling and retailing, while on the other hand they are stimulated by many structural market problems for the generic product.

Criteria on the institutionalization of sector marketing

Sector marketing can be carried out by various types of marketing organizations. At the outset, some. of these have been reviewed and certain criteria have been suggested which can be helpful in choosing the right type of organization. The establishment of commodity boards is now discussed on the basis of these criteria.

The first criterion is that sector marketing, having important societal objectives, requires an organization based on public law. Commodity boards were established under the Industrial Organization Act of 1950. The societal objective of the boards is the improvement of the exchange process between the successive companies in the marketing channel to the benefit of both the companies and the general public. To achieve this objective, functions like market research do not need the cooperation of all sector members in order to be effective, but other functions like minimum price schemes for liquid milk and bread will only work if every member adheres to the rule. Financial support for promotional campaigns and 'research and development' projects for the generic product should also be compulsory for all sector members. Otherwise the so-called 'prisoner's dilemma' will break down collective action. An organization based on public law therefore seems very well suited for some of the marketing functions now performed by commodity boards. Under a private based structure the promotional and research functions of the commodity boards might be at risk.

The second criterion is the fitness to a desirable economic system. The establishment of commodity boards in the Netherlands was based on fundamental views about the optimal economic structure of society. Today the general view is that the Industrial Organization Act of 1950 has not proved to be the ideal basis for structuring Dutch socioeconomic life. Only in agriculture have commodity boards been set up. Political and societal support for this system has substantially weakened. Also participants in the existing commodity boards have not been participating in the system as much as they used to. For instance, the largest trade union in the food industry, the 'Voedingsbond FNV', no longer designates members for the commodity boards on which it is entitled to be represented. This union holds the view that commodity boards should have a stronger hold on investment programmes of individual companies in order to solve structural problems in the industry, like overproduction and overcapacity. However this authority was not granted to commodity boards by the Industrial Organization Act of 1950. Also employers are not in favour of granting such authority since it does not fit in with the Dutch economic system, which is an economy based on free enterprise, but at the same time influenced by government policies. Although employers consider commodity boards useful organizations they are anxious that they will not interfere with the functions of individual companies.

This fading enthusiasm of society, politics and even sector members for the commodity board system hardly provides encouragement to boards to engage in new functions required by the changing market situation. Instead, there is continual pressure from sector members and the government to improve the efficiency of operations. Consumer organizations want the authority of commodity boards over regulations on product quality and packaging to be curtailed and the Food and Drugs Act to be the authority.

The third criterion is the flexibility to adapt to changing industry structures. The differences in marketing activities, the evolution of commodity boards in the various sectors of Dutch agriculture, as reviewed previously, and also the present day evolution of some boards demonstrate their flexibility. An important reason for the commodity boards adapting flexibly to the changing structure and activities of the sector is that many members of the commodity boards are also members of the cooperative groups and other private bodies engaged in marketing of the generic product. The flexibility of commodity boards to changing market situations in recent times goes together with the sharing of more functions with private bodies in the sectors. It implies a loss of the authority of the boards.

The fourth criterion is sufficient authority. The organization should have sufficient authority to realize its functions efficiently. Are commodity boards more or less powerful than other possible sector marketing organizations? Some of these are industry boards, which represent those members at a specific stage of the marketing channel only, e.g. farmers; cooperative unions and private organizations of producers and traders in a particular sector of the Dutch agriculture; national marketing boards, which also trade in products; informal cooperation between companies to handle specific marketing problems of the generic product.

Reward as a basis of authority is difficult to evaluate. Sector marketing functions, like market research, promotion and research and development influence the income of individual sector members only indirectly. Also the quality of people rather than the structure of the organization seems to be more decisive in this respect. Central cooperative organizations and marketing boards with trading power can integrate various marketing acitivites into a joint marketing programme better than the commodity boards, and this gives the former a greater reward potential.

- Within the authority granted, the coercive power of the commodity, industry and marketing boards with trading powers is stronger than other types of sector organizations, since their authority is based on public law. Commodity boards have a smaller marketing programme than many central cooperative organizations and therefore have fewer issues on which they can exert coercive power.
- Expertise does not seem a strong basis of authority for commodity boards since they delegate marketing functions to specialized organizations or participate in working parties with them.
- Legitimacy is a strong power basis for commodity boards within the authority granted by law. This is a positive point in favour of commodity boards, particularly for the raising of funds for marketing functions.
- Sector members seem less eager to identify themselves with commodity boards than with central cooperative organizations.

From this discussion of institutional authority of commodity boards, it cannot be concluded that they are stronger or weaker than other organizations concerned with sector marketing. Points in favour of commodity boards are the authority invested in them to levy sector members in order to finance marketing projects, and the presentation on a board of all members of the marketing channel for a product. This latter point may at the same time be a weakness because the diversity of interests of different channel members impedes innovative action.

Conclusions

It appears from the analysis that commodity boards have not become the marketing organizations of the various agricultural sectors, as was expected with the passing of the Industrial Organization Act in 1950. Rather, they have become one of a number of useful sector marketing organizations.

From the beginning, commodity boards differed a great deal in importance between sectors, because of the existence of other marketing organizations, like central cooperative organizations, and because of differences in concentration and product differentiation of industries at the time a board was established. Since then industrial concentration, product differentiation, and the CAP of the European Economic Community have challenged the existence of the boards. On the other hand the large number of structural changes in the marketing of the generic product have become a stimulus to the commodity boards, particularly in the field of market research, research and development, and promotion.

Both the positive and negative factors influencing marketing by commodity boards underline the need for systematic cooperation between the boards and other marketing organizations operating within the sector. They also demonstrate the need for continuous assessment by employers and workers, of the marketing tasks granted to the commodity boards.

References

1. ABBOTT, J. C. and CREUPELANDT, H. C. (1966) *Agricultural Marketing Boards: Their Establishment and Operation.* FAO Marketing Guide No. 5. Rome, FAO
2. DE VOS, G. (1979) Agricultural marketing boards in the Netherlands. In *Agricultural Marketing Boards – An International Perspective*, pp. 239–269. Ed. by S. Hoos. Cambridge, Mass., Ballinger Publishing Company
3. DOBSON, W. E. and SALATHE, L. H. (1979) The effects of federal milk orders on the economic performance of the US Milk Markets. *American Journal of Agricultural Economics*, **61**, 213–228
4. FORBES, J. D. (1982) Societal control of producer marketing boards. *Journal of Macromarketing*, **2**, 27–37
5. HOOS, S. (Ed.) (1979) *Agricultural Marketing Boards – An International Perspective.* Cambridge, Mass., Ballinger Publishing Company
6. IZRAELI, D. and ZIF, J. (1977) *Societal Marketing Boards.* New York, John Wiley
7. JESSE, E. V. (1979) Social welfare implications of federal marketing orders for fruits and vegetables. US Department of Agriculture Economics, Statistics and Cooperatives Service, *Technical Bulletin*, No. 1608, 29 pp. Washington DC
8. KOHLS, R. L. and DOWNEY, W. D. (1972) *Marketing of Agricultural Products*, 4th ed. New York, Macmillan
9. KOTLER, P. (1980) *Marketing Management: Analysis, Planning and Control*, 4th ed. Englewood Cliffs, NJ, Prentice Hall
10. LANDAU, S. (1966) *Institutionalized Monopolies in Agriculture, a Comparative Study of a Developed and Developing Economy.* Master of Social Sciences Thesis, The Hague, Institute of Social Studies
11. McCARTHY, E. J. (1981) *Basic Marketing: A Managerial Approach*, 7th ed. Homewood, Illinois, R. D. Irwin
12. MEULENBERG, M. T. G. (1968) Handel und Marketing. *Agrarwirtschaft*, **17**, 339–345
13. PURCELL, W. D. (1979) *Agricultural Marketing: Systems, Co-ordination, Cash and Future Prices.* Reston, Virginia, Reston Publishing Co.
14. SOCIAAL ECONOMISCHE RAAD (1985) *Jaarverslag 1984*, 's-Gravenhage
15. STANTON, W. J. (1975) *Fundamentals of Marketing*, 4th ed. New York, McGraw Hill Inc.
16. STERN, L. W. and EL-ANSARY, A. I. (1982) *Marketing Channels*, 2nd ed. Englewood Cliffs, NJ, Prentice Hall Inc.
17. TER WOORST, G. (Ed.) (1984) 45 Jaar Land–en tuinbouwcoöperaties in cijfers, *Coöperatie*, **46** (485), February

Chapter 20

Policies, markets and food system development in marginal areas

Bruce M. Koppel

Introduction

Among national and international actors in the food system, perceptions of food problems are a mix of technological, administrative and socioeconomic elements focused in some cases on 'first generation' production problems and, in other cases, on 'second generation' marketing problems. However, attention is increasingly being given to the development in both production and marketing terms of what might be called 'secondary regions' – regions where the cultivation of basic foodgrains traditionally has not appeared to be an optimal use of land, where large-scale irrigation infrastructure is not technically or economically feasible, where the role of animal and fish production in existing local food systems is often significant, and where wild ecosystems and shifting cultivation may represent significant portions of regional land use. Nevertheless, it is widely believed that the strategy of intensifying food production in such regions presents significant long-term potential. Can that potential be reached without thoroughly re-evaluating existing mixes of technology, institutional, and economic policies?

Secondary regions and marginal areas

Secondary regions are most often associated with substantial amounts of arable land classified as marginal. That classification, however, is crude. In fact, determining precisely how much of the world's potentially arable land is marginal is difficult. Measures based on land use, soil capability, opportunity cost, ecological degradation, market system performance, accessibility, geographical location and urban functions are among the leading criteria[2,6,7,12,19,21]. Each criterion represents a different assumption about what marginality is. In addition, each is sensitive to assumption made about technology and levels of production needed. It follows that 'marginal' is a characterization that includes some problematic biases and assumptions.

For example, in agroeconomic terms, marginal refers to limited land capability and the levels of technology and management needed to compensate for soil deficiencies and climatic liabilities. It is a characterization that is relative to specific land uses. What is a profitable application of inputs for one crop may be a losing proposition for another crop. In political-economy terms, marginality refers to the consequences of limits on local government initiatives, and restrictions on financial markets. In geographical terms, marginal refers to low accessibility: an organization of economic functions in space which penalizes less accessible areas. In social terms, marginal often refers to low levels or unfavourable terms of assimilation into some dominant sociocultural pattern. The factors which are usually associated with the label, 'marginal' include: occupation, class, income, ethnicity, and religion. When people with marginal characteristics live in a contiguous area, the attribution of marginality may be extended to the area itself.

Instead of the term 'marginal', it may be more useful to choose a term, such as 'secondary', to refer to areas which combine mixes of agroeconomic, institutional, and spatial marginality. It is important to emphasize that marginal areas are not necessarily unimportant, particularly to those directly dependent on them. In many of the less developed countries, secondary regions may contain the majority of land and water that are harvested for food under available technology.

The challenges of developing secondary regions

What are the challenges facing development of the food systems in secondary regions? The first challenge is that the major thrust for developing the food systems in secondary regions usually comes from the primary regions. Expanding urban populations need to be fed. Former agricultural lands, converted to non-agricultural uses by demands for industrial and residential sites or abandoned because of residential and industrial pollution, need to be replaced. Countries that are deficit producers and countries that have inadequate capacities to ensure that what production there is reaches urban consumers at low prices, have usually been impelled to exercise either or both of two options: they have imported food (if they had the foreign exchange) and they have used concessionary food aid. Since the early 1970s, however, and particularly since the so-called 'second oil shock' of 1979, many of these same countries do not find themselves in a position to finance food imports. At the same time the level of concessionary food aid available has declined substantially. In this situation, development strategies which maximize possibilities for mineral and agricultural exports from marginal areas, thereby generating foreign exchange and restoring food imports, will attract considerable support. Strategies also emerge to substantially increase basic food production in marginal areas, exporting that production to primary regions and urban areas.

The second challenge is that technology support systems, both public and private, for formulating and implementing development options for secondary regions, are still emerging. Included here are conventional agricultural research and extension infrastructure. What is most crucial and what remains to be developed are modes of appropriate programmatic interaction between conventional technology support systems for agriculture and the local institutions and characteristic farmer resource endowments found in secondary regions[11]. Also included in the list of 'first' region components of an agricultural support system, in search of appropriate modes of interaction with 'second' regions, are (a) the policy frameworks within which factors are priced and markets influenced, (b) the factor and output market infrastructure, and (c) more generally, the administrative capacities of both public and private actors who attempt to influence food system development[9]. For example, a wide range of 'non-formal' or traditional mechanisms already exist for acquiring and transferring technological knowledge from site to site and between generations[17]. The bases for relating these to primary region institutions, however, are weak – often because it is assumed that such mechanisms are anachronistic and not useful.

A third challenge is that, in many cases, the ecology within which agriculture functions is both complex and more delicate than the ecologies that have seen the major development of cereal grain production. The complexity is a product of the dominance of diversified ecosystems in contrast to the generally monocultural ecosystems characteristic of more developed primary agricultural areas. Drainage properties of marginal area soils tend to be problematic. Topsoil is often very thin; water and weather erosion are often advanced; micronutrient composition is often seriously deficient. In these situations, tillage practices and cropping choices, for example, can be crucial. Once the topsoil is lost, or once significant minerals or nutrient elements are depleted, replacement can be expensive if not impossible. Nevertheless, the extension into secondary regions of estate-type agriculture (often not for food production) and large-scale monocultural food production continues to be implemented. There are also attempts to replicate in marginal areas the technoeconomic package programmes developed originally for the green revolution. Because only a small proportion of the available agricultural land in marginal regions is planted to crops and varieties covered by the green revolution (primarily irrigated rice and wheat), it has been suggested that the potential for a second green revolution, i.e. an application of science and technology to create significant production opportunities, in so-called 'secondary crops' is present[4,5]. That potential, however, will be difficult to reach. One reason is that for many of the crops and varieties involved, there is only a limited pool of knowledge about what is grown, how it is grown, under what conditions it is grown, how it is used, and what variabilities, vulnerabilities and bottlenecks are typical.

The high yielding variety technologies are, in general, high input technologies. Varieties were crossed to optimize responsiveness to higher levels of nitrogen fertilization and careful water management. Plant architecture was altered to support heavier grain loads. However, given the large petrochemical content of many of the agricultural inputs, current yields will not be maintained easily. Although recent adaptive breeding efforts have tried to reduce high reliance on chemical inputs, the basic breeding model which optimizes the high-input premise has not been abandoned.

However, there are a number of other possible models. They range from breeding programmes based on line selection for adaptability, to more exotic approaches that improve the efficiency of carbon and nitrogen cycles, to ecosystem management approaches such as minimum tillage and biological and botanical pest control[3,13,14]. What is important to acknowledge for this discussion is that stable and high yields under suboptimal growing conditions are not easy objectives to pursue jointly if a high input regime is not to be part of the solution. Consequently, serious research efforts based on a different breeding model are seen as risky, with uncertain pay-off potential.

Many secondary food crops are grown in highly diverse environments from silviculture to monocropped fields to highly organized home gardens. These environments are not significantly modified compared to the alteration of natural ecosystems for wet rice culture. One implication is that breeding for generalized environments, a key premise of resource allocation within the international and many national agricultural research centres, will be only a limited possibility. Thus, canons of research investment and organization that have generated results for crops that have widely generalizable ecological settings, may not be appropriate bases for crops for which there is significant variation in agricultural ecologies.

The same variabilities point to levels of complexity that will make the design of policy and improvement strategies quite difficult. Production will occur under significantly different circumstances among producers with widely varied endowments. All this will complicate the pursuit of conventional strategies. For example, price support systems will have to confront not only different production costs, but will need to discount the costs of soil and water 'mining' associated with different production regimes. Widely scattered and diverse production situations will be associated with problems of variable output quality, conflicts between local and wider-area classification criteria, and product deterioration – all a challenge for marketing development. In many cases, economies will not be fully monetized, complicating pricing problems in the market chain.

These points illustrate an important caveat: the green revolution was considerably more than technological change; it was the mobilization of a policy and public investment system to exploit certain advantages that the technologies offered. Such investments were facilitated, in part, by relatively homogeneous (and generalizable) production conditions and by the feasibility of creating such conditions, e.g. through large-scale irrigation. The same assumptions may be displaced in marginal areas. The same strategies may be ecological as well as financial disasters.

There is little research on the significant secondary food crops now grown in secondary regions or the social, economic, or political characteristics of such farming systems. So-called 'poor man's crops' in many instances have virtually no 'back-up' research or special attention in food policy circles. What is known often will be primarily anecdotal and, in various ways, prejorative. In many instances, plants are viewed as nuisances when they have crucial roles in local ecosystems and marginal area economies. Three examples are sago, mangrove forests, and imperata grass[16,18,20]. Furthermore, the problems of combining local diversified food production with export crop production are typically underestimated, yet these are problems that can lead to many of the social costs of marginal area development strategies – including out-migration, land disenfranchisement, malnutrition, and rural violence[15].

Components of a strategy

Formulating feasible, sustainable options for secondary regions involves the intersection of three complex analytical concerns: farming systems research analysis, technology support system analysis, and administrative capacity analysis.

Farming systems research

It is first necessary to make a distinction between 'cropping systems research' and 'farming systems research'. Cropping systems research refers to the analysis of plant–plant and plant–animal combinations. When it incorporates an economic component, it is sometimes called agroeconomic research, but its main characteristic is to evaluate technological options to determine 'best' options under specified agroclimatic conditions. Farming systems research, in contrast, is directed at the social, economic, and political organization of cropping systems.

Farming systems research begins with an analysis of existing plant and animal ecologies and of the existing range of cropping systems. Range would be defined in terms of combinations present and variations in productivity levels. Special attention would be given also to water requirements of marginal area food crops, how water requirements are being satisfied, analyses of soil drainage properties, nutrient characteristics, and microbiology, and the impacts of existing land use patterns on the viability of the soil resource base. Understanding the development of specific cropping system regimes is important when determining the ecological pressures that have been, are, and will be present to hinder or support higher returns to land and labour and reduced yield variability. In other words, can current levels of productivity be maintained or increased without a significant alteration of production regimes?

Translating cropping systems research to farming systems research requires an expansion of scope that, while increasingly acknowledged in principle, largely remains to be practised. Issues which need to be examined include:

- *What capacities do households have to grow their own food?* What is and will be the capacity of marginal area households to purchase food? What are current and prospective patterns of food demand and consumption for marginal area households? These are especially important questions because, with increased commercialization of marginal area food economies and heightened emphases on exporting food from such areas, marginal area populations can find themselves more vulnerable to food security problems.
- *What is the role of the food system in supporting income and employment in marginal areas relative to other sectors?* How do changes in employment opportunities and wage levels in non-food sectors affect agricultural productivity, labour absorption and wage rates in the food system?
- *How do marginal area households adjust to changes in relative prices or availability of different foods?* What are consumption elasticities and intercommodity substitutabilities between and among secondary crops and primary cereal grains, and between and among locally produced and imported foods, with special attention within, as well as between, household comparisons? Are there social status effects in food preferences among marginal area populations? If so, what are these patterns and how might they affect local food systems as economic development and seasonal employment in urban areas grows?
- *How do marginal area communities deal with food security and localized variability in food supplies?* What relationships are there between the distribution of power, prestige and access to productive assets in the village and decision making within households about food production, storage, marketing and consumption? What are the characteristics of socioeconomic inequality? What are the relationships of inequality to patterns of resource use and management?
- *How are joint demands for food and fuel from biomass organized?* Are there existing or potential problems in managing renewable resources being used jointly for food and fuel in marginal areas? What are the impacts on marginal area food systems of demands for marginal area biomass to satisfy energy needs outside marginal areas?

All these issues would need to be examined to respond specifically to what appear to be relatively simple questions: what is the capacity of the existing food system to meet the income, nutrition, and employment requirements of a local population as well as the demands placed upon the system from outside the region? To what degree is the production problem technological and what are the technological problems? What administrative, organizational, and policy problems exist? What would be the impact on a farming system of technological, institutional and policy interventions or modifications? The last question is especially significant. It requires determining how vulnerable the stability of existing cropping systems is to the instabilities and uncertainties resulting from change in social, economic, and institutional environments.

Technology support system

There are many complex issues involved in determining how existing research systems can contribute to farming systems research. While there have been interesting attempts by some centres and national programmes, two facts remain: agricultural research is organized predominantly on a commodity basis and the tremendous variability in existing cropping systems is difficult to duplicate within any research organization's cropping systems programme. It is not surprising, therefore, that programmes tend to focus on one crop and then to build general cropping systems around that one crop. This can present considerable ecological and economic risks for prospective users.

The international agricultural research centres have been under considerable pressure in the area of farming systems research. A few years ago they were encouraged to pursue farming systems research. There is now general agreement that the international centres should limit their scope of work to development of farming systems research methodologies and training national research system staff in the use of such methodologies. It is not clear, however, that generalizable methodologies can be developed without more active participation in national programmes and attention to a considerably wider range of agroeconomic environments.

It is not surprising that, at high levels within national agricultural research systems, within international centres and the donor community, there is serious rethinking about the criteria for allocation of research resources and about the appropriate role of international centres. This discussion is complex, but one way of summarizing it is to make a distinction between efficiency (investment in rice research has led to higher average rice yields) and effectiveness (poorer farmers have not had real access to the new rice technology). Those who want to argue for more emphasis on effectiveness as well as efficiency criteria bear a significant methodological burden. They must develop objective measures for calibrating the impact of alternative research investments which give preference to those who are supposed to benefit from increased production possibilities, and assign values to environmental and ecological sustainment. Examples of the latter are maintenance of soil and water nutrient cycles, impacts on pest populations, and the conservation of non-renewable resources. These are essentially location-specific criteria, suggesting that national rather than international research centres will need to take leadership in this area.

If it follows that the more appropriate arena for strengthening technological support for marginal area development is the *national* agricultural research system, then a number of additional issues must be confronted. While national agricultural research systems have the mandate to respond to a more complex range of problems than any international centre, resource limitations and professional orientations both tend to converge on demonstrated higher pay-off topics. Under the best circumstances, the skills and attention of national system management are focused on coordinating diverse capabilities present in the system, responding to a variety of often inconsistent pressures for priority research directions, and building patterns of international cooperation that do not excessively deflect the system's goals. The capability of national agricultural research systems to respond to marginal area development will not be independent of the systems' capacities to deal with these issues[8].

Administrative capacity

This, in many ways, is an overarching category. Once technological and non-technological elements of the problems of secondary region food system development are clarified and specified, and once ecologically viable technological options are identified, implementing such options is extremely difficult. For example, most food policies operate through the market system. It assumes that the system, through its price and stock allocation mechanisms, will signal various incentives and disincentives to producers and consumers. However, market systems in secondary regions do not always transmit undistorted versions of such signals to producers or policy makers.

Market systems in secondary regions are often less specialized than those found in primary regions. An exception is the primary region market outlet in a secondary region. However, beyond these enclaves, sometimes in response to them, there is a specializing trend in secondary region markets. Marketing organization is changing from multipurpose periodic markets to a more firm-centred structure. This transformation can especially weaken the bargaining power of buyers and sellers in marginal areas. On the other hand, such specialization may be more efficient for assembling products destined for urban markets.

While most policy interventions in exchange systems assume that the systems can function simultaneously to allocate resources (through relative prices) and extract resources (through mediating internal terms of trade), the actual patterns of resource allocation and extraction are not always anticipated or desired. It follows that food policy must, not only be more sensitive to regional and subregional variations in market system operation, but must also seek alternative instruments for communicating incentives and disincentives. Cooperatives and other forms of organizational strategies are one example, but there are several others ranging from adjusting local government powers to modifying landholding systems.

Analyses of marginal area market systems and the impact of external market systems on marginal area economic organization require asking some rather basic questions and being receptive to some substantial complexities. Two major issues illustrate the point.

Who participates in market economies and why? In some cases, participation is a deliberately commercial behaviour, indicative of transition to, if not actually assimilation in, a large exchange system. However, in marginal areas, there is ample evidence that participation is episodic, supplementary behaviour – a way of compensating for problems such as inadequate availability of basic foods, lack of alternate employment, lack of fields etc. Such participation does not imply commitment to the economic behaviour, e.g. producing surpluses for cash, considered 'appropriate' by the market. Indicators of this are what is being sold, the points of sale, and the relationships between selling and buying behaviour within the same households. While these characteristics will be significantly influenced by transportation, processing, and financial infrastructure, the choices made *and* how these choices are implemented within the economy of the marginal area household are important and independent indicators of what participation actually means. The conclusion often rapidly made that participation means commercialization and market orientation may be simply incorrect.

How are marginal area markets organized and what are the impacts of endogenous as well as exogenous change on the performance of these markets?   The shift from periodic to firm-centred market systems is a common process in many marginal areas. It is a process of specialization that, in turn, encourages specialization among marginal area producers. Two characteristics of this process deserve special note. First, when specialization is driven by export demand (from other parts of the country for example) and an area concentrates on generating a surplus which puts it in competition with surpluses coming from more accessible regions, the net effect may be to further marginalize producers and sellers in secondary regions. Second, specialized market systems cannot always be expected to accept commodities other than those for which they are specialized. As experience with attempts to reduce opium production in Thailand have shown, substituting one product for another at the production end does not mean that a commodity formerly subject to poorly developed market arrangements can simply assume marketing efficiency by being plugged into a highly developed marketing system[10].

In dealing with these and related issues, it is important to consider the opportunity costs of standard public approaches to developmental objectives in the village and the region. How can public administration be improved or privatized? In a period of 'aid fatigue' and disillusionment with two decades of applied rural development experience, this question has attracted serious attention. It is leading to examinations of bureaucratic reorientation, reconsiderations of the roles of indigenous forms of community resource management, and new interest in the functioning of small-area market systems[1]. How does government affect transaction and information costs in the village? Any constructive development of secondary region market systems is going to have to build on sensible answers to this question. Exchange systems are resource management systems. There are organizational costs incurred in the maintenance and modification of resource management systems. How are these costs distributed? There are many other questions. How are linkages between marginal and primary regions institutionalized in commodity, capital and labour markets? What assumptions do programmes of public intervention typically make about investment and risk-taking behaviour outside the public sector? More generally, what are the existing organizational and administrative capacities and how do they compare to the capacities assumed by various strategies?

Conclusion

Much of what we know about how to guide food system development comes from experience in defined area development within relatively well-endowed regions. The extrapolation of these lessons to a different context, different in social, economic, political, ecological and edaphic terms, can lead to a chain of consequences that are not pleasant. We will need to improve our understanding of how market systems are functioning and what functions they are serving, how market systems are changing in both structural and functional terms, how the gains and losses of participation in the system are distributed, how broader changes in the macroeconomic, political, and social environment are influencing market systems, and what roles market systems play in linking shorter-term problems of food stability in primary regions to longer-term problems of food security in secondary regions.

Traditional food policy analysis, built on simplistic but purportedly universal assumptions about economic behaviour and market commitment, may be misleading for marginal areas. Policy analysis will need to be significantly more amenable to a contextual understanding of economic organization in marginal areas, the multiple dimensions of individual and collective economic behaviour, and very possibly a substantially broader perspective on the scope and roles of exchange systems. All this should lead to enhanced recognition that food policies are doing considerably more than just to influence factor allocation through manipulation of price-formation processes. Food policies are institutional policies, influencing the organization, feasibility and effectiveness of economic activities. Food policies are also technology policies, influencing the choice and valuation of factors.

In all this, the nexus between patterns of indigenous organization and exchange and the assumptions made about these patterns by the policy system loom large as an area that is crucial for the future of marginal areas. It is also a principal context in which examinations of market systems, as the link between 'first' regions and 'secondary' regions, might well be emphasized.

References

1. COWARD, E. W., KOPPEL, B. and SIY, R. JR (1983) *Organization as a Strategic Resource in Irrigation Development*. Honolulu, East–West Center Resource Systems Institute
2. ECKHOLM, E. (1976) *Losing Ground: Environmental Stress and World Food Problems*. New York, W. W. Norton
3. GRAINGE, M. S., AHMED, S., MITCHELL, W. C. and HYLIN, J. (1984) *Plant Species Reportedly Possessing Pest-Control Properties – A Database*. Honolulu, East–West Center Resource Systems Institute, RM 84-1
4. GREENLAND, D. G. (1975) Bringing the green revolution to the shifting cultivator. *Science*, **190**, 841–844
5. JENNINGS, P. (1976) The amplification of agricultural production. *Scientific American*, **235**, 181–194
6. JOHNSON, E. A. (1970) *The Organization of Space in Developing Countries*. Cambridge, Mass., Harvard University Press
7. KELLOGG, C. and ORVEDAL, A. (1969) Potentially arable soils of the world and critical measures for their use. *Advances in Agronomy*, **21**, 109–170
8. KOPPEL, B. (1979) The changing functions of research management. *Agricultural Administration*, **6**, 123–139
9. KOPPEL, B. (1981) Food policy options for secondary regions. a framework for applied research. *Food Policy*, **6**, 33–46
10. KUNSTADTER, P. (1979) *Hmong (Meo) Highlander Merchants in Lowland Thai Markets*. Paper prepared for United Nations University–Chiang Mai University Workshop on Agro-Forestry for Rural Communities. Chiang Mai, Thailand
11. LACY, W. B., BUSCH, L. and MARCOTTE, P. (1983) *The Sudan Agricultural Research Corporation: Organization, Practices, and Policy Recommendations*. Lexington, Kentucky, Department of Sociology
12. MORGAN, W. B. (1978) *Agriculture in the Third World: A Spatial Analysis*. Boulder, Colorado, Westview Press

13. NATIONAL ACADEMY OF SCIENCES (1976) *Making Aquatic Weeds Useful. Some Perspectives for Developing Countries.* Washington, DC, NAS
14. NATIONAL ACADEMY OF SCIENCES (1979) *Tropical Legumes: Resources for the Future.* Washington, DC, NAS
15. PAIGE, J. M. (1975) *Agrarian Revolution: Social Movements and Export Agriculture in the Underdeveloped World.* New York, The Free Press
16. PHILIPPINE COUNCIL FOR AGRICULTURE AND RESOURCES RESEARCH (1977) *Proceedings of the International Workshop on Mangrove and Estuarine Area Development for the Indo-Pacific Region.* College, Laguna (Philippines), PCARR
17. RUDDLE, K. (1974) *The Yukpa Cultivation System: A Study of Shifting Cultivation in Colombia and Venezuela.* Berkeley, University of California Press
18. RUDDLE, K. (1978) *Palm Sago: A Tropical Starch from Marginal Lands.* Honolulu, University of Hawaii Press
19. SANCHEZ, P. A. and BUOL, S. W. (1975) Soils of the tropics and the world food crisis. *Science,* **188,** 598–603
20. SHERMAN, G. (1980) 'What 'green desert'? The ecology of Batak grassland farming. *Indonesia,* **29,** 148–173
21. TROLL, C. (1966) *Seasonal Climates of the Earth: World Maps of Climatology.* Berlin, Springer Verlag

Chapter 21

Implementation of food distribution policies: a case study in south India

Barbara Harriss

Introduction

Any public intervention consists of a modification of the mobilization and/or distribution of resources. By intervening in the markets of the food economy, a government may thus change the ways in which resources are allocated within the food marketing system. It may change the prices acting as signals from some or all consumers to some or all commercialized producers. A government may therefore either alternatively or simultaneously change the rate and direction of extraction of resources from agriculture via the private marketing system. By such interventions, the state also provides an arena of action, an arena which in turn interacts with, and reflects the actions of, a wider policy.

Here, a case study is presented of the implementation of public policy for foodgrain distribution and consumption in Coimbatore District in south India. Since it is not possible to divorce public policies affecting consumption from those affecting the acquisition on the part of the state of commodities for consumption, the record of implementation of state trading policies for rice with reference to south India is first considered.

Implemented interventions in state trading in food

The partial socialization of trade changes the distribution of physical resources. In the early 1970s, government procurement of rice at prices lower than those on the free market in many regions of India resulted in compensating distortions to this market such that all rural and urban people dependent on the market for supplies of rice in surplus-producing regions subsidized the target groups eligible for the 'fair price' rice of the public distribution system. The target groups comprised a limited number of low income people in cities, certain deficit states such as West Bengal and Kerala, and the deficit districts on state borders.

Commodities

Both the Central Government's Food Corporation of India (FCI) and civil supplies corporations of individual states have found it necessary to diversify, as devices to increase their turnover in order to reap economies of scale and to reduce trading

This chapter was originally an article in *Food Policy*, 1983, Vol. 8, No. 2, pp. 121–130.

risks. In the late 1970s, the acquisition from procurement and imports of a large buffer stock of foodgrains led to a withdrawal from intervention in procurement. It has also led to the distribution of fair price commodities to concentrations of government servants and to captive markets such as the army, police, hospitals and prisons, and the distribution of a limited quantity as grain payment for routine repair work done on behalf of local government institutions, during times of peak agricultural demand for agricultural labour[10].

Technology

The partial socialization of trade leads to a significant change in technology in the direction of large size and capacity in both storage and processing. The lack of viability of such technology except at high capacity utilization has led to attempts to develop much more highly centralized distribution systems, to subsidies, and most importantly to the perpetuation of institutional links with private trade, the latter controlling lower cost and more versatile technologies.

Finance

The partial socialization of trade has changed the mobilization of financial resources. Paradoxically, both State and Central Government trading corporations emphasize the commercial base to their operations in their annual reports. Meanwhile, the civil supplies corporations indulge in internal cross-subsidization between profit and loss-making trade and require intermittent bailing-out from the state governments' general revenues. FCI, by contrast, now needs Rs10 (Rs = rupees) per individual in India in subsidy from Central Government revenues. Even the reforms mooted for Food For Work and Employment Guarantee Schemes require resources from general funds to cover an increase in technical personnel administering the grain payment schemes. FCI has failed in its one clearly financial objective: to be a source of credit for farmers. Both FCI and the civil supplies corporations have been destinations of credit from international financial institutions, notably the World Bank via the Agricultural Refinance and Development Corporation for investment in physical infrastructure. But state trading is not profitable for the state. Its circumscription by other financial, trading, infrastructural and policy-making institutions of Central and State Government is used to justify patterns of operation requiring subsidy.

Beneficiaries of state trading

That state trading is perpetuated is indicative that a number of interests are served by its perpetuation. First, the FCI does not harm the interests of powerful surplus producers of wheat and rice in north India where its procurement prices exceed market ones. Elsewhere, since procurement at low prices directly from producers is easily and massively evaded[19], the interests of large surplus producers are not materially threatened.

Second, the relationship between private food merchants and the food parastatals is profoundly ambiguous. On the one hand coercion and conflict are characteristic. Movement restrictions cut off supplies and force merchant-millers into speculative passivity as agents of the state. Powerful merchants can criminally syphon resources out of public distribution and into the risky and highly profitable black market resulting from movement restrictions. The legitimate need of the state to be vigilant against such activity can turn into rank oppression of private merchants on occasion.

Yet, on the other hand, collaboration with the state may not be against private mercantile interests. The existence of markets distorted by the state[1] provides opportunities for illegal excess profit making through blackmarketing. Acute market imperfections may allow the spawning of large numbers of petty dealers smuggling profitably across the trading cordons[9,18]. Furthermore, the state needs private merchants, who mediate in the management of labour, whose technology operates at lower costs than that in the control of the state, and who reduce the fixed cost component of state trading operations by the expedient of their intermittent co-option. In turn this relationship allows contract millers to trade and process freely whenever food distribution policies are liberalized.

Third, international interests are served by these institutions being a market for technology and for credit underwritten by the Indian State (by means of paid-up capital, direct and indirect subsidies).

The rapidly growing institutions and programmes of Central Government which independently circumscribe state trading are used to justify high levels of subsidy. State trading involves a continual reinvesting in purely mercantile activities. These tend to promote monopolies which thwart investment in the expansion of commodity production on which both the private and state mercantile sector depend for their further appropriation of resources.

Implemented interventions in food distribution and consumption

State trading has rarely involved a regular release of supplies onto the open market to contain retail prices below specified ceilings. It has generally functioned as a relief or welfare system via a separate network of Fair Price Shops (FPS), whose supplies, until recently at least, were dominated by imported wheat. The creation of a separate 'fair price' network leads to the evolution of a multiple pricing system. The high retail prices of the black market and the residual market (in districts where procurement is coerced) puts pressure on 'fair price' retailers to reduce the difference between the markets, and then to pocket it.

The record for the Fair Price Shop system is as follows:

- The uptake of publicly distributed foodgrains is variable, depending on local production and on the relationship between controlled 'fair' prices and uncontrolled black or residual market prices.
- Consumers face problems of lack of physical access to state trading outlets, of adulteration, and poor quality of grain and, at times, of corruption and blackmarketing.
- Generally, however, it is supply rather than demand which is the key constraint on fair price sales.
- Even though low income groups in urban areas undoubtedly benefit from FPS, those of rural areas are rarely covered by the network. Rural people dependent on markets for food may even subsidize it themselves by virtue of their paying prices for grain inclusive of a hoist which compensates food traders for the losses made by compulsory levies to state trading agencies at fixed prices lower than market ones. (*See* studies for Uttar Pradesh, Kerala, Andhra Pradesh and Karnataka, respectively, as follows: Singh[17], George[5], Subbarao[20], and Harriss[11].)

Public distribution of food: a case study

Coimbatore District is a deficit region for foodgrains, sensitively located on a state border and a focal entrepôt in the private, inter-regional foodgrains distribution system. A major activity of the State Civil Supplies Corporation here, besides the storage and processing of rice, is therefore the final distribution of essential commodities through the system of Fair Price Shops. There are 665 in the district as a whole consisting of 134 urban retail cooperatives and 457 rural cooperatives, 35 Civil Supplies Corporation stores in Coimbatore City, and 11 such stores in rural areas, 28 private shops and 'private cooperatives' run by the managements of large textiles and engineering factories for their workers.

The District Supply Office budgets the supply of the commodity sold in the shops and it is the responsibility of the Civil Supplies Corporation to get goods moved from its storage points to the retail outlets, a service for which it is paid by the cooperatives and private merchants. Finance is coordinated by the State Bank of India.

Marketing arrangements for foodgrains under the Fair Price shop system may vary from complete non-market distribution with quantities and prices fixed to sales at open market prices but with rationed quantities, or, as with cereals between 1978 and 1981, sales at fixed 'fair' prices and (with 'rationing' at up to 24 kg per purchase) almost unlimited quantities. Even though issue prices are low the distributive margin is quite large (from 43% for superfine rice to 31% for coarse rice). However, it is not as wide as in the public distribution system of Karnataka (47% for fine rice and 42% for coarse rice) or in FCI's distribution system.

Lack of effective rationing leads to offtake in inverse proportions to local harvest sizes. In 1977, with short local supplies of grain, 53 451 metric tons of cereals were disbursed through the public distribution system – enough to provide each cardholder with 74 kg of rice and wheat. But in 1978, 9.2 kg per cardholder were sold and in 1979, 19 kg (*Table 21.1*). Furthermore, these latter quantities cannot influence market prices. No coarse grains, which are the foodgrains eaten by low income groups in the district, have been sold.

Our case study focuses on one taluk within the district. Avanashi Taluk betrays its deficit status as a cereals producer by the fact that it accounts for 7% of Coimbatore District's ration cards but 16% of its publicly distributed rice. In Avanashi Taluk there are 48 Fair Price Shops. The 7 shops located in urban areas accounted for 30% of the total turnover in 1979/80. Two of the outlets are owned by the Civil Supplies Corporation while the rest are cooperatives. The two Civil Supplies Corporation's outlets comprise 12% of total turnover in the taluk. A total of 48 405 cardholders are eligible to use the stores – 1008 per store on average. This is half the constituency of the average shop in the state as a whole, and identifies this rural region as one of the most intensively and unusually well-provided in Tamil Nadu.

The size distribution of shops in Avanashi Taluk over the period January 1979 to May 1980 is shown in *Table 21.2*. Distribution is strongly skewed, the total turnover of the biggest firm being equal to that of the bottom 35% of firms. Nevertheless, in terms of the value of turnover, this largest firm is two-thirds of the average size of private firms for the state as a whole (Tamil Nadu State Commercial Taxes Department, Regional Office, Coimbatore, 1979, unpublished data).

The retail outlets of the Fair Price Shop system are very small shops. The Fair Price Shop requires a monthly turnover of Rs4500 at 1979–80 prices (Rs54 000 per year) in order for it to be privately viable. The average turnover in Avanashi Taluk is Rs28 000, about half of the viable turnover. In these petty sales, cereals form a minor component in comparison with sales of sugar and kerosene. Over the 17 months from January 1979–May 1980, only 228.4 metric tons of rice and 47.7 metric tons of wheat were sold through the Fair Price Shop system in Avanashi Taluk – enough for 4 kg of rice and 1 kg of wheat per cardholder per year (Tamil Nadu State Civil Supplies Corporation data[21]). This is one week's calories at FAO norms of 2400 a day.

Foodgrains were distributed unequally. Ninety-four per cent of rice and 30% of wheat went to the urban clients of just four stores. The remaining rural stores sold an average of two quintals of rice and five quintals of wheat a year: a single bullock card load.

TABLE 21.1. Releases of rice and wheat by Civil Supplies Corporation to Fair Price Shops, Coimbatore District, 1977–80 (metric tons)

	Rice (metric tons)				Wheat (metric tons)		
	1977	1978	1979	1980	1977	1978	1979
January	3724	2371	323	292	722	473	163
February	6072	327	288	191	748	288	48
March	6714	359	197	207	1218	283	31
April	2053	349	317	99	914	221	35
May	4342	209	356	102	854	284	22
June	3525	350	769	–	1815	154	96
July	4148	334	1193	–	859	216	54
August	4787	443	4381	–	1106	102	52
September	4848	502	2931	–	990	69	13
October	4413	309	1629	–	1040	193	104
November	3856	622	603	–	842	196	102
December	4969	444	912	–	981	76	58

Source: Notes on Civil Supplies, Coimbatore Distric, Tamil Nadu State Civil Supplies Corporation, Coimbatore, 25/5/80.

TABLE 21.2. Turnover of FPS 1979–80 (17 months) in Avanashi Taluk

$10^{-3} \times$ Turnover (Rs)	Number of shops	Percentage
0–9.9	6	13
10–19.9	12	26
20–29.9	9	19
30–39.9	5	10
40–49.9	3	6
50–59.9	4	8
60–69.9	3	6
70–79.9	3	6
80–89.9	2	4
90–99.9	–	–
100–149.9	–	–
150–199.9	–	–
200–249.9	1	2

Note: Mean – Rs 40 000; Median – Rs 25 000; Mode – Rs 15 000.

Source: Tehsildar, Avanashi Taluk, July 1980.

The 48 stores employ 133 people, 2.8 for the average store. In 1979 the annual turnover per person was just Rs10 200. In the state as a whole each shop receives an annual subsidy of Rs2400, roughly enough to cover the low labour costs – Rs100 per person per month in the smaller shops.

It is doubtful that the turnover increases in drought years will compensate in the long term for indifferent performance meanwhile. Thus the Fair Price Shop system must be justified on welfare grounds. However, such a justification is not obvious when the inventories of such stores are inappropriate for the needs of the poorest, when the packaging of commodities is in excessively large units for them, when sales are for cash, not credit, and when quality is often low and supplies not always dependable. In Avanashi Taluk in years of normal production the system operates with a bias to the needs of the cardholding urban population.

Grain payment schemes

While the public distribution system distributes resources mainly to urban areas, the increase of landless and the massive increase of landless women and children going into the rural workforce (60.5% and 78% increases respectively between 1964–65 and 1974–75)[6] testify to increasing rural distress. The acquisition of sizeable buffer stocks in public control has enabled the Central and State Governments to justify the distribution of rice as grain payments. Two schemes were introduced: Food for Work and Employment Guarantees.

Food for work

Food for Work was inaugurated by the Government of India in 1977 with three objectives:

● To generate additional gainful employment.
● To create durable assets.
● To use surplus foodgrains to develop human resources.

Fifty to one hundred per cent of wages were to be in grain. In 1978–79, in the country as a whole 286.4 million man days of work were provided and 2.5 million metric tons of foodgrains were distributed[7]. The project has now been incorporated into India's Basic Needs Strategy.

In Tamil Nadu the scheme went into operation in April 1979, work projects being sanctioned by the Panchayat Union Commissioners and actually inspired by local contractors and landlords. Rice for payment is drawn on the Tamil Nadu Civil Supplies Corporation and replaced by supplies from the Central Government buffer in the possession of the FCI. The Central Government allocated 73 000 metric tons to Tamil Nadu for 1979. This would provide all year round food for 50 000 people at 4 kg/day. The Central Government allocated 27 000 metric tons for 1980–81 (work all year round for 18 500 people). Even so the Central Government claimed that, 'liberal releases through the public distribution system and Food for Word programme have prevented an increase in urban market prices for fine cereals', but this is with reference to a state with a population of over 50 million[13,15].

Balaji and Ramachandran studied the implication of this programme so far in two drought-prone districts of Tamil Nadu[2]. While it represents a considerable increase in potential funds for expenditure on public works, it provided highly inadequate employment for agricultural labour in the first year of operation: between 2.6 and 4.6 man days, least in the most backward areas and maldistributed through time to coincide with peak demand for agricultural labour and with the rainy season. There was no effect on wages and workers were paid below the Tamil Nadu State statutory minimum. The work has rarely enhanced assets. It comprises petty maintenance, often left incomplete. No financial allotment for materials needed in rural works has been included.

Basu[3], in a separate study, has pointed out that if grain payment schemes are simply substituting for pruned routine activities then the net employment generated may be far less than what is implied in statements on man days of work supplied under the programme. Furthermore, payment in grain in Tamil Nadu amounted to 11–14% of total payment for work done. Grain received was 28–37% short of entitlement. Irregular supplies led to late payment and the employment of contractors, contrary to Central Government guidelines[6].

A Planning Commission evaluation covering 80 villages in 10 states in 1980 confirmed the general nature of the specific observations here, including the retrogressive role of contractors, who manipulated muster rolls, sold rice in the open market, and paid labour lower cash rates[8]. Dandekar and Sathe[4] found that 90% of the beneficiaries in Maharashtra continued to be below the poverty line. Finally, in the case of Tamil Nadu, the rice from the Civil Supplies Corporation was of such poor quality that it was almost inedible, some over five years old. This brought work to a halt in Tirunelveli District too[12]. Panchayat Unions were not allowed to take fine rice and to pay Tamil Nadu Civil Supplies Corporation the difference, nor were workers allowed *ragi* instead.

It is a paradox of this programme that Coimbatore District, one of the richest and most industrialized of the state, should have cornered 30% of the entire state's allocation to this programme in 1979, its first year of operation (Tamil Nadu Civil Supplies Corporation, 28 September 1979, unpublished data). In the year ending April 1980 the District Development Department's own evaluation recorded that 1675 metric tons of foodgrains had been used, that Rs1118611 had been disbursed and that employment had been given to 12708 men and 8065 women. For these

TABLE 21.3. Food for Work projects, 1979–80

	Annur	Avanashi	Palladam	Tirupur	Pongalur	Sultanpet	Sulur
Total number of projects	131	91	30	33	9	77	36
Road repairs							
Number of projects	102	77	23	30	6	37	31
Total cost (thousands of Rs)	282.6	242.5	92.5	94.8	88.5	294.8	146.3
Percentage total of FFW	36	52	89	70	70	43	87
Average cost (thousands of Rs)	2.8	3.2	4.0	3.2	14.8	7.9	4.7
School repairs							
Number of projects	27	9	7	3	2	17	5
Total cost (thousands of Rs)	247.0	116.1	13.9	39.0	25.6	110.8	21.0
Percentage total of FFW	32	25	11	30	20	16	12.5
Average cost (thousands of Rs)	9.2	12.9	1.9	13	12.8	6.5	4.2
Irrigation							
Number of projects	17	5	–	–	–	–	–
Total cost (thousands of Rs)	233.1	104.0	–	–	–	–	–
Percentage total of FFW	30	23	–	–	–	–	–
Average cost (thousands of Rs)	13.7	20.8	–	–	–	–	–
Others*							
Number of projects	3	–	–	–	1	21	1
Total cost (thousands of Rs)	19.5	–	–	–	11.6	244.0	20
Percentage total of FFW	2.0	–	–	–	10	41	3
Average cost (thousands of Rs)	6.5	–	–	–	11.6	11.6	20
Percentage of total financial component	32	19	4	5	5	28	7
Rice component							
Allotted (metric tons)	369	568	47	65	nd	99	85
Distributed (metric tons)	342	497	47	16	12.5	52	45
Distributed as percentage total allotted	93	88	100	25	nd	52	53

* Includes 2 children's nurseries, 2 agricultural stores, 5 repairs to periodic market infrastructure, 3 sheds, repairs to 6 Panchayat Union buildings, repairs to a bus-stand and a mosque, and the construction of a dispensary.

people this amounted to 27 days' rice at 3 kg/day plus Rs53.8 in cash, such that the programme's impact is of higher significance than in Ramnad or Dharmapuri. Nevertheless, for the district as a whole it amounts to about six days employment per head of estimated rural population. Of the 1458 works started, only 569 had been completed within the first 12 months. The utilization of the allotted rice for the district amounted to 70% by July 1980. The durable assets created were repairs to public buildings such as maternity centres, schools, rural stores, tree planting and soil conservation, and repairing irrigation tanks and channels (Coimbatore District Development Office, Collectorate, Coimbatore, 1980, unpublished data).

In the second year of operation the district's plan was less ambitious, calling for 595 projects, 1590 metric tons of rice and Rs7.17 *lakhs* of money(1 *lakh* = 100 000 rupees).

The seven blocks or Panchayat Unions comprising our study region have made up 55% of the entire district's Food for Work Schemes, 54% of its finance and 60% of the district's rice allocation to Food for Work. *Table 21.3* summarizes achievements under Food for Work in its first twelve months of operation. Our region may be subdivided into two types of subregion, blocks which implemented the programme and blocks where implementation was weak. Three blocks, Annur, Avanashi and Sultanpet, account for 80% of the region's total programme finance, 90% of its rice and 90% of its schemes. Thirteen per cent of the allocation to the entire State went to these three blocks. Thus, although Coimbatore District provided slightly more work and rice under the Food for Work scheme than districts such as Ramnad and Dharmapuri, the programme's implementation has been extremely patchy in a spatial sense. It is evaluated in terms of its stated objectives.

As regards the durability of assets created, the great majority of schemes were routine and mostly petty repairs. Fifty per cent of Food for Work resources were invoked for roads and highway maintenance and one-quarter went to schools. Among the three implementing blocks, only 43% of resources went to roads and 24% to schools. In these blocks, a third of the resources went to infrastructural schemes such as tanks, canals and wells, and assets such as Panchayat Union buildings and nurseries, agricultural stores, a dispensary, a bus-stand and facilities for a weekly market; the latter two alone might be used by those who built or repaired them.

By contrast, roadworks accounted for 80% of Food for Work resources and the remainder went to schools in the four blocks which were poor implementers. The material allowances for road repairs were inadequate. In using free mud for repairing tarmac roads, Food for Work workers were not creating durable assets. They were, however, ensuring for themselves the need for more repair work after the next rains. It is known that, contrary to Central Government guidelines, labour contractors have been used in Avanashi Taluk. They respond to pressure from transport contractors eager to establish bus routes and the location of Food for Work projects may be affected by them.

The Government of India stipulated that between 50 and 100% of the resources allocated should comprise payment in grain. In our seven blocks this amounted to 40%: 43% in implementing blocks and 27% in non-implementing blocks. The latter is still twice as great as the maximum proportion of rice in Ramnad and Dhamapuri Districts. Furthermore, while 55% of the rice allocated was actually paid out in non-implementing blocks, 86% was distributed in implementing blocks. The meaning of these statistics is qualified by cases of refusal of mouldy rice from stocks over two years old. Workers were prepared to accept wages lower than those stipulated provided payment was in cash. Poor quality Food for Work rice was then sold to merchants who double boiled it and wholesaled it in Kerala (A. Rutherford, 1981, personal communication).

On the creation of gainful employment, the author could not obtain block-wise data on actual numbers employed. It is clear, however, from data on financial and grain resources, that employment was enormously concentrated in the three implementing blocks and only these could have had any impact on wage rates or work for agricultural labourers.

The distribution through time of rice in the first year of operation is given in *Table 21.4*. That of implementing blocks is more evenly distributed than that of poor implementers, though, for both, the months of October to January are the months of peak activity. These are also peak times for demand for agricultural labour and coincide with the north-east monsoon. Therefore, Food for Work competes for agricultural labour. It does not complement it in the off-season.

TABLE 21.4. Distribution of rice under Food for Work and Employment Guarantee Schemes in 7 blocks in Coimbatore District, 1979–80

	Implementing blocks*		Poorly implementing blocks[†]	
	(total metric tons)	(%)	(total metric tons)	(%)
July 1979	5.7	0.6	2.3	2.1
August	20.3	2.2	2.7	2.5
September	12.8	1.4	3.6	3.3
October	61.2	6.8	19.4	17.9
November	114.8	12.8	11.4	10.5
December	178.1	19.9	21.3	19.7
January 1980	94.3	10.5	37.5	34.7
February	14.2	1.6	2.8	2.6
March	149.8	16.7	3.8	3.5
April	54.6	6.1	0.5	0.5
May	22.8	2.5	2.9	2.6
June	31.9	3.5	na	–
July	131	14.7	na	–

* Annur, Avarashi, Sultanpet.
[†] Sulur, Palladam, Tirupur.
Pongalur did not supply monthly data.
na = not available.
Source: Original data from Panchayat Unions.

Employment Guarantee Scheme

In September 1979, a second food distribution scheme went into operation. The Employment Guarantee Scheme had as its objective the creation of employment and skills for the unemployed to make them self-employed in due course. Employment is guaranteed within 30 days to those able-bodied people over 18 who are not beneficiaries of rural development, small farmer or drought-prone area development projects and who have registered as unemployed. If no employment is found within that period a dole of Rs1 per day paid in rice at Rs1.50 per kg is provided. For those given work, payment is Rs6 a day in rice (4 kg).

The study of Ramnad and Dharmapuri Districts showed that no funds were allowed under the scheme for labour, compared with a materials component of Rs

1 *lakh* per Panchayat Union. Employment exchanges had not been established, employment had not been given nor had the dole. The scheme simply did not exist[2].

Tamil Nadu State's allocation of Rs4 *crores* (compared with Karnataka's allocation of Rs 30 *crores*)[14] represents about 1.5 days employment for all agricultural labour (1 *crore* = 10 × 10^6 rupees).

An attempt to implement the scheme has been made in Coimbatore District. Of the 28 721 registered unemployed by July 1980, 55% had been given work, though the District Development Officer acknowledged that, as with Food for Work, jobs had been provided in the peak agricultural season. Projects planned under the Employment Guarantee Scheme for 1980–81 totalled 766 at a cost of Rs7.4 million and necessitating 2343 metric tons of rice. The Employment Guarantee Scheme is therefore a larger scheme here than is Food for Work.

The case study region of seven blocks is far less prominent a sink for investment under the Employment Guarantee Scheme than it is under the Food for Work Scheme, comprising 31% of the projects under employment guarantee, 25% of money costs, and 32% of rice. As with Food for Work, there are contrasts between the same implementing and non-implementing blocks. The three implementing blocks corner 60% of projects in this region, 70% of finance, and 80% of the rice. *Table 21.5* gives details of progress during the first year. Employment has been provided only for road repairs, including some larger projects in the implementing blocks but dominated by petty maintenance in non-implementing blocks. Road mending is the only 'skill' for which 'training' is provided. This is hardly a job in which one can become 'self-employed in future'. However, it is clear that considerable menial employment was provided in certain places – 70 000 man days in Avanashi, an implementing block contrasted with 6400 man days in Pongalur, a poor implementer.

TABLE 21.5. Details of Employment Guarantee Scheme in 7 blocks of Coimbatore district

Block	Number projects	10^{-3} × total cost (Rs)	Percentage grand total	Roads as percentage project	10^{-3} × average cost project (Rs)
Annur	62	824.3	47	100	13.3
Avanashi	62	668	38	100	10.8*
Sultanpet	14	49	3	100	3.5
Pongalur	18	57.1	3	100	3.2†
Sulur	29	55	3	100	1.9
Palladam	14	36.8	2	100	2.6
Tirupur	22	47.5	3	100	2.2

* Rice disbursed = 278.9 metric tons = 4.5 metric tons per project = 1124 man-days/project.
† Rice disbursed = 25.6 metric tons = 1.4 metric tons per project = 355 man-days/project.

These grain payment schemes are to be expanded since it is stated by the Government of India that they have 'potential to become a focal programme for the generation of rural employment in the coming years'[8]. Suggested reforms to these grain payment schemes imply an increase in state bureaucracy. The Central Government, having renamed them the National Rural Employment Programme, has advised state governments to appoint technical personnel at block level to supervise projects, to appoint field officers to monitor schemes and to create a new agency to be responsible for the delivery of foodgrains from FCI and Civil Supplies

Corporation stores to work sites. Private contractors could then be banned. But there is little to indicate the removal of alleviation of constraints like finance. Hence the grain payment schemes may be expected to continue to be of little importance even as welfare measures except in small pockets.

Conclusion

The public distribution of foodgrains provides (subsidized) employment for government shopkeepers and reduces the financial burden, to Central and State Governments, of large buffer stocks. It has been claimed that such schemes are at best the application of a disguised famine code, enabling the survival and reproduction of those with nothing but their labour power but without any attempt to transform agrarian production relations. It is claimed that this subsidizes the production of the labour force available to landlords and to capitalist farmers, though it is the poor rather than the landlords who become dependent on the emerging 'welfare state'. Evidence shows that even in pockets where the scheme has been 'intensively' implemented, it has had none of the impact necessary for this type of explanation to have force.

References

1. AULAKH, H. S. and KAHLON, A. S. (1978) The role of zonal policy in creating an imperfect market structure. *Indian Journal of Agricultural Economics*, **33,** 59–67
2. BALAJI, M. and RAMACHANDRAN, V. K. (1980) *A Report on the Implementation of the Food for Work Programme and Employment Guarantee System in Ramanathapuram and Dharmapuri Districts.* Madras Institute of Development Studies, Madras, Mimeo
3. BASU, K. (1981) Food for Work programmes: beyond roads that get washed away. *Economic and Political Weekly*, **12,** Nos 1–2
4. DANDEKAR, V. M. and SATHE, M. (1980) Employment Guarantee Scheme and Food for Work Programme. *Economic and Political Weekly*, **15,** 12 April
5. GEORGE, P. S. (1979) *Public Distribution of Foodgrains in Kerala: Income Distribution, Implications and Effectiveness.* Research Report No. 7. Washington DC, International Food Policy Research Institute
6. GOVERNMENT OF INDIA (1978) *Food for Work Programme: A Guideline.* New Delhi, Ministry of Agriculture and Irrigation, Department of Rural Development
7. GOVERNMENT OF INDIA (1980) *Economic Survey 1979–80.* New Delhi
8. GOVERNMENT OF INDIA (1980) *A Quick Evaluation of the Food Programme: An Interim Report.* New Delhi, Programme Evaluation Organisation, Planning Commission
9. HARRISS, B. (1979) *Paddy and Rice Marketing in Northern Tamil Nadu.* Madras, Sangam Publishing Company for Madras Institute of Development Studies
10. HARRISS, B. (1984) *State and Market: The Political Economy of Exchange in a Dryland Region of South India,* Chaps 4,8,9. New Delhi, Concept Publishing Co.
11. HARRISS, B. (1986) *Coarse Grains, Coarse Interventions.* New Delhi, Twenty-First Century Publishing Trust
12. *Hindu* (1980) 12 May
13. *Hindu* (1980) 10 June
14. *Hindu* (1980) 3 Nov.
15. *Hindu* (1980) 23 Nov.
16. RAJ, K. N. (1981) Peasants and potatoes. *Mainstream*, **19,** 4–6 and 40
17. SINGH, V. B. (1973) *An Evaluation of Fair Price Shops.* Delhi, Oxford IBH Pub. House
18. SIVAKUMAR, S. S. (1978) Aspects of agrarian economy in Tamil Nadu: a study of two villages. *Economic and Political Weekly*, **13,** No. 20
19. SUBBARAO, K. (1978) *Rice Marketing System and Compulsory Levies.* Delhi, Institute of Economic Growth
20. SUBBARAO, K. (1981) What is a 'surplus state'?: an analysis of the public distribution. *Artha Vignana*
21. TAMIL NADU STATE CIVIL SUPPLIES CORPORATION (1980) *Hindu,* 7 April

Part IX

Cross-cultural consumer food buying habits

The food system of any country is a complex and dynamic process. For consumers, food is one of the most important product areas. For the food industry, it is of utmost importance to keep in touch with the consumers' expectations in order to match the needs and demands generated with the changing prerequisites and conditions of supply. In the first chapter, a model is presented for analysing the impact on the food industry of changing food consumer attitudes and behaviour. This analysis, based on certain enduring variables in consumer condition, focuses upon eating habits, customs and the nutritional role of these habits. The analysis indicates that the food industry needs a deeper understanding of consumer needs, wants and problems in order to be able to offer a satisfactory supply of products and services in this area in the 1980s and beyond. In particular, there seems to be a need for improvements in the area of information and communication.

The second chapter examines ethnic food shopping behaviour in the Metro Halifax area. The Halifax area is a mosaic of many cultural groups and it is thus believed that a study of this nature may prove to be highly beneficial to the Metro Halifax area vendors, manufacturers, and retailers as well as to public policy makers in designing better marketing strategies for reaching these different market segments. The objectives of this study are to determine what differences, if any, exist between ethnic and non-ethnic purchase behaviours in the Metro Halifax area. This empirical study should provide a sound basis for policy-making purposes and should direct attention to those areas where further investigation is most needed for improvement in the living standards of ethnic and non-ethnic food consumers.

Marketers have frequently utilized the concept of interpersonal communications to facilitate acceptance of innovative products and new brands. The purpose of the third chapter is to examine whether one aspect of interpersonal communications, opinion leadership, can be put into effective use in accelerating the acceptance of an innovative food retailing institution, the supermarket, in Saudi Arabia, and to discuss several strategies from implementation of which the Saudi supermarket operators can benefit.

Chapter 22

Food consumption and consumer behaviour in the future

Solveig R. Wikström

Introduction

When exploring the future for food consumption there are difficulties and uncertainties. The more dynamic and complex the area of research, the more these difficulties increase. The food area has been, and most certainly will remain, both complex and dynamic in the 1980s and beyond.

An approach for analysing this complex area is illustrated by the model depicted in *Figure 22.1*. The time perspective is the '80s' and beyond. Changes in consumer

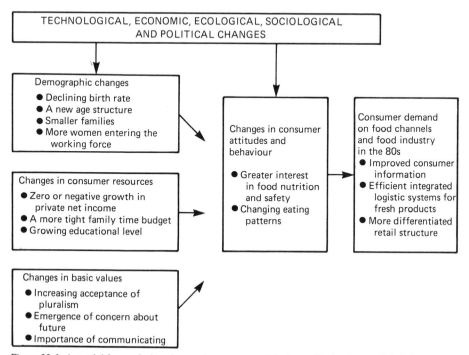

Figure 22.1. A model for analysing changes in consumer attitudes and behaviour and their impact on the food industry in the 1980s

attitudes and behaviour, a central component in the model, can be identified in two ways. This is done first by focusing upon trends in the system's environment and in the consumer's situation, and by analysing the implications of such for attitudes and consumer behaviour in the future. Important environmental variables are related to technological* and economic development, together with changes in the political system and the organization of the societal institutions. When it comes to changing consumer prerequisites and their impact on consumer attitudes and behaviour, it will be necessary to consider demographic changes, changes in consumer resources and basic values. The second way is by continuing to identify trends in consumer attitudes and behaviour from available consumer surveys, consumer audits and household buying records, and from other sources such as food production and retailing statistics.

With data on changing consumer attitudes and behaviour, it is possible to identify aspects of their impact upon industry and the types of adjustments that may be needed to maintain or improve prevailing market conditions. The scope of the analysis may hold relevance for Western industrialized countries. The attitudes and variables concentrated upon in this study are summarized as follows:

- The kind of food people consume compared to what they need for nutritional reasons.
- Eating habits, customs and traditions.
- Requirements and priorities when it comes to some central quality aspects of food: taste of food and the importance of food as a delight and reward, convenience in food supply, food prices and food costs, nutritional requirements and demand for safe products.

The analysis of the effects upon the food industry will take into consideration different aspects and different levels in the production/consumption systems of a country. These are summarized below:

- Effects on the total demand for certain product lines; people, for instance, tend to eat more fruit and vegetables, less fat and sugar.
- Effects on marketing and distribution; as people become more healthy and fitness conscious, food marketing needs to emphasize nutritional and food safety aspects.
- Effects on logistic systems; the increasing demand for fresh food calls for improvements in integrated systems for harvesting, packing, storing and transportation.
- Effects on retail systems; with a more differentiated household structure and more pluralistic consumption patterns, there is a need for further differentiation of the retail structure.
- Effects on the catering industry; with all family members being outside home during work days this market will expand and this places responsibility for new products and increasing quality on the catering industry.

When, in this context, analysing how, and in what directions, the future attitudes and behaviour of food consumers will change, it is possible to take into consideration only some of the more enduring variables affecting the production/ consumption interface.

* Technology is seen in a broad sense as the development and application of new knowledge.

Some environmental variables affecting attitudes and consumer behaviour in the food system

The external variables are to be seen as part of the food marketing system's environment. Environmental variables (uncontrollable factors) are defined as those affecting the system without the possibility of the system affecting the variables in desired directions. From a system's perspective, the environment is often classified in technological, economic, ecological, sociological and political variables[2]. These variables set the boundaries for the system's performance. Not only is consumer behaviour affected by these external variables, but also by the components of other systems: the business units as well as the government agencies. These variables also interact. To illustrate environmental effects, changes in technological and economic variables will be considered with their concomitant effects.

New technologies, such as new packaging and preserving methods, affect all activities in the food system by offering possibilities to mechanize, rationalize and develop new products and services. This thus generates economic and functional benefits for the food consumer and shopper. New technological breakthroughs, together with new applications of existing technologies, have a considerable potential for improving the performance of food systems on the medium-term horizon. Genetic technology, for example, has recently opened up quite new opportunities for generating breeds and crops with fundamentally new qualities.

Economic conditions affect the food system by the effect they have on both demand and supply of products and services. Available forecasts point in the same direction: a considerable increase in costs for food processing and distribution; increasing commodity costs with the rising cost level; rising processing, transportation and storing costs through high energy prices; increasing food prices as a result of rising protectionism. These changes can be related to zero or limited increases in expected net household earnings as a result of, among other things, declining productivity rates in the Western economies. The Western World is apparently facing a new economic order in the '80s' where economic development and growth can no longer be taken for granted. The psychological effects of these new conditions may prove more important than the real economic outcome.

Some internal variables affecting attitudes and behaviour of the consumer in the food system

As was pointed out earlier, there are certain changes in the demographic structure, and in consumer resources and basic values, which have large implications for the future development of the food system. Let us consider each of these changes in turn.

Demographic change and geographical changes

There are declining birth rates in most Western countries and this creates zero or negative population growth. The implications of this are considerable in a number of different areas: stagnating consumer goods markets, smaller families, a shrinking youth market, a relative increase in market catering to the needs of the older groups.

A further important and perhaps related trend is for both husband and wife to work outside the home. Some 85% of women in Sweden already have jobs, while in the USA the comparable figure is 65%. This trend, too, has far-reaching consequences for the food system, It provides a better family income, but simultaneously creates new patterns of demand, more convenience products, services and informational and educational facilities. Since there is no longer a professional housewife catering for the shopping, cooking and serving, the commercial food system is automatically assigned a new role.

A geographical trend of importance is the further growth of urbanization in the form of large multicentred agglomerations like the Ruhr and the West Midlands, and large metropolitan regions dependent on a single core city but with settlement areas which continue to expand into the environs, as in Paris, Madrid and Rome[5]. These aggregates are both time and energy consuming, and are dependent upon external supplies of fresh food. For these markets, the distance in time and space between production and consumption is long and circuitous. This creates a demand for efficient logistics and transportation systems, and for effective preservation techniques for 'fresh' foods.

Changing consumer resources

When discussing consumer resources, money, which creates the ability to buy, is the most important one. In most industrialized countries in the Western World today there are lower expectations for economic growth in private consumption. There are countries with a negative growth in private net income: this is a break from a long trend of constant growth. The effects of this expected reduction in income and purchasing power in numerical terms are rather small. The psychological impact upon consumer behaviour, however, may be much longer and more enduring. Up until now, we have had very little knowledge about the accumulated effects of such changes on the household budget. The impacts may be considerable when taking into consideration, as parallel trends, new consumer values and increasing educational levels. Through changing food consumption patterns, there are possibilities to cut cost without any harmful effects on health and nutrition. This, however, requires both a readiness to change eating habits and a willingness to obtain knowledge about food nutrition and its effects on health and fitness. Further, a more negative attitude towards overconsumption of food and to problems of being overweight would contribute considerably to changing food habits. With a decline in household income, and with rising food prices and changing values, there are possibilities for a shift in food consumption patterns which may considerably affect demand for certain food products.

Another important resource affecting food consumer attitudes and behaviour is education. In the '80s' several countries are entering the 'educational society' where the main part of the population has an educational background to the high school level or higher. As an example of the growth of educational level attained, it can be mentioned that, in the USA, the time children spend at school increased by 35% between 1956 and 1978[10]. In Sweden, more than one-third of the population had high school education as a minimum in 1979; this reached nearly 50% in 1980 and, in 1990, it is expected to have reached 60%[9]. To this should be added increased adult education. One consequence of this will be a higher capability amongst food consumers to process information and more awareness, although this does not necessarily mean they are more knowledgeable. There is also a stated positive relationship between educational level and consumer aspirations. In other words, with higher education levels, consumers become better equipped to pursue their personal goals.

Changing basic values

What will then be the priorities of the food consumers in the '80s'? What changes can be foreseen? It has, to some extent, to do with changing basic values. Values can be seen as both the result and the cause of changes. There are certain basic value changes which are difficult to explain. They seem to be independent processes taking place in society, having little to do with demographic structures and economic resources.

Some new basic social trends of relevance for consumer behaviour in the food system have been identified by Skelley in the USA[8]. Not all of these social trends are yet visible in Europe. Below, some of the more important emerging basic social trends are described:

- Rising acceptance of pluralism, flexibility and variation in all areas of life, in lifestyles, in departure from rigid standards and requirements, in compensation, and in eating patterns; possible consequences of this will be an easier climate for changing food consumption habits.
- Emerging new conservatism and trust towards professional knowledge: declining antibusiness reactions, less support for government intervention, erosion of egalitarian spirit, more support for elitism. Possible consequences of this will include an easier climate for the food industry to get credibility and trust by offering safe products, and make it easier for the consumers to place trust in food experts about nutrition and health claims.
- Re-emergence of concern about the future; less 'living for today', more commitment to preventative measures, continuing concern about physical fitness and vitality. An illustrative example of this latter trend is that, in the '60s', young men talked about how much they drank over the weekend, but now they talk about how long they have run. Possible consequences of this may include an increasing concern for the nutritional role of food, more concern about food as a way of physical fitness and vitality, and a better climate for improving food consumption patterns.
- Communications as a panacea for everything: in private life, at work, in public policy, in buying behaviour. The move is away from protectionism and towards communication as the basis for public policy. A possible consequence of this may be greater consumer interest in information processing, and in expression of views. This opens up opportunities for businesses to involve themselves in developing communication with the consumers as an aspect of normal competition.
- Return to technology; commitment to 'the natural' is starting to reverse; the attack on materialism and technology starting in the '60s' is now 'fading off'. Possible consequences of this will be: a new openness for highly processed food, less commitment to 'the natural', and for home-made and home-grown foods.
- New emphasis on the family and role for women: a new concentration on the family, but in a form which certainly will not mean a return to the home by women. There will be incrased investments in the home on the purchase of new

appliances for food preparation which will facilitate the demand for convenient food products. This new trend will have far-reaching effects on the efficiency of food retail systems.

From these general changing social trends some tentative conclusions can be drawn about how food consumer attitudes and behaviour may be affected in the future, and also how the prerequisites of food business may change. We can also look at the available data on consumer attitudes towards food and food consumption and identify changing habits. If it is possible, however, to explain the phenomena, and to place them in a logical context, the findings will have greater reliability and applicability.

Future directions of consumer attitudes and behaviour in the food system

Certain changes are taking place in the attitude and behaviour of consumers who are actors in the prevailing food system. Let us look at these changes in more depth.

Towards improved matching of nutritional and food consumption needs

There is apparently an imbalance between what people eat and what they need to eat for nutritional reasons and physical fitness. At present this imbalance exists in two ways. First, an apparent tendency towards overeating. According to a USA study, almost half of the families (44%) indicated that at least one member of their family was overweight. Furthermore, one out of five consumers (21%) reported that they had either started or had been on a diet in the week preceding the interview[13]. Second, there is an apparent tendency towards an overconsumption of expensive proteins such as fish, meat and eggs, and an underconsumption of fruit and vegetables and basic foods, such as potatoes, bread, grain, cereal, milk and cheese[1].

By eating less and choosing a different pattern of food ingredients consumers could both become more healthy and fit and considerably cut their food expenditures. American consumers are generally worried about high prices of food[6]. Swedes are also worried, but to a lesser degree[11]. Why do consumers maintain this imbalance? There are several possible explanations for this:

- Deeply rooted habits are hard to change. People eat the way they used to do when physical work was hard.
- Lack of knowledge. There is a manifest interest in nutrition among the majority of the consumers both in the USA and in Sweden, but actual behaviour has been little affected by this.
- The perception of what tastes good and what bad: basic foods have a low gourmet reputation, while steaks and sweets are highly valued. Food consumers generally have a perceptual bias.

There are, however, reported changes in food consumption patterns in a more positive direction. According to the Woman's Day Study[13] consumers reported eating more of chicken, salads, fruits and cheese, and eating less of cakes, biscuits, sweets, crisps, pretzels, butter, bread and meat. Swedish consumers also report the same kind of changes. Consumption statistics, however, provide little support for these types of changes, which may indicate that food habits are hard to change in practice.

The budget problem is attached, not only to minor changes in food consumption, but also to more intense bargain hunting in shopping[3]. A quotation from the Woman's Day report indicates major shifts in eating habits towards a more casual life style:

> The new values with their stress on self-fulfilment, the new role of women, more relaxed and casual life style, less formality and rigidity – run counter in many ways to the rigors of adhering to a set routine of three meals a day, regular mealtimes, making sure that every meal is balanced, or sticking to a menu in which certain foods are appropriate for only certain meals. The result of these changing values has been the adaption of a support for new and different concepts of nutrition, many of them supported by leading nutritionists – and all of them with important planning and merchandising implications.

According to L. Borell (head of a Swedish research company specializing in qualitative research and who carry out interviews on changing consumer attitudes and behaviour), major changes have occurred in the Swedish eating habits in recent times which, to a certain extent, follow the same directions as in the USA. With all family members working or being outside home, and with a tight time budget, few families serve a proper dinner at home during week days. The main meal is lunch which is eaten out. Eating at home is concentrated at weekends with Friday night as a particular family dinner evening. This has implications for shopping patterns. For the weekend there is planned shopping, but during weekdays people pass by a store just to get something to eat.

With increasing educational level, higher aspirations, growing interest in nutrition and price issues and more flexible eating habits, considerable changes in food consumption patterns are possible in the future. The consequences of this may be quite severe for certain parts of the food industry. With a zero population growth, even minor shifts in demand could cause considerable economic problems for the food business firms concerned.

Requirement of different food quality aspects

There are four central quality aspects of food in focus in this chapter. These are: (a) taste and food as a pleasure, (b) convenience, (c) nutrition and the demand for safe food, (d) food prices and food cost. These quality variables should not be seen as being isolated from each other. The problem from the consumer's perspective is that buyers have to, or think they have to, make trade-offs among these variables.

It has been postulated that there are shifts in the priorities, and that there are differences in priorities among different countries. In the USA, for example, consumers worry much more about high food prices than in Sweden, whilst the Swedes are much more concerned about additives and pesticides in food. Surveys indicate that industry does not seem to be fully aware of consumers' views and priorities. A recent pilot study conducted in Sweden about food quality priorities identified three important food quality dimensions which one out of five considered to be very important: food as a delight, food as nutrition and the safety of food[12]. Very few mentioned the price dimension. A deeper analysis revealed some clear attitude patterns; those who thought that nutrition qualities were very important also cared for the safety of food. On the other hand, those who thought that food as a delight was very important did not consider nutritional and safety aspects to have such a high priority.

These attitude patterns may, to some extent, explain why the importance of keeping food prices down in this context was ranked low, which is in contrast to the results of other surveys[6,11]. In a ranking situation for pronounced hedonists and puratinists, other qualities are more important, even if high prices can also be a problem *per se*. What about these variables in the future? The taste of food, and food as a delight, give an immediate reward compared to nutrition and safety. This quality is also easy to recognize. For a large majority, this variable has become more important in recent years[12]. It also seems probable that this quality dimension will keep its high rank in the future, even if other variables become increasingly important.

There are no recent surveys available highlighting the importance of convenience in food consumption. Tentative conclusions may, however, be drawn from the increasing employment of women outside the home to the effect that convenience will increase rather than decrease as a factor in the future. There are nevertheless conflicts between demand for convenience, on the one hand, and demand for nutrition and safety, on the other. For certain categories, however, food cost may prove a hindrance.

The interest in nutrition aspects, and worries about food safety and additives and pesticides in food, has increased considerably in recent years[4,6,11-13]. These aspects have become more important than the design and cost aspects of food. The taste and the cost of the food will most certainly continue to be important variables in the '80s'. The safety and nutrient aspects of food will, however, most probably have the greatest impact on changing food consumption patterns in the future.

At present, American and Swedish businesses are not fully aware of consumers' growing interest in nutrition and health aspects, and worries about unsafe products[4,6,11]. For instance, one consumer out of three in the USA and Sweden worries a great deal about unsafe products, but only one out of 20 business people think this is a problem for consumers. This insensitivity to consumer problems and reactions may lead to further consumer frustration and negative reactions from the market place, and may give rise to demands which could be costly to both business and consumers. It seems important at this stage for the food industry to improve credibility with consumers[7] and to develop efficient communication tools for the industry.

The efforts to keep the food budget down will most probably continue in the '80s', as one may expect further increase in the price level and little increase in net income. High price consciousness will continue as well as intense bargain shopping. High food prices may also be a motivation for people to learn more about nutrition and change the composition of their food consumption and purchasing patterns. The need for keeping the food budget down will, in the future, also be in conflict with the demand for convenient, tasty, healthy and nutritious food. What the people of the '80s' may increasingly demand is food which gives both immediate satisfaction, such as good taste and convenience, and long-run consumer welfare including high nutritional value and safer products. The challenge to the food industry for the '80s' lies, therefore, in diminishing the trade-offs which the consumers think they have to make at present between these important food quality variables.

Changing demands on different food industry levels

The main purpose of this chapter has been to indicate and illustrate how changes of attitudes and consumer behaviour concerning food industry in the future can be identified. With this as a basis, conclusions may be drawn about further consumer demands on the food industry. Corresponding changes in food industry should have the inputs discussed below.

Food marketing

- More consumer information and education about nutrition and food safety; this could be made a major marketing management goal.
- More nutritional labelling which is less technical, more descriptive and easy to understand.
- Less discrimination in the marketing between breakfast and dinner foods.
- More emphasis on healthy and nutritious snacks for people who may eat snacks instead of regular meals.
- More emphasis on diet and low calorie foods in product development.
- More convenience products that anyone in the family can prepare.
- More single-sized portions for families who do not eat together and for the increasing number of singles, and more packages where an arbitrary amount can be taken out and then reclosed.

Logistic systems

The demand on the logistic systems will have to increase for different reasons:

- By more efficient and better integrated systems costs could be cut.
- Stiffer standards of freshness for products will demand both faster and more logistic systems.
- Increasing emphasis on fresh fruit and vegetables will require improvements in integrated systems for growing, harvesting preservation, storing, transportation and packaging.

Retail systems

- More differentiated retail structure: convenience stores and fresh food stores versus discount stores and supermarkets.
- Improved communication systems with the consumers.
- More stress on nutrition for the dollar in the supermarket.
- More fast food chains offering nutrition, freshness and product safety.

Catering industry

- Expanding markets for the catering industry because all family members are outside home during the day in schools, work places and sport centres.
- Higher quality demands; dimensions to be stressed are freshness, nutrition, product safety and variety.
- Variation and flexibility in building up meals is important, particularly those tied in with physical fitness.

Conclusions

By systematic analysis of variables affecting consumer food attitudes and behaviour, possible future changes may be identified. There are also surveys available indicating new trends of importance for predicting future consumer behaviour. As has been shown, this is a complex and dynamic area where both facts and feelings are affecting consumer behaviour. It is important that food scientists and the food industry at all levels develop a deeper insight to changing consumer conditions affecting the food area, such as income, family structure, time budget and values, and new trends when it comes to attitudes and behaviour.

The challenging mission or task for the food industry is, not only to match the demand for better nutritional values of the food, for safe products which are tasty and convenient to prepare and for reasonable food prices; but also to overcome the prevailing communication problems with consumers as well as with their spokesmen. An improved supply will not result in more satisfied, safe and secure consumers. The marketing of products and services has also to adapt to the changing consumer conditions. In order to achieve good matching, the industry needs to open up a dialogue with the consumers, reacting to their demands both in reshaping products and in their marketing. It also needs to explain why certain demands cannot be met and what trade-offs must be made.

In shaping consumer attitudes and behaviour, there are strong feelings involved. Keeping in close touch with the consumers is therefore of the utmost importance, both for consumer satisfaction and for business profitability. Conflicts and rumours in this area can, in a very short time limit, eliminate the total demand for a product.

References

1. AGNSÄTER, A. B., VON DÖBELN, W. and RING, B. (1977) *It pays to know about Basic Food.* Consumer Information Department, Consumer Coops Association
2. CHURCHMAN, C. W. (1968) *The Systems Approach.* New York: Delta Publishing Co.
3. GENERAL MILLS AMERICAN FAMILY REPORT 1974-75 (1975) *A Study of the American Family and Money.* Conducted by Yankelovich, Skelley and White, Inc., Minneapolis
4. GREYSER, S. (1977) *Consumerism at the Crossroads.* A National Opinion Research Survey of Public, Activist, Business and Regulator Attitudes towards the Consumer Movement. Sentry Insurance
5. HALL, P. (1977) *Europe 2000.* London, Gerald Duckworth & Co. Ltd
6. HARRIS, L. *et al.* (1978) *A Survey of the Public, Community Leaders and Consumer Activists on Consumerism.* Report No. 48, Vol. III. New York, L. Harris and Associates
7. HOLLINGWORTH, D. (1975) How can we improve credibility with consumers of the Food Industry and the Nutrition Authorities. In *Nutrition and the Public.* Proceedings from symposium at Marabou, Sundbyberg, Sweden: Swedish Nutrition Foundation
8. SKELLEY, F. (1981) *The Attitudes of the Consumers.* Proceedings from Marabou International Symposium, Stockholm, Sweden: Swedish Nutrition Foundation
9. SWEDISH CENTRAL BUREAU OF STATISTICS (1975) The IPF study. *The Education Growth 1970–2000,* Sweden
10. TOFFLER, A. (1980) *The Third Wave.* New York, William Morrow and Company
11. WIKSTRÖM, S. *et al.* (1981) *Swedish Consumerism at the Crossroads.* Research Report No. 2, Lund University, May. (In Swedish.) A progress report from 1979 is available in English
12. WIKSTRÖM, S. (1981) *Consumer Priorities in Food Consumption, a Pilot Study.* Lund University, Department of Business Administration. A Working Paper
13. WOMAN'S DAY FAMILY FOOD STUDY (1978) *Nutrition, a Study of Consumer's Attitudes and Behaviour. Towards Eating at Home and Out of Home.* Conducted by Yankelovich, Skelley and White, Inc.

Chapter 23

A comparison of ethnic and non-ethnic food shopping behaviour: a Canadian case

Erdener Kaynak

Introduction

The shopping behaviour of individuals and various market segments in North America have been studied from innumerable perspectives, and many of the concepts and findings have helped marketers gain a better understanding of shoppers. The results have often provided a basis for more effective marketing strategies[6]. Research has also shown that the differences in food shopping behaviour among ethnic and non-ethnic consumers in developed countries tend to be reflected in their selection of food retail outlets and their responsiveness to specific marketing policies[11,13].

Most of the prior research on food retailing among both ethnic and non-ethnic consumers of North America has been primarily on macroeconomic studies[2-5] or studies of specific market processes and institutions[1,7,9,12,14-16,19,20]. The primary objective of this study is, then, to examine the shopping and consumption patterns of ethnic and non-ethnic individuals living in Metro Halifax*, Nova Scotia, Canada. Such characteristics as type of retail institutions patronized, important elements in the purchase decision process, sources utilized to acquire information about food products, transportation to markets and the use of credit are investigated. The results should be useful to both marketing academics and retail managers because they indicate the types of similarities and differences that may exist between ethnic and non-ethnic shopping behaviour patterns in Metro Halifax.

The literature related to the shopping practices of food consumers in North America shows that the pattern of shopping and purchasing behaviour for food among ethnic market places is dissimilar to that for consumers in the non-ethnic market places. What can this poor performance of food retail institutions in ethnic market areas be attributed to? According to the results of a limited number of surveys conducted in the USA, there is not much concern on the part of the large food retail outlets operating in non-ethnic market areas with the needs and wants of consumers residing in ethnic market areas.

---

* Metro Halifax includes Halifax, Dartmouth and Bedford.

Methodology

The study is aimed towards describing and analysing the characteristics and differences existing between ethnic and non-ethnic Nova Scotians with regard to their respective food shopping behaviours. This study will also evaluate the views of respondents with regard to what selective criteria are important when a consumer is choosing a food retail outlet. Respondents' opinions were also measured with regard to which food product attributes were important. The theoretical proposition was that shopping behaviour will vary between the ethnic and non-ethnic groups of Nova Scotia.

Data collection method

The data were collected through the use of a mail questionnaire. A focus group interview was conducted among a group of food shoppers of Halifax in order to limit and define the topics under study, as well as to pretest the questionnaire. The questionnaire was highly structured and contained relatively few indirect questions. The respondents were informed that their food shopping behaviours were being studied but they were not notified that they would be grouped according to their ethnic origins. This is an emotional subject and it was not believed that they would have reacted to this favourably. Dichotomous, structured response questions, multiple choice questions and Likert rating scales constituted the main inquiry format. Two open-ended questions were also asked. The questionnaire was highly structured to aid in the case of data collection and analysis.

Selection and measurement of variables

A number of independent variables were selected that would give an indication of the respondents' perceptions and attitudes toward the various attributes that are salient to them, with regard to the purchase of food products and the selection of food shopping outlets. Questions were also included to determine who constitutes the buyer, influencer and decision maker of each respondent's household.

Classification variables such as age, sex, income, ethnic origin, number of people per grocery budget, were used in order to describe and segment the survey respondents and to add meaning to the analysis.

Identification of target population and sample selection

The target population consisted of individuals residing in the Spryfield area of Halifax. This target group was chosen because it was believed that the population residing there was representative of the ethnic composition existing in the Metro Halifax area. Three hundred and sixty questionnaires were hand delivered to residents of the area. The respondents were asked to complete the questionnaire and were notified that it would be picked up two days later. The respondents were also asked to leave the questionnaire outside their door if likely to be absent at the designated time. After two callbacks, a 61% response rate was obtained and 10% were deemed to be unusable. The latter 10% were not utilized in the analysis due to the fact that the respondents were unwilling to complete the question concerning their ethnic origins. Survey results are based upon 184 responses.

Limitations

This study only pertains to the purchase of grocery products, therefore, it may not be used to draw any predictive conclusions concerning the purchase behaviour relating to clothing or any other consumer goods.

The sample was a restricted sample, interviewing only residents of one particular area in Metro Halifax. The sample consisted predominantly of married couples with relatively lower incomes by comparison with the population at large. The age group fell mostly between 20 and 40 years and is fairly representative of the whole Nova Scotia population. The limitations of the sample make the results useful only for exploratory purposes and not for the purpose of drawing concrete conclusions.

The survey was carried out in the summer of 1981. It is difficult to say whether or not the respondents may have answered differently if they had been interviewed at a different time. All types of factors could have caused their response to vary. There was no control over who filled out the questionnaires. The answers given truly represent the general tendency as regards the ethnic and non-ethnic food shopping process, and it may not necessarily tell us what happens with respect to purchase behaviour of the household or if the answers merely reflect how the respondent personally perceives the situation.

The Likert rating scale may have been difficult for some respondents to answer. Others may have simply been unwilling to supply the true answer. The question pertaining to 'what is your ethnic origin?' could have been couched in better terms. Some 11% of the respondents failed to answer this question. Others simply said that we Canadians should not be so concerned with ethnic origin and should think of ourselves as 'Canadians only'. Many of Scottish and Irish origin did not know where to include themselves. Many answered for the 'other' category that they were Canadians even though they had already replied yes to this previously mentioned question. There was no way of knowing if all members of the household were from the same or different ethnic origins. However, the proportional representation of the ethnic groups was representative of the proportions in the population at large.

To overcome some of the above-mentioned difficulties in the future, a longitudinal rather than cross-sectional design scale might also be utilized. As well, the respondents' educational level may need to be included and the class interval categories for income need to be adjusted. Income is a very sensitive subject for non-Canadian respondents. It is illegal for some of these subjects to be working in Canada without a working visa. For this reason, the researcher needs to ensure the respondent of anonymity and be very tactful when dealing with this item. If handled properly, a question dealing with the occupation of the respondent would enhance the validity of the overall study.

Future researchers should also determine if the respondent's entire family is ethnic or whether, through marriage, assimilation has occurred. Lack of this information could severely limit the subsequent conclusions drawn from the results of the study. Further research should also deal with choice and purchase behaviour of products other than food stuffs.

Dependent variable

The dependent variable, ethnic versus non-ethnic food shopping behaviour was operationalized through responses to the question: 'Are you Canadian born?' One hundred and thirty-six respondents were classified as non-ethnic and 48 as ethnic food shoppers.

Independent variables

Three sets of variables were used for profiling the two food shopper categories of Metro Halifax. The first set of variables was related to information sources utilized by food shoppers. Second, respondents were asked how important a list of factors was in choosing a food retail outlet to shop in as well as the type of brands preferred. The third set of independent variables was socioeconomic and demographic characteristics of respondents themselves. These variables included sex, marital status, household size, age and income.

Findings

Demographic characteristics

The demographic and socioeconomic profile of the ethnic and non-ethnic food shoppers of Halifax were defined by household size, sex, marital status, age, income and ethnic origin of the respondents. Socioeconomic and demographic characteristics of ethnic and non-ethnic food shoppers are shown in *Table 23.1*.

TABLE 23.1. Socioeconomic characteristics of ethnic and non-ethnic food shopper groups

Variable		Ethnic		Non-ethnic
Sex				
Female	(120)	56.4		71.7
Male	(64)	43.6		28.3
Marital status				
Married	(158)	76.9		92.5
Other	(26)	23.1		7.5
Household size				
1 to 3	(150)	76.9		84.9
4 to 6	(34)	23.1		15.1
Age				
Under 40	(156)	92.3		83.0
40 or more	(28)	7.7		17.0
Income				
Under C$20 000	(82)	32.7		61.6
C$20 000–C$29 999	(90)	59.6		35.9
C$30 000 or more	(12)	7.7		2.5
Ethnic origin				
British	(84)		45.7	
Asiatic	(28)		15.2	
French	(22)		12.0	
Other Europeans	(16)		8.8	
All others	(34)		18.3	
Total			100.0	

Food retail store selection process

Ethnic food shoppers and non-ethnic ones did differ in the factors they considered in choosing a food retail store in metropolitan Halifax. The importance attached by each group to various factors was measured. With regard to the importance of canned food available, the mean was 3.2 and the highest percentage of ethnic and non-ethnic responses fell in the score of greater than 3 on the Likert scale. Thus, the variety of canned foods available did not appear to be of primary importance to either group (*Table 23.2*). When the importance of customer service was measured, it is obvious that this store attribute is much more important to the ethnic group and there was a statistically significant difference between the two groups on this factor. It can be seen that the importance of the proximity of store location is slightly more important to non-ethnic groups. With regard to the importance of food quality it is obvious that both groups of respondents feel that quality is of prime importance. Most respondents reported that a well-organized layout was important; however, responses are fairly well diversified from categories 1 to 4.

From *Table 23.2*, one can draw a number of tentative conclusions. First of all, we really do not know why the store was selected in the first place. Second, there may not be much difference between ethnic and non-ethnic Canadians' food store selection behaviour. Third, the only significant differences are the store personnel, how they treat customers and if they keep the place neat, a finding previously identified by Sturdivant[8,17,18].

TABLE 23.2. Importance of factors in choosing a food retail store in Halifax

Factors[*,†]	Mean scores[‡]				P
	Ethnic	Rank	Non-ethnic	Rank	
Availability of canned foods	3.31	11	3.13	11	NS
Customer service and assistance	2.03	6	2.68	8	0.04
Proximity of location	1.79	5	1.83	5	NS
Overall quality of food sold	1.18	1	1.15	1	NS
Well-organized layout	2.08	7	2.26	7	NS
Availability of frozen foods	3.49	12	2.89	10	NS
Availability of meat counter	1.54	3	1.60	3	NS
Price of products sold	1.44	2	1.25	2	NS
Spacious shopping conditions	2.44	8	2.81	9	NS
Availability of produce counter	1.54	3	1.64	4	NS
Instore displays	2.79	9	3.43	13	NS
Store neatness	1.64	4	2.24	6	0.02
Availability of a speciality area in store	3.00	10	3.32	12	NS

[*] Comparisons are made by using the chi-squared test.
[†] The response to each statement was obtained on a five-point scale where 5 = not important at all, 1 = very important.
[‡] Although the statements used here do not generate interval scale data, the mean scores are presented to provide the general tendency exhibited by the respondents.
$P < 0.05$.
NS = not significant.

With regard to the importance of the availability of frozen foods, the two groups placed different weights on this attribute. The mode for the ethnic group was divided between ratings 2 and 3 whereas the mode for the non-ethnic falls in category 4. The overall mean was 3.0. It can be seen that frozen food availability is more important to the ethnic group. However, no significant difference was found. Both the ethnic and non-ethnic respondents feel that the variety and availability of meats is very important for deciding at which food store they will shop. The overall mean was 1.6. A mode of 1 for both groups was reported. The groups were highly similar.

With regard to the importance of price, both ethnic and non-ethnic respondents rated this attribute as being of prime importance. The overall mean was 1.3 and the modal tendency for both groups was one. The groups again show little variation.

With regard to the importance of spacious shopping conditions, the majority of non-ethnic respondents rated the attribute as being 2 on the Likert scale. The majority of the ethnic group rated it as 3, with no significant difference between the two groups. With regard to the importance of available produce, this attribute was rated overall as being fairly important with a mean of 1.6. The ethnic group, however, tended to rate this attribute as more important than the non-ethnic group rated it. However, no significant difference was found between the two groups.

With regard to the importance of displays, this attribute was not rated as having prime overall importance. The mean score was 3.2. More of the ethnic group rated this attribute as falling in the 1–3 category, whereas the majority of the non-ethnic respondents rated it as being 3–5. No significant difference between the two was found. With regard to the importance of store neatness, a relatively high majority of the ethnic group rated this as being of high importance. The modal tendency for the non-ethnic group was 2; the overall mean was 1.9; a significant difference was found. With regard to the importance of a specialty area in the store, the majority of non-ethnic respondents reported that this attribute was not very important at all. However, the majority of ethnic respondents were fairly equally divided between the modes 2 and 3. No significant difference was found.

With regard to the importance of Imperial weight, both groups felt that this information was very helpful. The importance of metric weight on the label was perceived as being somewhat useful by the majority of the respondents, with the ethnic group perceiving it to be slightly more beneficial. The highest percentage of respondents felt that price per unit on the label was very helpful. Of the three labelling devices, the price per unit was found to be by far the most useful to both groups of respondents. Although the non-ethnic group perceives it to be slightly more useful, overall there was no significant difference found between the two groups.

Food shopping related activities

It is obvious that the majority of respondents, both ethnic and non-ethnic, do not frequently read the newspaper for food specials. The majority of the ethnic population reads the paper only once a week, whereas the majority of the non-ethnic population fell into another category making comparison difficult.

With regard to the type of transportation used on their shopping trips, the majority of ethnic and non-ethnic respondents reported that 'by car' was the most prevalent type of transportation used. The other forms of transportation were utilized fairly equally between the two groups, and there was no significant difference between the two groups. The second most important means of transportation used by both groups was walking.

With regard to the store shopped at, more of the ethnic respondents shop at either Sobeys or IGA. The non-ethnic respondents' choice of store seems fairly equally divided between the Capital Store, Sobeys or IGA. There was no significant difference found between the two groups on this score. The majority of respondents for both ethnic groups tend to shop at their usual store between 50 and 100% of the time. In other words, both ethnic and non-ethnic food shoppers were store loyal.

With regard to the importance of different factors in meal preparation for Halifax shoppers, the majority of the ethnic group had a bimodal response evenly divided between categories 2 and 3 (*Table 23.3*). The majority of respondents did not feel that a meal requiring four ingredients was all that important. The modal response for both groups was 3. Inexpensive ingredients seemed to be slightly more important for the non-ethnic group, the modal pressure being 2. For the ethnic

TABLE 23.3. Importance of different factors in meal preparation for shoppers of Halifax

Factors*,†	Mean scores‡		P
	Ethnic	Non-ethnic	
Speedy preparation	2.67	3.09	NS
Use of few ingredients	3.10	3.42	NS
Use of expensive ingredients	2.72	2.34	NS
Use of frozen food	3.26	3.04	NS
Can be prepared ahead of time	3.10	3.21	NS
Nutrition value	1.26	1.30	NS

* Comparisons are made by using the chi-squared test.
† The response to each statement was obtained on a five-point scale where 5 = not important at all, 1 = very important.
‡ Although the statements used here do not generate interval scale data, the mean scores are presented to provide the general tendency exhibited by the respondents.
P < 0.05
NS = not significant.

group the mode was category 3. With regard to the attribute that the meal can be frozen, the non-ethnic group felt that this was more important than did the ethnic group: the mode was 2. The ethnic group had a bimodal response of categories 2 and 5. The fact that a meal can be prepared ahead of time was not seen by respondents as being all that important. The non-ethnic mode was 3 and the ethnic group's bimodal response fell into categories 3 and 4. Nutrition was by far the most important attribute for all groups; 75.5% of the non-ethnic group rated this as being very important, as did 79.5% of the ethnic group. There was no significant difference found for any of the above.

Brand preference

Both ethnic and non-ethnic groups were more loyal to national brands throughout. Although there are no statistically significant differences between the non-ethnic and ethnic groups with regard to their usual brand purchases, some variations in their purchasing behaviour were observed. With regard to the purchase of dairy products and laundry detergent, non-ethnic respondents are more likely to purchase either no name brands or they are not sure of which brand they usually purchase. Ethnic groups appear to be much more loyal to national and store brand dairy products than are the non-ethnic groups. On the other hand, in the purchase of coffee, soft drinks, soups, desserts, juice and tea, the ethnic group appeared to be far more likely to buy no-name brands than the non-ethnic group or they were not sure which brand they usually purchased (*Table 23.4*).

The majority of respondents of the ethnic group tend to purchase brandname dairy products, coffee and soft drinks more frequently than do the ethnic. The non-ethnic group, on the other hand, tend to purchase brandname soups and tea

TABLE 23.4. Type of brand preferred by food shoppers of Halifax

Type of brand	Dairy product (%)		Tea (%)		Coffee (%)		Soft-drinks (%)	
	Ethnic	Non-ethnic	Ethnic	Non-ethnic	Ethnic	Non-ethnic	Ethnic	Non-ethnic
National brand	92.3	77.4	68.4	86.3	73.7	89.8	79.4	80.0
Private brand	7.7	13.2	18.4	9.8	15.8	8.2	5.9	11.1
No name brand	–	1.9	10.5	3.9	7.9	2.0	8.8	2.2
Not sure	–	7.5	2.7	–	2.6	–	5.9	6.7
Total	100.0	100.0	100.0	100.0	100.0	100.0	100.0	100.0
	df = 3		df = 3		df = 3		df = 3	
	$P < 0.1787$		$P < 0.1845$		$P < 0.2002$		$P < 0.5156$	

Type of brand	Fruit juice (%)		Laundry detergent (%)		Desserts (%)		Soups (%)	
	Ethnic	Non-ethnic	Ethnic	Non-ethnic	Ethnic	Non-ethnic	Ethnic	Non-ethnic
National brand	65.8	57.7	69.2	73.6	60.6	71.7	82.1	96.0
Private brand	23.7	36.5	23.1	15.1	15.2	15.2	7.7	4.0
No name brand	7.9	5.8	5.1	9.4	3.0	–	2.6	–
Not sure	2.6	–	2.6	1.9	21.2	13.0	7.7	–
Total	100.0	100.0	100.0	100.0	100.0	100.0	100.0	100.0
	df = 3		df = 3		df = 3		df = 3	
	$P < 0.4043$		$P < 0.6987$		$P < 0.4702$		$P < 0.1053$	

TABLE 23.5. Frequency of purchase of selected food products by shoppers

Brand name of selected food products* †	Mean scores‡		P
	Ethnic	Non-ethnic	
Dairy products	1.38	1.47	NS
Tea	2.18	2.15	NS
Coffee	2.02	2.43	NS
Soft drink	1.77	2.45	0.04
Juice	1.79	2.13	NS
Laundry detergent	2.23	2.06	NS
Desserts	2.62	2.87	NS
Soups	1.77	1.60	NS

* Comparisons are made by using the chi-squared test.
† The response to each selected brand name food product was obtained on a five-point scale where 5 = never, 1 = all the time.
‡ Although the statements used here do not generate interval scale data, the mean scores are presented to provide the general tendency exhibited by the respondents.
NS = not significant.

TABLE 23.6. Usefulness of information sources utilized by food shoppers of Halifax

Information sources utilized* †	Mean scores‡		P
	Ethnic	Non-ethnic	
Television	4.08	4.47	NS
Radio	4.10	4.09	NS
Newspapers	2.90	3.02	NS
Store flyers	2.95	2.75	NS

* Comparisons are made by using the chi-squared test.
† The response to each selected brand name food product was obtained on a five-point scale where 5 = not important at all, 1 = very important.
‡ Although the statements used here do not generate interval scale data, the mean scores are presented to provide the general tendency exhibited by the respondents.
NS = not significant.

more frequently than do the ethnic group. In general no significant difference was found. On the whole, the non-ethnic group tends to purchase brandname laundry detergent more often with the ethnic group having bimodal responses, the responses being divided between categories 1 and 2. With regard to the purchase of brandname desserts, the ethnic group has a modal response of 2 where the non-ethnic group has a modal response of 4. No significant difference was found (*Table 23.5*).

Information sources utilized

With respect to the information sources utilized regarding food purchases, a substantial majority of both the ethnic and non-ethnic groups perceived television and radio information sources as being of very little importance at all. In contrast, the majority of the ethnic groups found newspapers to be a very important food information source, while the majority of the non-ethnic groups rated newspapers as being not very important at all. The reason for this trend is that non-ethnics do not consider newspapers to be an important source of information. With regard to store flyers, both groups seemed to perceive this information source as being fairly important with the majority of the non-ethnic group (26.9%) rating it as very important. The majority of the ethnic group (41.0%) rated it as 2 on the Likert scale. No significant difference was found on any of these cross-tabulations (*Table 23.6*).

A sigificantly higher proportion of non-ethnic respondents prepared a detailed shopping list before shopping. These respondents also usually stuck to only buying the items which they had on the list. On the other hand, ethnic shoppers did not prepare a list as often and the majority of this group never stuck to buying only the items that they had on the list. A significant difference was found when the answers to the question 'do you usually prepare a list' were tabulated ($P<0.05$) and a significant difference ($P<0.01$) was found when answers to the questions 'do you usually stick to buying only the items which you have on the list?' were cross-tabulated.

When respondents were asked which sources of food store information they usually search for, the majority of respondents stated that they usually search for bargains. Approximately 30% more of the non-ethnic group always shopped for bargains. There emerged a statistically significant difference between the two groups at a $P<0.06$ level. The majority of respondents did not search for helpful menu suggestions, with the ethnic group making up a slightly higher percentage in the ethnic category. The ethnic group usually searched slightly more frequently for new products with the modal response of 3. The modal response for the non-ethnic group was 4; this was non-significant ($P<0.34$).

With regard to coupons, the most frequently cited score for both groups was 4 with the non-ethnic group tending to use coupons much less frequently than the ethnic group. There is no significant difference ($P<0.17$). A significant difference was found with regard to the persuasive abilities of in-store contests. Neither group seemed to find this type of promotional effort excessively persuasive. However, the non-ethnic group found it much less persuasive than did the ethnic group and this was significant at $P<0.01$.

The non-ethnic respondents shop less often for food than do the ethnic respondents. The majority of respondents, however, shop between 3 and 4 times per month for food. The percentage of ethnic respondents that fell in this category was 56.4% while the percentage of non-ethnic respondents was 39.6%. Frequency of purchase by ethnic and non-ethnic food shoppers is shown in *Table 23.7*. Both groups most frequently cited that they spend between C$101 and C$150 on food for one month. On average the non-ethnic group appears to spend more on food than does the ethnic group (*Table 23.8*).

TABLE 23.7. Frequency of monthly food purchases by food shoppers of Halifax

Frequency of food shopping[†]	Percentage breakdown*	
	Ethnic	Non-ethnic
< 1	–	3.8
1–2	23.1	28.3
3–4	56.4	39.6
> 5	20.5	28.3
Total	100.0	100.0
Number of respondents	78	106

* Comparisons are made using the chi-squared test.
[†] No statistically significant differences were observed between ethnic and non-ethnic shoppers.

TABLE 23.8. Food expenditures of food shoppers of Halifax

Monthly food expenditures[†]	Percentage breakdown*	
	Ethnic	Non-ethnic
C$50.00	–	–
C$51–C$100	23.1	17.3
C$101–C$150	35.9	38.5
C$151–C$200	25.6	30.8
> C$200	15.4	13.5
Total	100.0	100.0
Number of respondents	78	106

* Comparisons are made using the chi-squared test.
[†] No statistically significant differences were observed between ethnic and non-ethnic shoppers.

With regard to which members of the family decide where to shop, what to buy and actually do the buying, the wife has a distinct role across both ethnic and non-ethnic groups. She is more frequently cited by both groups as conducting all of the above activities. Husband and wife together rank second in all 3 cases.

With regard to who influences the purchaser on what to buy, the above relationship applies only to the ethnic group, i.e. the wife is again the usual influencer. On the other hand, the non-ethnic group replied with a bimodal response equally divided between the husband and the syncratic influence of husband and wife.

Managerial implications

With regard to the characteristics that are important to consumers in relation to deciding upon which food store they will shop in, the following characteristics were cited as being most important: (*a*) overall quality of food sold, (*b*) price of products sold, (*c*) availability of meat counter, (*d*) store neatness, (*e*) proximity of location, (*f*) customer service and assistance and, (*g*) well-organized layout.

These store attributes held much salience for both the ethnic and non-ethnic groups. The availability of frozen foods and food displays were not seen as being very important for either group. Significant differences were found between the two group's perceptions of the importance of a specialty area, the neatness of the store and customer services. Neatness and customer services were perceived to be of more importance to the ethnic respondents, whereas a specialty area was perceived to be more important to the non-ethnic group.

A marketing manager should emphasize, in his promotional appeals, the important evaluative criteria that are stressed by all his customers. If a localized approach is utilized, he should then place emphasis on the above as well as stressing the neatness of the store and customer services when advertising to ethnic groups and the existence of a specialty area when aiming for the non-ethnic population. In order to maximize the effectiveness of the marketing mix, the manager must ensure that the location of the store is not distant from the clientele, that the quality and variety of meats and produce are excellent, that customer services are adequate and that prices are not excessively high.

The results of the study indicated that newspapers were not read frequently by either group. In contrast to the other media types, however, the ethnic group stated that they found newspapers to be a very important source of information regarding food purchases. The non-ethnic group was consistent in their responses as they again rated newspapers as a relatively unimportant source of information. Store flyers were regarded by both groups as being a fairly important information source with the majority of the non-ethnic group rating store flyers as very important. Little salience was attributed to either television or radio as information sources by either group.

On the basis of the findings of this study, it appears that promotional tactics aimed toward the non-ethnic group should stress store flyers. Promotion aimed toward the ethnic population should, however, emphasize the use of newspaper advertisements. The use of television and radio do not seem to constitute a valid promotional device about food purchasing whether they be ethnic or non-ethnic consumers.

It is obvious that most of the ethnic and non-ethnic groups shop at the same store over 50% of the time. Promotion should therefore be aimed at making consumers patronize the store as the consumer is likely to become store loyal. Promotional reminders and reinforcers should serve to maintain this state of affairs.

With regard to what qualities are important to consumers in preparing a meal, nutrition was ranked as being of prime importance for both groups. The answers pertaining to the other criteria stated in the questionnaire showed mediocre results and did not stand out to any great extent. Marketers should therefore emphasize the nutritional aspects of their food products. It should be remembered though, that although inexpensive ingredients were not rated as being very important in this question, price was mentioned earlier as being quite important. Marketers should be aware, however, that quality seems to be of more importance to consumers than price. Promotion can be fairly well standardized in this case as there are no significant differences between the ethnic and non-ethnic groups.

No significant differences were found between the ethnic and non-ethnic groups regarding the purchases of brands of products. All respondents tend to more frequently purchase national brands, with store brands being purchased with a little less frequency. This again leads to the assumption that quality is more frequently perceived as being more important than price. Marketers should thus emphasize this point and retailers should ensure that their shelves contain these brand products. Consumers on the whole tend to be fairly brand loyal, on the basis of this study, and this should be stimulated so that it eventually leads to brand insistence. The marketer of no name brands should stress the fact that his products do have quality and, just because the price is lower, the products are not necessarily inferior.

Non-ethnic shoppers much more frequently prepare detailed shopping lists and do not deviate from these to a great degree. Ethnic shoppers, on the other hand, do not prepare lists as often and do not tend to stick to lists that they do prepare. This constitutes a statistically significant difference between the two groups and can help the marketer in preparing his promotional campaign. It appears that ethnic consumers are much more likely to be waylaid into buying products that they had not thought about purchasing previously. In-store promotions should serve to help induce these consumers to select advertised in-store products. On the other hand, advertisements that reach the non-ethnic group before they go shopping may help to plan their purchasing lists and may induce them to attend the store in question.

Bargains seem to be more important for the non-ethnic group, although no significant difference was found between the two groups. This ties in with the fact that the non-ethnic group frequently utilizes store flyers and prepares a detailed shopping list ahead of time. Thus, when utilizing information sources, it seems that the non-ethnic group plans ahead and searches for this information. The ethnic group does not seem to search as much for bargain information and does not plan ahead as much. Therefore, in-store promotions will help to sway the latter group's decisions. Search does not take place to such a high degree for helpful menu suggestions or new product ideas for either group. Thus, it seems that food store information sources are not utilized to a large extent for the former two purposes.

Non-ethnic individuals shop for food less often than do ethnic individuals. This could perhaps be explained by the fact that the non-ethnic shoppers plan ahead more often. Both groups appear to shop between 3 and 4 times per month. Promotion could perhaps be staggered to meet once-a-week shopping. This may also have a relationship to the stocking of the retail outlets, e.g. no fresh produce available on Monday. Retailers must ensure that shelves are fully stocked throughout the week.

The non-ethnic group appears to spend slightly more on food purchases than do ethnic individuals, although this difference was not statistically significant. This could perhaps be explained by the fact that the non-ethnic incomes were a bit higher than those reported by ethnic groups. Ethnic groups also emphasized the variety of fresh produce as being more important and, since produce is generally less expensive than meat, this could help to account for the lower food bills.

The wife plays the most prominent part in the decision making, buying and influencing role with husband and wife team coming second. Children's influence is perceived as being minimal, perhaps due to the fact that they must generally be preschoolers. This is evidenced by the fact that the majority of the respondent's ages were between 31 and 40 years old. Promotional appeals should thus be geared mainly toward the household wife. These results may, however, have been influenced by the fact that the majority of the respondents were female, 71.7% of the non-ethnic group and 56.4% of the ethnic group.

Overall, few statistically significant differences were found between the ethnic and non-ethnic groups. The following results seem to be the most valuable: (*a*) customer services and neatness of the outlet are more important for the ethnic groups, (*b*) specialty areas are more important for non-ethnic individuals, (*c*) non-ethnic individuals tend to make detailed shopping lists and seldom deviate from them, (*d*) in-store contests are not as persuasive for non-ethnic shoppers. Further promotional appeals can take these factors into account to varying degrees depending on the type and nature of the store and its clientele.

References

1. ALEXANDER, M. (1959) The significance of ethnic groups in marketing new-type packaged foods in Greater New York. In *Proceedings of the American Marketing Association,* pp. 557–561. Ed. by L. M. Stockman. Chicago, Illinois: American Marketing Association
2. BARTH, F. (1970) *Ethnic Groups and Boundaries.* Boston, Mass., Little, Brown and Co.
3. BARYMPLE, D. J. (1972) Consumption behavior across ethnic categories. *California Management Review,* **14,** 65–70 and 110–111
4. BERKMAN, H. W. and GILSON, C. C. (1978) *Consumer Behavior: Concepts and Strategies.* California, Dickerson Publishing
5. BLUM, M. L. (1977) *Psychology and Consumer Affairs.* New York, Harper and Row
6. GREEN, R. T. and LANGEARD, E. (1975) A cross-national comparison of consumer habits and innovator characteristics. *Journal of Marketing,* **39,** 34–35
7. HOLLOWAY, R. J., MILLELSTAEDT, R. A. and VENKATESAN, M. (1971) *Consumer Behavior Contemporary Research in Action.* Boston, Houghton Mifflin Co.
8. JOYCE, F. and GOVONI, N. A. P. (Eds) (1971) *The Black Consumer.* New York, Random House
9. KASSARJIAN, H. H. and ROBERTSON, T. S. (1973) *Perspectives in Consumer Behaviour.* Illinois, Scott, Foresman and Co.
10. LESSIG, V. P. (1971) *Personal Characteristics and Consumer Buying Behavior: A Multidimensional Approach.* Washington, Washington State University Press
11. MARTINEAU, P. (1968) Social classes and spending behavior. *Journal of Marketing,* **23,** 121–130
12. PATTERSON, M. (1975) French agencies have no golden touch – just a better feel for the Quebecois test. *Marketing,* Oct. 27
13. RICH, S. U. and JAIN, S. C. (1968) Social class and life cycle as predictors of shopping behavior. *Journal of Marketing Research,* **5,** 41–49
14. ROBERTSON, T. S. (1970) *Consumer Behavior.* Glenview, Illinois, Scott, Foresman and Co.
15. ROMANUCCI, R., DE VOLA, L. and DE VOLA, G. (Eds) (1975) *Ethnic Identity Cultural Committees and Change.* California, Mayfield Publishing Co.
16. SHORT, K. C. (1970) Shopping patterns in Newcastle, NSW. In *The Hunter Valley Research Foundation Monograph,* No. 33. Research Centre Newcastle
17. STURDIVANT, F. D. (Ed.) (1967) *The Poor Pay More: Consumer Processes of Low-income Families.* New York, The Free Press
18. STURDIVANT, F. D. (1969) *The Ghetto Market Place.* New York, The Free Press
19. TAMILIA, R. D. (1979) International advertising revisited. In *Contemporary Perspectives in International Business.* Ed. by H. W. Berkman and R. I. Vernon. pp. 197–205. New York, Rand McNally and Co.
20. THOMPSON, D. N. and LEIGHTON, D. S. R. (Eds) (1973) *Canadian Marketing: Problems and Prospects.* Toronto, John Wiley & Sons

Chapter 24

Using interpersonal communications to facilitate the adoption of an innovative food retailing institution

Ugur Yavas
Secil Tuncalp

Introduction

Historically, an innovation has been defined as any thought, behaviour or thing that is new because it is qualitatively different from the existing norms[3]. It, then, naturally follows that the supermarket with its reliance on multiline product assortment, mass merchandising strategy, self-service method of operation and one-price-for-all policy is a major innovation by the food retailing standards prevailing in many countries[7,13]. Within the last few decades a plethora of writings has been devoted to the introduction of supermarkets into the retail food markets in less developed countries. Commentators felt that, among others, the following benefits would accrue as a result of transferring supermarkets to the less developed countries[14]:

- Supermarkets buy in large volume; retailers would use their greater buying power to drive down the food intermediaries' allegedly excessive margins and create efficiency in distribution.
- Supermarkets have a large sales volume; the resultant rapid stock turnover would permit retailers to lower food prices while realizing adequate profits on reduced margins.
- The lower food prices made possible by supermarkets would lead to a substantial increase in the real income and purchasing power of consumers, since food expenditure makes up about 50% of total living expenditure of a family.
- Supermarkets sell branded, packaged products; consumers patronizing these stores would thus have assurance of uniform quality, price and honest measure.
- Supermarkets have frozen food departments; with supermarkets as the dominant food retailing institution, more agricultural output would be frozen, lessening spoilage and stabilizing supplies and prices.

The efforts to transfer supermarketing technology to less developed countries, however, have met with lacklustre success[7].

Several explanations can be offered for the limited success of supermarkets in less developed countries. By their nature, supermarkets encourage one stop shopping. Evidence, however, shows that consumers in such less developed countries as Israel, Morocco and Turkey tend to patronize several stores during the same shopping trip[2,9,24]. Once a week or less frequent grocery shopping is another

268

convenience offered by supermarkets. On the contrary, though, consumers in less developed countries prefer to engage in grocery shopping on a rather frequent basis. In Brazil, for instance, shoppers patronize food stores, on the average, four times a week. In Bolivia, 90% of the consumers shop at least once a day[8]. The modal grocery shopping frequency in Turkey is twice a week[24]. Moroccan shoppers carry it to the extent that they buy certain staples such as bread each meal time[2].

Yet another plausible explanation for the failure of supermarkets to attain any degree of significant penetration in less developed countries is that consumers perceive risk in shopping at these innovative food outlets. Hilger[10], for instance, found that patronage of public operated small grocery stores in Mexico over US-style supermarkets was partially attributable to less risk associated with the public stores. Studies conducted in Turkey and Saudi Arabia also lead to the conclusion that perceived risk may be a determinant of the consumers' decisions to patronize supermarkets[25,26]. This was inferred from the product purchase patterns of the Turkish and the Saudi shoppers. For instance, even those Turkish shoppers who designated themselves as supermarket patrons purchased what might be characterized as 'high-risk' grocery items (e.g. fresh produce, meat, poultry, fish, milk) at other outlets. In Saudi Arabia, supermarkets' appeal to high-risk perceivers was only for canned goods, bottled water, crackers/biscuits, gourmet foods and frozen foods.

The study

The purpose of this study is to investigate empirically the feasibility of utilizing interpersonal communications in facilitating the acceptance of supermarkets in Saudi Arabia. A study addressing this issue is relevant and significant for at least two reasons.

On the theoretical side, there has been a growing interest in the diffusion of innovations framework to understand, predict and influence the adoption rate of new products, brands, ideas and practices[5]. A common thread which runs through the contemporary consumer behaviour writings is that dissemination of information via interpersonal communications has a major impact on an individual's adoption decision[21]. This is because consumers associate varying degrees of risk with an innovation and seek information capable of reducing perceived risk. It is claimed that communicating to the potential adopters through an opinion leader (a form of interpersonal communication) enhances the effectiveness of the message[6]. Despite the attention paid to opinion leadership as a mechanism to facilitate the adoption of innovations, its role in achieving this end in regard to diffusion of supermarkets is overlooked.

On the practical side, the study findings may yield invaluable insights for supermarkets operators. The first modern supermarket, the Souks, in the Kingdom of Saudi Arabia was opened as recently as 1979 in Dhahran. Receiving technical help from the Southland Corporation, owners of 7–11 convenience stores in the United States, and operating under a British management, the Souks Company extended its penetration into the grocery market by opening other stores in such diverse locations as Damman, Jubail, Al-Khobar, and Qatif by 1982. Similar to its namesakes in the shopping areas and bazaars throughout the Middle East known as 'suqs', the overall objective of the Souks Company was to create a one-stop shopping environment. Thus, in concept, the Souks was similar to the supermarkets found throughout North America and western Europe.

The uniqueness enjoyed by the Souks chain was short lived. Toward the end of 1979, the Tamimi and Fouad Food Company entered the grocery market by opening two giant supermarkets in Dammam and Al-Khobar. These supermarkets were put under the management of Safeway Inc., US multinational retailer. Already, a third Safeway store is operational in Jeddah and a fourth one was added with the opening of a unit in Riyadh in late 1982.

Despite the mushrooming of supermarkets in a very short timespan, their main appeal, nevertheless, is to the expatriates, notably the Westerners who have come to the Kingdom in increasing numbers within the last decade to participate in massive development projects. As noted before, though, many Saudi consumers perceive risk in patronizing supermarkets. Naturally such risk must be minimized for supermarkets to further penetrate the market and establish a solid customer base for the future. This becomes especially important in view of the Saudi government's 'Saudization' goal which is expected to result in a significant decline in the amount of expatriate manpower during the Fourth Development Plan period (1985–90).

Necessary conditions

The efficacy of opinion leadership in facilitating adoption of an innovation depends on the extent to which certain conditions are met. These include:

- Opinion leaders and opinion recipients should be sociodemographically similar: this is because people with similar characteristics interact and engage in subject matter related conversations with greater frequency[17,22].
- Opinion leaders should be actively involved with the subject matter: this is because opinion recipients turn to opinion leaders for advice due to their perception that opinion leaders are more informed about the subject matter than they are[18]. Thus, the more the opinion leader has 'expert' credentials, the more persuasive he is.
- Opinion leaders should be more attentive to and be more convinced of the value of messages disseminated by the mass media about the subject matter. This is because according to a theory of interpersonal flow of communications, opinion leaders act as vital links in the transmission of information from the mass media to the opinion recipients. In the so-called 'two-step flow of communication hypothesis', opinion leaders are direct receivers of information from the relevant mass media sources and, in turn, they interpret, legitimize, and transmit the information to others. Thus, communication from the mass media does not necessarily affect the audience directly but works through a web of interpersonal networks where opinion leaders play the key role as middlemen[12].

Method

Research questions

Based on the necessary conditions set forth in the preceding section, three research questions were formulated to guide the current investigation.

- Are opinion leaders sociodemographically similar to opinion recipients?
- Are opinion leaders more involved with grocery shopping/supermarket patronage relative to opinion recipients?
- Do opinion leaders place a greater degree of importance on supermarket advertisements relative to opinion recipients?

Data gathering

Data pertaining to these questions were collected from a non-probability sample of 137 Saudi consumers residing in the three cities of Dhahran, Al-Khobar, and Dammam in the Eastern Province. The data collection instrument was a structured questionnaire. The questionnaire was originally prepared in English and translated into Arabic by using the back-translation method[4]. To further ensure that the Arabic version was similar in meaning to the original English version, the cross-linguistic comparability of the questionnaire was also tested with the faculty members of a local university who were bilingual.

To measure opinion leadership, the key variable of the study, King and Summers'[15] self-designated scale was used. The selection of this particular scale was based on several considerations. First, the scale consists of a parsimonious set of seven straight-forward questions making it easy to administer. This is important because Saudis not accustomed to survey research are reluctant to participate in lengthy studies. Second, in measuring opinion leadership, the self-designated technique is especially appropriate since it measures the respondent's perception of himself, which is what actually affects his behaviour. Third, the scale has been used and tested for its reliability in previous studies, not only in the United States[20,27] where it was originally developed, but also in other countries including Saudi Arabia[28,29]. Cronbach's alpha reliability coefficient computed on the data of this study was 0.70 and it lended further evidence that the scale demonstrates satisfactory internal consistency[19].

In dividing the respondents into dichotomous categories of opinion leaders and opinion recipients, typical opinion leadership scores are rank ordered, and the upper 23–30% of the respondents are classified as opinion leaders[23]. After arraying the respondents' opinion leadership scores, the first quarter of the respondents were labelled as opinion leaders and the remainder were classified as opinion recipients.

Results

To explore the assumption that the first condition be a requirement for determining the feasibility of opinion leadership in facilitating the acceptance of supermarkets, opinion leaders and recipients were compared in terms of seven sociodemographic characteristics. The hypotheses, the statistical techniques applied in testing them, and the results obtained are summarized in *Table 24.1*. A significance level of 0.10 was used during the analysis[16].

Since none of the sociodemographic differences was statistically significant at the chosen level, it was concluded that opinion leaders and recipients are similar in sociodemographic profile. In other words, the two groups share similar characteristics with respect to tenure in the Eastern Province, number of people in the household, education level, marital status, age, occupation, and sex. Therefore, the first necessary condition is successfully met.

TABLE 24.1. Sociodemographic profile: summary of hypothesis-testing results

Hypothesis*	Statistical test used	Acceptance/rejection of hypothesis[†]
Length of residence in the community	t-test	Accept
Number of people in household	t-test	Accept
Education	Chi-squared	Accept
Marital status	Chi-squared	Accept
Age	Chi-squared	Accept
Occupation	Chi-squared	Accept
Sex	Chi-squared	Accept

* The hypothesis was that opinion leaders and opinion recipients are not different with respect to the listed conditions.
[†] The decision to accept or reject the hypothesis of no difference was based on the 0.10 level of significance.

Data exhibited in *Table 24.2* suggest that the other two necessary conditions are satisfied as well. Indeed, opinion leaders are more involved with various aspects of the subject matter compared with opinion recipients. As can be seen from the table, 58% of the opinion leaders patronized supermarkets while almost 61% of opinion recipients preferred to do their grocery shopping in other types of outlets. Although the majority of both opinion leaders and recipients were the primary grocery shoppers in their households, the incidence was significantly higher among the opinion leaders. Furthermore, 61% of the opinion leaders made the decision regarding which particular brands of grocery products to purchase. In contrast, 45% of their counterparts designated themselves as the primary grocery brands decider in their households. Interestingly, but not surprisingly, opinion leaders placed a higher degree of importance on grocery advertisements.

TABLE 24.2. Subject matter and media involvement

Type of involvement	Opinion leader	Opinion recipient	Acceptance/rejection of hypothesis*
Primary grocery shopper in the household			
Respondent	96.8[†]	83.1	
Somebody else	3.2	16.9	Reject[§]
Outlet patronage			
Supermarket	58.1[†]	39.3	
Grocery store/souk	41.9	60.7	Reject[§]
Primary grocery brands decider in the household			
Respondent	61.3[†]	44.9	
Somebody else	38.7	55.1	Reject[§]
Importance attached to grocery advertisements	2.96[‡]	2.50	Reject[¶]

* Decision to accept or reject the no-difference hypothesis was based on the 0.10 level of significance.
[†] Values given as percentages.
[‡] Mean value.
[§] Comparison is made by using the chi-squared test.
[¶] Comparison is made by using the t-test.

Summary and conclusions

The findings of the study suggest that opinion leadership has the potential to facilitate adoption of supermarkets in Saudi Arabia. Having determined this, some specific strategies can be offered to supermarket operators to implement the concept.

First, supermarket managers can stimulate word-of-mouth communication among the opinion leaders and opinion recipients. This can be achieved by advertising designed to prompt opinion leaders to talk to their peers, friends, and neighbours. Messages such as 'tell a friend about supermarkets' should be valuable in achieving this end. Word-of-mouth communication can also be stimulated by advertising designed to prompt opinion seeking through such messages as 'ask your friends about supermarkets'.

Second, campaigns sponsored by supermarkets could use themes that simulate the opinion leadership process by developing advertisements that are high in conversational value. For instance, ads could feature scenes in which one person tells another about some aspect of supermarket shopping and the two then discuss the value of that behaviour. Opinion leadership could also be simulated through using a testimonial approach wherein someone who has recently shopped at a supermarket conveys the consequences of that experience to others. Ads, additionally, could feature testimonials by celebrities, sports figures, or other well-known people. For example, the Japanese manufacturer Toshiba uses a famous Saudi singer, Mohammed Abdo, in promoting its hi-fi products. A well-known football player, Majed Abdullah, frequently appears in ads praising the products of a textile manufacturer. In the past Toyota was able to increase its sales by 18.8% in the highly competitive Saudi car market by using the former heavy-weight world boxing champion Mohammed Ali who is a devout Moslem[11]. It is only logical to assume that supermarket chains will benefit from employing such celebrities in their campaigns.

Third, opinion leaders can be used to encourage trial shopping in supermarkets by the opinion recipients. For instance, a type of discount arrangement could be instigated to serve as inducement for opinion leaders who bring along their friends or neighbours to shop in a supermarket. In a similar vein, supermarkets could create an exclusive club atmosphere (this outlet is not for everybody, but . . .) by giving such privileges as discount cards, keys to loyal customers. The privileges could be emphasized in campaigns through messages like 'a key to Safeway opens new doors . . .' or 'key holders get 5% discount at . . .'. The process of supplying certain 'heavy' supermarket shoppers with attractive privileges and selecting them into the so-called club would have the effect of creating opinion leaders.

Advertising messages should be communicated to the opinion leaders through magazines, newspapers and outdoor media. Newspapers and magazines with large circulations including *Asharg Al-Awsat* (No. 1 Arabic daily newspaper), *Al-Jazirah, Al-Youm* and *Al-Majalla* (No. 1 weekly news magazine) should be the primary channels. Ads stimulating the word-of-mouth communications must be particularly directed at women since they are socially very active, always visiting friends and relatives. In this case ads should be placed in *Al-Sayidaty* which is the No. 1 family magazine.

It should be added that while radio and TV commercials are not currently allowed in Saudi Arabia, supermarket chains located on the coastal areas can utilize TV and radio stations broadcasting from nearby Arab countries.

The rapid transformation in Saudi society could complement implementation of opinion leadership in facilitating the acceptance of supermarkets. 'Saudi Arabia is no longer anything like the image that once prevailed of an exotic, closed society or an austere Islamic desert Kingdom opposed to the benefits of modern civilization'. This positive attitude toward change signals brighter prospects for the acceptance of innovations including supermarkets in Saudi Arabia.

Future research directions

While the unifying framework and the findings of this study provide some useful insights concerning the application of opinion leadership in accelerating the adoption of supermarkets, a number of questions remain unanswered. To fill the gaps future research is needed.

This study examined the feasibility of opinion leadership to facilitate adoption of supermarkets in one region of Saudi Arabia. To determine if any regional and subcultural differences might affect the conclusions drawn here, the study should be replicated in other provinces of the Kingdom. A richer basis for a more comprehensive understanding can also be obtained by undertaking similar studies in other such Gulf countries as Bahrain, Kuwait, Qatar, and the United Arab Emirates. Furthermore, this study has focused on the use of opinion leadership among the indigenous population only. Because a substantial proportion of the people living in Saudi Arabia are expatriates coming from less developed countries including India, Pakistan, and other Arab countries, this study should be replicated among specific nationality groups. Such studies where the modern supermarketing scene of Saudi Arabia would serve as a laboratory could shed further light if an opinion leadership pattern appears valid on a cross-cultural basis. Additionally, the implications of these studies might prove useful to supermarket administrators in showing if they can benefit from a standardization strategy when entering markets in the less developed countries.

As a closing note, it appears that investigation of issues relating to acceptance of supermarkets provides a challenging area of research for the students of food marketing. It is hoped that this study will lead to a more deliberate and thorough exploration of some of the questions raised.

References

1. A NEW REALITY (1983) *Saudi Business,* **21**
2. AMINE, L. S. (1983) Food marketing in a developing country: the case of Morocco. In *Managing the International Marketing Function. Creative Challenges of the Eighties,* pp. 21–28. Ed. by E. Kaynak. Halifax
3. BARNETT, H. G. (1953) *Innovation. The Basis of Cultural Change.* New York, McGraw-Hill
4. BRISLIN, R., LONNER, W. J. and THORNDIKE, R. M. (1973) *Cross-Cultural Research Methods.* New York, John Wiley & Sons
5. BROWN, L. A. (1981) *Innovation Diffusion. A New Perspective.* London, Methuen and Co. Ltd
6. ENGEL, J. F. and BLACKWELL, R. D. (1982) *Consumer Behavior.* Chicago, The Dryden Press
7. GOLDMAN, A. (1981) Transfer of a retailing technology into less developed countries: the supermarket case. *Journal of Retailing,* **57**, 5–29
8. GOLDMAN, A. (1974) Outreach of consumers and the modernization of urban food retailing in developing countries. *Journal of Marketing,* **38**, 8–16
9. GOLDMAN, A. (1982) Adoption of supermarket shopping in a developing country: the selective adoption phenomenon. *European Journal of Marketing,* **16**, 17–26

10. HILGER, M. T. (1980) Consumer perceptions of a public marketer in Mexico. *Colombia Journal of World Business,* **15,** 78–82
11. JAMEEL, G. (1982) Outdoor advertising in Saudi Arabia. *International Advertiser,* March–April, 36 and 39
12. KATZ, E. and LAZARSFELD, P. F. (1985) *Personal Influence.* New York, The Free Press
13. KAYNAK, E. (1981) Food distribution systems: evolution in Latin America and the Middle East. *Food Policy,* **6** (2), 78–90
14. KAYNAK, E. (1975) *Food Retailing Systems in a Developing Economy.* Bedfordshire, Cranfield Institute Press
15. KING, C. W. and SUMMERS, J. O. (1970) Overlap of opinion leadership across consumer product categories. *Journal of Marketing Research.* **7,** 43–50
16. LABOVITZ, S. (1968) Criteria for selecting a significance level: a note on the sacredness of 0.05. *The American Sociologist,* **3,** 220–222
17. MOCHIS, G. P. (1976) Social comparison and informal group influence. *Journal of Marketing Research,* **13,** 237–244
18. MYERS, J. H. and ROBERTSON, T. S. (1972) Dimensions of opinion leadership. *Journal of Marketing Research,* **9,** 41–46
19. NUNNALLY, J. C. (1967) *Psychometric Theory.* New York, McGraw-Hill
20. RIECKEN, G. and YAVAS, U. (1983) Internal consistency reliability of King and Summers' opinion leadership scale: further evidence. *Journal of Marketing Research,* **20,** 325–326
21. ROGERS, E. M. (1983) *Diffusion of Innovations.* New York, The Free Press
22. ROGERS, E. M. and BHOMIK, D. K. (1970) Homophily–heterophily: relational concepts for communication research. *Public Opinion Quarterly,* **34,** 523–538
23. SUMMERS, J. O. (1970) The identity of women's clothing fashion opinion leaders. *Journal of Marketing Research,* **7,** 178–185
24. YAVAS, U., KAYNAK, E. and BORAK, E. (1982) Food shopping orientations in Turkey: some lessons for policy makers. *Food Policy,* **7** (2), 133–140
25. YAVAS, U., KAYNAK, E. and BORAK, E. (1981) Retailing institutions in developing countries: the determinants of supermarket patronage in Istanbul, Turkey. *Journal of Business Research,* **9,** 367–379
26. YAVAS, U. and TUNCALP, S. (1984) Perceived risk in grocery outlet selection: a case study in Saudi Arabia. *European Journal of Marketing,* **18,** 13–25
27. YAVAS, U. and RIECKEN, G. (1982) Extensions of King and Summers' opinion leadership scale: a reliability study. *Journal of Marketing Research,* **19,** 154–155
28. YAVAS, U., RIECKEN, G. and HAAHTI, A. (1982) Reliability assessment of opinion leadership concept: a cross-national study. *The Finnish Journal of Business Economics,* **31,** 239–246
29. YAVAS, U., RIECKEN, G. and HAAHTI, A. (1984) Further evidence on the cross-national reliability of King and Summers' opinion leadership scale: an extension to Saudi Arabia. In *Proceedings of the XIIIth Annual Conference of the European Marketing Academy,* pp. 633–648. Ed. by W. F. V. Raaij and F. J. C. M. Schelbergen. Breukelen, The Netherlands School of Business

Part X

Cooperative marketing of food products

The first chapter examines the connection between cooperative organization and cooperative market share in the agricultural systems of the 10 EEC countries. Although the data available are far from ideal, it is clear that a consistently high market share for agricultural cooperatives tends to be associated with three tiers of strong organization. While it was farmers' enthusiasm for cooperation that historically established high cooperative market shares and thus permitted the growth of strong organizations, it is now probable that the development of organizational structures of the kind mentioned above produces a managerial style inimical to the original ideals of the cooperative pioneers.

The second chapter is concerned with some characteristics of the agrofood industry in Spain, Greece and Portugal, countries that have recently entered the European Community. The analysis is based on an examination of the ways in which the agroindustry and food consumption patterns influence the economic development of these countries. Also discussed are problems of agreements between the food industry and the agricultural sector, and the role played by public administration.

Chapter 25

The structure of cooperative marketing in European agriculture

Gordon Foxall

Introduction

Cooperative market shares are significantly smaller in the United Kingdom's agricultural sector than in the farming industries of the remainder of the European Community. In the EEC as a whole, cooperatives are responsible for the collection, processing and marketing of over 60% of farm produce and for the supply of some 50% of farm production inputs. The corresponding proportions for the UK are 14 and 23%, respectively. Certain member states of the Community have cooperative sectors whose share of agricultural marketing is three times that of the UK: in the Netherlands, for instance, the figure is 55% and in West Germany it is about 50%[10]. There is a positive link between the market performance of the cooperative sectors of EEC member states and the type of organizational structure which represents and directs primary cooperatives and their members[12,14,15]. Those states with the largest cooperative market shares have tended to possess strong, central organizations capable of directing and coercing their members.

The UK lacks central cooperative organizations capable of acting to advance the cause of cooperation as other European cooperative systems can. Although about a quarter of the approximately 600 UK farm cooperatives have some experience of coordinated action, this has taken the form, for the most part, of rather weak *associations* of primary cooperative societies. Second-tier or *federal* cooperatives are rare.

This chapter investigates the relationship between cooperatives' market performance and the structure of the cooperative organizations responsible for it, throughout the expanded EEC. Its purpose is to raise policy issues by means of a comparative study of international food marketing organizations. First, it discusses the nature of cooperative marketing in agriculture; second, it compares the cooperative market performances of the agricultural systems of the Community; and third, it draws attention to the patterns of organizational structure and behaviour which accompany the various market performances.

The nature of cooperative marketing in agriculture

Agricultural cooperation in Europe has usually arisen because of farmers' needs to increase their collective power in the market in order to raise their individual incomes. Collective action may enable them to reduce the costs of farm production inputs by means of bulk buying, to exploit scale economies in production and distribution, to integrate production and/or marketing vertically, and to create countervailing power *vis-à-vis* the buyers of farm produce[3,7]. Cooperative organizations may make their greatest contribution to farmers, however, by providing market information which would not otherwise be collected by the individual farmer; federal cooperatives, in particular, may provide the marketing intelligence which enables production and marketing to be coordinated[27]. But it is the perception of more concrete economic benefits of cooperating that persuades most farmers to join and remain members of farm cooperatives[16,17]. Cooperation in the UK has always been seen as an alternative form of business organization to those otherwise available; where a primary cooperative acting alone has been unable to achieve the economic benefits demanded by its members, it has always had the option to act jointly with other societies. Second-tier cooperative organizations represent one means of such joint action through which farmers might seek the more efficient use of their transport facilities, managerial talent, investment programmes or purchasing procedures. Mergers and joint consultative arrangements can achieve such objectives, but second-tier organization uniquely requires an additional managerial stratum and some loss of autonomy on the part of existing members and managers[13,18].

Second-tier organization is especially problematical in the UK. The democratic principles upon which British cooperation is founded require that trade will take place predominantly with other cooperative members, that share capital will be limited, members' dividends being paid in proportion to their trade, that each member shall have one vote, that membership shall not be artificially restricted and that information will be regularly disclosed to members[15]. So central are these principles to the practice of cooperation that organizations which flout them may lose their registration under the Industrial and Provident Societies Acts: the cooperative societies and companies so registered are exempted from monopolies legislation and restrictive practice acts which render illegal the collusive price fixing of otherwise independent businesses. But it is the one member : one vote provision which is especially relevant.

Cooperative performance

The extent to which cooperative marketing can be said to be of importance within a country's agricultural sector is indicated, in general terms in *Tables 25.1* and *25.2*.

On the basis of these figures, Denmark, Holland, Luxembourg constitute a group in which cooperative performance is of crucial importance to agricultural production, processing and marketing. There, cooperative market shares are consistently high for all the major sectors of agricultural production and marketing (with the exception of meat and livestock in Holland and Luxembourg). The second group, among whose members cooperation remains of constant and sustained though smaller significance, comprises France, West Germany, Belgium and Ireland. Finally, Italy, the UK and Greece form a group whose members are characterized by lower market shares generally, albeit across a wide range of agricultural product markets.

Numerous factors partially explain these differences in market share. Financial, legislative, agricultural, social and related factors have all played a part in the

281

TABLE 25.1. Cooperative market shares (percentage turnover/production) for EC agricultural produce*

Product–market	Denmark	Holland	Luxembourg	France	West Germany	Belgium	Ireland	Italy	UK
Dairy									
Milk collection	87	88	80	47	79	70	100	30	(100)†
Butter	92	93		47		70	100	57	
Cheese	79	94		33		80	65	39	
Milk powder		86		51		80	76		
Drinking milk	78	80		59		50	47	12	
Yoghurt				33					
Condensed milk		80							
Meat and livestock									
General			30	31	18		25		
Pigs/pigmeat	90	27		30	20	15	35	11	7
Cattle/beef	55	14	25	30	19		20	2.5–6	6
Sheepmeat				22					
Poultry	50			40		3	61		
Fish	15						75		
Crops									
Cereals	50	60	90	70	52	12		5.4	15–20
Potatoes		100	90	30					12
Fruit		84	70	40	30	65	34	22	19
Vegetables	50+	84		30	46			8.6	10
Flowers		90							
Plants		60							
Mushrooms		80		77					
Hops						40			
Wool		65							31
Sugarbeet	14	63		16				15	
Eggs	65	20	90	25			64	5	19
Wine				68	35			40	

Sources: COGECA (1983), *The Agricultural and Fisheries Co-operatives in the EC* Brussels; Foxall, G.R. (1982) *Co-operative Marketing in European Agriculture*, Aldershot, Gower.
* Most figures are for 1980; occasionally figures are for 1979 or 1978 where these are the latest available. *See* original sources for notes on the nature of the figures and text for their interpretation.
† The UK Milk Marketing Boards are producer controlled though not cooperatively-constituted organisations.

TABLE 25.2. Cooperative market shares for Greece, 1978*

Product–market	Percentage turnover attributable to cooperatives	Product–market	Percentage turnover attributable to cooperatives
Apricots	21.2	Olives, table	15.0
Butter	11.0	Peaches	18.4
Cheese, hard	10.0	Poultry meat	11.4
Cheese, soft	15.0	Raisins	28.0
Cotton	21.5	Ready meals	25.8
Cotton seeds	16.2	Stawberries	34.0
Currants	20.0	Tobacco, raw	8.0
Figs, dried	36.9	Tomato juice	24.3
Fodder	56.0	Tomato paste	39.8
Fruit, canned	25.9	Tomatoes, peeled	12.5
Fruit juices	16.3	Vegetables, canned	42.2
Milk, pasteurized	60.2	Wine	45.0

Source: COGECA (1983), *The Agricultural Cooperatives in the EC*, Brussels.
* Latest figures available.

development of cooperative marketing systems that are either relatively strong and extensive or weak and concentrated[15,24,28]. The need for farmers to combine in order to effect countervailing power against the purchasers of agricultural produce, the development for various reasons of an alternative, non-cooperative merchandising system for farm output, the size of farming units and general economic conditions and social mores have contributed in various combinations to the pattern of cooperative performance apparent in these tables. But, *cooperative organization* is another factor which contributes very significantly to sustaining the pattern of cooperative marketing.

Cooperative organization and behaviour

Group 1: Denmark, Holland, Luxembourg

These three countries are characterized by extensive cooperative organization. In the case of Denmark and Holland, this comprises three elaborate tiers of national, federal and primary cooperatives – a well integrated and complex vertical structure. The relatively small size of Luxembourg has tended to encourage horizontal rather than vertical organization and strong central organization coupled with a local cooperative system where rationalization and concentration are apparent.

An interesting factor in all three states is the integration of each of these layers of organization into a pyramid-shaped structure, each organization tending to be a member of another organization in the next layer. The possibility that the central cooperative organizations of each country can plan and direct the behaviour of cooperative societies throughout the country, and thus have a major impact upon the actions of individual farmers, to whom those central cooperatives are somewhat remote organizations, is a strong one. When the norm is for cooperatives at the secondary and tertiary level to be highly specialized in terms of the commodities they handle, as in Denmark and Holland, the individual farmer, specialized in his enterprise, faces considerable pressures to conform. The integration, moreover, of the cooperative marketing system with cooperative credit and insurance organizations strengthens the possibility that cooperative business might, for essentially economic reasons which carry their own internal logic, become divorced from the democratic, farmer-oriented structure intended by the initiators of cooperative agriculture.

Three aspects of the behaviour of cooperative organizations in these countries are pertinent to this discussion: the concentration of the cooperative sectors, notably at primary level; the role of joint ventures between cooperative and non-cooperative organizations (which might circumvent the farmer control which is essential to most cooperative constitutions); the role of cooperatives in exporting.

The tendency in Denmark is towards a single national organization or a small number of regionally based federals dominating each commodity sector. For example, the cooperative dairies numbered 1100 in 1962; in 1980 there were 154 and a single national or handful of regional organizations is likely to become dominant in the near future. Similarly, the 61 cooperative bacon factories which existed in 1961 had become 18 by 1980 and just 8 multifactory cooperatives now control that market. By the 1980s, there was a single cattle organization comprising 28 cooperatives whereas there had been 58 societies in this sector two decades earlier. National cooperatives have been established in eggs and poultry, and seeds. It is expected that a single, national requisite (supply) cooperative will dominate the provision to farmers of feedstuffs, fertilizers and chemicals. This cooperative, the Danish Agricultural Supply Association (Dansk Landbrugs Gorvvareselskak, DLG), was founded by the merger of four requisite societies in 1969. Some local requisite societies are fully integrated with DLG and the number of local requisite societies, once as high as 1800, is now 353[10].

One reason for the ease with which central cooperatives appear able to formulate and implement plans for the economic and physical rationalization of entire sectors is that members are likely to concur initially in this process insofar as it simplifies a complicated organizational structure. It is certainly likely to reduce the notorious complexity of the Danish system of agricultural organization. McLean-Bullen and Pickard[21] note that: 'The organisation of Danish agricultural institutions is complex in the extreme. Many organisations are linked one to the other by ties of ownership, part-ownership, interlocking membership and the like'. Furthermore, structural change within the agricultural system may not appear remarkable in a country where cooperation is so extensive and so closely integrated with the local community.

Cooperative and non-cooperative organizations often work closely together in Denmark for sound economic reasons. Furthermore, cooperatives often own companies which are non-cooperative in constitution and have even established a fund to finance such companies. The one member : one vote system which pervades cooperatives' principles in Denmark may ultimately prove inconsistent with such development which, 'however logical commercially, is liable to look a little ominous to a community of farmers to whom cooperation was an activity in which they and their neighbours were included on a more or less share and share alike basis'[21].

Some idea of the scale of cooperative organization is apparent from the involvement of cooperatives in exporting; over 90% of the export of butter and of pigs and pigmeat is administered by cooperatives. The system is dominated by large organization, is experiencing rationalization on a grand scale and is changing in character as economic forces increasingly replace the social and ideological origins of cooperative action among farmers. As Bager[2] has written:

> Danish producer cooperatives enjoy a fairly widespread reputation among cooperators, because they were among the first to be formed, and because they have gained dominant positions in the marketing or agricultural products in Denmark. However, rapid changes of the cooperative sector and the agricultural structure in Denmark during the last decades have raised doubts about the viability of these cooperatives. At the end of this century there will probably be only one dominating, countrywide producer cooperative left in each cooperative sector. It is therefore questionable whether such complex, remote, large-scale organisations can retain a cooperative character, or whether they will follow their own dynamics, mainly determined by the socioeconomic context, and carried out by managing directors.

A broadly similar pattern is apparent among Dutch cooperatives. Agricultural organization and enterprise are specialized yet complex and both cooperative and non-cooperative organizations exist to represent farmers' interests nationally. Most Dutch farmers belong to more than one cooperative. Cooperatives have frequently merged in a process of sustained rationalization, exporting is important, cooperative banks supply a large proportion of cooperative finance, and the cooperative businesses.

Farmers' general needs are met through requisite cooperatives and service cooperatives such as those which offer labour relief, insurance and credit. There is no need for the farmer to trade at all outside the cooperatives, which supply some 60% of farm incomes[25].

Luxembourg has, to all intents and purposes, only one body through which cooperatives are organized: Centrale Paysanne Luxembourgeoise (CPL), which operates both centrally and locally. There is evidence of increasing power for the centre. Economic development has meant that 'the gradual decrease in the activity of local cooperatives has run parallel with the rapid development of central organization'. Since 1945, CPL has pursued a strategy of centralization in production and marketing by creating a viable organizational structure for cooperation. While CPL is not itself a cooperative and there are 'various cooperative businesses in the country . . . they are nearly all subsidiaries of the Central Paysanne, and they do not really engage in active competition with each other'[20].

Cooperative marketing is closely integrated with cooperative buying on behalf of farmers and the farmer whose production requirements are met by his cooperative association is unlikely to look for alternative channels of distribution. CPL is also integrated into the food processing industry and is increasingly involved in exporting and in international processing and marketing. Thus, 'over time small independent cooperatives have withered in the face of the apparently more efficient central organisation . . . but what is disquieting is that farmers seem to be losing control over this machine and many of them are uneasy about its methods of operation' (see McLean-Bullen and Pickard[20]).

Group 2: France, West Germany, Belgium, Ireland

France and West Germany also have three tiers of cooperative organizations which exert pressure for conformity on farmers and primary societies. In Belgium and Ireland, while they have important cooperative organizations, these are not used to formulate and implement plans in the same way as the cooperatives considered previously. The difference appears largely to be one of attitudes towards and expectations of cooperation in the various countries.

Cooperatives in France have been used as a means to the end of regional development and the Government has intervened to ensure that this end is achieved. French cooperation is 'being carried along on a policy of concentration, consolidation and planned expansion'[23]; the central planning required for this is made easier by the industrialization not only of production but also of marketing activities. The resulting opportunities for production–marketing integration and the fact that the cooperative sector is taking advantage of them are evidenced by the observation that, by the late 1970s, cooperation accounted for over 20% of the entire French agricultural and food sector and two of the four largest firms in France were agricultural cooperatives[9]. A factor in the strong development of French cooperatives is the 1972 legislation which permits the creation of SICA (collective agricultural societies), whose members and users may include higher proportions of non-farmers than the true cooperatives permitted. These non-farmer members include such representatives of the agrofood industry as dealers, slaughterers and retailers[11]. Exports play an important part in the activities of cooperatives in dairy products (where the cooperatives control 58% of exports), cereals and oilplants (50%), livestock and meat (36%), wine and alcohol (35%), fresh fruit (60%) and canned fruit and vegetables (50%)[10].

West Germany also shows evidence of a strong, central organization which can plan and compel reorganization and rationalization. The Raiffeisen movement, to which all primary cooperatives must belong for auditing purposes, has used its regional unions to implement a strategy of merging local societies. Whereas there were 19 400 primary cooperatives in West Germany in 1960, there were only 7229 by 1982. Carpenter[5] represents this movement as somewhat monolithic, bent on monopolizing agricultural markets. She writes:

> the way in which the cooperative movement is organised has led to a situation where the flow of capital is principally 'upwards' from the primary societies to the regional and national levels, while the direction of decision-making and policy formation is from the national and regional levels down to the primary society.

The regional unions 'have now developed into bodies with extensive advisory powers, and have become the major instruments for implementing policy decided at a national level'. The individual farmer, the individual primary society cannot influence let alone reverse such national policy[5]. (*See also* Schiffgen[29].)

Belgium and Ireland present cooperative organizations which, while they belong in this category by virtue of their market performance positions, differ from those of France and West Germany. The Belgian Boerenbond, the organization which represents Belgian farmers and to which most cooperatives are affiliated, has a far more extensive organizational structure (which embraces social and religious as well as economic and agricultural forces) than does Irish cooperation. But in neither country does there seem to be a will to use organization to compel farmers in ways inimical to the cooperative character of their systems.

The Boerenbond certainly does not lack influence over farming and business life in Belgium, but there is a greater willingness to see organizations as means rather than as ends in themselves and to establish organizations only where there is evidence that they are needed. There is comparatively little central planning in the cooperative sector of Belgium and independence in some agricultural sectors, accompanied by a willingness to create alternative marketing channels, and to innovate outside the cooperatives[20].

Ireland is more difficult to classify. Cooperative organization is based primarily on a central representative body, the Irish Cooperative Organizational Society, and local cooperatives. Although the committee system found in Ireland is far more extensive than that in the UK, for instance, and there seems to be a greater willingness to use organization, Ireland's cooperative market performance cannot be explained simply on the basis of organization[4].

Group 3: The UK, Italy, Greece

Although it is possible to speak in terms of three tiers of cooperative organization in the UK, this structure is quite different in intent and practice from the cooperative organizations considered so far. There is an overall UK *representative* body for farm cooperatives and each of the four countries within the UK has its own national ('second-tier') representative organization. But these are bodies which are hardly in a position to plan and coerce in the ways in which the cooperative centrals of Denmark, Holland, France and West Germany clearly can. The minority of British cooperatives whose managers and members have some experience of second-tier organization have, on the whole, been involved in simple information-sharing arrangements between cooperative societies at the primary level. Few have faced the problems of federalization in which disparate members and managers must devise means of sharing power or accommodating each other's viewpoints. British cooperatives are not, on the whole, integrated into the agrofood industry, any developments in this direction have generally been confined to the grading and simple preparation for market of farm produce. The small proportion of farm requisites purchased from cooperatives scarcely indicates the integration of cooperation in farm life and business. Loyalty to requisite societies tends to be low[16,24].

Italy, on the other hand, has a plethora of organizations and they are increasing rather than decreasing in number. But Italian cooperation lacks central coordination. Cooperatives compete with each other on the basis of their communist or non-communist affiliations as well as commercially. Cooperative strength varies very much from region to region. Farmers in Italy appear to show strong temperamental disapproval of cooperation as an act in itself and this is unlikely to produce the kind of cooperative system that can plan and integrate, coerce and restructure. The growth in the numbers of cooperatives may attest to the popularity of cooperation among some groups, in some areas, but it is also indicative of lack of coordination and planning. It suggests growing competitiveness between cooperatives themselves rather than the regrouping of primary societies into powerful coalitions. Production and marketing are seldom integrated even though, in some livestock marketing chains, cooperative abbatoirs may undertake slaughtering, cooperative butchers may purchase their output and cooperative retailers may sell the meat[22].

Rather less is known about Greek agricultural cooperatives. The available accounts give the impression, however, that they are far from extensive and powerful[10,26]. Second-tier and national organizations appear to be set up as market conditions and the need for countervailing strength arises. Although there is a consistent cooperative presence, the cooperative sector hardly dominates. There may be more production–marketing integration than appears at first sight, because Greek cooperatives own some 18% of food processing installations, but the overall picture supports the argument of this chapter with respect to the association between cooperative organization and market share.

The overall conclusion for this group must reflect the low degree of organizational power available at second and third-tier levels, without denying the outline structure of organization beyond the primary cooperatives[1,24,26].

Conclusions

Comparing the countries in groups 1 and 3, it is obvious that a consistently high market share for agricultural cooperatives *is* associated with three tiers of strong organizations, able to plan and, moreover, implement plant with export responsibility, production–marketing integration, and positive attitudes on the part of farmers at least towards the idea of cooperation. (Even here the relationship is not uncomplicated: Greek cooperatives have achieved important export markets in some cases.)

It is pertinent to ask, however, whether the countries which have been allocated to group 2 actually constitute a homogeneous set in terms of the structure and behaviour of their agricultural cooperatives. All four countries belong between the extremes posed by the other groups, but France and West Germany are clearly rather different from Ireland and Belgium. What these four countries have in common is a viable *alternative* to cooperative distribution channels and a willingness on the part of farmers to use them.

Historically, the extent of farmers' enthusiasm for cooperation and their loyalty to the societies they established no doubt led to the creation and role of secondary and tertiary cooperative organizations. What is being suggested here, however, is that insufficient attention has been paid to the fact that the causal relationship may now run the other way. The victim of strong organization at levels beyond the primary cooperative is member control and the loss of genuine democracy in the running of farmers' organizations must radically alter the nature of those organizations. Where the conflict between member control and managerial power is resolved in favour of the latter, the concept of cooperation hardly applies. Much of the commercial development which has taken place in the countries of group 1 and in France and West Germany is simply the result of logical business practice. Farmers may benefit from it economically on occasion or in the long run. But the resulting form of organization is quite different from that existing in some other countries' cooperative systems and this raises questions of the nature of cooperation and cooperatives and the rationale for state aid which have been discussed elsewhere[16,17,19].

References

1. ANONYMOUS (1976) Italian agricultural co-operation. In *Yearbook of Agricultural Co-operation 1976*, pp. 119–125. Ed. by F. H. Webster. Oxford, Plunkett Foundation
2. BAGER, T. (1982) Measures to retain the co-operative character of Danish producer co-operatives. In *Yearbook of Agricultural Co-operation 1981*, pp. 25–32. Ed. by J. E. Bayley and C. E. McKone. Oxford, Plunkett Foundation
3. BARON, P. J. (1978) Why co-operation in agricultural marketing? *Journal of Agricultural Economics*, **29**, 109–117
4. BOLGER, P. (1977) *The Irish Co-operative Movement*. Dublin, Institute of Public Administration
5. CARPENTER, S. M. (1979) The integration of agricultural co-operation in West Germany. In *Yearbook of Agricultural Co-operation 1978*, pp. 35–46. Ed. by F. H. Webster. Oxford, Plunkett Foundation
6. CCAHC (1977) *Co-ordination of Co-operatives*. London, Central Council for Agricultural and Horticultural Co-operation
7. CCAHC (1979) *Benefits of Co-operation*. London, Central Council for Agricultural and Horticultural Co-operation
8. CCAHC (1979) *Second Tier Co-operatives*. London, Central Council for Agricultural and Horticultural Co-operation
9. CFCA (1978) *Les Co-operatifs Agricoles en France*. Paris, Confederation Française de la Co-operation Agricole
10. COGECA (1983) *The Agricultural and Fisheries Co-operatives in the EEC*. Brussels, General Committee for Agricultural Co-operation
11. DELAGNEAU, B. (1976) The SICA: aims, functioning and evolution in France. In *Yearbook of Agricultural Co-operation 1976*, pp. 101–118. Ed. by F. H. Webster. Oxford, Plunkett Foundation
12. FOXALL, G. R. (1978) Marketing development in agriculture. *Oxford Agrarian Studies*, **7**, 75–86
13. FOXALL, G. R. (1980) Some consequences of the extension of federal organisation among agricultural co-operatives in the United Kingdom. In *Yearbook of Agricultural Cooperation 1979*, pp. 43–49. Ed. by E. Bayley. Oxford, Plunkett Foundation
14. FOXALL, G. R. (1981) Is more co-operation the answer? *Journal of Agricultural Economics*, **33**, 55–63
15. FOXALL, G. R. (1982) *Co-operative Marketing in European Agriculture*. Aldershot, Gower
16. FOXALL, G. R. and McCONNELL-WOOD, M. M. (1976) *Member–Society Relations in Agricultural Co-operations*. Newcastle upon Tyne: The University
17. GASSON, R. (1977) Farmers' approach to co-operation. *Journal of Agricultural Economics*, **28**, 27–37
18. KIRK, J. E. and ELLIS, P. G. (1969) *Horticultural Marketing Co-operatives*. London: Wye College

19. LE VAY, C. and BATEMAN, D. I. (1981) Why aid agricultural co-operatives? *Agricultural Administration*, **8**, 97–107
20. McLEAN-BULLEN, A. and PICKARD, D. H. (1975) *Livestock Marketing Systems in EEC Countries: Belgium and Luxembourg.* London: Wye College
21. McLEAN-BULLEN, A. and PICKARD, D. H. (1975) *Livestock Marketing Systems in EEC Countries: Denmark.* London: Wye College
22. McLEAN-BULLEN, A. and PICKARD, D. H. (1976) *Livestock Marketing Systems in EEC Countries: Italy.* London: Wye College
23. McLEAN-BULLEN, A. and PICKARD, D. H. (1977) *Livestock Marketing Systems in EEC Countries: France.* London: Wye College
24. MORLEY, J. A. E. (1975) *British Agricultural Co-operatives.* London: Hutchinson Benham
25. NCR (1983) *Agricultural and Horticultural Co-operation in the Netherlands.* The Hague: National Co-operative Council for Agriculture and Horticulture
26. PANHELLENIC CONFEDERATION OF UNIONS OF AGRICULTURAL CO-OPERATIVES (1978) The Greek farmers' co-operative movement. In *Yearbook of Agricultural Co-operation 1978*, pp. 109–128. Ed. by F. H. Webster. Oxford, Plunkett Foundation
27. PICKARD, D. H. (1970) Factors affecting success and failure in farmers' co-operative associations. *Journal of Agricultural Economics*, **21**, 105–119
28. SARGENT, M. (1982) *Agricultural Co-operation.* Aldershot, Gower
29. SCHIFFGEN, W. (1979) The Raiffeisen movement. *Agricultural Administration*, **6**, 245–251

Chapter 26

Cooperation in the agrofood industry: Spain, Greece and Portugal

Giovanni Cannata

Introduction

The implications for Common Market agriculture of the enlargement of the EEC to include Greece, Spain and Portugal have been the subject of frequent analysis. But little has been written about the repercussions in the agrofood complex of the Community and of the individual member nations. The reason for this probably lies in the lack of available information about the agrofood industry in these three countries. This chapter examines the organization and overall functioning of the production sector and indicates some of its critical points.

This analysis was carried out with exclusive reference to one part of the more general agrofood system and does not deal with relations outside the agricultural sector nor with the non-food uses of final production. It is based on the activities included in Article 13 of the Universal Industrial Classification of the United Nations. Where possible, food industries in the strict sense and beverage industries have been separated from tobacco industries, which are included in Article 13.

The inadequate statistical apparatus in use in the three countries, especially in Portugal and Greece, outdated census data, the scarcity of food surveys and the general absence of a real body of food statistics specific to each country set serious limits on carrying out the study. The extremely poor state of research on the entire complex agrofood system[1] necessitated a direct survey of data and components for each subsystem. The country for which some analyses are available is Spain (see Arroya[1], Fenollar[6], Jimenez[8] and Briz[2]). A recent seminar promoted by the European Association of Agrarian Economists was also dedicated to the problems of the agrofood industry. Publications on the Portuguese agrofood industry are much more limited (however see [3,10]). An analysis using input–output matrices is reported by Palmeiro[12]. Literature for Greece is almost non-existent. The analysis for Greece was based on unpublished material included in studies by the EEC[4] and the OECD[11].

The lack of basic information makes it impossible to address many questions and issues. Thus, we cannot examine factors outside the domain of agriculture, or analyse the ways in which agriculture and the overall economy have benefited from the industrialization of the agricultural sector. We cannot examine in detail the

This chapter was originally an article in *Food Policy*, 1982, Vol. 7, No. 2, pp. 125–132.

reasons for an exchange between agriculture and industry or evaluate the eventual mechanisms of agreements between the two sectors, which are beginning to appear on the production scene in those countries.

In addition, little is known about the social changes brought about by the food industry in the countryside as well as in society at large: new methods of production, new ways of consuming food and new ways of living have all had their effect.

The agrofood industry in the three countries

It is difficult to unify the issues which emerge from the analysis of the different countries, mainly because of the incompatibility of the available sources of information. (In the case of Spain and Greece, data from the census can be used, while for Portugal the annual surveys only account for 80% of employment and gross product.) Nevertheless, some overall conclusions can be drawn. First, it should be emphasized that in general the sector in all three countries has the characteristics of a handicraft concern, exhibiting considerable atomization. Average employment per plant, as shown in *Table 26.1*, hovers around 5–7 units, a figure that nevertheless compensates for the simultaneous presence in the statistics of concerns of particularly small size, such as those in the bread or beer-making industries and those connected with the sugar industry. The weakest organizational

TABLE 26.1. Plants and employees in the agrofood industry in Spain, Greece and Portugal (1979)

Production activities	*Spain*		*Greece*		*Portugal*	
	Plants	*Employees*	*Plants*	*Employees*	*Plants*	*Employees*
Olive oil	2783	12 648	4004	8065	3223	15 000*
Vegetable oils and fats	227	6667	200	2746	32	2657
Butchery, meat processing	5552	48 483	501	3651	301	4561
Dairy industry	1198	24 307	1875	6957	114	6590
Preserved vegetables	1032	30 342	778	16 377	74	6082
Preserved fish	602	19 754	79	907	146	14 085
Milling	7084	21 180	2364	7576	145	4686
Pasta industry	86	3164	254	1507	23	1725
Bread-making, baked goods	23 777	98 469	8025	27 852	2349	31 435
Sugar industry	52	5465	18	1490	6	1776
Cocoa, chocolate etc	690	11 623	458	5611	138	3723
Animal feedstuffs	800	12 305	225	1031	96	4014
Diverse food industries	1280	13 987	1102	5515	142	2757
Ethyl alcohol industry	697	6734	1927	3255	9	2238
Wine industry	5912	25 668	447	2894	32	1045
Brandy and liqueur industry	148	703			90	748
Brewing	52	14 801	24	1602	8	3465
Soft drinks production	1330	20 168	372	4557	103	3994
Food and drink industry	53 302	376 468	22 653	101 593	7031	108 617

* Estimated.
Source: Instituto Nacional de Estatistica, *Censo industrial de Espana 1978*, Madrid, 1979; Office National Statistique de Grèce, *Résultats du récensement des industries manifacturières, artisanat et des industries extractives, 1973*, Athens, 1975; Instituto Nacional de Estatistica, *Estatistica industriais 1977*, Lisbon, 1978.

structure in general seems to be in Greece, where the census counted only little more than 4 employees per plant. This situation is often associated with the use of a temporary labour force which, while on the one hand means low production costs, on the other results in less qualified workers, makeshift plants and a quality which does not always conform to the standards of international markets. Atomization is particularly marked in those areas which are 'sensitive' to participation in the European Community, namely, the oil, preserved vegetable and wine industries.

It is worth noting that there are a limited number of cooperative organizations in the agrofood sector, even though in Spain, for example, there has recently been an increase in the number of cooperatives and collectives. It should likewise be pointed out that in countries, such as Portugal, which have been marked in the last few years by profound social and political change (sparked off by the April revolution, and the reforms associated with it, and subsequently cooled by the resurfacing of centre–right social groupings), the movement toward cooperative associations has been characterized by both forward and backward steps.

At the other extreme of managerial organization, especially in Spain and Greece, the multinational food industry, backed by European and US capital, seems to be taking hold. Through the supply of technology, it conditions some of the most dynamic or modern sectors and, in a few strategic cases, the economy of those countries. As an example, one need only consider the repercussions of multinational intervention in the animal feedstuff sector, which were felt not only in the whole sector of livestock and livestock products, but also in related areas, such as the food oil sector.

The multinationalization process has found ample space in broad areas of the domestic market in food goods as well as in the cheap labour market, which has been an incentive to setting up facilities for production that will subsequently find an outlet on European Community markets. It is too soon to give an overall evaluation of this situation, especially when one considers the scanty information base. But there is no doubt that the multinational agrofood enterprise is destined to have considerable influence on the existing order, drastically modifying the eating habits of the populations involved as urban–industrial models of development take hold, i.e. as urbanization increases, more women join the labour force, family structure becomes less traditional, and eating habits change: less fresh produce and more convenience foods are consumed.

Agroindustry, food consumption and economic development

Unfortunately, as studies of food economy are limited in all three countries (with some exceptions for Spain), any attempt to reconstruct the dynamics of the food process and assess the importance of the agroindustry in the national economy must be based mainly on an analysis of national accounts for the years available. As the data for all three countries show, the agrofood industry assumes a role of some importance in the larger category of manufacturing industries in terms of its contribution to GNP, even though, in comparison with other production sectors, such as the textile, footwear, clothing and furniture industries, more modest growth rates have been registered in recent years. This is probably due to the backwardness of some parts of the agrofood sector. Productivity per employee also remains low.

Where a comparison is made between the evolution of the agricultural sector and the dynamics of total GNP, the historical tendency holds true. Agriculture plays a diminishing role in the overall economy, though it still accounts for a significant share of employment. The decreasing importance of agriculture has been accompanied by a process of investment contraction in the whole agrofood sector. In Spain, investments declined from 9% of the total in current prices in 1966 to little more than 4% in 1978.

In all the countries under study, the last decade has witnessed a growing ratio between domestic product of the agrofood industry and domestic product of agriculture. Even though the food industry does not always use raw materials of national origin (as in the case of a second phase of processing), nevertheless, this tendency toward manufacturing, which characterizes just about the whole of the European food economy, seems significant. The preceding data should be read in conjunction with the data in *Table 26.2* on private consumption and food consumption patterns in different spending categories and for different market groupings of goods.

The diminishing importance of food consumption in the whole of private consumption goes hand in hand with a tendency toward a broadening of the range of goods which make up the basket of food expenditure and, above all, with a shift in spending itself toward what are currently considered 'luxury' items[6].

Thus, a more consistent tendency can be observed toward livestock products, such as meat, milk and eggs, as well as toward those products that go under the statistical heading 'others' and account for all the new food preparations typical of a more modern society. Nevertheless, the last few years of the 1970s saw a marked slowdown in this process due to the significant reduction in consumption caused by inflation and the consequent rise in the cost of living that has characterized all of the economies of Europe.

Relations between agriculture and industry

The analysis of the relations between agriculture and industry and of the various forms of integration of the two sectors, particularly agriculture and manufacturing, takes on a different character for different countries and, more specifically, for different social strata and production conditions in the agricultural sectors of the countries themselves. The response of the family enterprise to industrial initiative is different from the capitalist enterprise. The quality of production that is achieved varies to a large degree according to the way in which the agricultural producer is able to relate to the manufacturer. Studies on agreements between industry and agriculture are almost non-existent in all three countries, although there are a few exceptions in Spain. Of particular interest is the work of Langreo[9] and Fenollar[5], in addition to the conclusions of a field study conducted in areas of agricultural development[7]. Some forms of integration began at the end of the 1950s in Spain with the appearance in a few sectors of large-scale industry and foreign capital investment. The agreements currently in effect, mainly concerning products not subject to government regulation, are distinctly different in form and modality according to the product and the province of the country. Despite the fact that there are attempts to set up agreements between agriculture and industry, there is no existing legislation in this regard, although a basic law on the matter, which would establish the essential content of the agreements, is now under examination

TABLE 26.2. Patterns of private consumption and food consumption according to market categories

	Private consumption	Food consumption	Bread and cereals	Meat	Fish	Milk, cheese, eggs	Oils and fats	Fruit and vegetables	Sugar and sweets	Coffee, tea, cocoa	Others
Spain											
1970	100	100	100	100	100	100	100	100	100	100	100
1971	102	102	99	101	105	100	105	108	100	97	103
1972	106	105	103	101	106	103	105	116	100	99	118
1973	115	115	112	118	108	109	110	127	101	108	128
1974	123	123	115	135	101	124	116	130	104	117	139
1975	125	125	124	133	104	131	117	130	109	122	145
1976	128	129	124	141	107	136	122	125	114	126	150
1977	129										
Greece											
1970	100	100	100	100	100	100	100	100	100	100	100
1971	107	103	103	108	99	104	105	97	103	108	109
1972	114	107	103	113	100	106	108	102	109	123	116
1973	123	113	105	21	108	111	112	106	111	129	126
1974	122	112	107	124	93	116	109	107	108	120	89
1975	131	120	105	131	98	118	110	122	110	156	124
1976	139	122	113	138	97	114	114	115	119	148	130
1977	146	124	115	149	97	116	116	106	113	127	151
1978	154	129	114	154	99	116	120	110	127	115	174

Note: 1977 = 100.
Source: Data from national accounts. Data not available for Portugal.

by the Coortes. This law would regulate, in the interest of all parties concerned, agricultural producers, manufacturers and consumers, the quantities to be consigned, the related procedures, the forms of technical assistance and advice to producers, the qualities to be consigned, the conditions for penalization and arbitration etc. Forms of agreements between agriculture and industry are most frequent in horticultural production, particularly in the production of tomatoes, peppers and asparagus, for crops grown in the valley of the Ebre and the Rioja–Navarra, and in the newly irrigated areas, such as the Badajoz region where tomatoes are grown for processing. There are also some agreements between agriculture and industry in the growth of oil seeds and hops, and in the sugarbeet industry.

The problems of agreements between agriculture and industry in Spain continue to be the limited organization of the sector and the relative inability to form cooperative associations. However, more significant experiments in integration can be found in the livestock products' sector, particularly in the raising of hogs and sheep, with the supplying of fodder, and butchery and meat preparation.

Integration of the sectors is negligible in the Portuguese economy where no important initiatives can be noted, except for a few efforts in the newly irrigated areas. In the Greek economy, however, there is a system of compulsory agreements in the growing of tomatoes for processing and sugarbeet. Annually, the state administration fixes the maximum area that agricultural producers can cultivate, for which they receive a license that specifies, among other things, the industries to which the producer can consign his crops. The designated area constitutes a ceiling for the grower. This system of voluntary agreements is spreading, though with difficulty, in the growing of beans, peas and asparagus.

The role of public administration

A significant problem in the examination of the agroindustrial system of a country is the definition of the role of public administration and of the operational centres which formulate the policy of the sector. In all three countries there is serious fragmentation of responsibilities among different centres of economic policy. For this reason, there are recurrent demands on the part of the public administration for the constitution of a single centre which would organize and coordinate public activity – a kind of Food Ministry. Of the three countries, again Spain is the one which, though with some contradictions, can rely on a more efficient administrative apparatus, essentially based on the authority of the Ministry of Agriculture and the Ministry of Industry – the former for the area of primary manufacturing (which also includes processes of simple handling of agricultural products), and the latter for the area of secondary manufacturing. From the point of view of administrative control, Spain can rely on a regulatory structure for public initiatives that, with the elimination of the individualized system of concessions to enterprises, programmes the activity itself.

For this purpose, sectors of particular industrial importance (*sectores industriales de interes preferente*) and zones of agroindustrial development (*zonas de preferente localizacion industrial agraria*) are designated, within which interested firms can benefit from a system of incentives and technical assistance. Firms can be broken down into three categories: *empresas liberalizadas, empresas condicionades*, and *empresas exceptuadas*. While those in the first category are not bound in any substantial way and the respective localization is the fruit of free enterprise, those in the second category, in order to gain access to the system of benefits, must meet a series of minimal technical requirements. (These are usually firms connected with the meat cycle, dairy plants etc.) Firms of the third type, those related to the oilseed sector, wine production in the DOC zones (controlled quality zones) and the big slaughterhouses, are bound to a system of preventive authorization by the administration that allows them to be placed in a registry of agrarian industries.

The system of production activities protected by the Ministry of Industry also makes use of a mechanism comparable in certain respects to Italian State investment in the private sector. This mechanism serves to unite the initiative of cooperative plants or big producers and industrialists with firms financed by the Instituto Nacional de Industria. From the financial viewpoint, there seems to be many possibilities of using public funds through a plurality of channels, even though sometimes, due to bureaucratic and administrative constraints, this potential is not fully utilized.

Regional development of the agrofood industry

The location of agrofood industries is characterized differently in each of the three countries, although for sectors which process imported raw materials, plants are located on the coast.

Spain

A broadly sketched map of the distribution of the agrofood industry in Spain shows areas of major concentration. Among these are the Galizia region with the largest centre at La Coruña, the Basque–Cantabrica region, the Catalan–Mediterranean region with the most important centres at Barcelona, Tarragona, Valencia and Alicante, and the Betica region with the main centre at Sevilla.

Thus, the Spanish agrofood industry is located peripherally with respect to the centre of the country and the capital, which connects the Galizia region with the Basque–Cantabrica region, which is linked to the Mediterranean–Catalan region, and the Betica region.

It should be pointed out that the area of greatest development is the Mediterranean–Catalan region, because in this region there is an equilibrium between supply and demand for manufacturing products. This is not the case, for example, in the Basque–Cantabrica area, marked by centres of high production, such as Oviedo, nor in areas of heavy consumption, such as Vizcaya.

More specifically, it can be noted that about half of the plants are located in centres of less than 5000 inhabitants, which is also related to the close connection between agriculture and industry for some types of production. While this may seem to be a limiting factor in certain respects, e.g. because it is impossible to take advantage of external economies that could be registered in plants located in larger areas, it could be advantageous if sufficiently exploited by the Spanish Government. In fact, a growth of the food industry in small centres, with an abundant labour force, which would not need to be trained from scratch, and with considerable experience could have a role of some value.

The agrofood industries (except for plants involved in sophisticated, second phase processing) have a potential relationship with the area that supplies them with raw materials. Putting this into practice would not require a great deal of initial investment, as in the case of some manufacturing or basic industries.

Moreover, it can be estimated that a job in this sector costs on the average 1.7 million pesetas, compared with 9.3 million in the organic chemical industry, 8.4 million in the steel industry, and 3–4 million in inorganic chemicals. Undoubtedly, agroindustrial development, where coordinated and controlled by the public administration, as has happened to some extent in Spain, can have a positive effect on agriculture. By guaranteeing employment levels and inducing a process of modernization, growth is stimulated. This is confirmed by the satisfactory level of the multiplier of final demand calculated on the basis of the input–output tables for the Spanish economy.

Portugal

The Portuguese food industry is particularly concentrated in the coastal areas. The vegetable oil and fat industry is more heavily concentrated in the three port areas of Lisbon, Setubal and Oporto, which account for more than 80% of production capacity, valued at around 600 000 metric tons of oleiferous seeds.

The Azores, because of the abundance of forage crops, play a role of some importance in the production of dairy products in individual factories that contribute to Portuguese production, which is spread over all regions of the country and exploited in special 'certified production zones' with the making of cheeses, such as *quejes de Serra*. Firms producing preserved vegetables are located mainly in the south–central regions where a growth in horticulture has been registered, as in Alentejo. The preserve industry is most widespread in the districts of Lisbon, Santarem and Portalegre.

Industrial concentration and availability of storage facilities, both for raw materials and for products, confirm the model of localization on the cost for sectors connected with mill products and so on, for the production of flour, pasta, animal feedstuffs etc. Olive oil and wine production are more evenly distributed throughout the territory, and in both cooperation plays a more significant role, in view of the small quantities of products turned out by each concern (more than 50% of wine production comes from winegrowers who produce less than 100 hectolitres per year).

Greece

As for industry in Greece, the most significant sector for which complete information is available is the preserved vegetable sector. However, apart from a few exceptions, such as milling and preserving fish, in general the industry in Greece is distributed throughout the whole country, obviously retaining handicraft characteristics in the more depressed areas. In this way, maintaining its location near the regions where raw materials are produced, the agrofood industry has been able to erode regional imbalances. However, there are areas of concentration in the Peloponnese and central and eastern Macedonia, as well as Attica and the adjacent islands.

Unlike its counterpart in Spain, the preserved vegetable industry in Greece is quite young, dating from the beginning of the 1960s. This does not mean that it does not have considerable potential for expansion, as shown by the growth of the tomato industry, which has produced elements of crisis in the traditional production geography of the Mediterranean area.

The sector can rely on about 60 plants, half of which were set up in the 1960s and a good many more of which were started immediately after 1970. From the viewpoint of internal location, it is important to note that in recent years there has been a movement of plants away from the islands. At one time the islands accounted for about 40% of production. Current production capacity is valued at over 200 000 metric tons per year at a plant utilization rate that hovers at about 70%. The region of Ilia, however, has an excess of production capacity and processes raw materials from other zones.

Conclusion

The research which has been discussed in this chapter is concerned foremost with an examination of the organizational and institutional elements of the agrofood industry in the three countries. It does not deal, therefore, with the problem of competition nor with the issue of the costs to the different member nations connected with the entry of these three countries into the European Community. On the basis of first findings, Spain will be the only new member country which is potentially more competitive, if one considers the whole of the food industry and not just particular sectors (the tomato and olive oil sectors, just to give an example).

This is because a process of industrialization of the food sector has at this point been set in motion in that country; because the large multinational enterprises have played a role in conditioning, but also in stimulating the entire production fabric; because forms of association are slowly being consolidated; because the country's agriculture, in its organization and existing land structure, is better prepared for an evolution toward more modern systems of market participation; because the social changes brought about in the process of the country's development and the increasing concentration of the population in urban areas imply new food habits and, therefore, a new way of utilizing the products of the land.

References

1. ARROYO, J. P. (1976) La realidad industrial agraria espanola. *Editorial Agricola Espanola,* Madrid
2. BRIZ, J. (Ed.) (1980) Espana y l'Europe verte. *Editorial Agricola Espanola,* Madrid
3. COMMISSAO NACIONAL DE FAO (1978) *Industrias alimentares em Portugal.* Ministerio de Negocios Etrangeiros, Lisbon
4. EEC (1980) *Etude sur la concentration, les prix et les marges dans le complexe alimentaire grec,* Brussels, EEC
5. FENOLLAR, R. J. (1976) Las relaciones agricultura-industria: la agroindustria en Espagna. *Boletin de Restudios Economicos,* No. 32
6. FENOLLAR, R. J. (1978) *La formacion de la agroindustria en Espagna 1960–70.* Ministerio de Agricultura, SGT, Madrid
7. GAMIZ, A. (1976) Agricultura familiar y dependencia en la producion baio contacto. *Agricultura y Sociedad,* No. 1
8. JIMENEZ, M. M. (1975) La industria agroalimentaria espanola. *Economia industrial,* No. 137
9. LANGREO, A. (1978) Analisis de la integracion vertical en Espana. *Agricultura y Sociedad,* No. 8
10. MINISTERIO DE AGRICULTURA E PESCAS (1980) *Elementos sobre industrias agroalimentaires em Portugal,* Lisbon
11. OECD (1980) *La politique agricole de la Grece,* Paris
12. PALMERRO, M. L. F. (1978) *Analise exploratoria do complexo agro-alimentar industrial atraves des matrices multisectoriais de 1970 e 1974.* Ministerio de Agricultura e Pescas, Lisbon
13. TERRON, E. (1978) El futuro de la alimentacion. *Agricultura y Sociedad,* Oct.–Dec., pp. 151–160

Part XI

Future directions and trade patterns for food marketing

The prime objective of the first chapter is to help development policy makers and planners in less developed countries evaluate proposed changes in food marketing systems, by enabling them to compare and contrast different alternatives in terms of their efficiency for producers, consumers and intermediaries. To this end, the first chapter (*a*) explains why Western capital-intensive mass marketing technology, even a stripped-down model of it, is ill-suited to serve low- and middle-income consumers in the less developed countries; (*b*) sketches out elements of intermediate marketing technologies that better fit the implementation of basic needs strategies, which will increasingly dominate approaches to development during the decade of the 1980s and beyond; (*c*) suggests elements of a guideline for marketing decision makers in the developing world as well as in agencies providing technical and financial assistance to such countries. A presentation is given of a development banker's preliminary ideas on a pragmatic guide to those technologies appropriate to different parts of marketing channels for consumer staples in urban areas of less developed countries, the main purpose of this being to provoke constructive dialogue. The presentation is coloured by the author's professional experience in Latin America and the Caribbean.

The distributive industry in Finland has been undergoing some structural changes since the beginning of the 1960s. The most important changes are examined in the second chapter in the context of the following main change fields traditionally considered in channel theory: (*a*) institutional changes, (*b*) functional changes, (*c*) changes in relationships among channel system members, and (*d*) changes in relationship between the system and its task environment.

Chapter 27

In search of appropriate marketing technology for the less developed countries

Frank Meissner

Introduction

Marketing can and has been defined as a business activity, a frame of mind, a group of institutions aimed at facilitating exchange of ownership as well as physical transfer of products and services, a process of physical concentration, the processing and dispersion of goods, a creator of time, place, form, and possession utilities, a set of devices for adjusting forces of supply and demand. Marketing can be considered to be the design, organization, and implementation of socioeconomic action programmes and projects aimed at effectively creating time, place, form, and ownership utilities related to satisfaction of basic needs. In addition to physical distribution of goods and services over space and time, marketing thus includes policy-oriented research, product selection, planning, and design, pricing, communication aimed at making the market 'transparent', thus facilitating open interplay of forces of supply and demand.

Being a behavioural discipline, marketing must not only deal with trading institutions and the flows of goods and services, but also with people and information flows. It not only deals with public acceptance of new products but also with public acceptance of new ideas. It strives for tangible improvement of the standard of living as well as for creation of a better overall quality of life. The main activities of marketing are defined as follows: the identification of unmet basic needs, the development of products and services to meet these unmet basic needs, pricing, the search for channels of distribution to the target markets, and communication to potential consumers about availability of products and services capable to satisfactorily meet specific unmet basic needs (freely adapted from Hughes[7]).

Selective appropriateness of Western mass marketing technology

Over the last quarter century Western literature on marketing consumer staples within less developed countries often recommended transfer of relatively capital-intensive mass marketing technology as a solution to problems of less developed countries related to the distribution of consumer staples. The

This chapter was originally presented as a paper in *Economic Analysis and Agricultural Policy*, 1982, Ed. by E. Day, Iowa State University Press, 2121 South State Avenue, Ames, Iowa 50010, USA, with the permission of the Publishers.

horizontally and vertically integrated systems surrounding institutions known as supermarkets were hailed as generators of substantial benefits due to economies of scale, self-service, and shortening of the distribution channel. Supermarkets supposedly help bypass the public wholesale markets, replace the crowded, old-fashioned, noisy, disorderly, and picturesque but dirty food stands in municipal retail bazaars, and do away with pesky street vendors who cause permanent health and safety hazards in busy downtown areas. In short, the small, limited-line retailer of consumer staples, plus the long, labour-intensive, haphazardly coordinated distribution chain, were arrogantly brushed aside as inadequate, inefficient, and irrelevant. For an early manifestation of this approach see Galbraith and Holten[5]. Subsequently, Professor Galbraith intellectually more than redeemed himself. Some of the relevant insights, gained since then, are revealed in Galbraith[4].

Sounds logical does it not? The trouble is that, from some 25 years of hindsight plus evidence of many bankrupt supermarkets in less developed countries, the above counsel turned out to be largely wrong. In short, Western marketing technology is too big and too expensive for the less developed countries. It does not create the jobs needed to absorb the rapidly expanding labour force, and it is not appropriate for the very small farm and business enterprises that make up the bulk of economic activities in less developed countries.

[See introduction to Meissner[9], which had the provocative title 'A new ethnocentric myopia? Rise of Third World demands marketing be stood on its head'[5]. The provocation worked wonders. This chapter is therefore to serve as 'mass response' and acknowledgement of the valuable comments and criticisms received. Special thanks are extended to Professor Louis P. Bucklin (University of California, Berkeley), Ronald Stucky (Santa Clara University), Tannira R. Rao (University of Wisconsin-Milwaukee), Victor E. Childers (Indiana University), Eleanor Branttley-Schwartz (Cleveland State University), Edward W. Smykay (Michigan State University), Hans Mittendorf (United Nations Food and Agriculture Organization in Rome), and Klaus Moll (United Nations Industrial Development Organization in Vienna).]

Entering the 1980s the development profession humbly returned to square one. Gradually appreciation is beginning of variations in the traditional, labour-intensive food retailers as, by and large, an appropriate technology suitable for marketing staples to the bulk of the world's population – neither so primitive as to offer no escape from low production and low income nor so highly sophisticated as to be cut out of reach for poor people and therefore ultimately politically and economically unacceptable. Within this context it becomes evident that 'the supermarket, even in its more rudimentary version, is ill-equipped to service the low- and middle-income consumers in developing . . . countries; . . . if gains in distribution are to be obtained, they must be secured through improvement in domestic or intermediate technologies'[2].

Inappropriate supermarket mass marketing technology is by no means an affliction confined to less developed countries only. Thus the mid-1979[1]:

decision by Safeway Stores to close its supermarket in central Anacostia (a district of Washington DC) – which threatens to leave an estimated 10 000 black, low income residents nothing but small, high priced food markets is a national trend. The number of supermarkets in cities has declined by about 50% during the last 10 years; in the District of Columbia, the number has dropped from 91 to 40. From a pure business point of view supermarkets are failing in the face of limited space, high labour costs, shoplifting, vandalism, and employee turnover.

As a result the high-cost corner mom-and-pop grocery stores, likely to be owned by recent, hard-working immigrants – entrepreneurs from such less developed countries as South Korea and Vietnam – are thriving. Their traditional technology of grocery marketing is apparently far more suitable for poor Americans than is the supermarket.

No wonder that in a limerick on the 'Extra Cost of Being Poor' the USDA's *Farm Index* of May 1970 (*p. 15*) launched the following definition:

Poor is:
Paying more for many of the necessities of life than others do.
Trying to balance spending and income with no savings to cushion emergencies.
Buying in amounts you can afford, not being able to take advantage of twofers and threefers.
Buying whatever quality shoes and trousers you can manage on your time payments.
Buying more interest on credit terms because it takes longer to pay.

Supermarkets, an institution as American as McDonald's hamburgers, have not as yet penetrated the less developed countries. The main reason is that supermarkets are primarily merchandisers of processed foods, which few poor people can afford to buy. Also, the lack of a sustained supply of uniform-quality produce, typical in the less developed countries, makes it difficult for supermarkets to organize efficient field procurement; as a result they have to go through central wholesale markets, just like their 'traditional' colleagues. Consequently, even in the relatively few unprocessed foods they sell, mostly fresh fruits and vegetables, capital-intensive supermarkets can hardly ever compete with the low prices charged by traditional labour-intensive huckster–higgler type retailers or ambulatory street vendors with little overheads. Consequently, supermarkets tend to be found in high-income areas of less developed cities, bringing the benefits of Western-type mass marketing to those who can best afford to pay for it.

The developed countries, in which supermarkets are flourishing, nowadays represent 30% of the global population. Projections of current population trends show that by the year 2000 their share is likely to be down to about 20%, and to a miniscule 10% by the year 2050. This seems to indicate that the current type of supermarket mass marketing technology is unsuitable for a growing proportion of the world population, a fact seldom explicitly recognized by the Western marketing establishment.

Search for appropriate marketing technologies

Multinational financial and technical assistance agencies, such as the Asian Development Bank (ADB), the Inter-American Development Bank (IDB), and the World Bank, seem to have understood instinctively that the technology of the Western supermarket is not well suited to serving the needs of low-income food buyers. They have therefore been searching for more appropriate technologies.

Thus, in IDB the bulk of food-marketing projects are aimed at improving *traditional* rural assembly centres, municipal retail markets, and wholesale producers, plus strengthening the corresponding software infrastructure such as establishment of grades and standards, mobilization of working capital for traders, in-service training of food retailers and wholesalers, and market news services.

From its very inception in 1961, IDB thus recognized the importance of distribution as a crucial supplement to its production-oriented agricultural projects such as irrigation, crop and livestock credit, land settlement, and rural development. As of January 1, 1981, the Bank approved 29 loans for marketing and agroindustries, totalling US$711.3 million. IDB loans amounted to US$298.6 million, or 41.9% of the total. Three major types of facilities form more than half of the marketing portfolio: agroindustries, grain storage, and public markets. IDB tends to assign high priority to marketing and agroindustry projects that satisfy at least four major requirements: to provide effective incentives for farmers to increase production; to improve facilities at different stages of the marketing channel to assure urban and rural consumers timely and sustained supplies of reasonably priced basic foods and other staples; to help distribute equitably benefits from improved marketing among producers, intermediaries, and consumers; and to use relatively labour-intensive technology. IDB provides a substantial technical assistance aimed at: facilitating effective organization of small farmers for purposes of jointly selling their produce and for procuring production inputs; helping band together small intermediaries for purposes of mobilizing reasonably priced working capital resources; improving the management practices of individual assembly, processing, wholesale, and retail firms. This type of 'software' often represents up to as much as 10% of the project cost.

In contrast, capital-intensive, mass-marketing 'supermarket' technology, which primarily tends to serve middle- and high-income consumers in Latin American countries, is considered to be a suitable area for private financing.

It often takes a great deal of courage to swim against the stream of benign neglect, and/or counteract. IDB's participation in financing public wholesale food markets is a case in point. This is because urban planners often fear that mass-marketing technology will make public wholesale markets obsolete, hearing so much about private supermarkets 'integrating backward' by buying directly from producers and performing the wholesaling function themselves in their own central warehouses.

In reality, even in the highly developed industrialized countries of western Europe where supermarket chains are rapidly becoming a crucial distribution channel for consumer staples, the volume of fruits and vegetables moving through central wholesale markets remains stable or tends to increase as years go by, amounting in most cases to over 70% of total consumption. Furthermore, in North America the newer central markets are actually broadening their functions. When adequate land is available, agroindustrial parks tend to become integral parts of the complex. The brand new, publicly financed, and highly profitable Maryland Wholesale Food Center in Jessup (near the Friendship International Airport of Baltimore) is an outstanding illustration. Indeed, the private Giant supermarket chain has constructed its central warehouse, considered the most modern in the world, next to the public wholesale produce market, a perfect example of symbiotic public–private agrobusiness that is evidently opening up many opportunities for creative complementary relationships between the private and public sector agrobusinesses.

In spite of floods of literature on marketing in less developed countries (*see Table 27.1*), no systematic policy-oriented study has so far been made of the growing body of experience with appropriate marketing technology of multinational and bilateral development agencies.

TABLE 27.1. Income levels in GNP per capita per year

Factors	Low	Lower and intermediate middle	Upper middle	High
Number of less developed countries				
Latin America and Caribbean	1	16	8	3
Asia	12	10	5	8
Africa	22	19	3	1
Total: 108	35	45	16	12
Food expenditure as percentage of disposable income[†]	over 60	45–60	35–45	under 35
Share of perishable products (fresh or processed fruit, vegetables, meat and fish) in cost of popular diets (%)[†]	under 30	30–40	40–50	45–50
Labour cost or minimum wages (US$/day)	< 2.00	2.00–3.75	3.75–6.00	> 6.00
Access to private motorized transport and refrigeration	Practically non-existent	Rare	Rapidly increasing	Common
Assembly of agricultural products at point of first sale[†]	Occasional surpluses in small lots of ungraded product brought to market either by farmer (on foot, cart, public bus) or picked up at farm by intermediary; quantities marketed fluctuate greatly	Large lots informally graded by buyer-trucker at farm or assembly market; truck transport common where adequate farm-to-market roads exist	Commercial producers specialize in production of food crops that reflect demand specifications; intermediaries bring produce to wholesale markets or farmers form marketing groups; as area of outreach broadens, supply tends to stabilize, grading and standards being accepted by trade	Increasing quantities of produce brought directly from farmers by retail organization; government standards established; production contract become common; supply sustained

TABLE 27.1. (*Continued.*)

Factors	Low	Lower and intermediate middle	Upper middle	High
Wholesale Assortments	Wholesale–retail combined in individual enterprises that specialize in a few products	Specialized wholesalers develop, concentrating individual enterprises on a few commodities (grain, fruits, vegetables, poultry, etc.)	Wholesale food distribution centres located in suburbs or adjacent open country, with sections specializing in comodities	As local agrobusiness grows, assortment broadens into processed and packaged goods, in addition to traditional perishables and grains
Facilities	Wholesale–retail markets tend to be centrally located close to traditional downtown of major cities; stalls average roughly 10–20 m^2	Special wholesale markets being constructed away from central city areas; stalls average about 40–80 m^2	Roads and transport facilities to serve the retail trade are being added to wholesale centres, which provide stalls averaging over 80 m^2	Wholesale terminals become agrobusiness centres, in which – in addition to highly specialized wholesalers – central warehouses of chain stores as well as agroindustries, public warehouses, etc., also tend to locate
Retail Public markets, bazaars, and periodic fairs	Stall tenants supply most of consumer staples bought by low- and middle-income families	As cities grow, traditional public markets become more and more crowded; inadequate facilities drive trade into other channels	Satellite public markets and periodic fairs being built, old central facilities renewed; stall sizes increase, refrigeration more frequently available	Specialization in perishables increasing; processed and packaged goods tend to bypass public retail markets

307

Itinerant vendors	Numerous street vendors handling tiny quantities of merchandise constitute bulk of the 'informal sector'	Itinerant vendors grow in importance, selling in streets surrounding the public markets as well as delivering to households in residential neighbourhoods	Relative importance of itinerants depends largely on degree of employment; the more unemployment, the more feasible and attractive is this sort of retailing, which is easy to enter
Neighbourhood grocery stores	Small, family-owned, fixed-location stores in houses of residential neighborhoods. Carry less than 100 items, annual gross turnover of under US$5000	Larger in size (20–40 m^2), tendency to specialize in fruits and vegetables, meat, fish, bread, etc; annual turnover over US$10 000	Retailers from public markets 'graduate' to neighbourhood stores in newer, low income areas
Self-service superettes and supermarkets	Individually owned, small stores primarily located in upper-middle- and high-income neighbourhoods; large proportion of packaged and processed foods imported and high priced; few local perishables carried	In middle-income neighbourhoods, clerk and self-service superettes appear; supermarkets broaden assortment, including fresh fruits and vegetables; local food processors start substituting some imported goods	Stores tend to band together in voluntary, cooperative, or corporate chains; local agroindustries provide increasing share of processed and packaged goods; increasing share of products bypass independent wholesalers
Facilitating public infrastructure Grades and standards	Transactions based on inspection of individual lots	Informal grading practiced by traders	

TABLE 27.1. (*Continued.*)

Factors	Low	Lower and intermediate middle	Upper middle	High
Marketing information system	Word of mouth	Rudimentary market news services being set up in public markets	Within framework of national development planning, provisions being made for drawing up systematic marketing improvement programmes and their gradual implementation; substantial technical cooperation from multinational or bilateral agencies frequently required	
Education, training and extension	Occasional consultancies by expatriate experts, scholarships for local personnel	Gradually increasing as outreach of local pilot facilities broadens		
Policy-oriented research	Rarely done due to lack of data, qualified professionals, and awareness of need for systemic analysis of alternatives	Getting to be more frequent as data base increases; more professionals become available; multinational, bilateral, and local agencies demand better quantitative guidance for better decision making		
Mobilization of sources of capital				
Fixed	Local public agencies tend to seek concessionary funds from multinational or bilateral assistance agencies		Increased capability of public sector to mobilize local government funds makes possible supplementation of foreign funds at ordinary capital rates	
Working	Inadequate at all levels, resulting in high interest and short-term lending	Wholesalers tend to dominate 'backward' finance of producers and 'forward' financing of retailers		Increasing ability of farmers and retailers to obtain funds from commercial public or private banks tends to diminish domination of marketing channel by wholesalers

World Atlas of the Child Washington DC, World Bank, 1979, p. 3.
Adapted and updated from: *Food Marketing in 13 Asian Cities*, Bangkok: Food and Agricultural Organization of the United Nations, 1975, pp. 10–11.

Adapted from: *Market Place Trade: Periodic Markets, Hakers and Traders in Africa, Asia and Latin America*. Ed. by H. T. Smith, Vancouver BC. University of British Columbia, 1979. The 17 essays in the book relate to Ecuador, Sabah, Ethiopia, Madagascar, Tran, Papua, Hong Kong, Singapore, Nigeria, Colombia, Tanzania, Liberia and Kenya.

Income levels were measured as: low, under US$280; lower and intermediate US$281–1135; upper middle, US$1135–2500; high, > US$2500.

The author himself pleads guilty as coeditor (with Dov Izraeli and Dafna N. Izraeli) of *Marketing Systems for Developing Countries* (1976). The two volumes contain papers presented at the First International Conference on Marketing Systems in Developing Countries, held in Israel, January 6–12, 1974. The meeting was cosponsored by the International Marketing Federation and Tel Aviv University. Volume 1 deals with marketing systems for products and services in individual countries. Volume II focuses on institutions and infrastructures for agricultural marketing.

One truism is valid, and will continue to be valid in years to come: a 'drought' of potentially bankable projects is the greatest challenge of multinational development agencies trying to improve agricultural marketing systems in less developed countries. In short, money can usually be found for a good project[10]. The intensive search of the Organization of Petroleum Exporting Countries (OPEC) members for suitable outlets for their huge funds available for investment is a case in point.

In fact, adaptation of marketing systems for effective use by urban and rural poor, including the small farmers, is a relatively new field of endeavour. It is so new a subject, that the conventional marketing profession tends to consider it somewhat 'far out'.

Policy implications

When Mohammed does not go to the mountain the mountain has to go to Mohammed. Academic marketing researchers have so far not been overly helpful in guiding development bankers in the identification, selection, pre-evaluation, preparation, analysis, and implementation of marketing projects. Let us sketch a few possibilities based on the observations presented so far.

In the less developed countries, consumption of processed and packaged consumer staples is evidently limited by low incomes. The supermarket tends to serve only a relatively small section of the middle- and upper-income urban residents. As a rule it therefore appears that within an overall development strategy aimed at satisfying the basic needs of the bulk of rural and urban populations, governments should (*a*) strive to use public funds for improving marketing of food and non-food consumer staples by upgrading and developing existing traditional institutions such as wholesale produce markets and municipal retail bazaars and by regulating street vending in large cities as well as the periodic fairs in rural areas and in small cities; (*b*) let the private sector take care of investment in mass-marketing supermarkets, which tend primarily to serve the higher-income populations.

For this upgrading to be effective, substantial investment is needed in the improvement of facilitating marketing functions, i.e. the 'software' (consultancy, training, and institutional strengthening) that makes it possible for the 'hardware' (storage, transport, processing, access roads, public markets) to be operated reasonably efficiently. For a 'menu' of software *see* Dam *et al.*[3].

Experience indicates that in 'marketing development packages' investment in fixed capital would frequently represent roughly 50–80% of the total cost; working capital, needed for procurement of the goods and financing of their movements through the marketing channel, would require in the neighbourhood of 15–30%, while technical assistance would range all the way from a relatively 'normal' 1–5% to as high as 20% of total investment.

Under traditional practice it is easy for multinational development agencies to justify financing the foreign exchange content of fixed capital investment. As it so happens, capital-intensive supermarket technology requires much more foreign exchange than investments in labour-intensive bazaar technology, which primarily consists of local costs. In order to assist in financing this sort of appropriate technology, multinational development agencies have to be flexible enough to help finance substantial parts of local cost components whenever required. Likewise, there needs to be a readiness to assist with provision of the often substantial 'software' of technical cooperation, without which the hardware cannot operate satisfactorily.

Multinational development banks, drawing on specialized United Nations organizations and/or the numerous bilateral assistance agencies, are nowadays well equipped to provide all sorts of technical cooperation software as well as capital for customary hardware. Selected references, cited at the end of this chapter, indicate that some multinational and bilateral agencies have attempted to revitalize existing public markets and fairs through modernization and provision of entrepreneurial services to traditional wholesalers and retailers, who are primarily serving low-income rural and urban populations. Yet, the 'marketing profession' in North America and western Europe has not shown much interest in this type of public-marketing reform[2]:

The research that has been conducted upon the feasibility of such policies is regretfully minimal. There has been no known cost–benefit analysis, no evaluation of improvement of facility appearance upon patronage, no examination of the sociology of the market vendors to accept direction and change and no examination of incentives necessary for introduction of private enterprise, through market builders or stimulating their vigor to improve existing facilities.

In short, capital-intensive mass-marketing technology, which requires a high degree of vertical integration along the marketing channel, seems likely to be of dubious value for the low-income populations during the foreseeable future. Alternative marketing development options, including revitalization of existing public markets through modernization, provision of entrepreneurial services, and in-service training of wholesalers and retailers, appear more promising. Evidence is gradually being accumulated showing that from such traditional institutions, when well managed, vigorious competition can emerge.

References

1. ASHER, R. L. (1979) How others save supermarkets. *Washington Post,* August 4, A13
2. BUCKLIN, L. P. (1977) Improving food retailing in developing Asian countries. *Food Policy,* **2,** 114–122
3. DAM, TH., LORENZL, G., MITTENDORF, H. J. and SCHMIDT-BURR, H. (Eds) (1978) *Marketing – A Dynamic Force for Rural Development.* Berlin (FRG): German Foundation for International Development
4. GALBRAITH, J. K. (1979) *The Nature of Mass Poverty.* Cambridge, Mass., Harvard University Press
5. GALBRAITH, J. K. and HOLTON, R. H. (1955) *Marketing Efficiency in Puerto Rico.* Cambridge, Mass., Harvard University Press
6. HOWELL JONES, D. (Ed.) (1980) *Meeting Basic Needs: An Overview.* Washington DC, World Bank
7. HUGHES, G. D. (1978) *Marketing Management: A Planning Approach.* Reading, Mass., Addison-Wesley

8. IZRAELI, D., IZRAELI, D. N. and MEISSNER, F. (Eds) (1976) *Marketing Systems for Developing Countries.* New York: Wiley
9. MEISSNER, F. (1978) A new ethnocentric myopia? Rise of Third World demands marketing be stood on its head. *Marketing News.* International Marketing issue, October 6
10. MEISSNER, F. (1981) *Managing Preinvestment for Agricultural and Rural Development Projects.* Atlanta, Ga., Institute for Food Technology
11. MEISSNER, F. (Ed.) (1979) *Nutrition as a Tool of Socio-Economic Development of Latin America.* Washington DC, Inter-American Development Bank
12. SHEPHERD, G. S. (1955) *Marketing Farm Products – An Economic Analysis,* 3rd edn. Ames, Iowa State University Press
13. STREETEN, P. and BURKE, S. J. (1978) Basic needs: some issues. In *World Development.* Washington DC, World Bank

Chapter 28

Predictions of changes in food wholesale trade in Finland

Eeva Helena Mäkinen

Introduction

The distributive industry in Finland has been undergoing structural changes since the beginning of the 1960s. The most important developments have been in the grocery sector, which accounts for most of the sales of consumer goods. In this chapter the author discusses why and how wholesaling is changing, and will continue to change. The issue is important, because today wholesaling in Finland is a large and growing industry, which also has a great impact on the development of the retail trade. The predictions about the future are useful, because they form a base for planning in the distributive sector and other industries.

Problem areas in future changes of wholesaling

Nature of changes

Changes of wholesaling can be analysed from many different angles, one of which is the rate of change. Possibilities of change are (a) slowing, (b) accelerating and (c) gradual steady development. Many researchers claim that the rate of change is accelerating and that those sectors of the distributive industry that have so far been affected relatively little by these changes are now being caught up in the process that will propel them through the 1980s and into the 1990s[3,17]. These changes will be markedly more dramatic than those of the past, placing more strain upon firm flexibility. There are, however, many factors favouring relatively slow rates of evolution[4,6,16]. At present, channel changes in Finland are constrained by the lack of capital and by organizational rigidity.

Explanations for various change processes do not provide a precise set of circumstances for predicting when changes will occur. Since the environmental factors of trade are continuously changing, changes would be a continuous process. The time dates for changes can be accidental (new innovations) or regular (fluctuations and trends). The theory of the so-called 'pendulum effect' partly explains and predicts the time dates for changes. Changes in the distributive system seem to indicate that there is a general tendency for changes to be carried too far, leading to corrective reactions of one kind or another in the system[7]. It has, for example, been suggested, that the emergence of cash-and-carry wholesalers was, at least in part, a reaction to the trend towards increase in size of wholesalers. Naturally, new technological innovations cause many technological changes in the distributive trade[36]. As to the origin of changes, one can distinguish between evolutionary, slow and planned changes. The rise of planned vertical marketing systems comes from the willingness of all the firms in the system to commit themselves to one over-riding channel strategy[9,18]. This development is followed by the more important role of central organizations and/or wholesalers in channel strategy: they have, in many countries, become change agents in channel development. (For a concept of change agent in channels, *see* Bowersox *et al.*[5] and Mårtenson[24].)

Scope of changes

Through classification of changes as types we have a framework for analysing changes more thoroughly. As a unit of analysis, a vertical marketing system can be used[9,16,25]. Probably the most obvious kind of change in the distribution system is the development of institutions belonging to it at the wholesale or retail level[9,14,16]. The evolution of the system can also be usefully analysed in terms of changes in the performance of a function or activity – by the improved management of the institution performing it and/or by re-allocation of functions among institutions at various levels[16] (for the types of changes of activities and functions, *see* Mininger[26]). In addition to this functional change, economic relationships among channel system members are significant change fields in evolving distribution structures[16,25]. One of the developmental issues is also the relationship between the system and its task environment, i.e. the interface between the system and the consumer, governmental authorities etc.[9,12].

The change process can be examined in the context of the following main change fields traditionally considered in channel theory:

- Institutional changes.
- Functional changes.
- Changes in relationships among channel system members.
- Changes in relationships between the system and its task environment.

Institutional changes

There are many theories of institutional change: stage theories, cycle theories, dialectic theories, challenge–response models, diffusion theories and theories concerning economics of the firm[31,34]. Stage theories are characterized by linear or curvilinear chronological progression. Retail institutions are hypothesized to have a historical trend towards an increase in complexity of functions and offerings[31]. Cycle theories emphasize a dynamic movement in which changes lead from simple to complex and then back to simple, or a dynamic movement based on some predetermined biological pattern. Dialectic theories resemble cycle theories and are based on arguments that one type of institution in an almost biological sense produces its opposite[14,31]. The best known explanation in the group of cycle theories is the theory of 'the wheel of retailing'. The hypothesis suggests that innovative retailers originate as low-margin operators, first challenging their mature competitors and eventually emulating them, thus providing an opportunity for still newer low-margin retail methods to evolve[1,24]. Bucklin developed the concept of the 'wheel of wholesaling' for approaching the problem of wholesale evolution[6]. New types of wholesalers emerge as the competitive capabilities of old-fashioned wholesalers decrease. There are many other variants of cycle theories (for a framework for studying institutional change, *see* Mårtenson[24]). More research will be required, however, before this concept can be accepted as an explanation of domestic patterns of change in wholesaling.

In addition to the wheel theory, the challenge–response model has been applied by some researchers[1,7]. When a new institution emerges, existing firms tend to resist it by attempts to discredit the innovator and secure the support of restrictive legislation. Such laws and the accompanying publicity have seldom, if ever, had any real effect on the direction of change or rate of change. Conventional marketing institutions are forced to adapt to new forms of competition by meeting the innovators' methods, at least in a modified form. Thus, independent grocery wholesalers and retailers meet the challenge of the corporate chains by forming chains of their own. Ultimately, this process leads to emergence of a new equilibrium, combining features of both the old and new chains.

Traditional applications of diffusion and innovation models to channels take the innovation as given and describe the diffusion of channel innovation according to an S-shaped curve. Arndt refers to the diffusion of cash-and-carry wholesalers in West Germany as an example[1]. Swan's analysis of innovation in distribution channels based on Parsons and Smelser's model focuses on the process leading to the formulation of an innovation. This view implies that innovation is more in the nature of a response to a problem rather than a creative insight on the part of entrepreneurs in some unceasing search for profits[34].

The preceding models concern mainly the changes of types of institutions. The other typical institutional changes comprise the number, size and productivity of institutions. According to Tietz, the basic wholesale model for determining subsequent changes includes the following forces: general socioeconomic evolution, changes in the number of suppliers and the customers of the wholesale trade, changes in performance of the wholesale trade and its market partners, location and space requirements with regard to the necessity of changing the use of surfaces in congested areas, changes in transportation systems, changes in the systems of communication brought about by progress in electronic processing[35]. Bucklin has also shown, with regression results, that determinants of the number and size of wholesale establishments may be derived from the economic environmental factors, such as the number of manufacturers and retailers and the developmental stage of the economic system, which offers markets for wholesalers. Wealthy areas also buy a large number of services from hospitals, governments and schools which, in turn, require supplies and equipment from wholesale sources. They offer new markets for relatively specialized wholesale firms[6].

Beyond these economic, ecological explanations the concentration explanation has been used to explain the institutional changes. On the basis of this, one would assume that the trend towards concentration is continuing or even accelerating in the distributive trades[22]. The concentration tendencies have been explained firstly by the economies of scale and operation[36]. Just as industrial development shows increased concentration based on the economies of scale, the same is also true of wholesaling if only because wholesaling is a product of its environment, including the technological situation. The other factor to be mentioned in this context is Galbraith's thesis that economic power is held in check by the countervailing power of those who are subject to it. The first begets the second. The long trend toward concentration has brought into existence not only strong sellers, but also strong buyers. The two develop together, not at exactly the same rate but in such a manner that there can be no doubt that one is the response to the other[11]. This concentration may occur through the ordinary processes of growth and amalgamation until a roughly bilateral oligopolistic situation develops. The most crucial section of Galbraith's thesis deals with distribution, but one can include wholesaling under this heading. It is evidently expected that the 'mass wholesalers' will provide the most significant development to offset the market power of the industrial oligopolist.

Functional changes

The efficient performance of functions (such as transportation, promotion, inventory and transaction) is the raison d'être of the channel. Consequently the evolution of the channel is analysed in terms of changes in the performance of a function – by improved management by the institution performing it and/or re-allocation of function among institutions[16]. Changes in functions and activities can be described by such dimensions as space, time, technique, quality and quantity[25]. The striving for economic efficiency forms the main explanation for changes in functions[23]. The total costs in vertical marketing systems are minimized by avoiding duplication of functions and allocating them to the objects most suited to perform them[9]. The determination of what channel structure is likely to be in the future led Bucklin to introduce his concept of a 'normative' or ideal channel. A 'normative' channel is that which would exist if all institutions in the extant (or real world) channel, and all potential entrants, were fully adapted to economic conditions such that there would be no tendency for new firms to enter, old ones to exit or to shift functions among themselves[13,23].

Changes in relationships among channel system members

Most scholars accept the notion that, to a significant degree, the structure of channels is a reflection of an economy's level of development. At low levels of development there is little specialization between distributive and non-distributive functions because of the small market size. As market size develops, firms start to specialize in distribution and specific non-distributive operations. With further development, the distribution firms specialize within the distribution function, thus becoming specific types of wholesalers, agents, and retailers. At the stage of highly developed economies, vertical integration appears and more direct distribution becomes a strong structural characteristic[23]. During this development process, both the institutional and functional structure of the distribution channel may change. As was the case with institutions and functions, such changes in institutional and functional structure result from scalar economies (Stiglers spin-off model) and from market-oriented forces[13].

By now, increased institutional integration has, in many countries, led to the rise of vertical marketing systems particularly in grocery, but also in other trades. None of the preceding explanations adequately explains channel evolution in advanced economies where channel management and planning occur. Guiltinan's five-stage model comes much closer to achieving that goal (*see Table 28.1*)[16].

Guiltinan offers the thesis that most channels in the economy no longer change strictly on the basis of a natural evolution and that modifications in the structure of

TABLE 28.1. Changes in channels explained by changes in distribution objectives

Stage and objectives	Primary source of influence on policies	Illustrative policies
(I) Contactual/communication	Product characteristics	M-W-R channel Little channel direction
(II) Coverage/capacity	Institutional effectiveness in reaching consumers	Intensive distribution Multiple brands
(III) Control	Channel member relationships and marketing	Franchising Administered systems Exclusive distribution
(IV) Cost	Economic efficiency	Voluntary Cooperatives
(V) Cooperation/consolidation	Access to capital	Vertical integration
Reducing macro- and micromarketing dissatisfaction	Consumerism and regulation of society	New marketing and distribution system

Adapted from Guiltinan[16].

a given channel can be explained by changes in the strategic distribution objectives of key channel members. Such members may be strong channel captains or developers of a new product or other institutions with a major interest in a given channel (*see* Mallen's question[23]: 'who should lead the channel' and Guiltinan[16]). Also Savitt refers to the impact of planning on patterns of development[31].

Although this comprehensive theory does not completely specify the order of all evolutionary changes, it facilitates the development of hypothesis on the rate, direction, and consequences of future changes in distribution channels[16]. Channels remain in stage one in certain cases; however, channels in most lines of trade move through subsequent stages toward stage five, because many economies of scale are evident and the locus of control is well defined. According to this theory channels remain in this last stage for prolonged periods of time.

We can ask what the objectives of distribution channels are after this fifth stage is reached, e.g. after the stage of vertical integration. What are the factors determining the development in the future? There are two possible answers to this question. One factor determining the development could be consumerism and the other could be the regulation of society to determine the way the economy produces and allocates goods and services.

Changes in relationships between the system and its task environment

During the last 10 years the voice and power of consumers have been growing stronger in most countries. There are several inter-related factors which, when combined, seem to feed the forces of consumerism. The increasing level of affluence and the problems associated with it are often mentioned as such factors[29]. The current consumerism differs from its predecessors in intensity. Another factor operating to sustain and reinforce today's consumer movement is that consumerism has, like the labour movement before it, been largely institutionalized[10]. On the other hand, a government has developed many measures of control over most distribution activities. Protecting consumers is a traditional goal of public policy toward distribution. Improvement of efficiency of distribution has been a more recent goal. Some aspects of governmental intervention are essentially supportive in nature. Financial assistance or provision of low-cost loans illustrates this phase of public policy. It may be limited to particular types or it may be available to all types of dealers.

Consumerism represents a challenge to marketing, and it is very possible that a new marketing system that is characterized by more governmental regulation will emerge out of this challenge. This new kind of distribution system could be called 'a negotiated distribution system'. This kind of development could mean a change in the present marketing systems in Finland.

The current state of food wholesale trade in Finland

Finland has a very advanced and modern system of distribution. The grocery trade in particular is highly organized. Groceries are the province of four centralized chains. Within each group there is close cooperation between the wholesale and retail fields, which together form a tightly knit distribution system.

Two of the chains are cooperatives, and two private. The cooperatives are E-osuuskunta Eka (the Cooperative Society Eka) and Suomen Osuuskauppojen Keskuskunta (SOK) (the Finnish Cooperative Wholesale Society). In 1983 the Central Cooperative Society (OTK), its local member societies and retail shops merged to form the Cooperative Society Eka. The big conglomeration includes central organization, stores and mobile stores. The private groupings are K-group and T-group. Kesko Oy (retailer-owned wholesale corporation) is the central trading-house for K-shops and mobile stores, with which it combines to form the group. Tukkukauppojen Oy (Tuko – The Central Organisation of Independent Wholesalers) combines private grocery wholesale companies and their client retailers. The T-group concentrates on the delivery of goods in daily demand and department stores.

These four systems account for roughly 90% of food retailing and over 50% of the total retail trade in Finland. The other wholesalers operate mainly in other fields. Keskusosuusliike Hankkija (Cooperative Wholesale Society Hankkija) is a central organization operating primarily for farmers. The structure and organizations of Finnish wholesale and retail trade is outlined in *Figure 28.1*[30]. *Table 28.2* provides the sales and the market-shares of the wholesale groupings[33] and *Table 28.3* the sales of all wholesalers in 1982[33].

Since the wholesalers of four chains operate in many fields, the current sales and market-shares of groceries can be best measured at the retail level. *Table 28.4* shows the number and sales of grocery outlets by type of shop and chain in 1982[20].

Future changes and evolution in wholesaling

Theories concerning changes in distribution channels are not very fruitful in predicting future changes in wholesaling. It is, however, vital to determine as accurately as possible future changes, because planning relies heavily on forecasting. Consequently a number of researchers have made predictions about future changes in wholesaling in Finland using different forecasting methods.

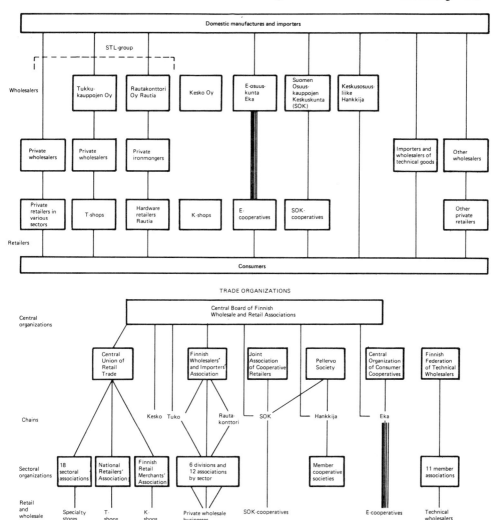

Figure 28.1. The structure and organization of Finnish trade. Partly redrawn from *Retail and Wholesale Trade in Finland*[30] with contributions of the author

This chapter is mainly based on predictions made by the author who forecaste future changes in grocery and food wholesaling with the Delphi method[13,28,36]. The purpose of the study was to forecast changes which will take place in wholesaling by 1990 in the most crucial 'change fields', e.g. structure of wholesaling, functions of wholesaling. Five rounds of questionnaires were sent to 36 experts from distributive trades and industry during the period between 1975 and 1976. These experts estimated the future direction and values of some developing and changing phenomena, predicted new changes and estimated dates for the expected changes. The study produced 36 quantitative forecasts, 25 forecasts about the dates of some expected changes and other information about future changes[22]. Some of the results have been replaced or completed with the predictions of another Delphi study, which was prepared in 1983 by 38 leading directors and planners in wholesaling and retailing on 'the automation in domestic trade' by 1990[2]. In addition to these Delphi forecasts, some time-series predictions by distribution researchers are cited, which are based on data collected from official census records[19] or statistics of information service firms[20]. Due to strong vertical integration in Finnish domestic trade also most important changes at the retail level are cited.

TABLE 28.2. Sales of wholesale groupings including subsidiaries in 1982

	Mill. FIM	Percentage share	Change 1982/81
Kesko*	16 533.7	13.2	14.6
SOK	10 454.3	8.4	9.8
OTK	7057.5	5.6	11.1
Hankkija	7833.0	6.3	14.3
Member enterprises of Finnish Wholesalers' and Importers' Association	20 045.6	16.0	12.8
of which T-group's wholesalers	8064.0	6.4	20.0
of which Rautia group's wholesalers	4486.5	3.6	12.7
Member enterprises of Finnish Federation of Technical Wholesalers[†]	33 227.7	26.6	14.7
Other wholesalers[‡]	29 958.4	23.9	
All wholesalers[§]	125 110.2	100.0	10.5

* Turnover.
[†]Excluding subsidiaries.
[‡] Partly incuding sales by groupings.
[§] Estimate.
FIM = Finnish mark.
Mill.FIM excluding sales tax.
From *Statistics on Retail and Wholesale Trade in Finland 1983*[33].

TABLE 28.3. Wholesalers' sales in 1982 (mill.FIM)

	Mill.FIM*	Percentage share	Change 1982/81	
			Value	Volume
Central wholesalers	36 518.9	29.2	11.6	0.3
Other general wholesalers	4693.6	3.8	7.7	−3.1
Food and beverages	17 055.8	13.6	16.6	3.7
Textile, clothing and leather articles	1603.9	1.3	11.1	3.9
Iron wares and construction materials	7072.4	5.7	13.8	6.9
Electric appliances and radios	4226.8	3.4	14.9	8.4
Motor vehicles	7376.3	5.9	12.3	7.6
Fuels	16 812.1	13.4	3.0	0.1
Investment articles and raw materials	14 594.2	11.7	6.9	0.7
Timber	2811.1	2.2	0.7	−6.2
Other production articles	4521.3	3.6	18.2	12.2
Medicines and drugs	2378.8	1.9	15.2	7.2
Other wholesalers	5445.0	4.4	9.6	2.2
All wholesalers	125 110.2	100.0	10.5	2.4

* Estimate.
From *Statistics on Retail and Wholesale Trade in Finland 1983*[33].

TABLE 28.4 Number of outlets and grocery sales by type of shop and chain, 1982

Type of shop	K-shops	T-shops	Other priv.	SOK-shops	E-shops	Total	Total (mill.FIM)	Share of sales (%)
Hypermarkets	11	–	–	12	7	30	1159	4.3
Department stores	43	50	15	201	72	381	3854	14.2
Supermarkets	298	156	25	112	82	673	7224	26.7
Self-service shops	1776	1226	274	596	751	4623	11 501	42.5
General stores	529	414	532	938	244	2657	1735	6.4
Total	2557	1846	846	1859	1156	8364	25 473	94.1
Specialized shops	29	22	592	2	44	689	617	2.3
Market hall shops	8	1	371	1	4	385	254	0.9
Total shops 1/1/83	2594	1869	1809	1862	1204	9438	26 344	97.3
Mobile shops	262	56	7	160	58	543	739	2.7
Total	2956	1925	1816	2022	1262	9981	27 083	100.0

Chain	1982 Total (mill.FIM)	Share of sales (%)
K-shops	10 793	39.9
T-shops	5516	20.4
Other private	2205	8.1
SOK-shops	5019	18.5
E-shops	3550	13.1

Number of outlets 9981 %: 4, 7, 46, 27, 11, 5

Breakdown of grocery sales 27 083 %: 19, 27, 42, 6, 3, 3

Breakdown of grocery sales 1982 (%)

K-shops 40 — T-shops 20 — Other 8 — SOK-shops 19 — E-shops 13

Mobile shops
Specialized and market hall shops
Grocery shops with full assortment

From Lind[20].

Development of vertical marketing systems

Conventional marketing systems in the grocery and food market have, in Finland, been displaced by vertically organized marketing systems as the dominant distribution mechanism in the Finnish distributive trade. Three groups were formed in the 1960s and one (T-group) in the beginning of the 1970s. This development reflects a need for developing fully coordinated marketing and other policies in the internally consistent distribution system. Guiltinan's stage 5, e.g. collaborative alignments, has been reached. In order to reduce or eliminate conflict, objectives of cooperation and consolidation have taken primacy[18]. This development has been slower than in Sweden[27], but faster than in Norway and in many other industrial countries[15].

Increased coordination, cooperation and growth of vertical marketing systems is expected to continue. The latest example of this trend was the big merger of the Central Cooperative Society, OTK, and its local member societies in 1983 into one big cooperative society. The other groups are expected to increase their internal cooperation within various functions. The growth of groups will bring about changes in the market shares controlled by integrated groups of grocery and food outlets. The sales of integrated groups will increase from their share of 90% of total grocery and food sales in 1973 to 95% in 1990 measured at the retail level[22]. The result will be a shift of channel power from the manfacturers to a few large organizations, which are able to exert strong pressure on manufacturers for price and service concessions. This trend towards growth of vertical marketing systems is consistent with Davidson's assumptions on the development of systems[8]. Galbraith's explanation seems suitable when summarizing the development in grocery trade. On the other hand, there are signs of deviation at the moment from the previous development. The total number of shops fell in each of the various chains in 1982, but the number of shops outside the chains increased. At the same time, a prolonged decline in the market share of the other private retail sector stopped. It is to be seen if the development is permanent[20].

Structural and institutional changes

One of the main fields of change is the institutional structure of the whole marketing system and of the wholesale and retail level. It is clear that the cost-reducing innovations have had a large influence on trade. This author's research has suggested that concentration has increased in Finnish distribution during the last 15 years at the wholesale and retail level[21]. As far as size is concerned a further increase of large units may be expected by 1990. The increase in size has meant a decrease in the number of firms and their establishments. Many small businesses will be squeezed out of the market and big business will grow both in absolute and in relative terms.

At the wholesale level mergers are likely to continue and will make for large more effective units within the T-group. In other groups the number of administrative units of central organization will be decreased. Also the number of warehouses in wholesaling is anticipated to further decrease from the present number. Those with numerous locations reduce the numbers of branches and warehouses which they maintain and concentrate their activities on larger regional depots. Another rationalization possibility is the introduction of more numerous large warehousing units maintained jointly by several wholesale companies by 1990[21]. This result is likely to create a few regional T-wholesale companies in the future.

Also the units in retailing are expected to decrease from the present total. For example the Finnish Cooperative Wholesale Society, SOK, has planned a new system, to be ready by 1986. There are nowadays about 180 SOK cooperatives, which are intended to be merged into 34 new cooperatives at a regional base. As to the establishment of retail firms in the whole grocery trade, it is estimated that at the end of 1987 there will be only 7500 outlets selling the whole assortment of groceries. Some 160 more large units will be opened, most of them supermarkets. This structural change in itself means changes in the sales of various types of outlets. In 1987 large units are expected to account for a share of at least 53%, self-service shops for about 42% and general stores for about 5%[20]. *Table 28.5* shows the anticipated transformation in the shop structure in 1982–87.

TABLE 28.5. Transformation of the shop structure 1982–87

	Number		*Number*
Hypermarkets	+ 5	General stores	− 851
Department stores	+ 34	Total	− 829
Supermarkets	+122	Mobile shops	− 134
Self-service shops	−139		

Along with this development, establishment will develop into more and more efficient units. Hypermarkets, department stores and supermarkets have a sales area of at least $400\,m^2$. Today these shop types represent only 13% of all retail outlets, but handle nearly half the total grocery sales. For wholesalers this development means increasing the sizes of orders for deliveries.

New types of units and a further acceleration of institutional life cycles, as the wheel theories anticipate, can be expected. In the private sector of trade a relatively new type of wholesaling is the cash-and-carry system and an increase is expected in the share of cash-and-carry outlets. The share is expected to account for 10% by 1990[21]. The number of articles is likely to increase and new types of articles, e.g. machines, textiles and toys, will be taken to assortments of cash-and-carry wholesalers[19]. Consequently, in wholesaling large warehouses with large assortments and cash-and-carry warehouses will form two opposing rival pools. Totally new types of wholesale units will be developed. Within T-group new types have already been created in recent years by dividing the commercial functions and the physical movement of goods and allocating these functions to different wholesale companies. This functional specialization is consistent with Bucklin's hypothesis on the development of wholesaling in developed countries[6,23]. New institutional types of retail units are represented by specialty shops, like delicatessen shops and new discount stores in groceries with low prices without service. In retailing, supermarkets and specialty shops will form their own pools. Up to now the share of specialty shops has been small.

As to the whole institutional structure of vertical marketing systems, it is difficult to make any predictions, because the developmental trends in cooperative and private sectors are different. In the cooperative sector, the big merger in 1983 totally integrated wholesale and retail level and even made it impossible to talk about different levels of wholesaling and retailing. The new cooperative society Eka can be seen as one firm which runs wholesaling and retailing cooperatives and other cooperatives, too. The other cooperative group, SOK, is expected to follow the same pattern in the future. The private groups are increasing the shares of cash-and-carry wholesalers, which can be seen as a kind of new level in the institutional structure of groups. In all groups, both the vertical and horizontal integration in institutional relationships will be strengthened (*see* Mattsson[25] for the concept of institutional integration).

Functional changes and physical distribution

The functional structure as a whole is not expected to change very much in the future. It is due to the permanency of functions in distributive trades[32]. Certain functions must be performed in distribution channels. Functional changes within marketing systems will occur primarily in vertical direction between wholesalers and retailers. A part of commercial activities will be transferred from cooperative and private stores to their central organizations. They will not restrict their activities to wholesaling alone, but appear quite willing to develop marketing systems including more manufacturing and retailing operations using their wholesale houses as operational focal points.

Functions (activities) that are expected to be partly or entirely transferred to the central organization (wholesalers) are assortment functions, financial functions, control of retail location, national marketing campaigning, spreading of information and advisory activities as well as educational activities.

The central organizations are increasingly responsible for making sure that retail outlets in their areas are provided with the local ranges they need. One task of central organizations is to plan, direct and supervise financing and the use of resources of retail stores. At the moment central organizations (wholesalers) are controlling retailers through advances of credit. This task is expected to increase considerably by 1990. There are no laws which prevent wholesalers from controlling retailers in this way. A further task is to plan, direct and supervise profitability investments and retail plants. They ensure the renewal of retail network by establishing new retail outlets and by developing existing ones to keep up with customers' changing needs. This task is expected to increase in volume by 50% from 1975 to 1990. Central organizations aid and advise cooperatives and private stores also in the planning and analysing of national marketing and distribution campaigns. This task of central organizations is expected to increase in volume by 50% from 1975 to 1990. More regular advisory services to support retailers knowhow are also increasing their responsibility. Every group has an educational centre for wholesale and retail staff. The education activities will also increase from the present state in the future. The education task ensures that the groups' wholesale and retail outlets within their operational areas are able to retain their competitive edge[22]. Central organizations (wholesalers) are channel leaders in Finnish grocery distribution (*see* Mallen[23] about channel leadership). This is needed to derive the benefits of various scale economies in vertical marketing systems.

The practical implementation of functions is expected to undergo considerable changes during the next few years. Techniques and facilities are being developed with the aim of reducing system cost and at the same time helping individual system members to cope with continually increasing demands for service. As to buying, assortment, inventory, packing and transportation activities, automatization and mechanization will considerably increase in the future. Interorganizational data systems by computers are expected to operate so efficiently that a chain can operate as smoothly as an individual firm by 1988. Moreover, central organizations' and retailers' inventory systems are expected to operate to control respective inventory levels and reordering by 1985. The flow of goods can be totally controlled until it reaches the ultimate consumer by 1985[22]. This development is possible by using various kinds of computers. The amount of small pocket computers is expected to be 2000–10 000 by 1990 in establishments[2]. There will be a vast range of different types of warehousing. The widespread use of fully automated warehousing is unlikely before 1988. At the moment there are 8–10 fully automated warehousing units and their number is expected to increase by 50% within 10 years. Also the number of warehousing robots and automatic handling systems is expected to increase considerably by 1990[2].

Packing and transportation activities will be automated and rationalized further. There will be a growth in the use of containers (70% of deliveries by 1987). The increasing optimal vehicle routing programmes will lower transportation costs in systems. Techniques of packing will develop and standardize. Intermodal packages are likely to be used extensively, e.g. for 95% of packages by 1986[22]. Also coding systems for products will improve. An example is the EAN code, which is now being introduced in the Finnish food trade. By 1985 the distributive trades and producers will be using the same coding system. Also at the retail level automation will increase rapidly. The number of automatic receptacles for returned bottles and self-service weighing scales will increase by about 25–35% in the period 1980–90. At the same time various pieces of equipment based on microprocessors will increase as well as various laser scanners and the use of computers as cash registers[2]. The use of electronic money and the use of home computers will change the ordering of goods from shops or warehouses.

Relationships between distribution and society

General economic development has made it possible for vertical marketing systems to grow and has increased and multiplied their tasks. This is especially true for the share of the wholesale system. In the future because of the growth in economic development, vertical marketing systems are also growing and their share of the GNP and employment is increasing. The growth is closely connected to developments in infrastructure. *Table 28.6* provides gross domestic product by kind of trade and forecasted values by 1990[19,33].

TABLE 28.6. Gross domestic product in basic values by kind of trade

					Forecasts	
	1970	(%)	1981	(%)	1985 (%)	1990 (%)
Trade	3762.5	9.4	18 080.4	9.6	10.3	10.3
Wholesale	1616.3	4.0	8661.0	4.6	5.3	5.4
Retail	2146.2	5.3	9419.4	5.0	5.0	4.9

The values are in millions of Finnish marks.

By reducing the consumer price per unit or retail services, efficiency in distributive trades may be valued as a means of improving consumer welfare. The new methods of appraising efficiency in wholesaling and retailing are largely connected with a supra-institutional analysis of physical distribution and merchandising problems. The distribution optimum is not the same for different institutions in a distribution channel and for the distribution channel as a whole.

The interaction of distributive trades, society and other interest groups will increase in Finnish distribution. By 1990 regulation by national or local authorities is expected to increase by 40% from the 1975 value. This will mean both increased restrictive and supportive activities concerning, for example, location of wholesaling and retailing establishments. The public authorities will employ increased land-use control. Also ecological–environmental considerations are just beginning to influence regulation.

Cooperation between central organizations and public authorities in planning land-use is expected to increase by 30% by 1990. Government may take actions to restrain various types of wholesaling and retailing. Anti-shopping centre legislation is expected to emerge at both the local and national levels. This legislation will restrain new shopping centres (over 2500–10 000 m^2) in favour of conventional down-town retailing. On the other hand strict regulation of shop hours in Finland prevents development of small shops specializing in supplementary service, like the convenience stores of the United States. However, the growth in the consumers' need to make supplementary purchases is also evident in Finland.

In the future, supportive government activities will be increased and developed. Thus, Finnish authorities are currently debating the question of whether reduction in the number of stores to achieve economies of scale does not overpenalize the aged and other immobile members of society, especially in rural areas. In general, the furthering of efficiency must be constantly reconciled with the problem of maintaining social equilibrium. Thus, financial assistance or provision of low-cost loans to stores in rural areas will also be a part of public policy in the future. Wholesale and retail institutions become more active in their relationships to government and other interest groups. This means also the growing activity of trade associations.

Conclusions

Today, wholesaling is a large and growing industry, which has a great impact on the development of the retail trade. The predictions about the future are useful, because they form a base for planning in the distributive sector. There is a lack of certain conceptual models for the analysis of the change processes in wholesaling. That is why analogies concerning retail change models are often used to describe and explain patterns of development in wholesaling and to predict, as best possible, future changes. Stage theories, cycle theories, dialectic theories, challenge–response models, diffusion theories and theories concerning economics of the firm form the theoretical framework for the changes discussed in this chapter. Based on theories and past development in trade, 'a change framework' can be constructed that lists the potential fields of change in which most changes will occur. This 'change framework' can be used as a tool to aid thinking when a forecast of future changes with different methods is prepared.

Studies made by the author and other researchers in Finland suggest that the following main changes will take place by 1990. The rise of vertical marketing systems in grocery trade can be seen as a development of a new institutional type. Increased cooperation and coordination as well as growth of vertical marketing systems are expected to continue. At the wholesale and retail level, systems concentration will continue. New types of units and a further acceleration of institutional life cycles can be expected. In all vertical marketing systems both the vertical and horizontal integration in institutional relationships will be strengthened.

The functional structure as a whole is not expected to change very much. Functional changes within marketing systems will occur primarily in a vertical direction between wholesalers and retailers. A part of commercial activities will be transferred from retailers to their central organizations, e.g. assortment, financial, investment, campaigning, information and educational activities. Horizontally there will be increased integration in the functions.

The practical implementation of functions is expected to undergo considerable changes during the next few years. Techniques and facilities are being developed with the aim of reducing system costs. Automatization, mechanization and computerization will considerably increase in the future.

The interaction of distributive trades, society and other interest groups will increase in Finnish distribution. This will mean both increased restrictive and supportive activities concerning, for example, location of wholesaling and retailing establishments. Also ecological–environmental considerations are just beginning to influence regulation.

A large part of the forecast developments will hardly materialize as predicted because many factors, which are not known at the moment, will affect the future system of distribution. The future development of the wholesale trade will be predominantly determined by economic, social and technical conditions.

References

1. ARNDT, J. (1972) *Norwegian Retailing up to 1980,* Oslo, Johan Grundt, Tanum Publisher
2. AUTOMATION DEVELOPMENTS IN DOMESTIC TRADE (1983) Jyväskylä University, 53. Jyväskylä: Jyväskylä University
3. BATES, A. D. (1977) Ahead – the retrenchment era. *Journal of Retailing,* **53,** 29–46
4. BELLENGER, D. N., STANLEY, T. J. and ALLEN, J. W. (1977) Food retailing in the 1980s: problems and prospects. *Journal of Retailing,* **53,** 59–70
5. BOWERSOX, D. J., COOPER, M. B., LAMBERT, D. M. and TAYLOR, D. A. (1980) *Management in Marketing Channels.* Michigan, McGraw-Hill
6. BUCKLIN, L. P. (1972) *Competition and Evolution in the Distributive Trades.* Englewood Cliffs, New Jersey, Prentice-Hall
7. BUZZEL, R. D., NOURSE, R. E. M., MATTHEWS, J. B. JR and LEVITT, T. (1972) *Marketing: A Contemporary Analysis.* New York, McGraw-Hill
8. DAVIDSON, W. R. (1978) Changes in distribution institutions. A reexamination. In *Marketing Channels and Institutions,* pp. 261–275. Ed. by B. J. Haynes. Columbus, Ohio, Grid Inc.
9. ERICSSON, D. (1976) *Vertical Marketing Systems. Design and Development.* Gothenburg, SIMS
10. FORNELL, C. (1976) *Consumer Input for Marketing Decisions. A Study of Corporate Departments for Consumer Affairs.* New York, Praeger Publishers
11. GALBRAITH, J. K. (1952) *American Capitalism. The Concept of Countervailing Power.* Boston, Houghton Company
12. GATTORNA, J. (1977) *Innovative Developments in Distribution: the UK Grocery Industry.* Bradford, MCB Publications
13. GATTORNA, J. (1978) Channels of distribution. *European Journal of Marketing,* **12,** 471–512

14. GIST, R. R. (1974) *Marketing and Society, Text and Cases,* Hinsdale, Illinois, Illinois, The Dryden Press
15. GRIPSRUD, G. (1975) *Distribution systems for grocery trade. A theoretical framework.* Project report No. 10. Oslo, Foundation for market and distribution research
16. GUILTINAN, J. P. (1974) Planned and evolutionary changes in distribution channels. *Journal of Retailing,* **50,** 79–91, 103
17. HILL, S. R. (1974) Distribution in Britain – the next ten years. *Journal of Retailing,* **50,** 23–29, 103
18. HYVÖNEN, S. (1983) *Coordination and Cooperation in Vertical Marketing Systems: A Model Verification.* Publications of the Helsinki School of Economics B-63. Helsinki, Helsinki School of Economics
19. IDENTIFICATION OF DEVELOPMENT TRENDS OF DOMESTIC TRADE UP TO 1990. GROCERY WHOLESALING AND SPECIAL GOODS' WHOLESALING AND RETAILING (1982). Publications of the Turku School of Economics, Series A-3. Turku, Turku School of Economics
20. LIND, T. (1983) Structure and development of grocery trade in 1978–1987. *Marker. Marketindex Group Newsletter,* No. 4-4S
21. MÄKINEN, E. H. (1975) *The Effect of Concentration Trends and Ratios on Competition in Domestic Trade.* Publications of the Turku School of Economics, Series A-3. Turku, Turku School of Economics
22. MÄKINEN, E. H. (1976) *Forecasts of Changes in Grocery Wholesaling up to 1990, A Study conducted by the Delphi Method.* Publications of the Turku School of Economics, Series A-6. Turku, Turku School of Economics
23. MALLEN, B. (1977) *Principles of Marketing Channel Management.* Lexington, Mass., D. C. Heath and Company
24. MÅRTENSON, R. (1981) *Innovations in Multinational Retailing.* Gothenburg, University of Gothenburg
25. MATTSSON, L.-G. (1969) *Integration and Efficiency in Marketing Systems.* Stockholm, EFI
26. MINNIGER, G. (1968) *The changes of Functions in Wholesale Firms selling Consumer Goods.* Cologne, Cologne University
27. NYDAHL, T. (1979) Only to groups, strategic pricing policies based upon market conditions. In *Åttiotalets handel,* pp. 64–67. Ed. by N.-E. Wirsäll. Stockholm, ICA
28. PILL, J. (1971) The Delphi method: substance, context, a critique and an annotated bibliography. *Socio-economic Planning Science,* **5,** 57–71
29. RENOUX, Y. (1974) Consumer dissatisfaction and public policy. In *The Environment of Marketing Management, selections from the Literature,* pp. 442–448. Ed. by R. J. Holloway and R. S. Hancock. New York, John Wiley
30. RETAIL AND WHOLESALE TRADE IN FINLAND (1980) A brochure. Helsinki, Central Board of Finnish Wholesale and Retail Associations
31. SAVITT, R. (1982) A historical approach to comparative retailing. In *Comparative Marketing Systems,* Vol. 20, pp. 16–23. Ed. by E. Kaynak. Bradford, MCB Publications
32. SIMS, T. J., FOSTER, J. R. and WOODSIDE, S. G. (1977) *Marketing Channels, Systems and Strategies.* New York, Harper & Row
33. STATISTICS ON RETAIL AND WHOLESALE TRADE IN FINLAND 1983 (1983) A brochure. Helsinki, Central Board of Finnish Wholesale and Retail Associations
34. SWAN, J. E. (1974) A functional analysis of innovation in distribution channels. *Journal of Retailing,* **50,** 9–23, 90
35. TIETZ, B. (1971) The future development of retail and wholesale distribution in western Europe: an analysis of trends up to 1980. *British Journal of Marketing,* **5,** 42–55
36. WALTERS, D. (1976) *Futures for Physical Distribution in the Food Industry.* Farnborough, Hants, Saxon House, D. C. Heath Ltd

Index

Abidjan, 57, 86
Afghanistan, 42
Africa, 31, 43, 44, 50, 65, 83, 151, 153, 155–157
Agricultural Refinance and Development
    Corporation, 232
Agriculture Loan Bank, 156
AGRIPAC, 89
Amman, 60
Argentina, 24, 32, 34
Asia, 44, 65, 141
Asian bazaar, 77
Asian Development Bank (ADB), 303
Asian Rural Market Centre Development
    Programme, 60
Australia, 34

Baghdad, 60
Bahrain, 167, 172
Bangladesh, 30, 31, 91
Barbados, 63
Baseline data, 121
Beatrice Food, 5
Behaviour macro (country level), 1, 5
  micro (firm level), 1, 5
Beirut, 60
Belgian Boerenbond, 285
Belgium, 280, 284, 285, 287
Benefit – cost ratio, 184
Benghazi, 116
Berbers, 99
Bogota, 69
Bolivia, 23
Bombay, 60
Brazil, 31, 40, 45, 57, 70, 128, 181, 269
British Cooperation, 280, 285
Burma, 34

Canada, 44, 255
Canadian Ministry of Consumer and Corporate
    Affairs, 119

Capital-intensive mass marketing technology,
    299, 311
Capital store, 260
Caribbean, 40, 299
Casablanca, 98, 102
Cash and carry, 8
Central African Empire, 31
Central Cooperative Society of Finland, 318, 322
Central Organisation of Independent wholesalers,
    318
Central Purchasing and Coordinating Office, 18
Centrale Paysanne Luxembourgeoise, 284
Certified production zones, 296
Chad, 31
Chile, 31
China, 41, 60
Chinese foodgrain imports, 94
Civil Supplies Corporation, 234, 236, 237
CMA West Germany, 207
Cobal, 57
Cobb – Douglas technology, 143
CODIMER – ASMAK, 98
Coimbatore District, 234
Colombia, 31, 49, 69, 128, 143
Colombo, 75
Collective agricultural societies, 284
Commerciogenic malnutrition, 161
Commodity Board for Fruit and Vegetables, 217
Commodity Board for Livestock and Meat, 214
Commodity Boards (Netherlands), 207, 213
Common Agricultural Policy (CAP), 214
Compensatory Fund, 102
CONASUPO, 49
Consumer environment of food distributors, 133
Consumer Research Evaluation Branch, 119
Consumption sector, 142
Controlled quality zones, 295
Cooperative organization, 282
Cooperative society Eka, 318
Cooperative wholesale society Hankkija, 318
CORABASTOS, 69
Credoc, 24
Cropping systems research, 224

US Agency for International Development, 100
US Model, 48
USA, 5, 6, 8, 10, 23, 34, 35, 43, 51, 70, 76, 80,
    115, 130, 132, 135, 155, 140–141, 182,
    248–251, 255, 326
Utility of purchase, 199

Vertical Coordination, 61
    marketing system, 3, 4, 322
Vietnam, 31

Wages and Salaries Review Commission, 155
West Africa, 39, 158
Western technology, 171
West Germany, 20, 279–280, 284–287
    council of, 40
Wheel of retailing, 314
Wheel of wholesaling, 315

Wholesale changes,
    functional, 316
    institutional, 314
    relationships among council members, 316
Wholesale markets,
    food, 64
    size, 65
    transfer and production, 69
Woman's Day Study, 250–251
World Bank, 40, 42, 48, 94, 232, 303
World Food Programme, 23
World Health Organization, 162

Yemen, 60
Yoplait, 101

Zambia, 156
Zones of agroindustrial development, 294